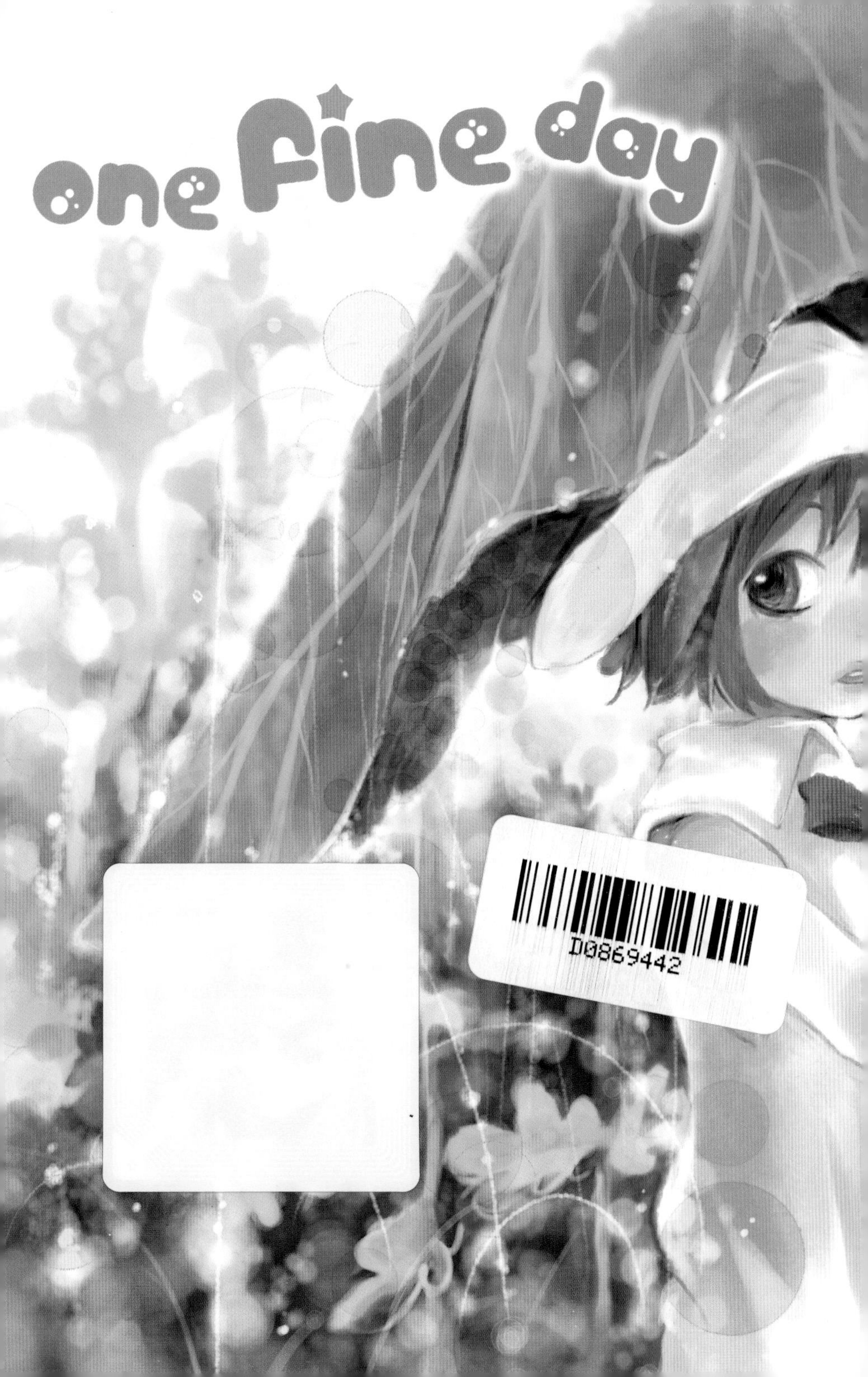
one fine day

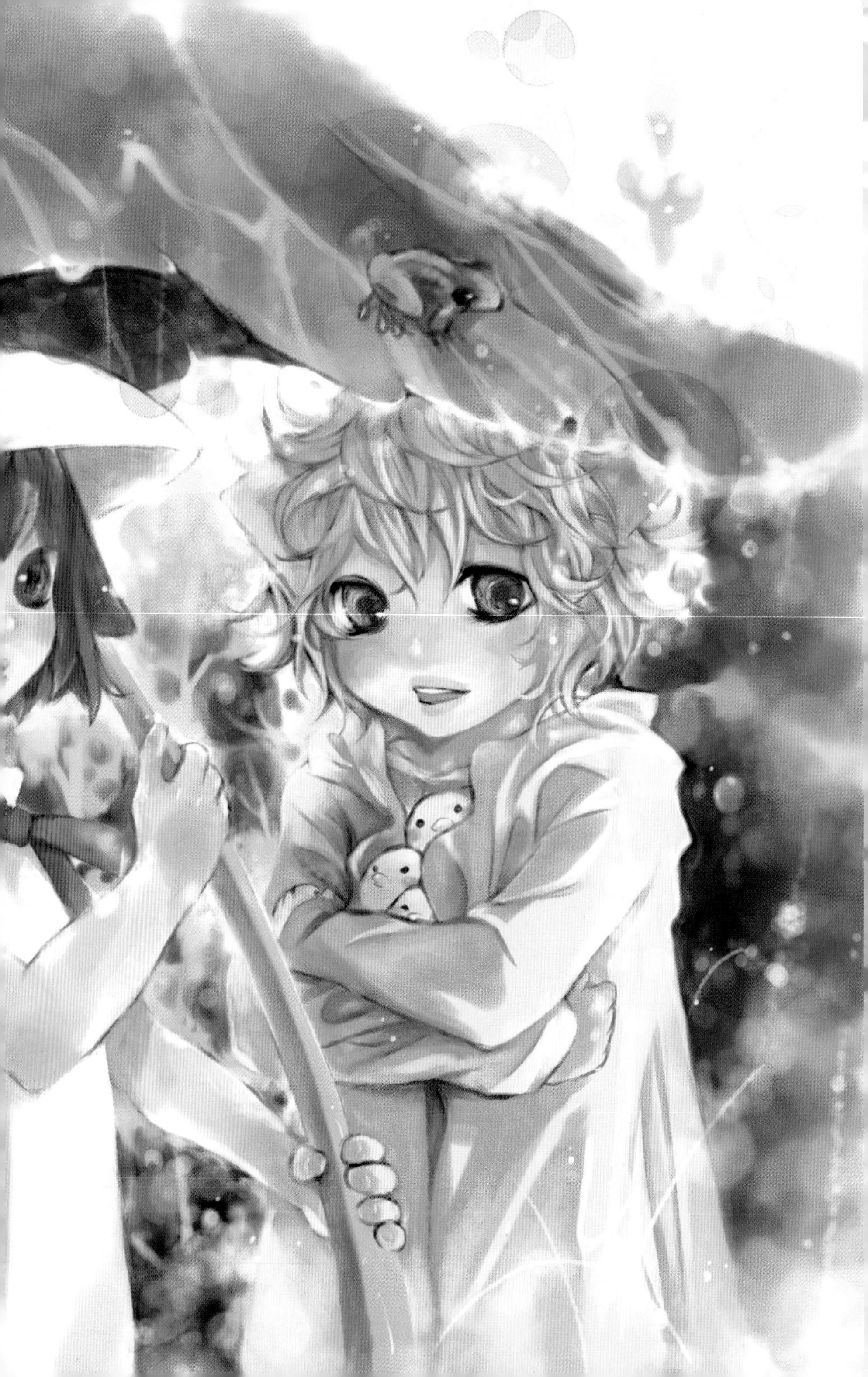

one fine day

SIRIAL
2

CONTENTS

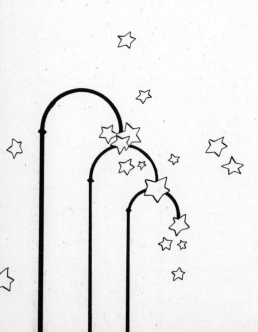

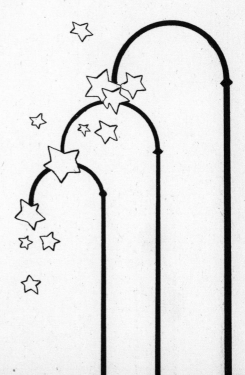

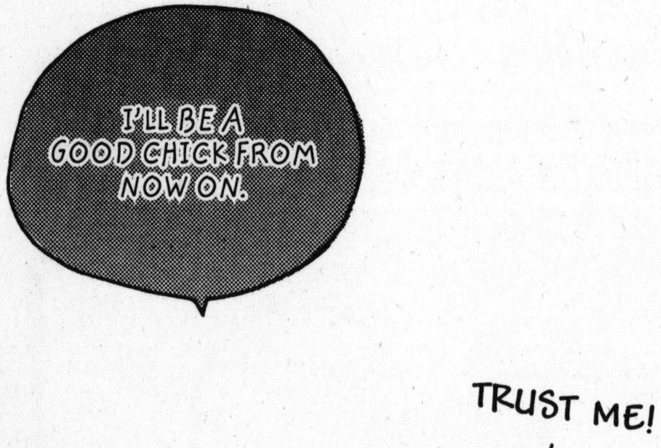
I'LL BE A GOOD CHICK FROM NOW ON.
TRUST ME!

DAY 14. PUPPY'S DAY OUT

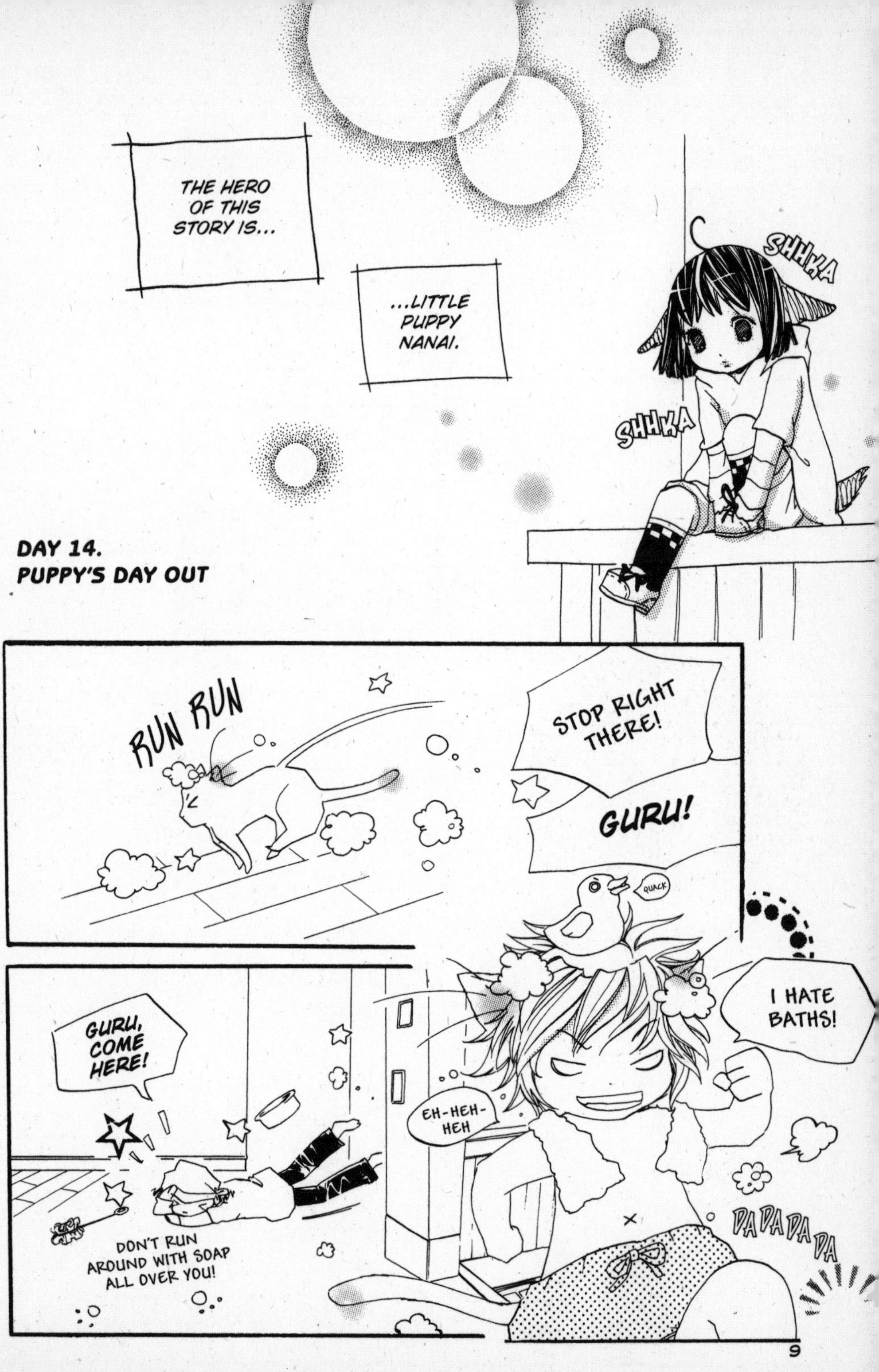
THE HERO OF THIS STORY IS...
...LITTLE PUPPY NANAI.
SHHKA
SHHKA
RUN RUN
STOP RIGHT THERE!
GURU!
GURU, COME HERE!
DON'T RUN AROUND WITH SOAP ALL OVER YOU!
QUACK
EH-HEH-HEH
I HATE BATHS!
DA DA DA DA

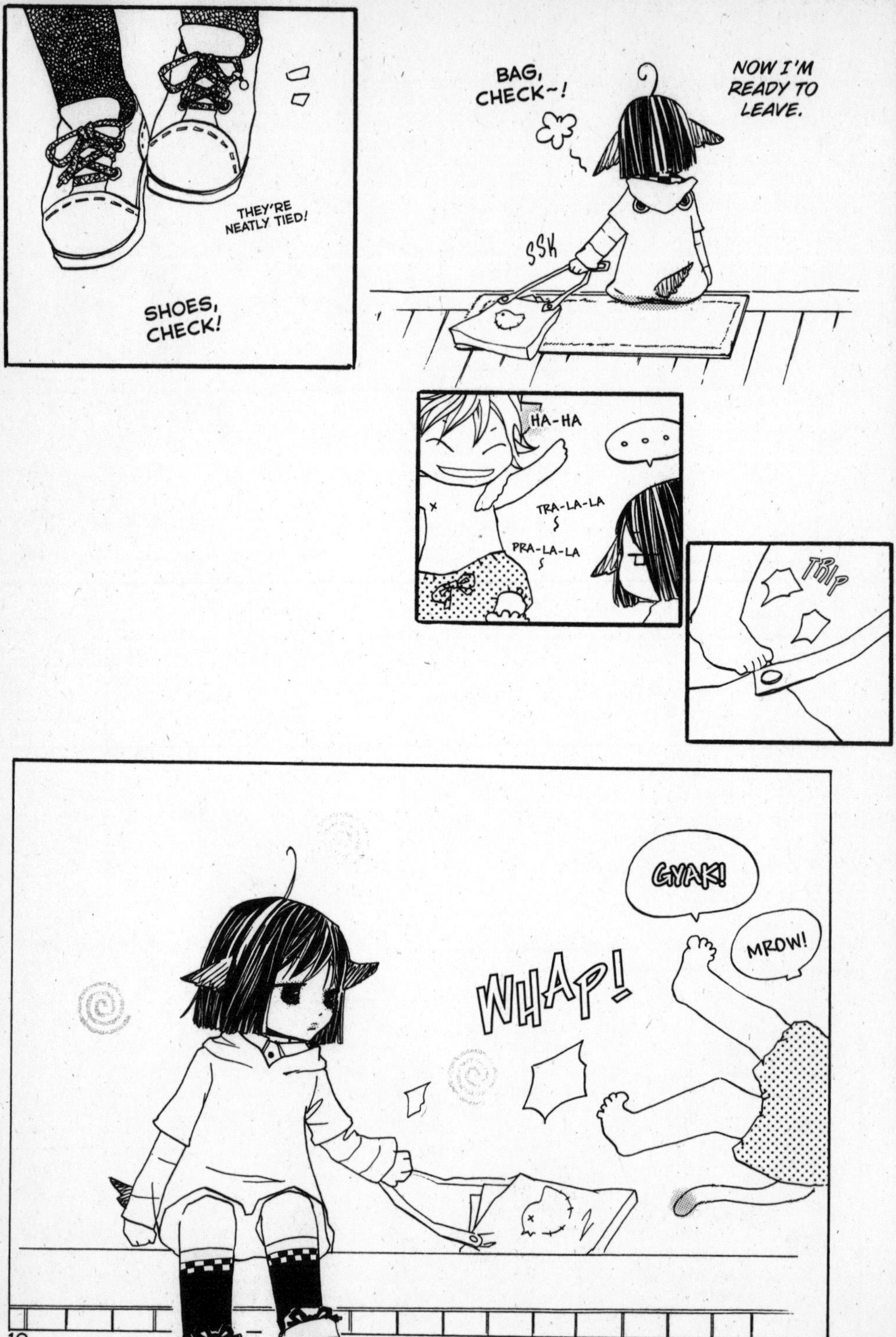
THEY'RE NEATLY TIED!
SHOES, CHECK!
BAG, CHECK~!
SSK
NOW I'M READY TO LEAVE.
HA-HA
...
TRA-LA-LA
PRA-LA-LA
TRIP
GYAK!
MROW!
WHAP!

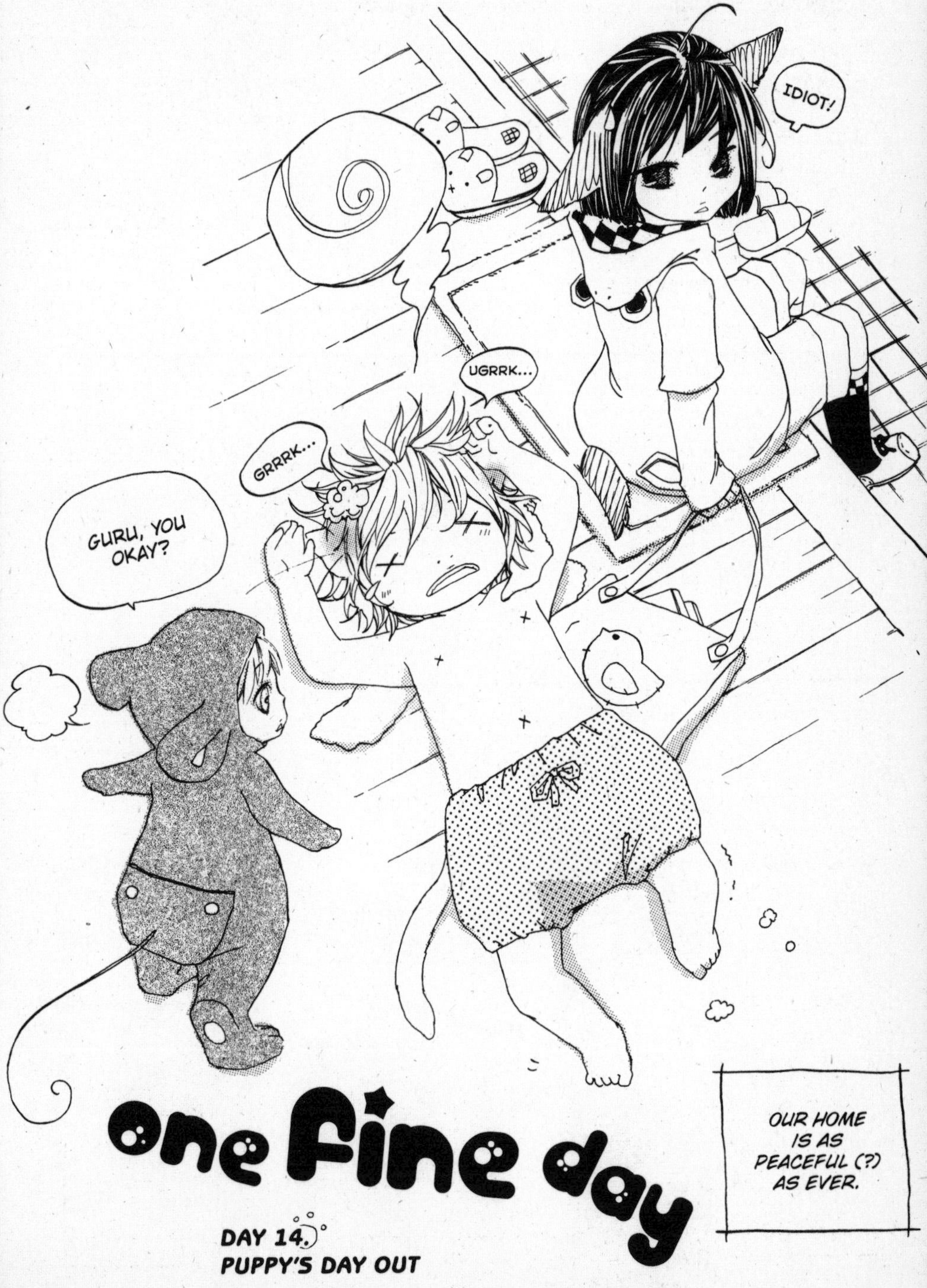
IDIOT!
UGRRK...
GRRRK...
GURU, YOU OKAY?
one fine day
DAY 14.
PUPPY'S DAY OUT
OUR HOME IS AS PEACEFUL (?) AS EVER.

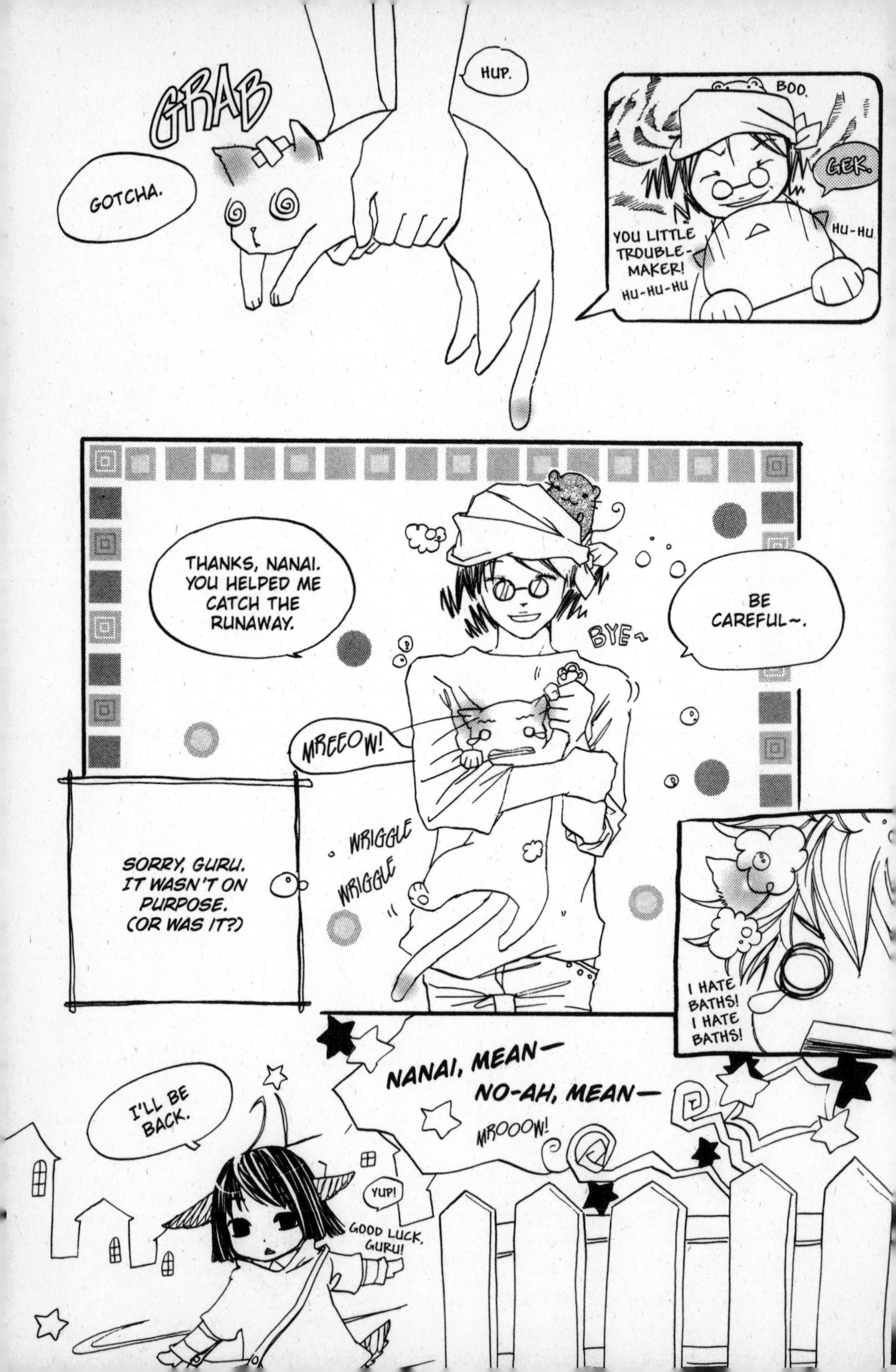
GRAB
GOTCHA.
HUP.
BOO.
GEK.
YOU LITTLE TROUBLE-MAKER!
HU-HU-HU
HU-HU
THANKS, NANAI. YOU HELPED ME CATCH THE RUNAWAY.
BYE~
BE CAREFUL~.
MREEOW!
SORRY, GURU. IT WASN'T ON PURPOSE. (OR WAS IT?)
WRIGGLE
WRIGGLE
I HATE BATHS! I HATE BATHS!
I'LL BE BACK.
NANAI, MEAN—
NO-AH, MEAN—
MROOOW!
YUP!
GOOD LUCK, GURU!

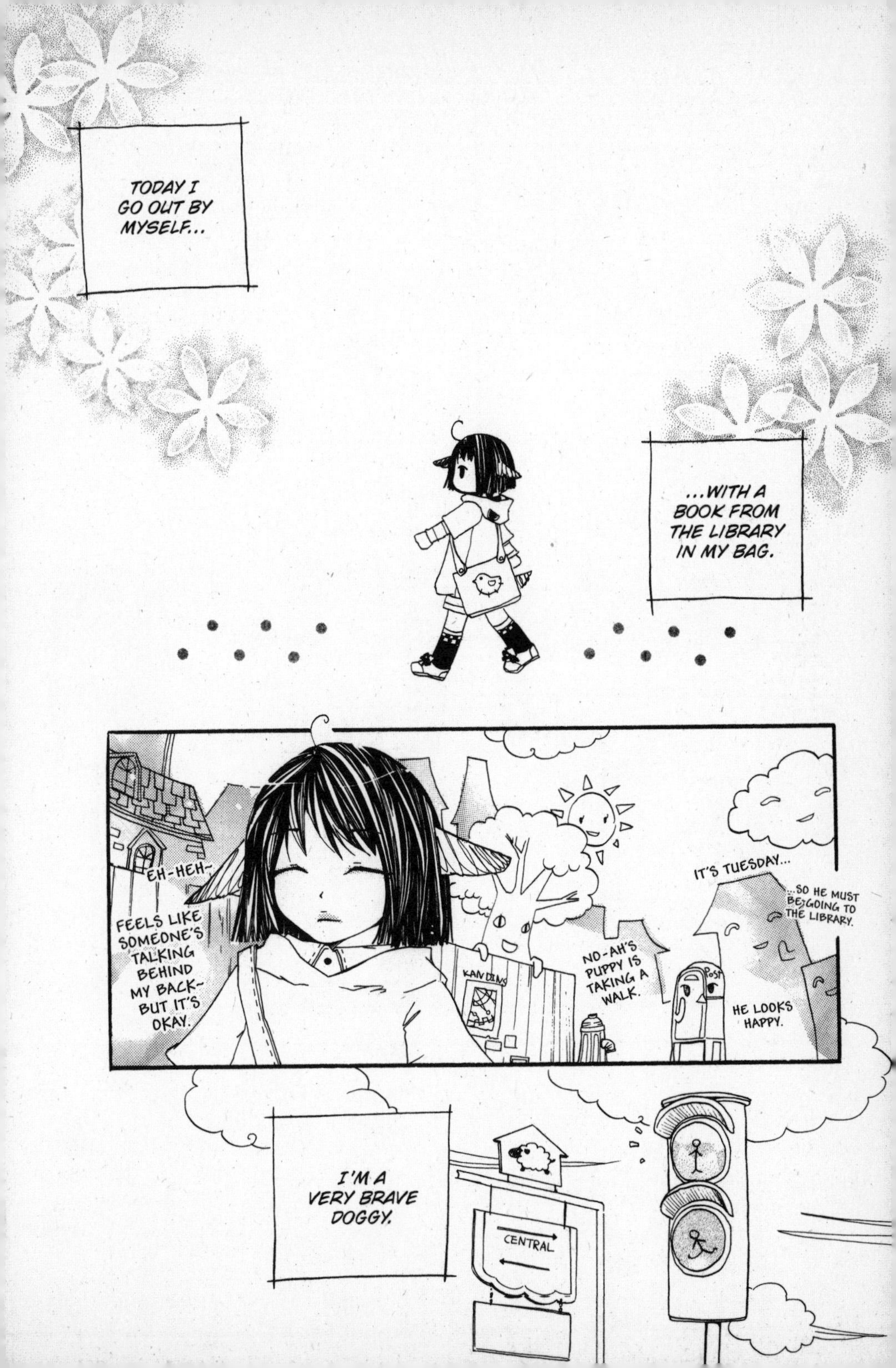
TODAY I GO OUT BY MYSELF...
...WITH A BOOK FROM THE LIBRARY IN MY BAG.
EH-HEH-
FEELS LIKE SOMEONE'S TALKING BEHIND MY BACK- BUT IT'S OKAY.
KANDINS
NO-AH'S PUPPY IS TAKING A WALK.
POST
IT'S TUESDAY...
...SO HE MUST BE GOING TO THE LIBRARY.
HE LOOKS HAPPY.
I'M A VERY BRAVE DOGGY.
CENTRAL

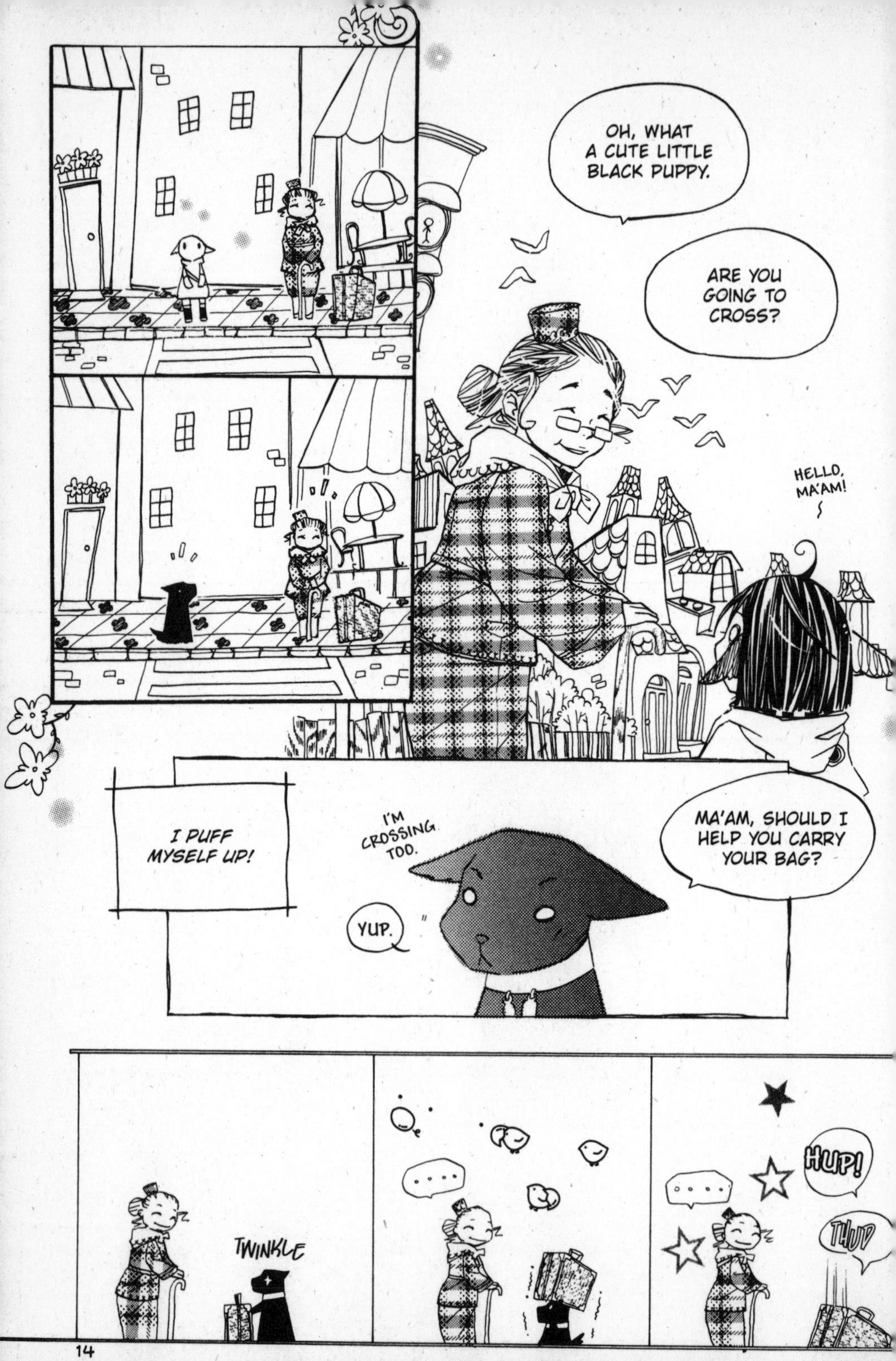

OH, WHAT A CUTE LITTLE BLACK PUPPY.
ARE YOU GOING TO CROSS?
HELLO, MA'AM!
I PUFF MYSELF UP!
I'M CROSSING TOO.
YUP.
MA'AM, SHOULD I HELP YOU CARRY YOUR BAG?
TWINKLE
....
....
HUP!
THUD

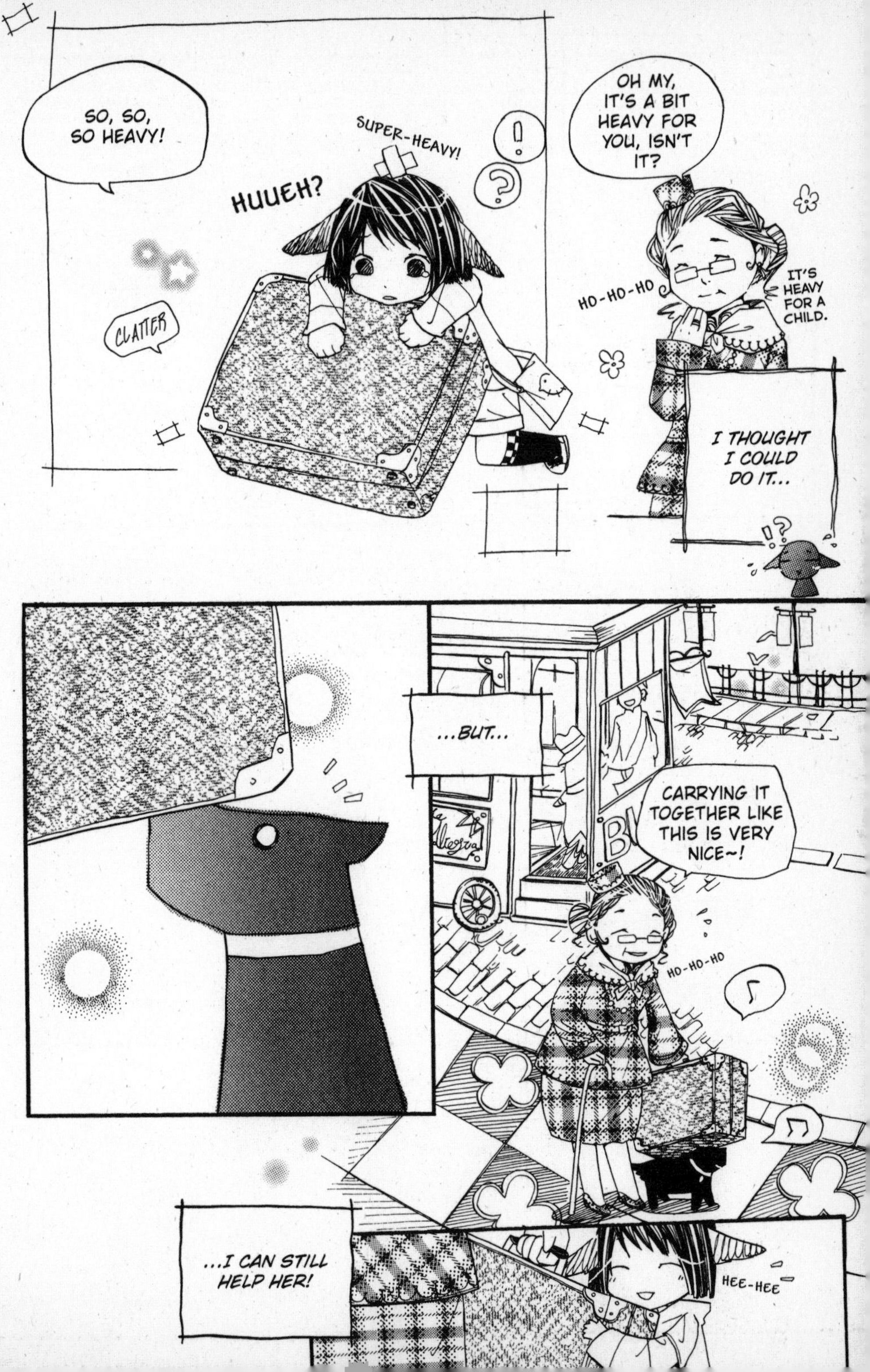
SO, SO, SO HEAVY!
SUPER-HEAVY!
HUUEH?
!
?
CLATTER
OH MY, IT'S A BIT HEAVY FOR YOU, ISN'T IT?
HO-HO-HO
IT'S HEAVY FOR A CHILD.
I THOUGHT I COULD DO IT...
!?
...BUT...
CARRYING IT TOGETHER LIKE THIS IS VERY NICE~!
HO-HO-HO
...I CAN STILL HELP HER!
HEE-HEE

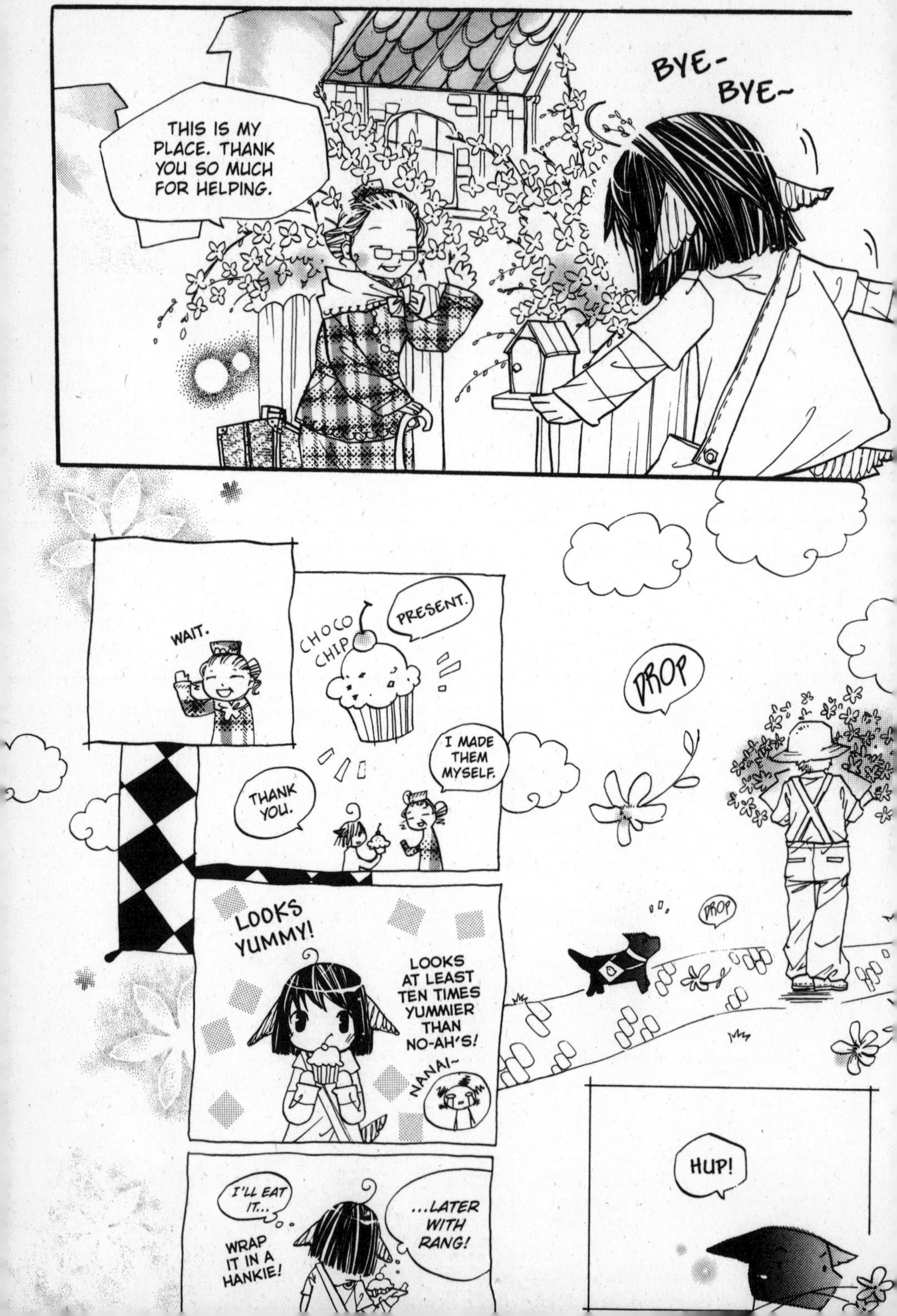
THIS IS MY PLACE. THANK YOU SO MUCH FOR HELPING.
BYE-BYE~
WAIT.
CHOCO CHIP
PRESENT.
THANK YOU.
I MADE THEM MYSELF.
DROP
DROP
LOOKS YUMMY!
LOOKS AT LEAST TEN TIMES YUMMIER THAN NO-AH'S!
NANAI~
I'LL EAT IT...
...LATER WITH RANG!
WRAP IT IN A HANKIE!
HUP!

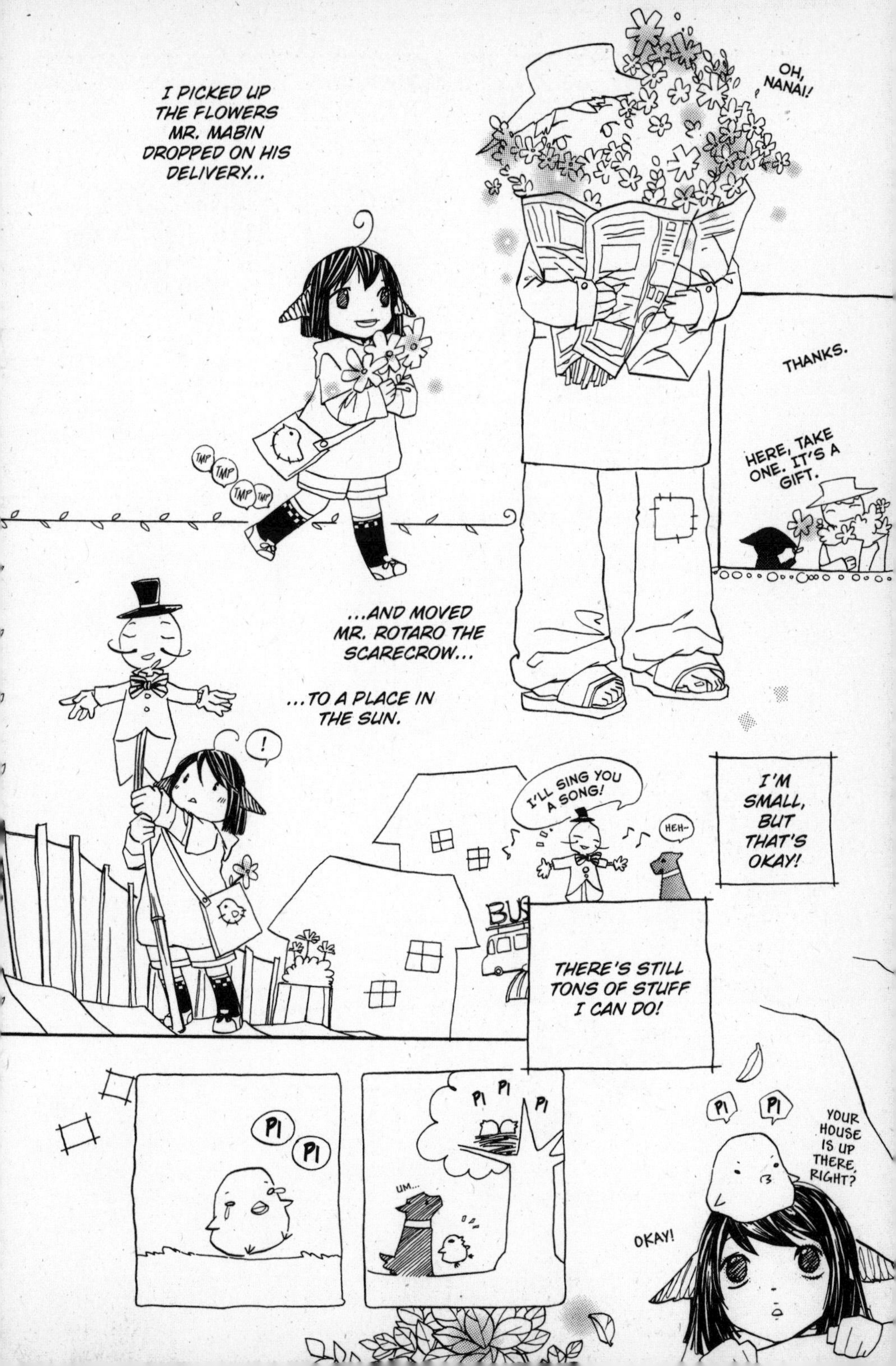
I PICKED UP THE FLOWERS MR. MABIN DROPPED ON HIS DELIVERY...
TMP TMP TMP TMP
OH, NANAI!
THANKS.
HERE, TAKE ONE. IT'S A GIFT.
...AND MOVED MR. ROTARO THE SCARECROW...
...TO A PLACE IN THE SUN.
!
I'LL SING YOU A SONG!
HEH~
I'M SMALL, BUT THAT'S OKAY!
THERE'S STILL TONS OF STUFF I CAN DO!
PI
PI
PI PI
PI
UM...
PI
PI
YOUR HOUSE IS UP THERE, RIGHT?
OKAY!

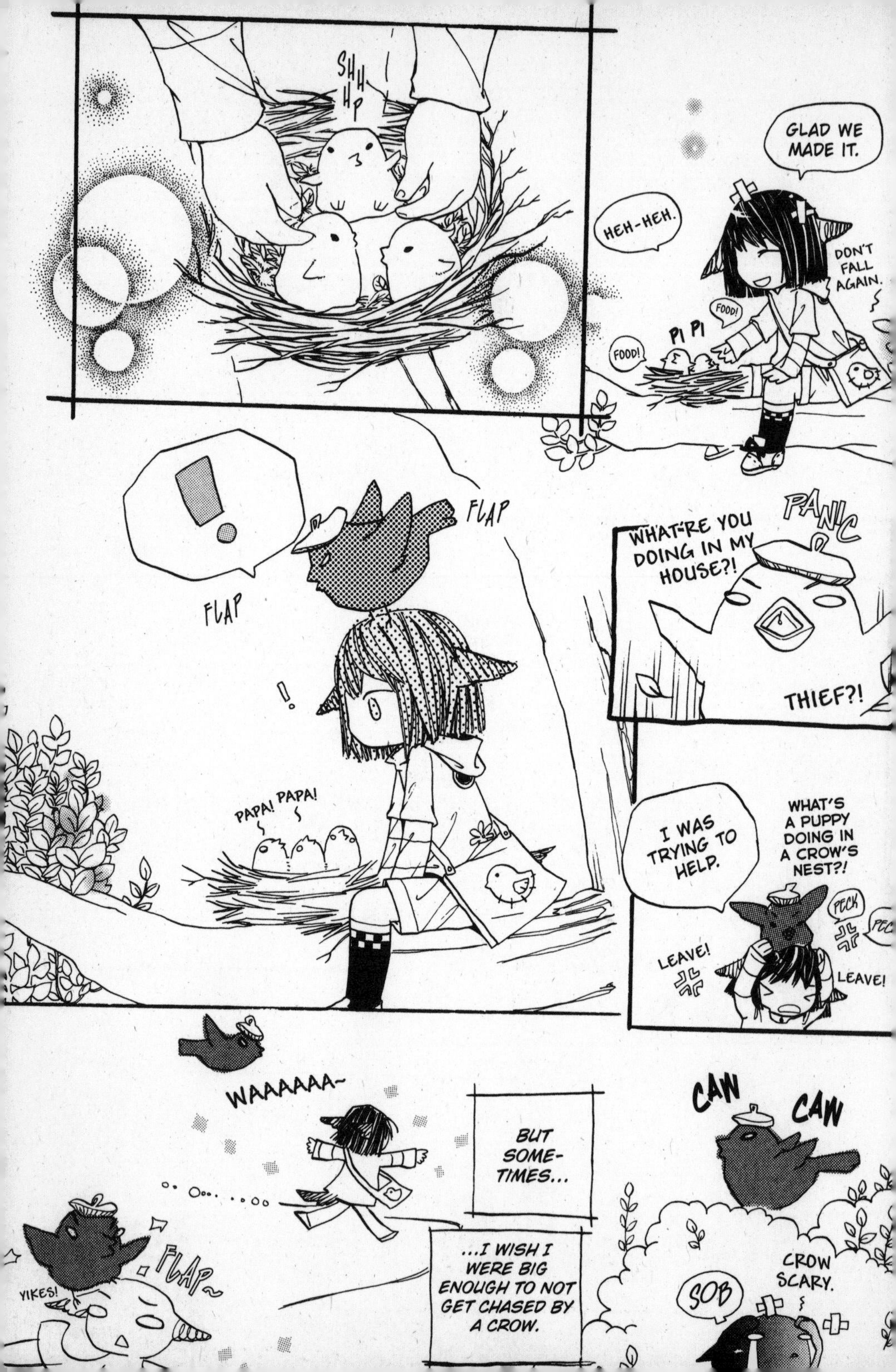
SHHHP
HEH-HEH.
GLAD WE MADE IT.
DON'T FALL AGAIN.
FOOD!
PI PI
FOOD!
!
FLAP
FLAP
!
PAPA! PAPA!
WHAT-'RE YOU DOING IN MY HOUSE?!
PANIC
THIEF?!
I WAS TRYING TO HELP.
WHAT'S A PUPPY DOING IN A CROW'S NEST?!
PECK
PEC
LEAVE!
LEAVE!
WAAAAAA-
BUT SOME-TIMES...
...I WISH I WERE BIG ENOUGH TO NOT GET CHASED BY A CROW.
YIKES!
FLAP~
CAW
CAW
SOB
CROW SCARY.

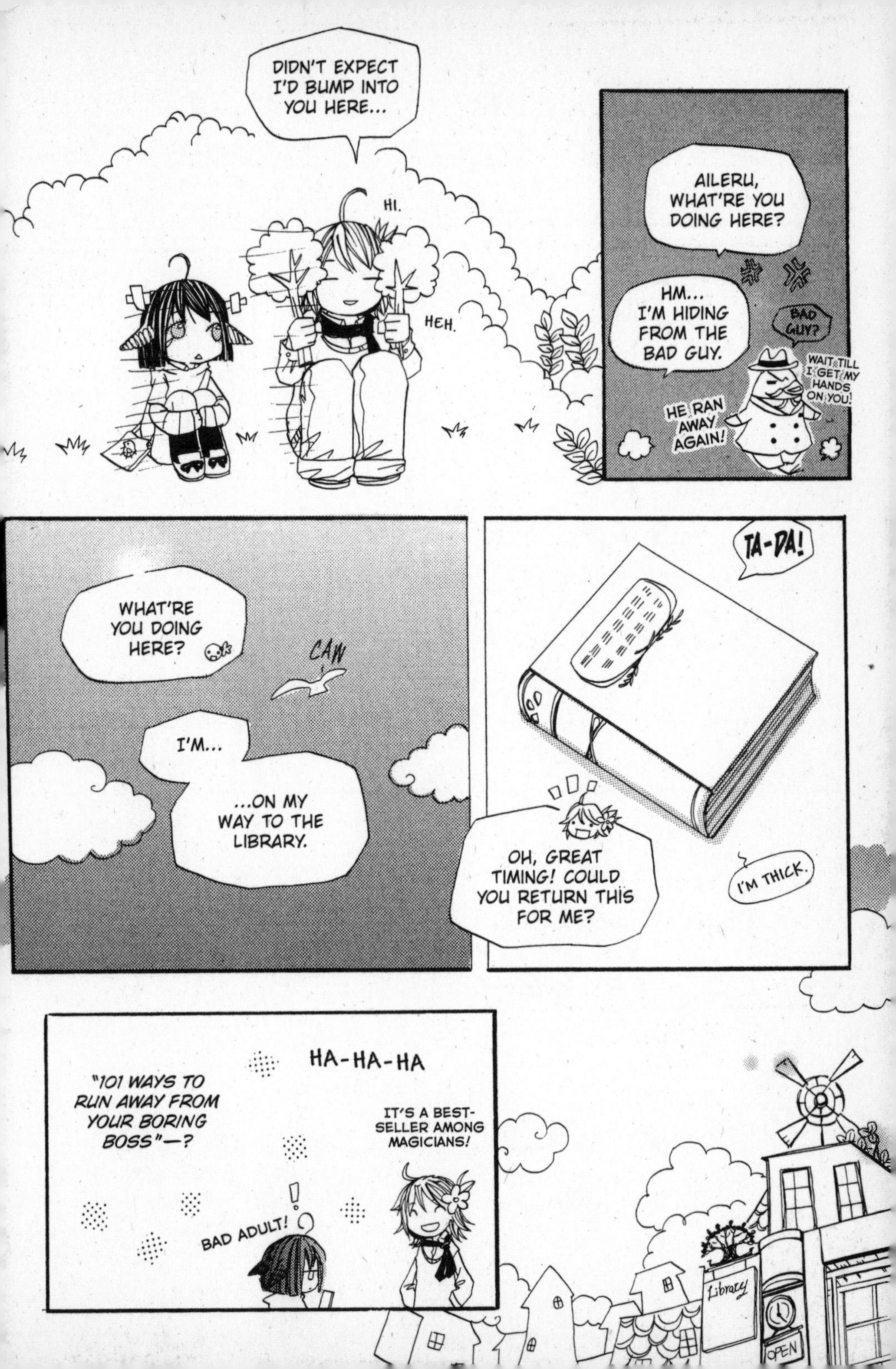
DIDN'T EXPECT I'D BUMP INTO YOU HERE...
HI.
HEH.
AILERU, WHAT'RE YOU DOING HERE?
HM... I'M HIDING FROM THE BAD GUY.
BAD GUY?
WAIT TILL I GET MY HANDS ON YOU!
HE RAN AWAY AGAIN!
WHAT'RE YOU DOING HERE?
CAW
I'M...
...ON MY WAY TO THE LIBRARY.
TA-DA!
OH, GREAT TIMING! COULD YOU RETURN THIS FOR ME?
I'M THICK.
HA-HA-HA
"101 WAYS TO RUN AWAY FROM YOUR BORING BOSS"—?
IT'S A BEST-SELLER AMONG MAGICIANS!
!
BAD ADULT!
Library
OPEN

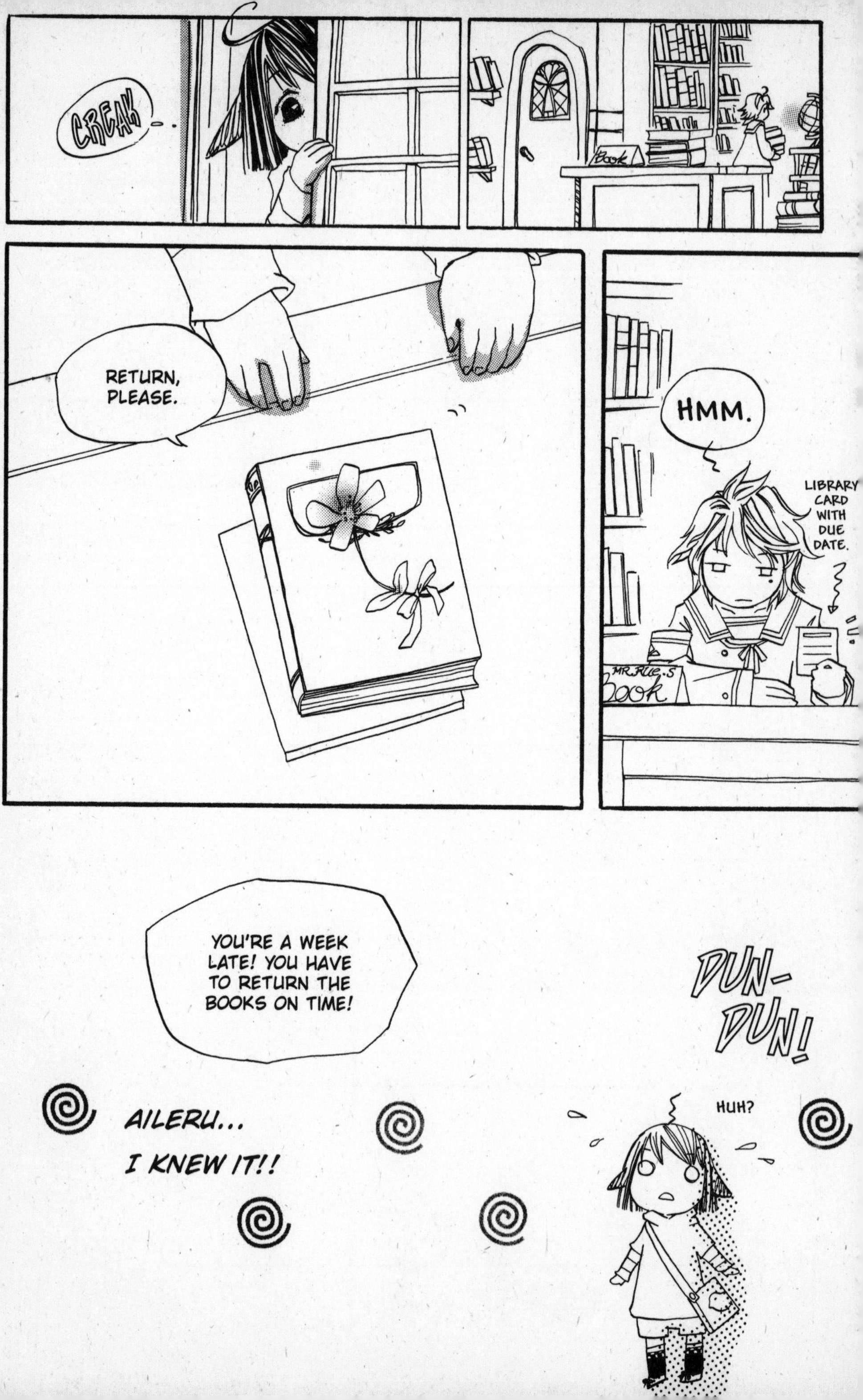
CREAK
RETURN, PLEASE.
HMM.
LIBRARY CARD WITH DUE DATE.
MR. RUE.S
Book
YOU'RE A WEEK LATE! YOU HAVE TO RETURN THE BOOKS ON TIME!
DUN-DUN!
AILERU...
I KNEW IT!!
HUH?

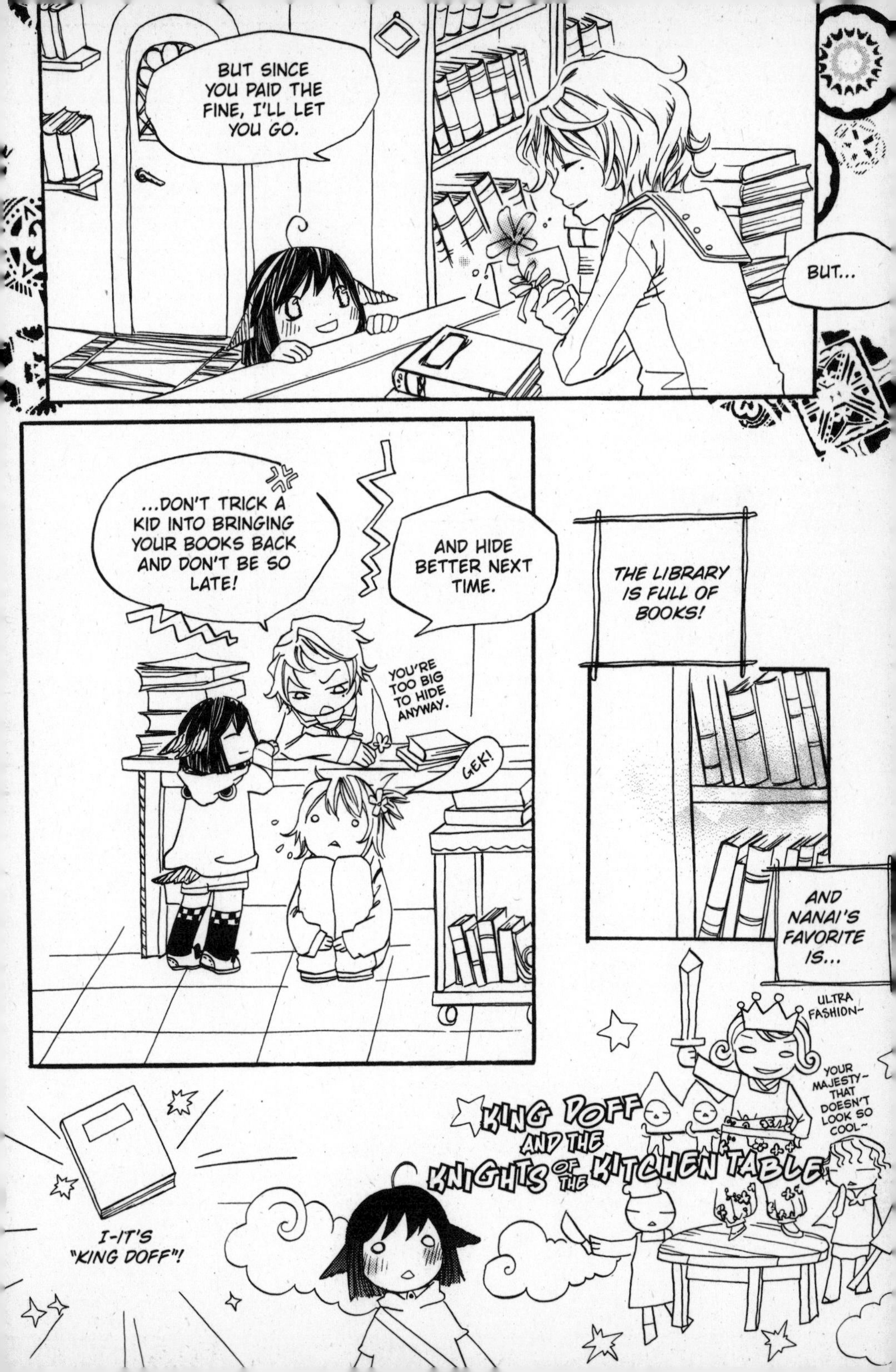

BUT SINCE YOU PAID THE FINE, I'LL LET YOU GO.
BUT...
...DON'T TRICK A KID INTO BRINGING YOUR BOOKS BACK AND DON'T BE SO LATE!
AND HIDE BETTER NEXT TIME.
YOU'RE TOO BIG TO HIDE ANYWAY.
GEK!
THE LIBRARY IS FULL OF BOOKS!
AND NANAI'S FAVORITE IS...
I-IT'S "KING DOFF"!
KING DOFF AND THE KNIGHTS OF THE KITCHEN TABLE
ULTRA FASHION~
YOUR MAJESTY— THAT DOESN'T LOOK SO COOL~

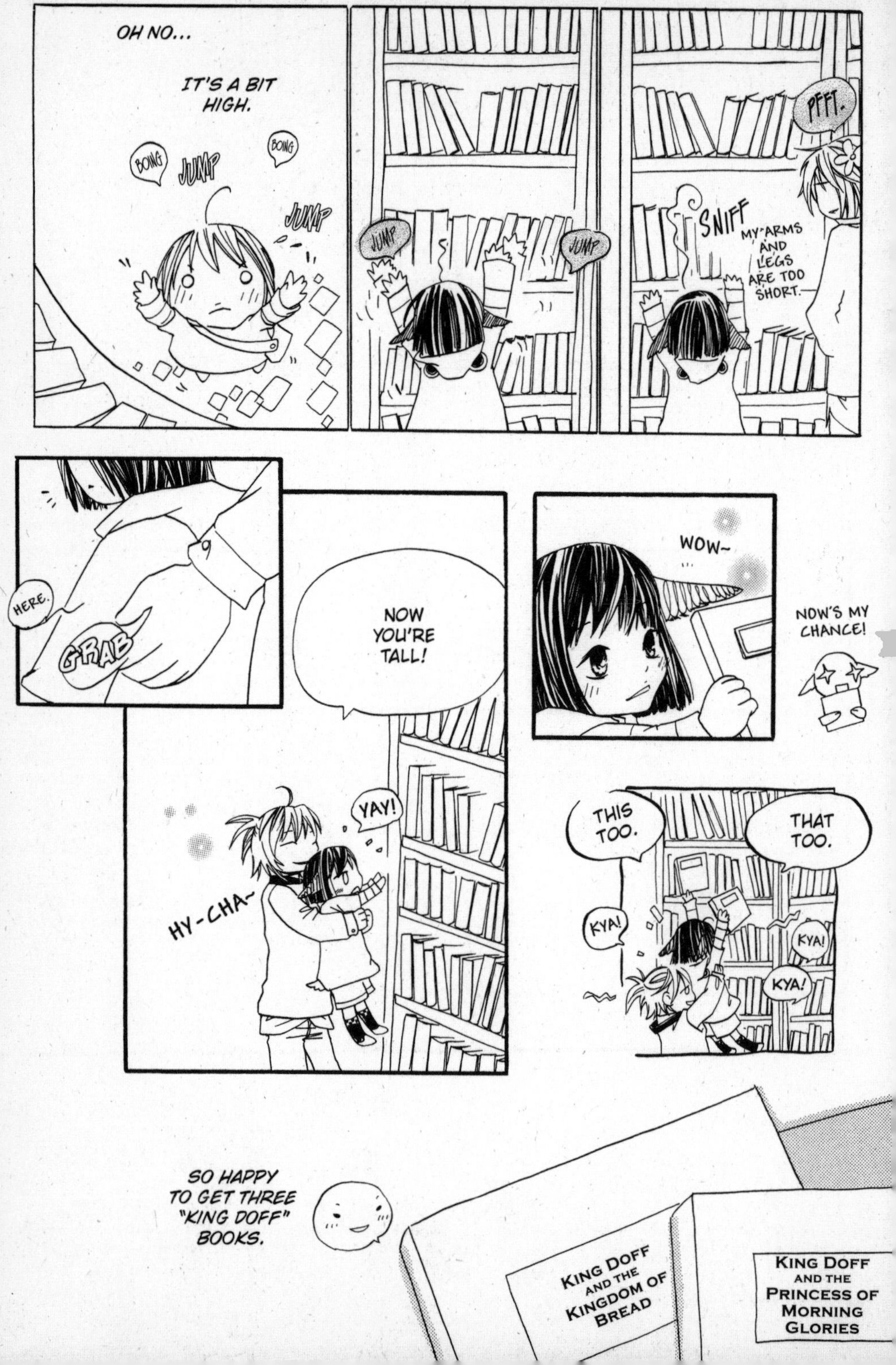
OH NO...
IT'S A BIT HIGH.
BOING
JUMP
BOING
JUMP
JUMP
JUMP
PFFT.
SNIFF
MY ARMS AND LEGS ARE TOO SHORT.
HERE.
GRAB
NOW YOU'RE TALL!
YAY!
HY-CHA~
WOW~
NOW'S MY CHANCE!
THIS TOO.
THAT TOO.
KYA!
KYA!
KYA!
SO HAPPY TO GET THREE "KING DOFF" BOOKS.
KING DOFF AND THE KINGDOM OF BREAD
KING DOFF AND THE PRINCESS OF MORNING GLORIES

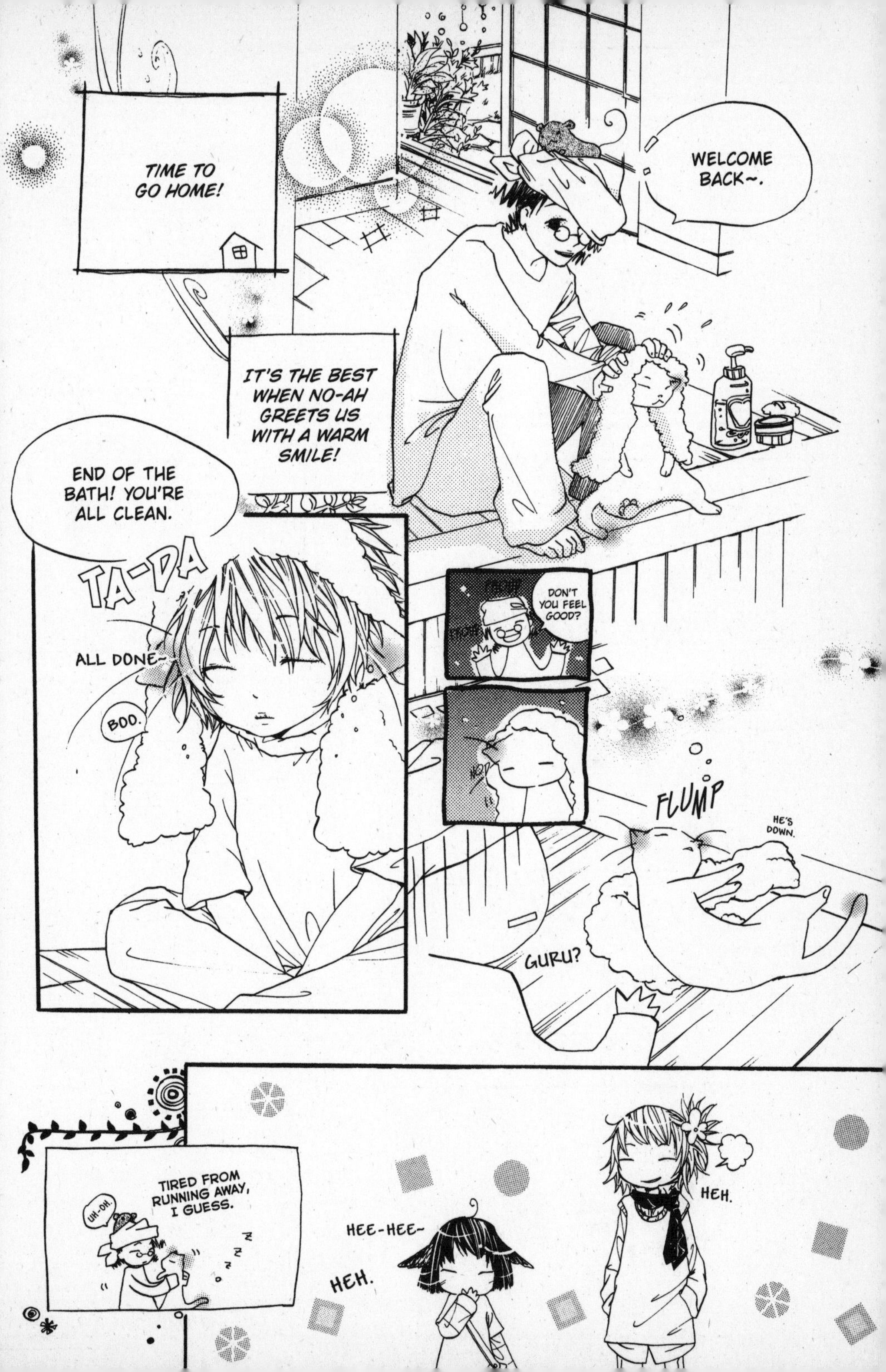
TIME TO GO HOME!
WELCOME BACK~.
IT'S THE BEST WHEN NO-AH GREETS US WITH A WARM SMILE!
END OF THE BATH! YOU'RE ALL CLEAN.
TA-DA
ALL DONE~
BOO.
DON'T YOU FEEL GOOD?
FLUMP
HE'S DOWN.
GURU?
TIRED FROM RUNNING AWAY, I GUESS.
UH-OH.
HEE-HEE~
HEH.
HEH.

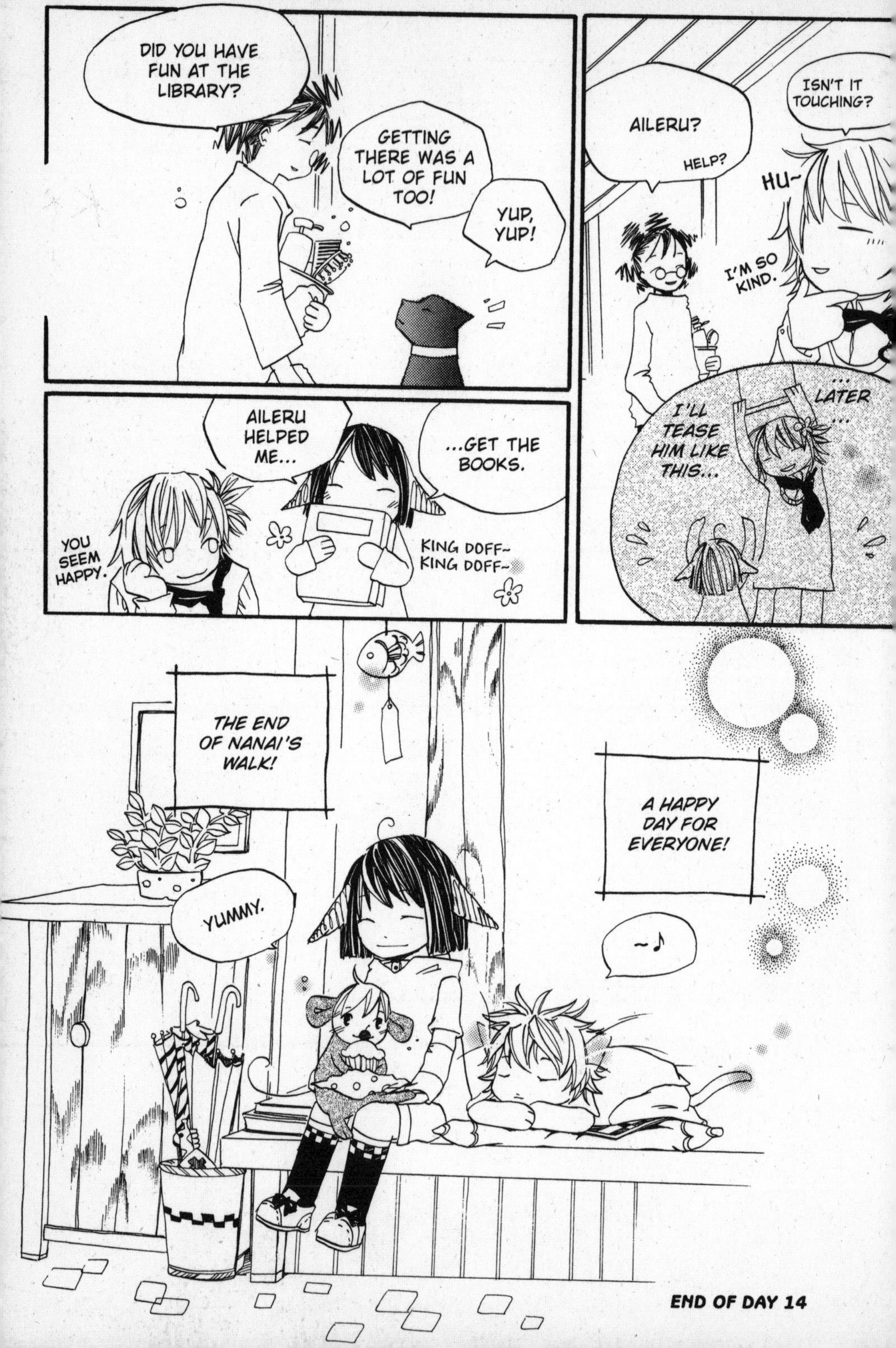
DID YOU HAVE FUN AT THE LIBRARY?
GETTING THERE WAS A LOT OF FUN TOO!
YUP, YUP!
AILERU HELPED ME...
...GET THE BOOKS.
YOU SEEM HAPPY.
KING DOFF~ KING DOFF~
AILERU?
HELP?
ISN'T IT TOUCHING?
HU~
I'M SO KIND.
I'LL TEASE HIM LIKE THIS...
...LATER...
THE END OF NANAI'S WALK!
A HAPPY DAY FOR EVERYONE!
YUMMY.
~♪

END OF DAY 14

DAY 15.
NIGHT WITH THE MOON

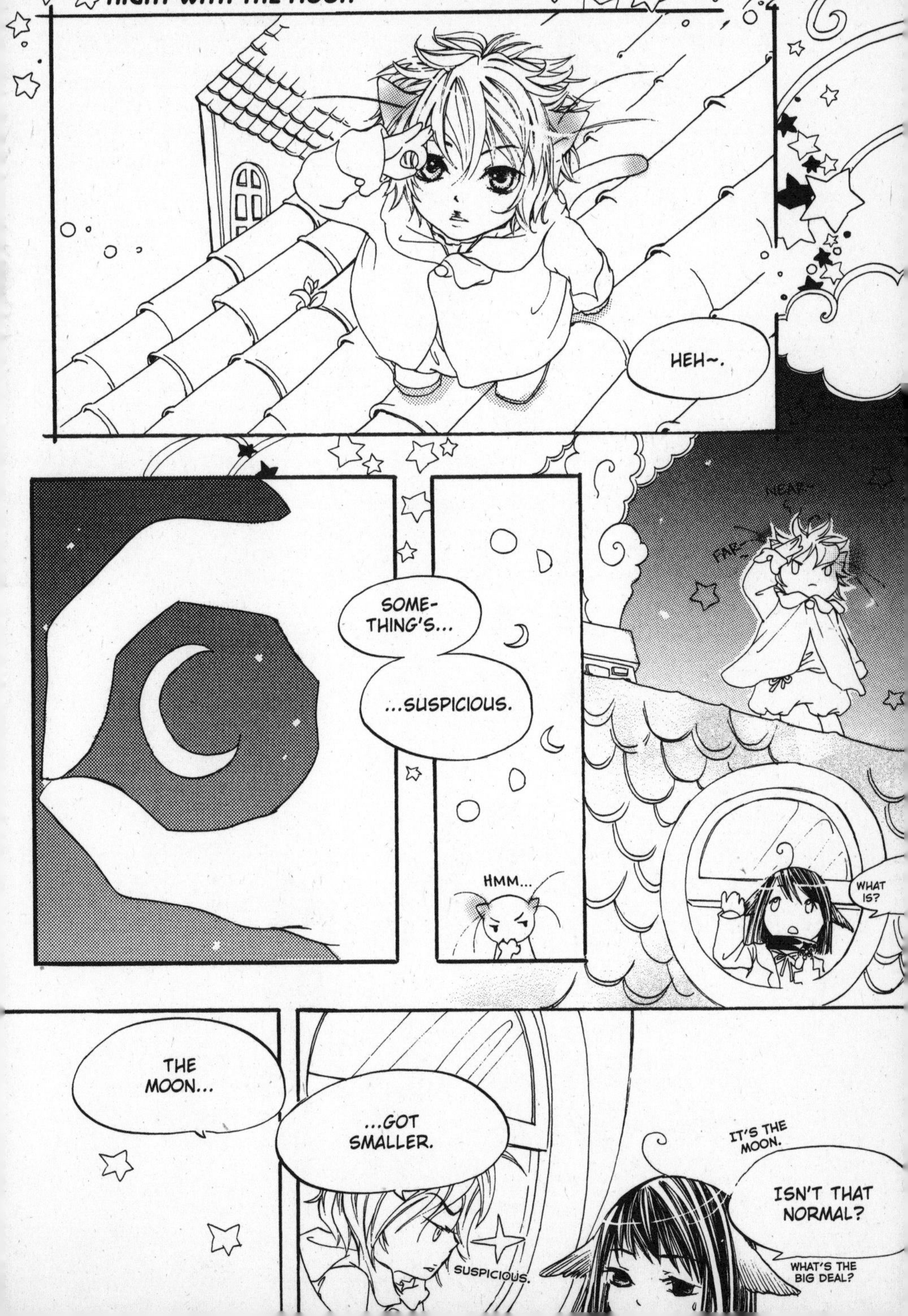
HEH~.
SOME-THING'S...
...SUSPICIOUS.
HMM...
NEAR~
FAR~
WHAT IS?
THE MOON...
...GOT SMALLER.
SUSPICIOUS.
IT'S THE MOON.
ISN'T THAT NORMAL?
WHAT'S THE BIG DEAL?

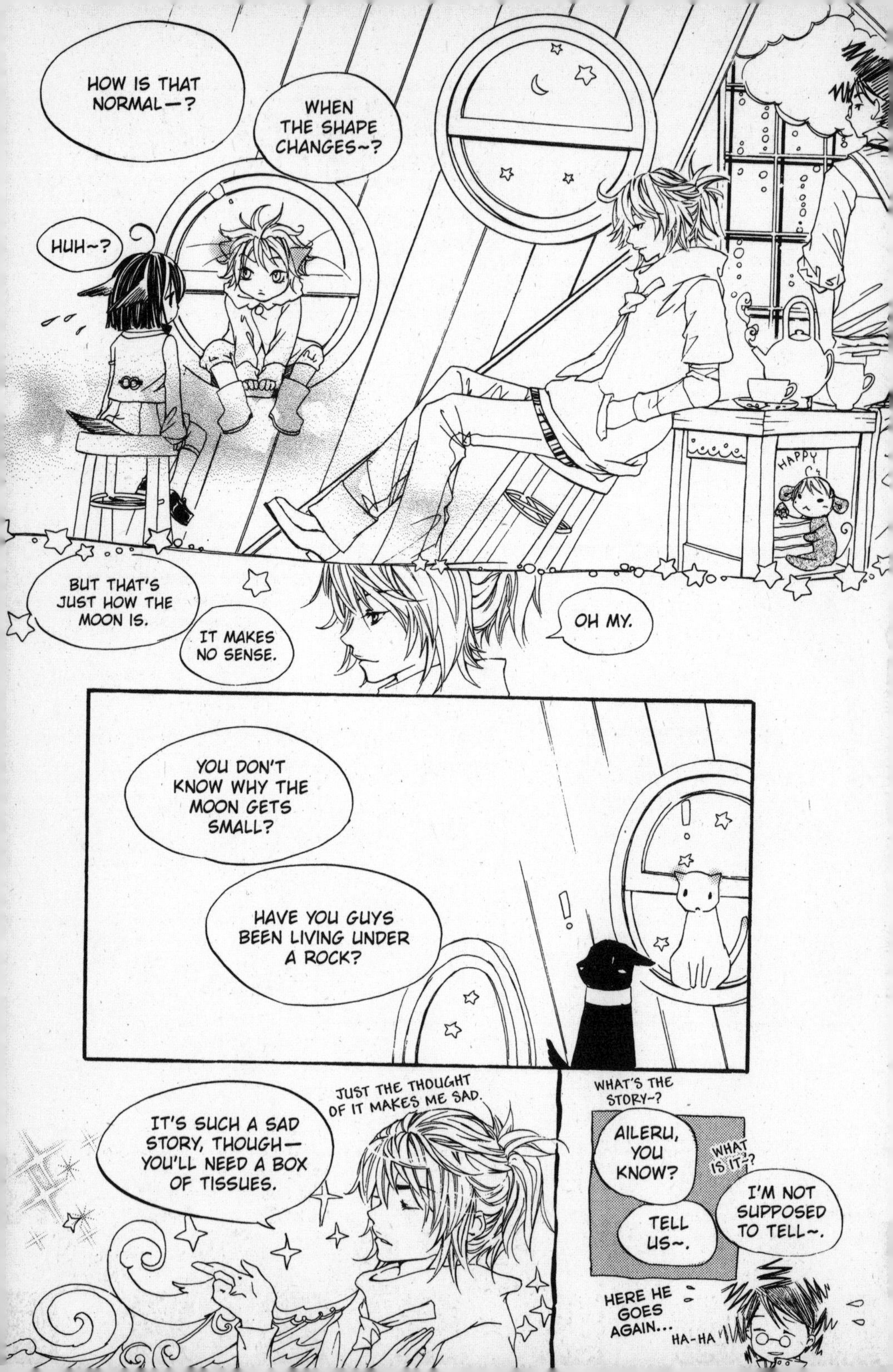

HOW IS THAT NORMAL—?
WHEN THE SHAPE CHANGES~?
HUH~?
HAPPY
BUT THAT'S JUST HOW THE MOON IS.
IT MAKES NO SENSE.
OH MY.
YOU DON'T KNOW WHY THE MOON GETS SMALL?
HAVE YOU GUYS BEEN LIVING UNDER A ROCK?
!
!
IT'S SUCH A SAD STORY, THOUGH— YOU'LL NEED A BOX OF TISSUES.
JUST THE THOUGHT OF IT MAKES ME SAD.
WHAT'S THE STORY~?
AILERU, YOU KNOW?
TELL US~.
WHAT IS IT~?
I'M NOT SUPPOSED TO TELL~.
HERE HE GOES AGAIN...
HA-HA

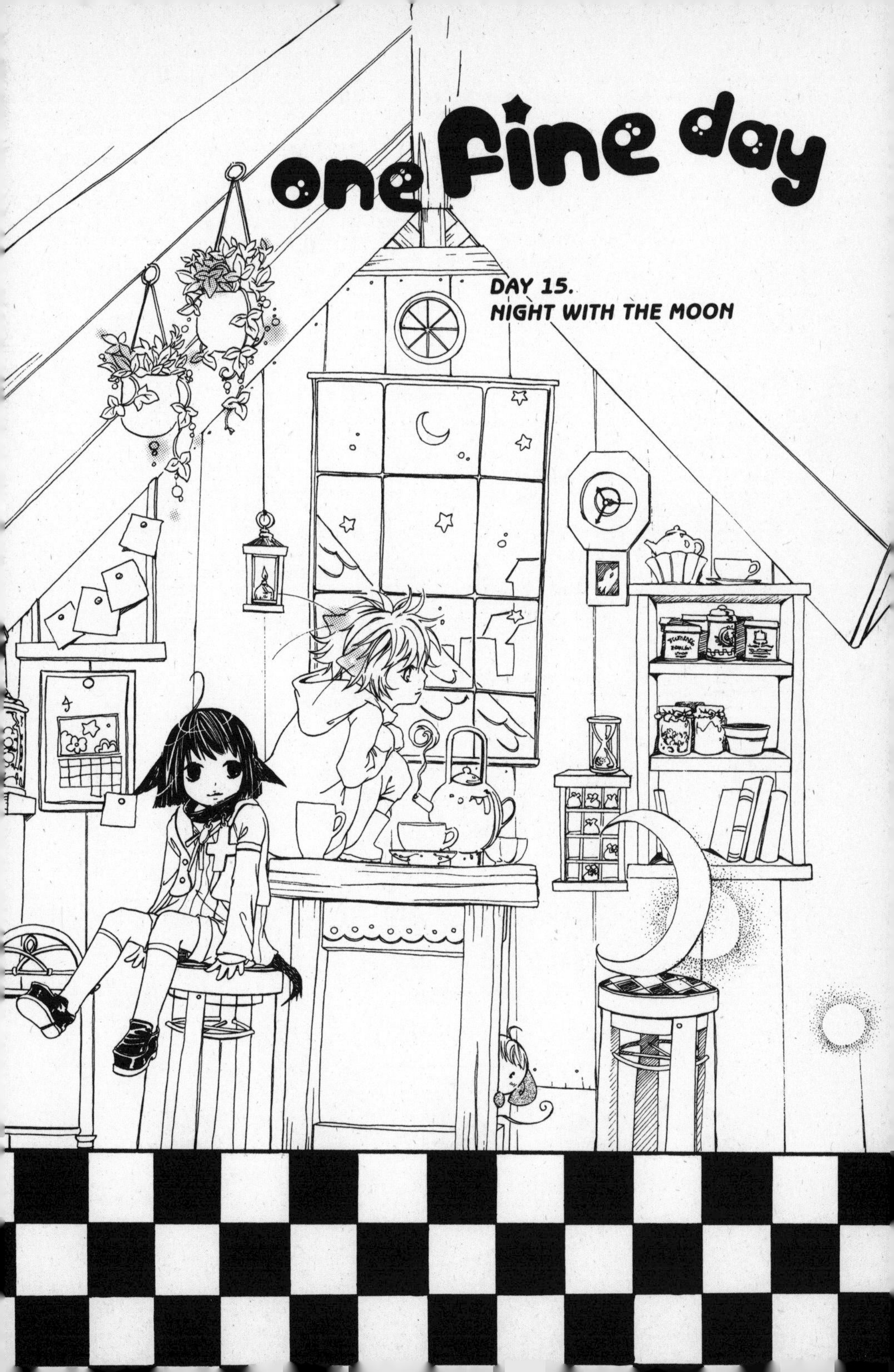
one fine day
DAY 15.
NIGHT WITH THE MOON

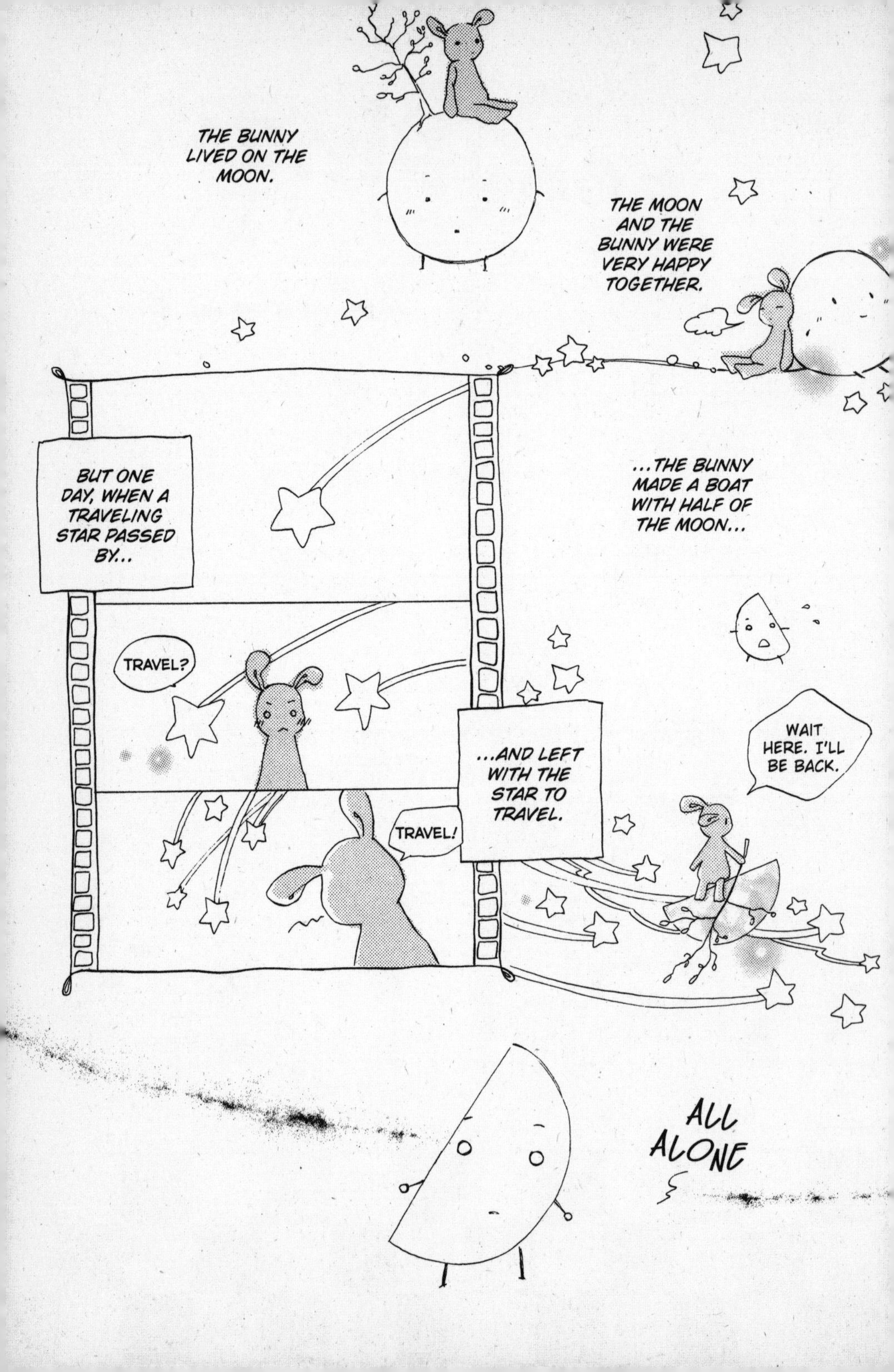
THE BUNNY LIVED ON THE MOON.
THE MOON AND THE BUNNY WERE VERY HAPPY TOGETHER.
BUT ONE DAY, WHEN A TRAVELING STAR PASSED BY...
TRAVEL?
TRAVEL!
...THE BUNNY MADE A BOAT WITH HALF OF THE MOON...
...AND LEFT WITH THE STAR TO TRAVEL.
WAIT HERE. I'LL BE BACK.
ALL ALONE

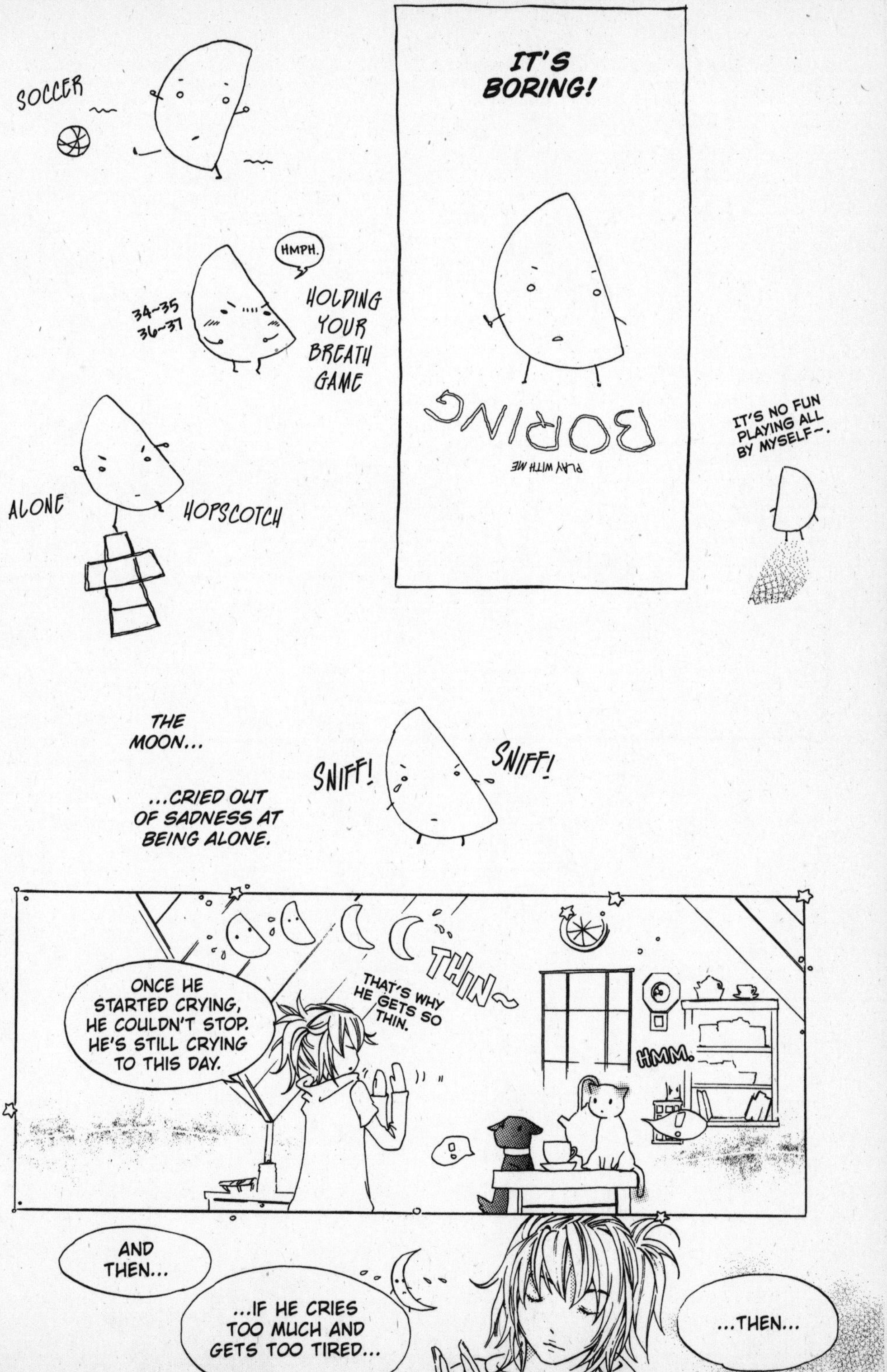

SOCCER
HMPH.
34~35
36~37
HOLDING YOUR BREATH GAME
ALONE
HOPSCOTCH
IT'S BORING!
BORING
PLAY WITH ME
IT'S NO FUN PLAYING ALL BY MYSELF~.
THE MOON...
...CRIED OUT OF SADNESS AT BEING ALONE.
SNIFF!
SNIFF!
ONCE HE STARTED CRYING, HE COULDN'T STOP. HE'S STILL CRYING TO THIS DAY.
THAT'S WHY HE GETS SO THIN.
THIN~
HMM.
AND THEN...
...IF HE CRIES TOO MUCH AND GETS TOO TIRED...
...THEN...

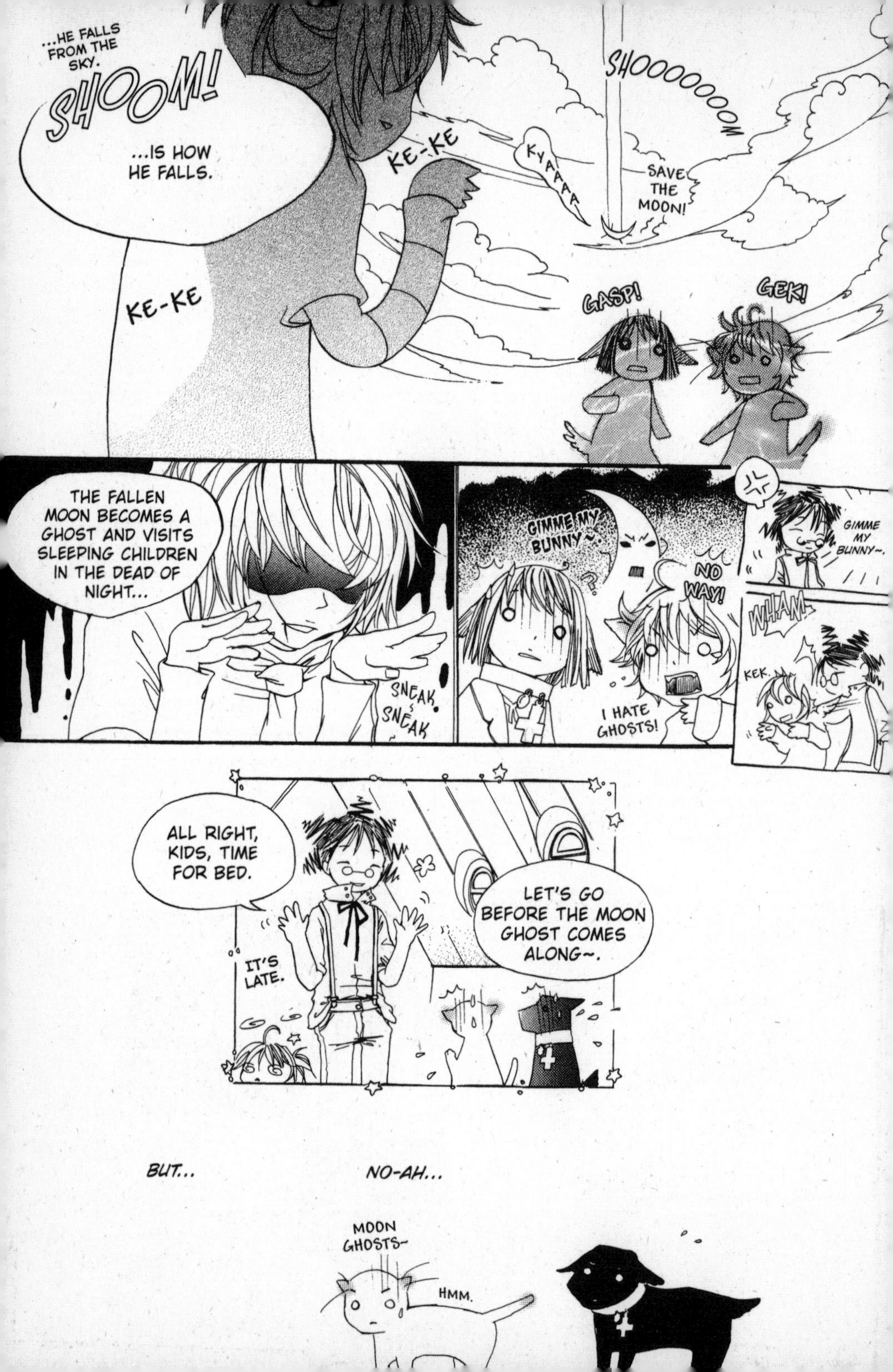
...HE FALLS FROM THE SKY.
SHOOM!
...IS HOW HE FALLS.
KE-KE
KE-KE
KYAAAAA
SHOOOOOOOOM
SAVE THE MOON!
GASP!
GEK!
THE FALLEN MOON BECOMES A GHOST AND VISITS SLEEPING CHILDREN IN THE DEAD OF NIGHT...
SNEAK SNEAK
GIMME MY BUNNY~.
?
NO WAY!
I HATE GHOSTS!
GIMME MY BUNNY~.
WHAM!
KEK.
ALL RIGHT, KIDS, TIME FOR BED.
IT'S LATE.
LET'S GO BEFORE THE MOON GHOST COMES ALONG~.
BUT...
NO-AH...
MOON GHOSTS~
HMM.

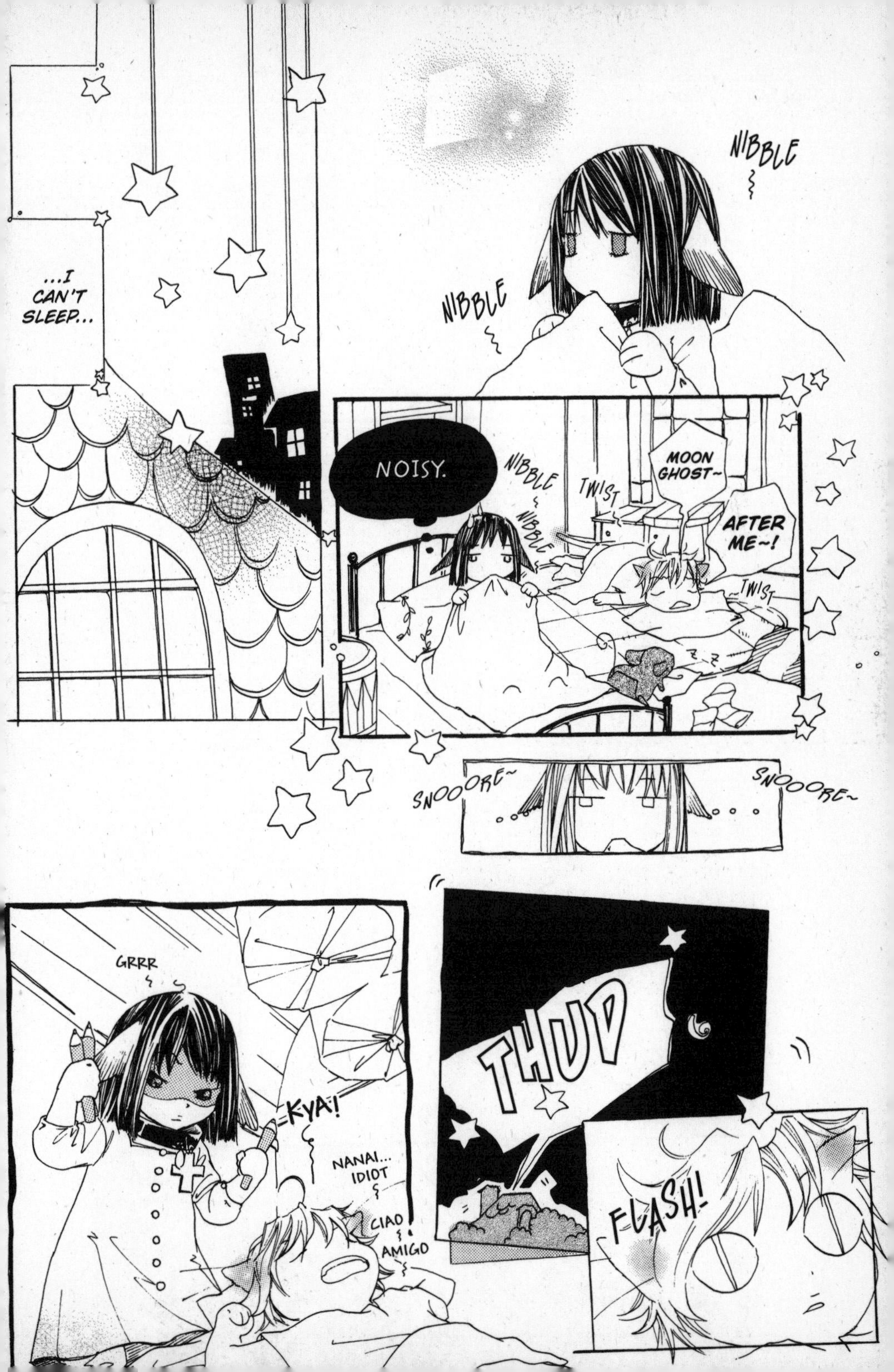
...I CAN'T SLEEP...
NIBBLE
NIBBLE
NOISY.
NIBBLE
NIBBLE
TWIST
MOON GHOST~
AFTER ME~!
TWIST
SNOOORE~
SNOOORE~
GRRR
KYA!
NANAI... IDIOT
CIAO AMIGO
THUD
FLASH!

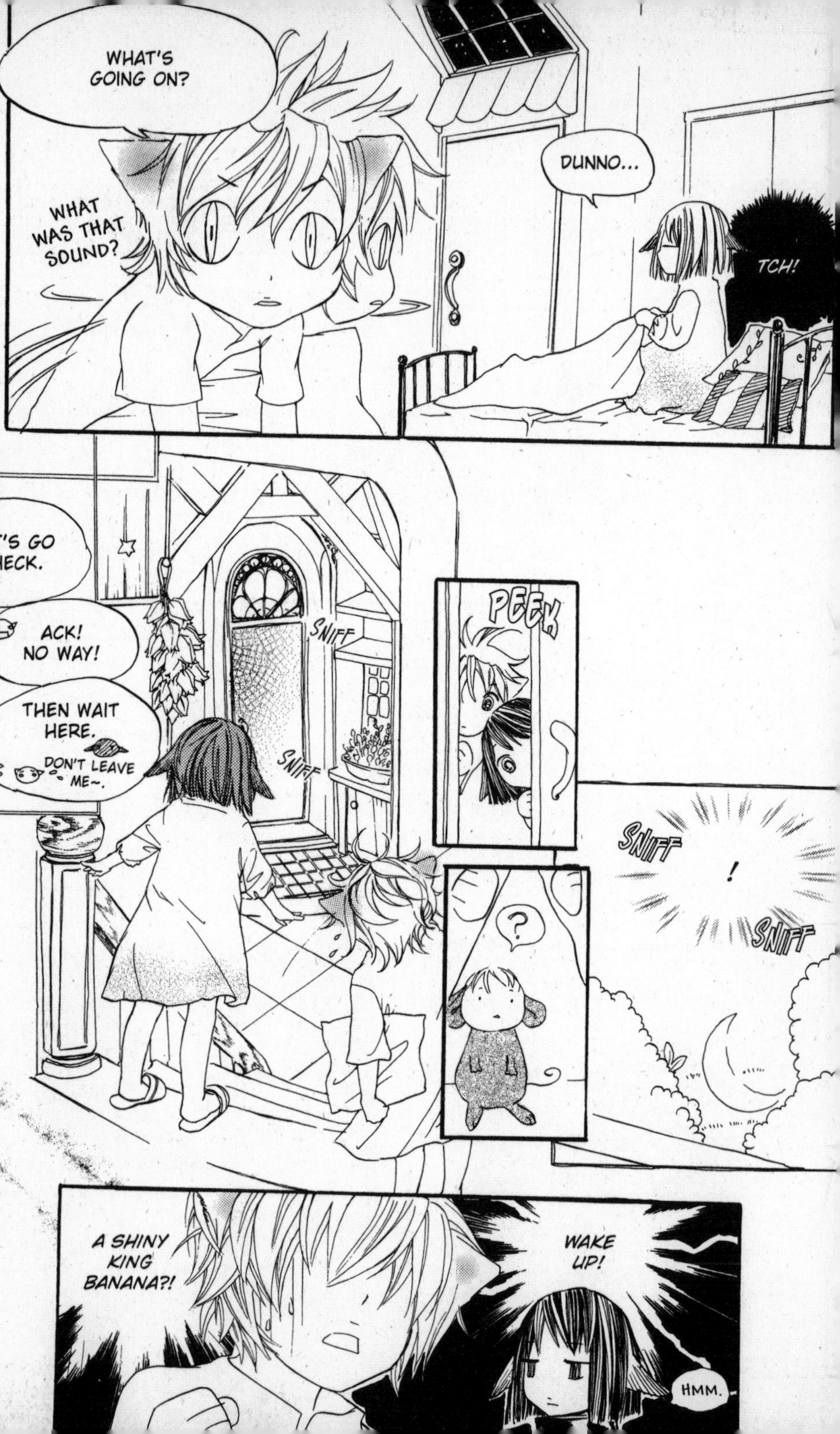
WHAT'S GOING ON?
WHAT WAS THAT SOUND?
DUNNO...
TCH!
LET'S GO CHECK.
ACK! NO WAY!
THEN WAIT HERE.
DON'T LEAVE ME~.
SNIFF
SNIFF
PEEK
?
SNIFF
!
SNIFF
A SHINY KING BANANA?!
WAKE UP!
HMM.

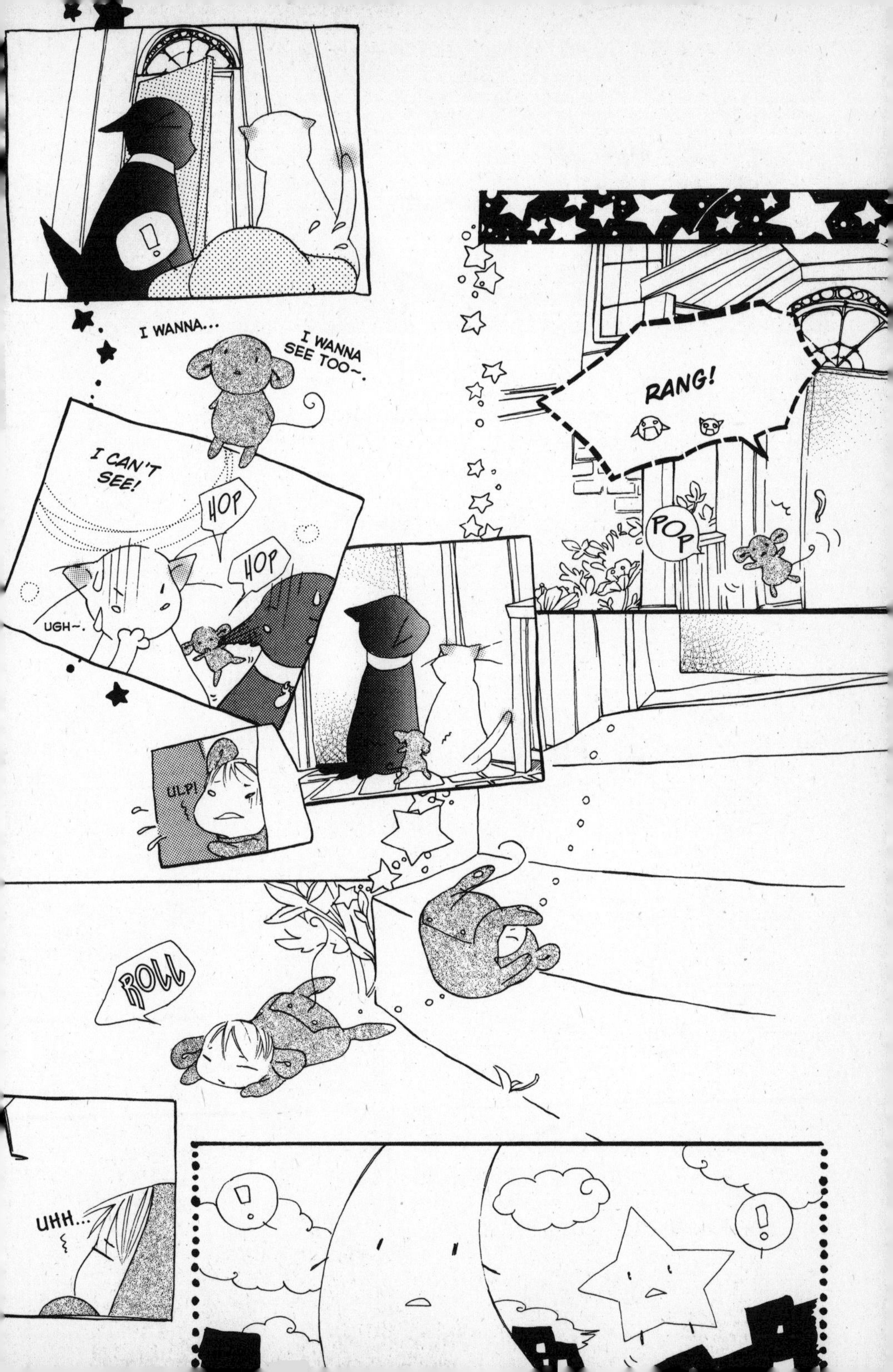
!
I WANNA...
I WANNA SEE TOO~.
I CAN'T SEE!
HOP
HOP
UGH~.
ULP!
RANG!
POP
ROLL
UHH...
!
!

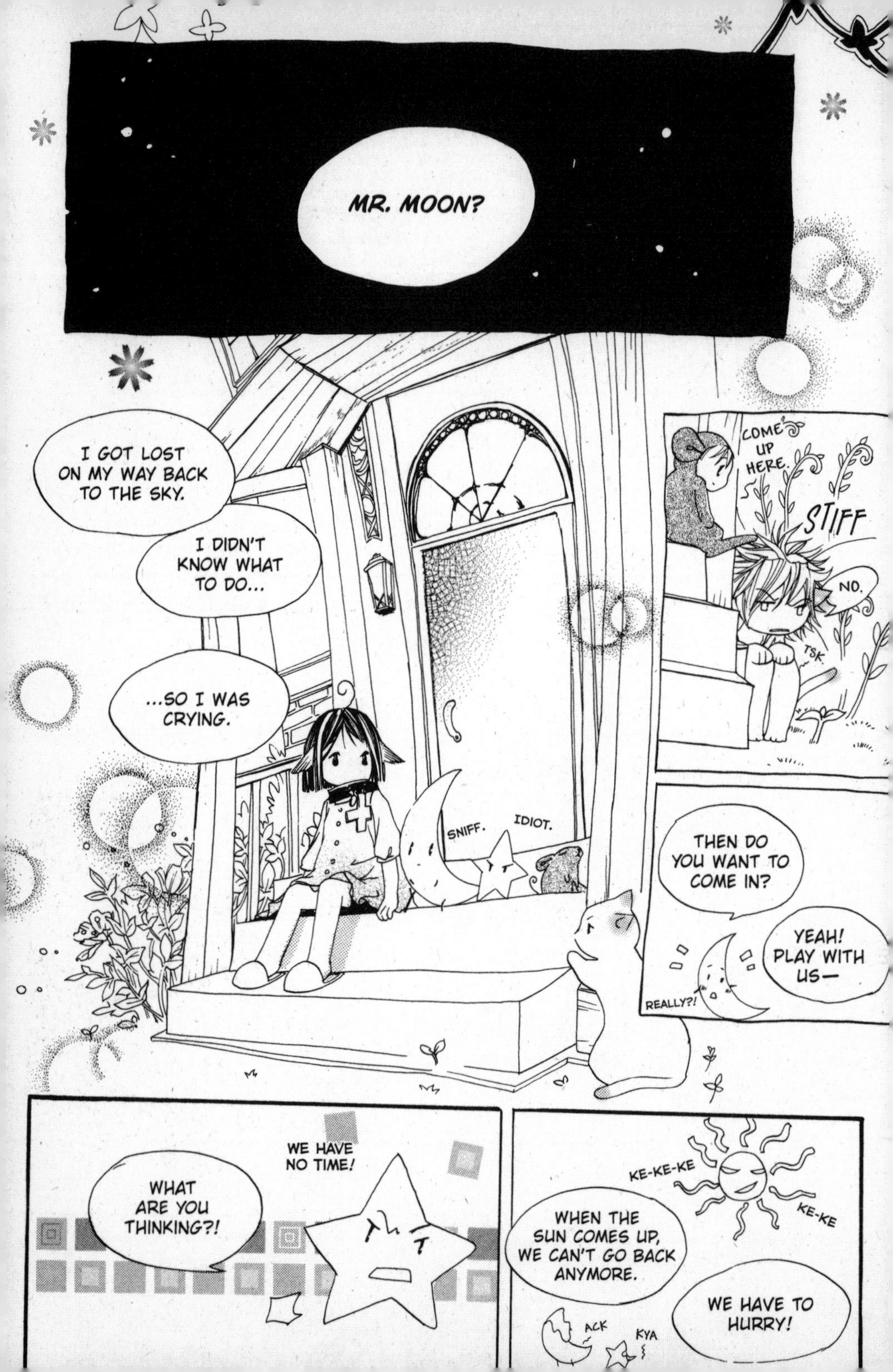
MR. MOON?
I GOT LOST ON MY WAY BACK TO THE SKY.
I DIDN'T KNOW WHAT TO DO...
...SO I WAS CRYING.
SNIFF.
IDIOT.
COME UP HERE.
STIFF
NO.
TSK.
THEN DO YOU WANT TO COME IN?
YEAH! PLAY WITH US—
REALLY?!
WHAT ARE YOU THINKING?!
WE HAVE NO TIME!
KE-KE-KE
KE-KE
WHEN THE SUN COMES UP, WE CAN'T GO BACK ANYMORE.
WE HAVE TO HURRY!
ACK
KYA

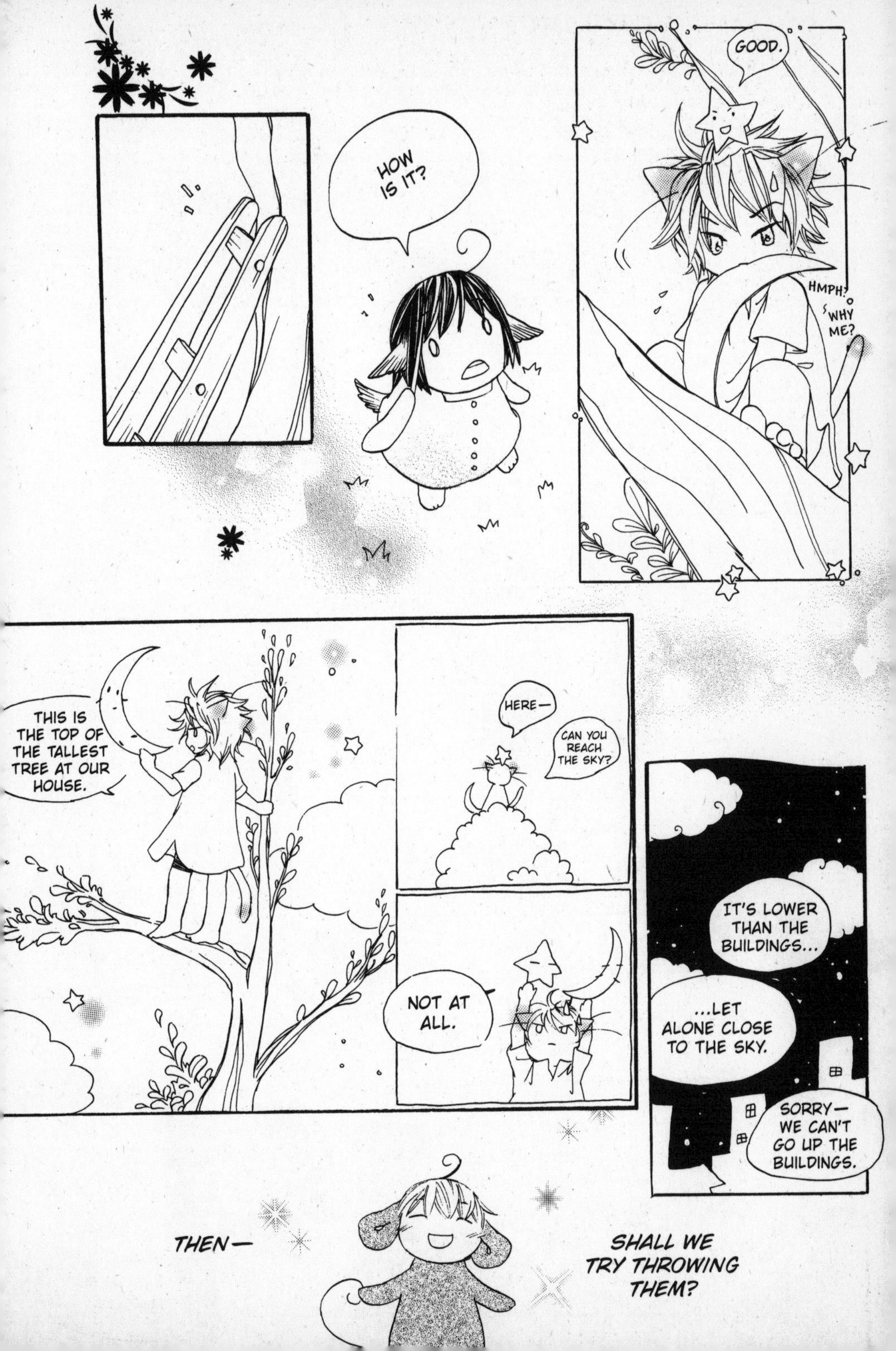
HOW IS IT?
GOOD.
HMPH? WHY ME?
THIS IS THE TOP OF THE TALLEST TREE AT OUR HOUSE.
HERE—
CAN YOU REACH THE SKY?
NOT AT ALL.
IT'S LOWER THAN THE BUILDINGS...
...LET ALONE CLOSE TO THE SKY.
SORRY— WE CAN'T GO UP THE BUILDINGS.
THEN—
SHALL WE TRY THROWING THEM?

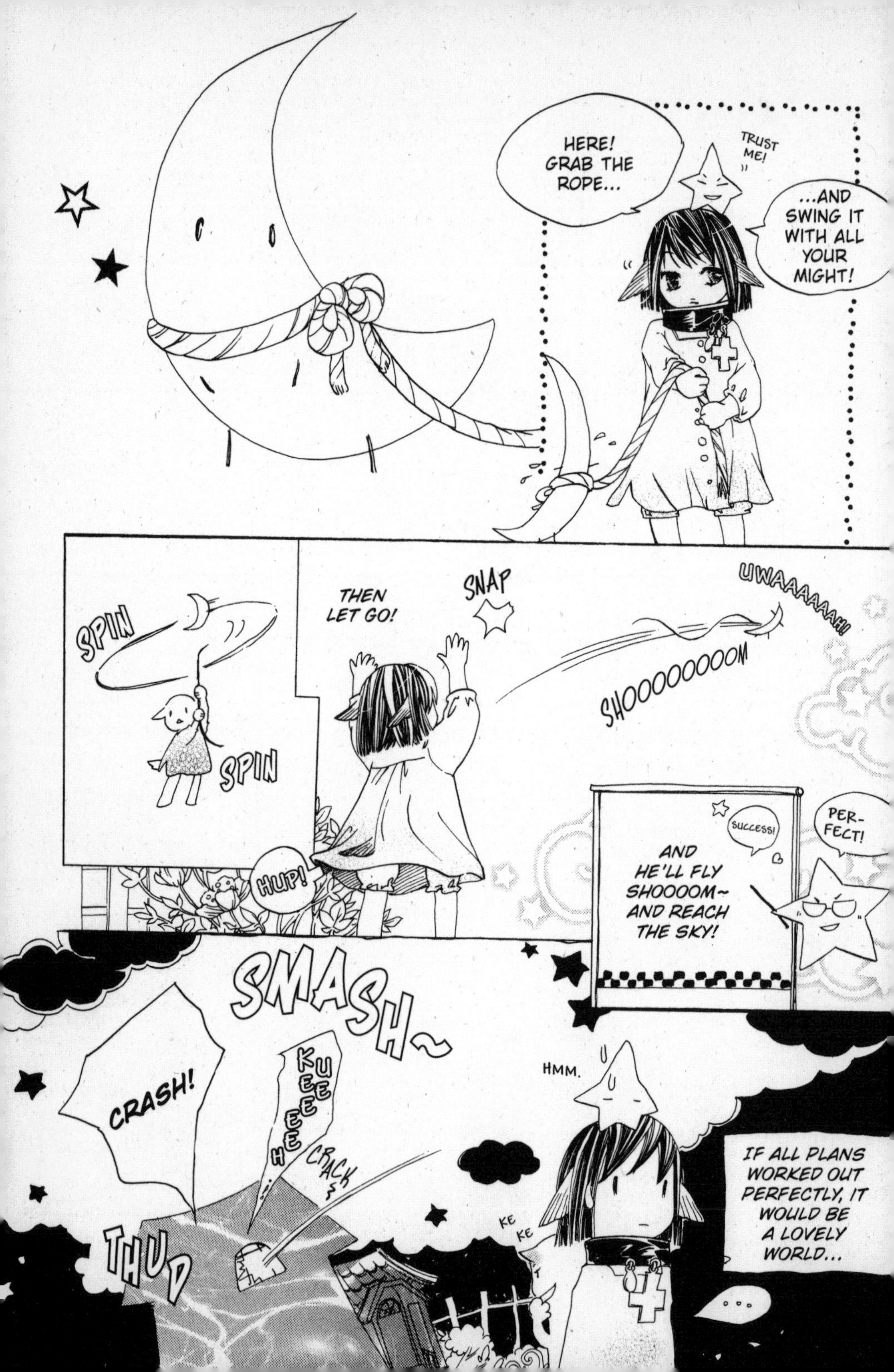
HERE! GRAB THE ROPE...
TRUST ME!
...AND SWING IT WITH ALL YOUR MIGHT!
SPIN
SPIN
THEN LET GO!
SNAP
UWAAAAAAAH!
SHOOOOOOOOM
HUP!
SUCCESS!
AND HE'LL FLY SHOOOOM~ AND REACH THE SKY!
PER-FECT!
SMASH~
CRASH!
KUEEEEEH
CRACK
THUD
HMM.
KE KE
IF ALL PLANS WORKED OUT PERFECTLY, IT WOULD BE A LOVELY WORLD...
...

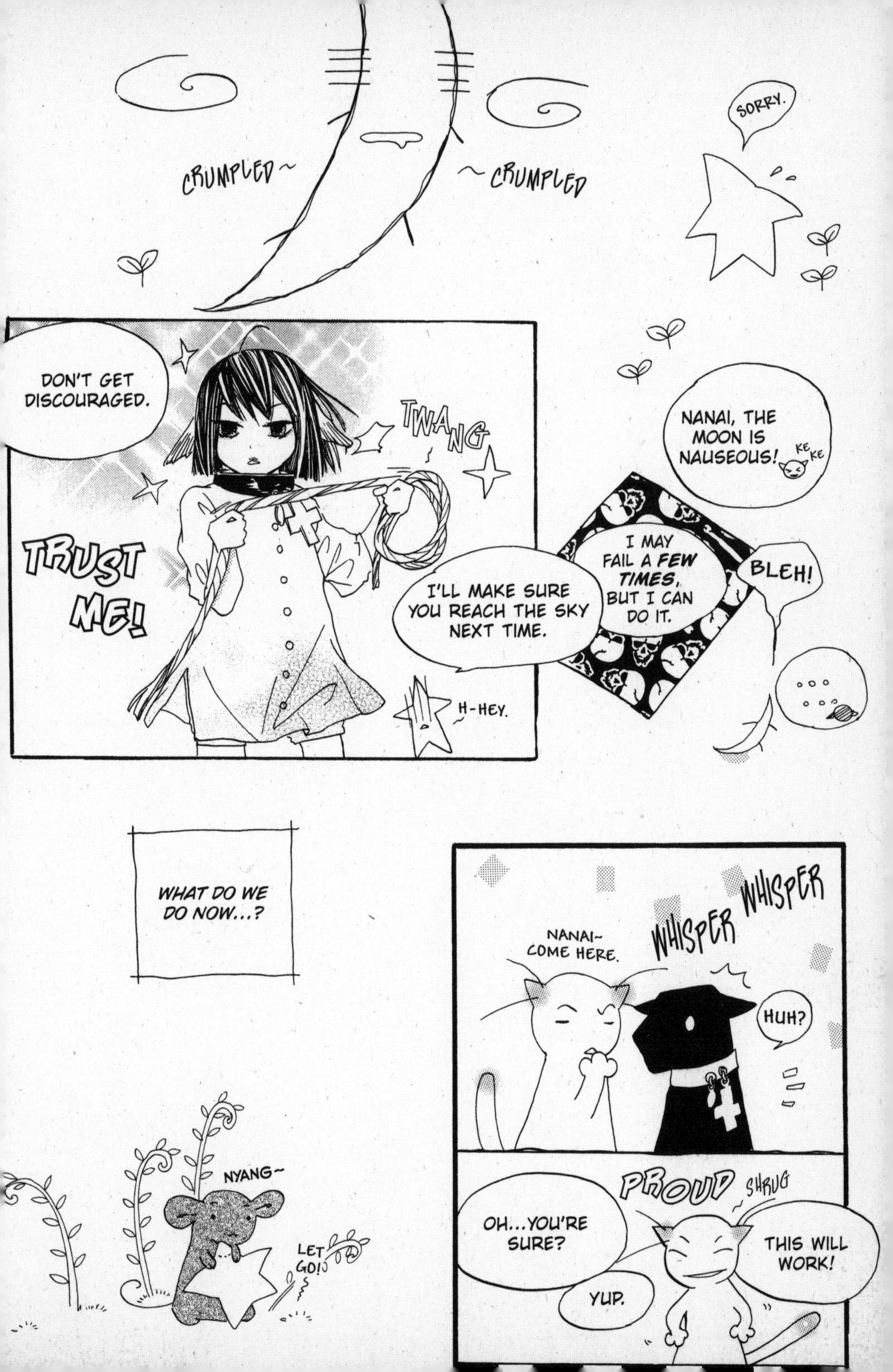
CRUMPLED~
~CRUMPLED
SORRY.
DON'T GET DISCOURAGED.
TWANG
TRUST ME!
I'LL MAKE SURE YOU REACH THE SKY NEXT TIME.
H-HEY.
NANAI, THE MOON IS NAUSEOUS!
KE KE
I MAY FAIL A FEW TIMES, BUT I CAN DO IT.
BLEH!
WHAT DO WE DO NOW...?
NYANG~
LET GO!!
NANAI~ COME HERE.
WHISPER WHISPER
HUH?
PROUD
SHRUG
OH...YOU'RE SURE?
THIS WILL WORK!
YUP.

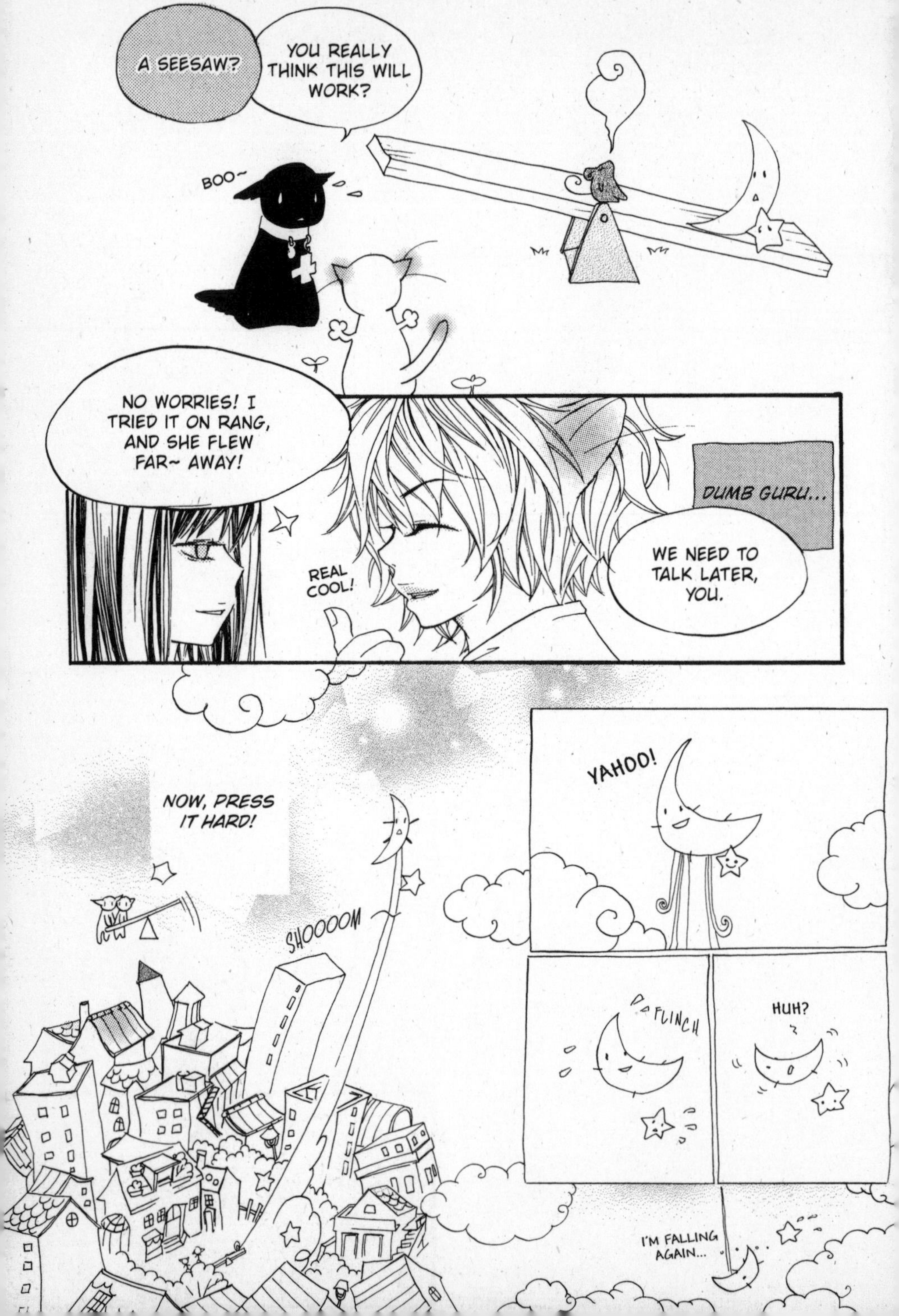
A SEESAW?
YOU REALLY THINK THIS WILL WORK?
BOO~
NO WORRIES! I TRIED IT ON RANG, AND SHE FLEW FAR~ AWAY!
REAL COOL!
DUMB GURU...
WE NEED TO TALK LATER, YOU.
NOW, PRESS IT HARD!
SHOOOOM
YAHOO!
FLINCH
HUH?
I'M FALLING AGAIN...

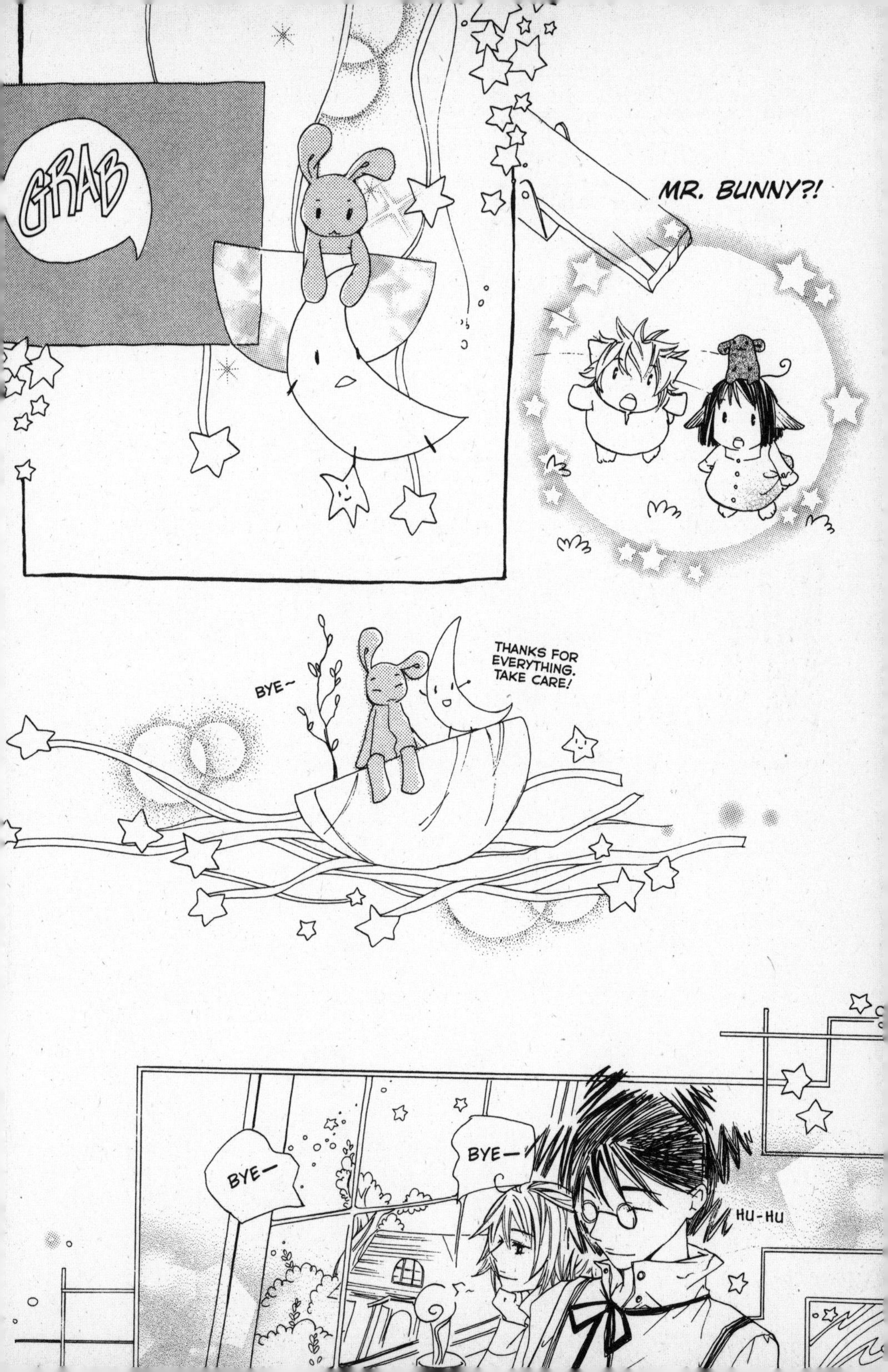
GRAB
MR. BUNNY?!
BYE~
THANKS FOR EVERYTHING. TAKE CARE!
BYE—
BYE—
HU-HU

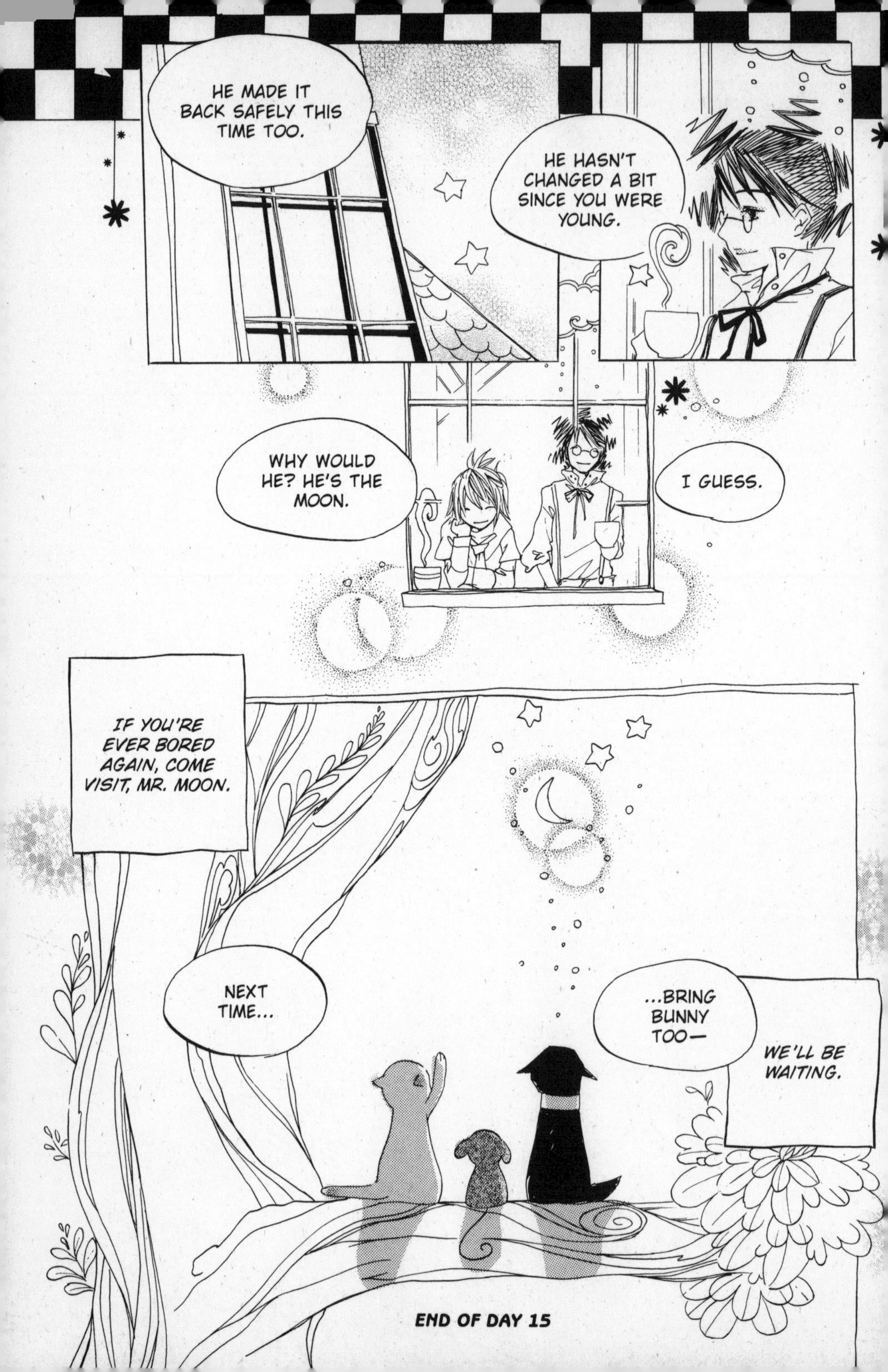
HE MADE IT BACK SAFELY THIS TIME TOO.
HE HASN'T CHANGED A BIT SINCE YOU WERE YOUNG.
WHY WOULD HE? HE'S THE MOON.
I GUESS.
IF YOU'RE EVER BORED AGAIN, COME VISIT, MR. MOON.
NEXT TIME...
...BRING BUNNY TOO—
WE'LL BE WAITING.
END OF DAY 15

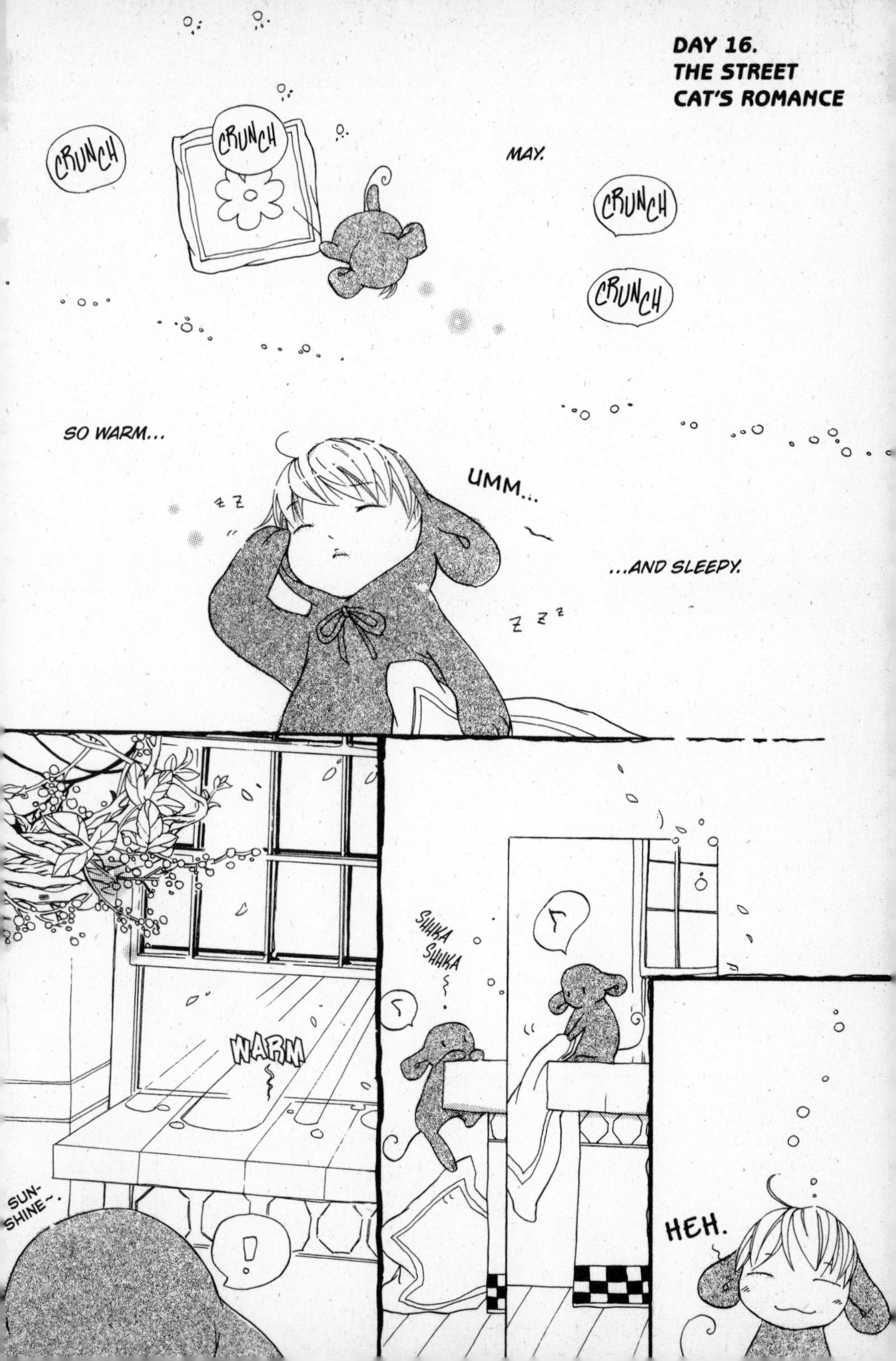
DAY 16.
THE STREET
CAT'S ROMANCE
CRUNCH
CRUNCH
MAY.
CRUNCH
CRUNCH
SO WARM...
UMM...
...AND SLEEPY.
WARM
SUN-SHINE~.
!
SHHKA SHHKA
HEH.

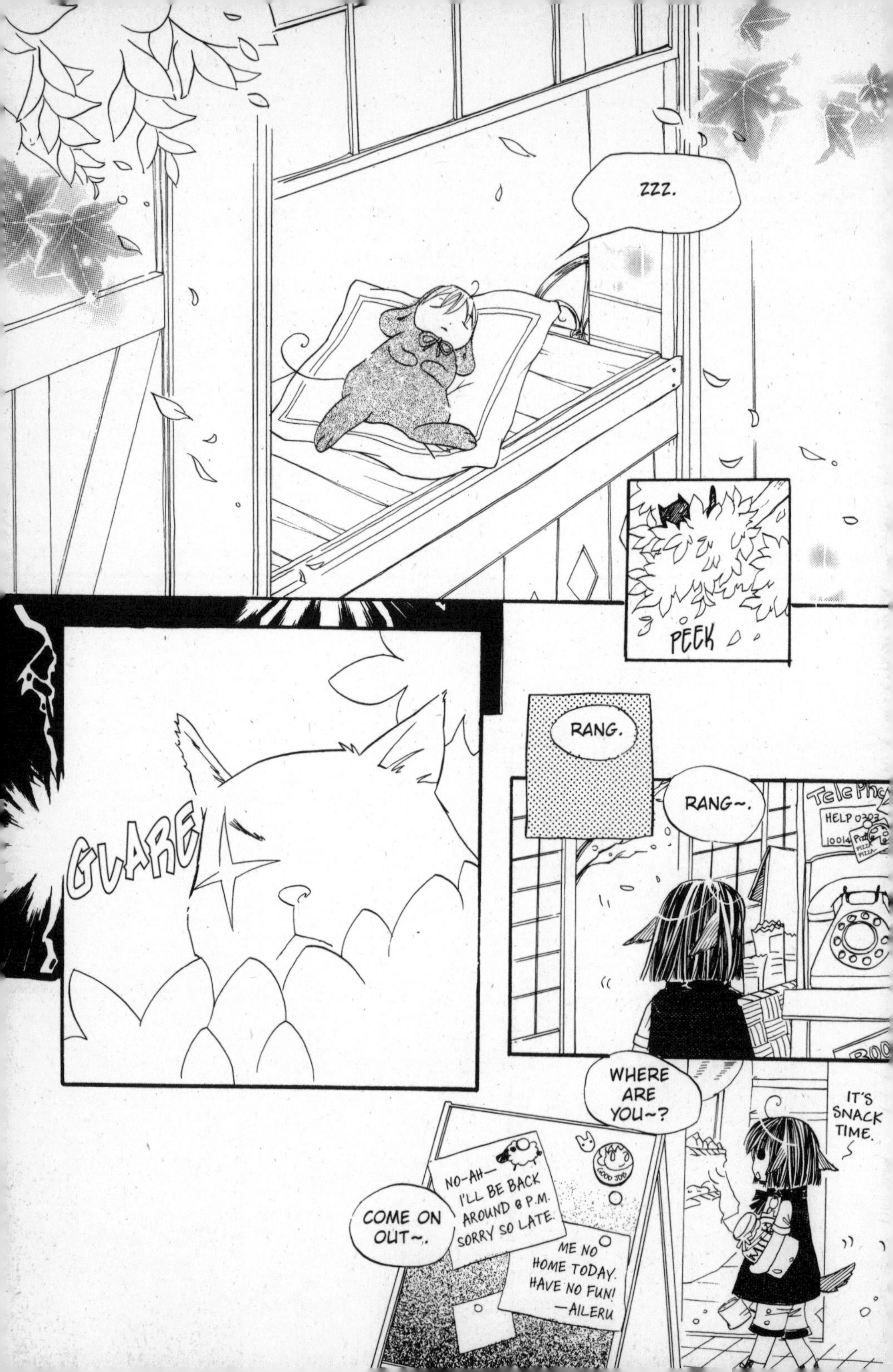
ZZZ.
PEEK
GLARE
RANG.
RANG~.
WHERE ARE YOU~?
IT'S SNACK TIME.
COME ON OUT~.
NO-AH— I'LL BE BACK AROUND 8 P.M. SORRY SO LATE.
GOOD JOB
ME NO HOME TODAY. HAVE NO FUN! —AILERU

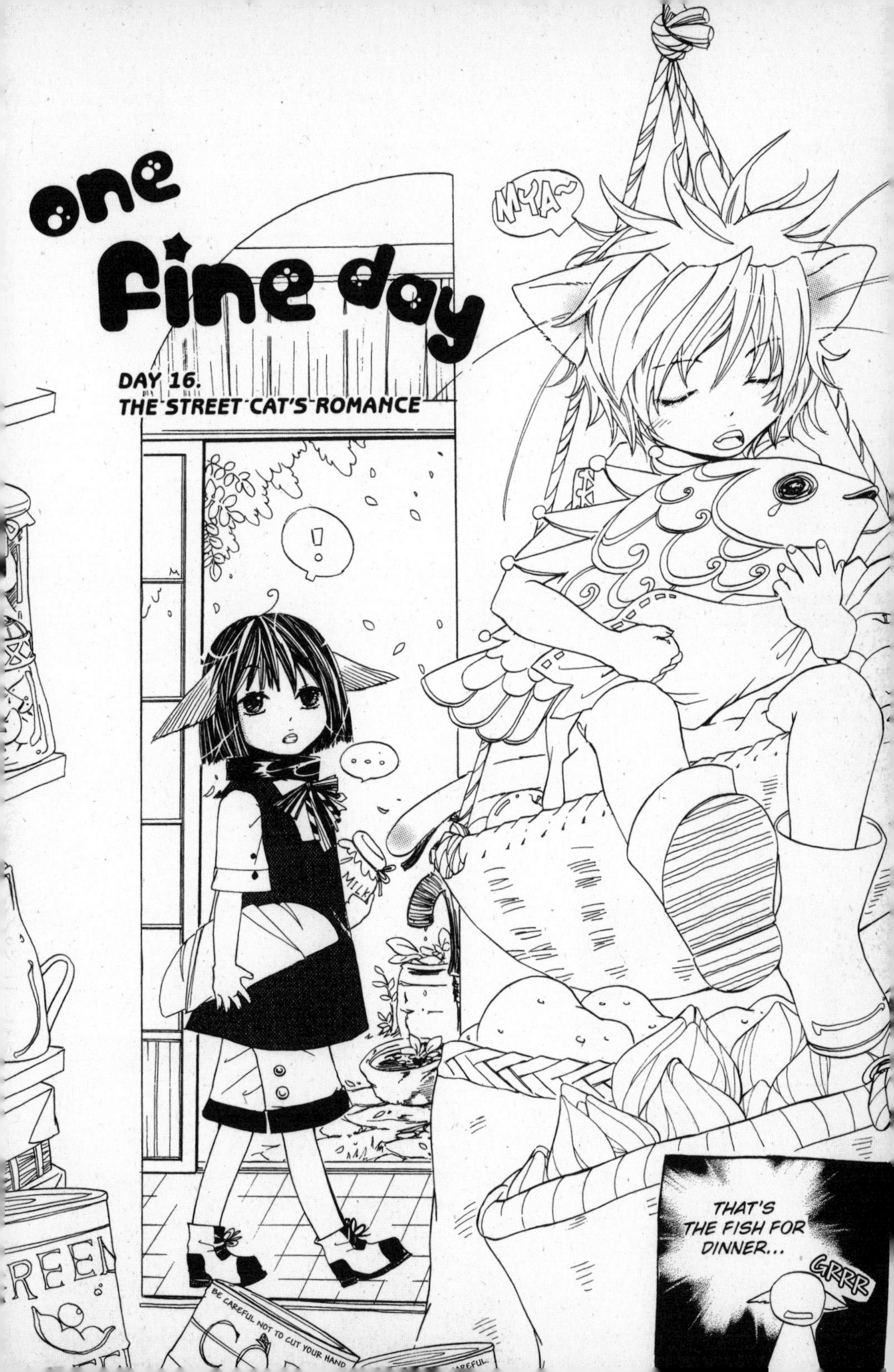
one fine day
DAY 16.
THE STREET CAT'S ROMANCE
MYA~
!
...
MILK
GREEN
BE CAREFUL NOT TO CUT YOUR HAND
THAT'S THE FISH FOR DINNER...
GRRR

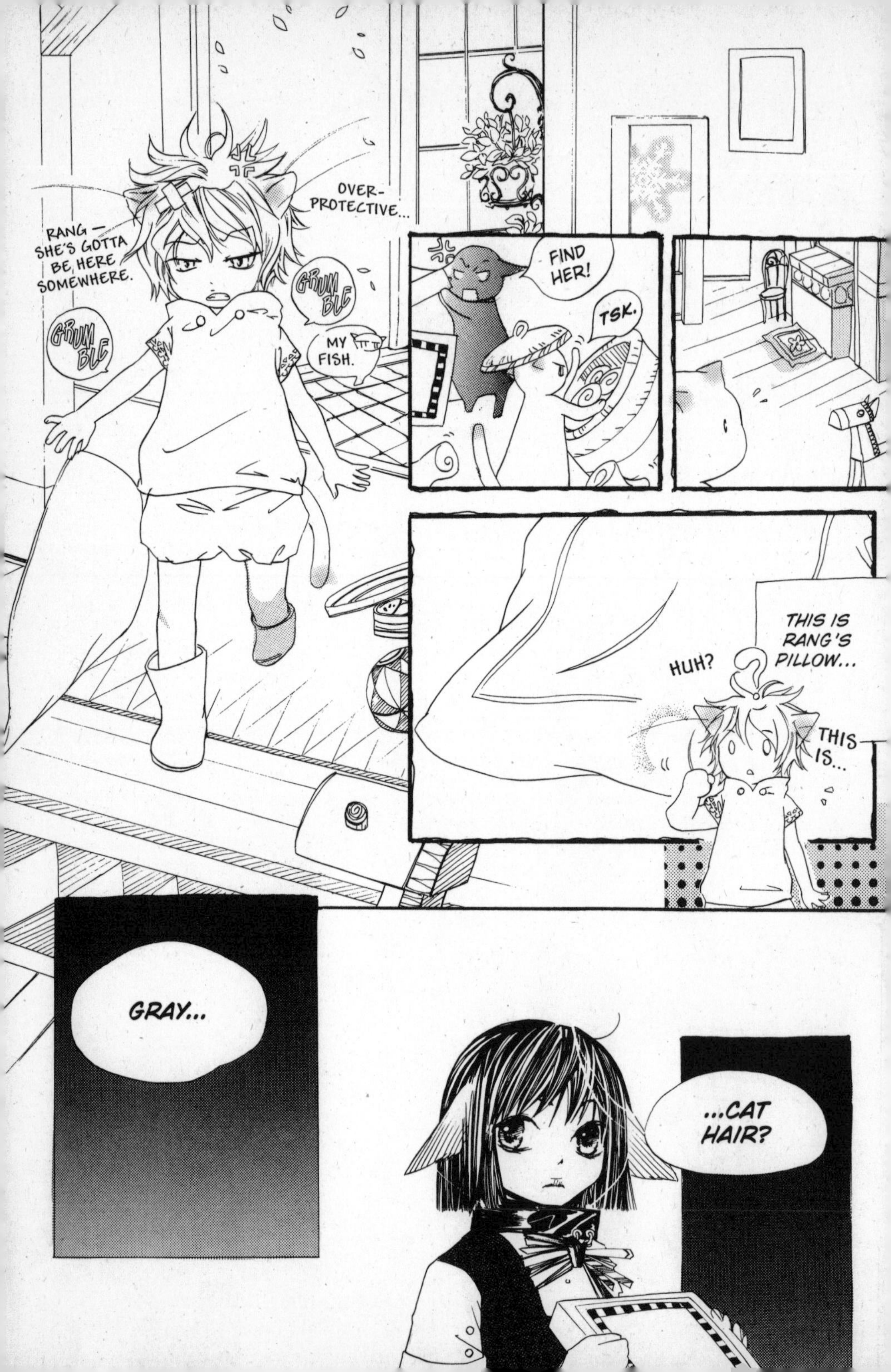
RANG — SHE'S GOTTA BE HERE SOMEWHERE.
OVER-PROTECTIVE...
GRUMBLE
GRUMBLE
MY FISH.
FIND HER!
TSK.
HUH?
THIS IS RANG'S PILLOW...
THIS IS...
GRAY...
...CAT HAIR?

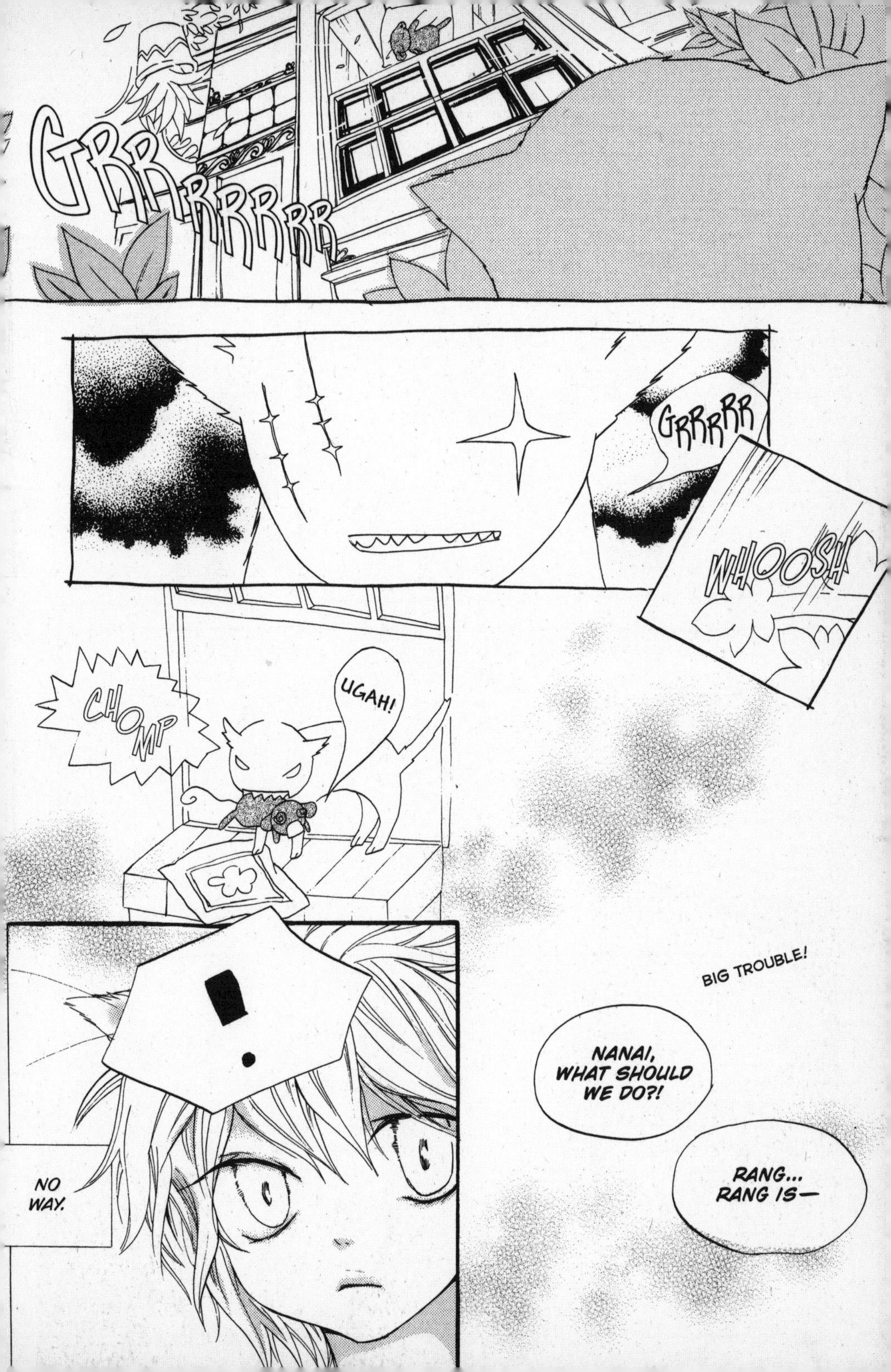
GRRRRRRRR
GRRRRR
WHOOSH
CHOMP
UGAH!
BIG TROUBLE!
NANAI, WHAT SHOULD WE DO?!
NO WAY.
RANG... RANG IS—

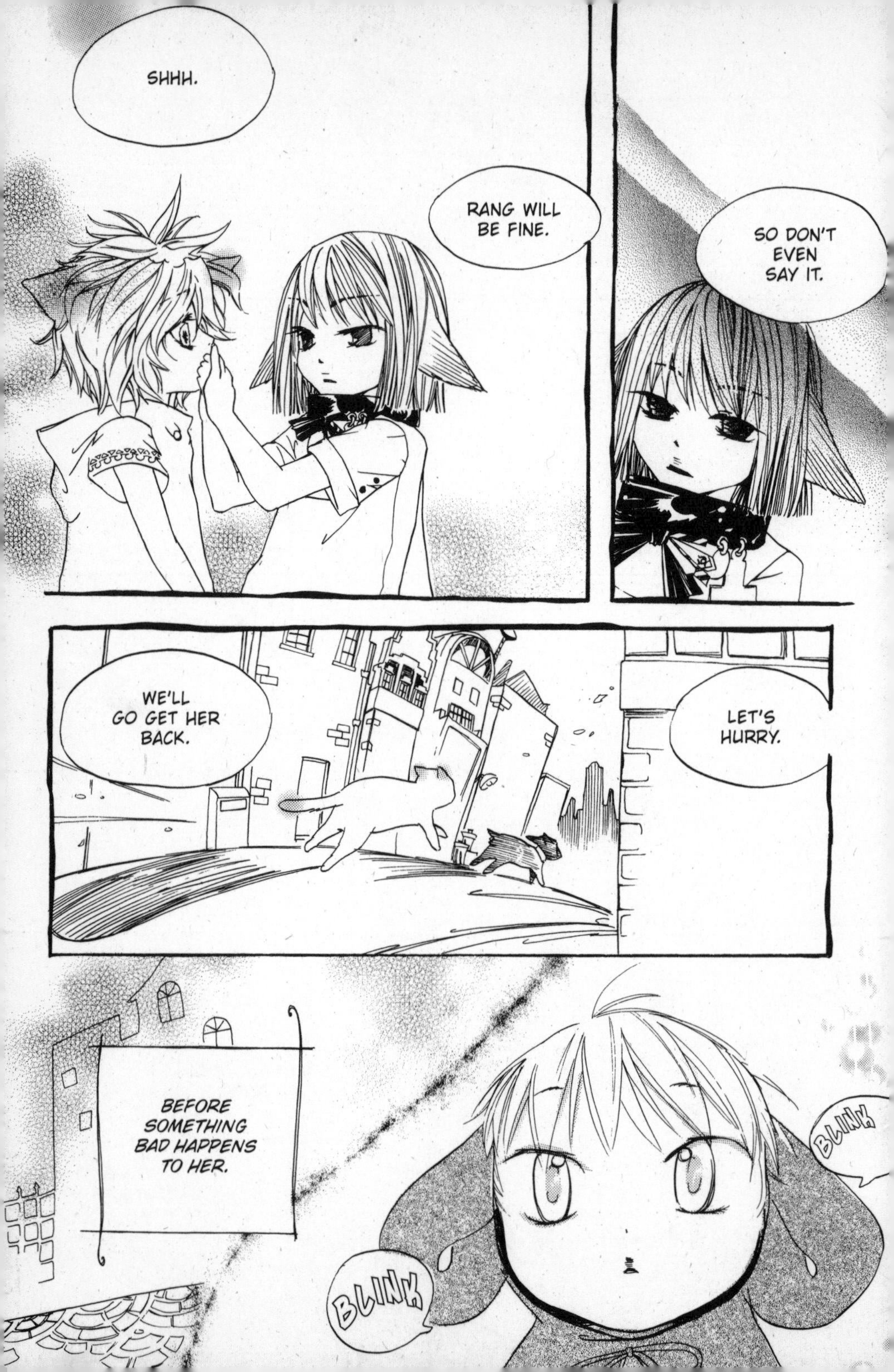
SHHH.
RANG WILL BE FINE.
SO DON'T EVEN SAY IT.
WE'LL GO GET HER BACK.
LET'S HURRY.
BEFORE SOMETHING BAD HAPPENS TO HER.
BLINK
BLINK

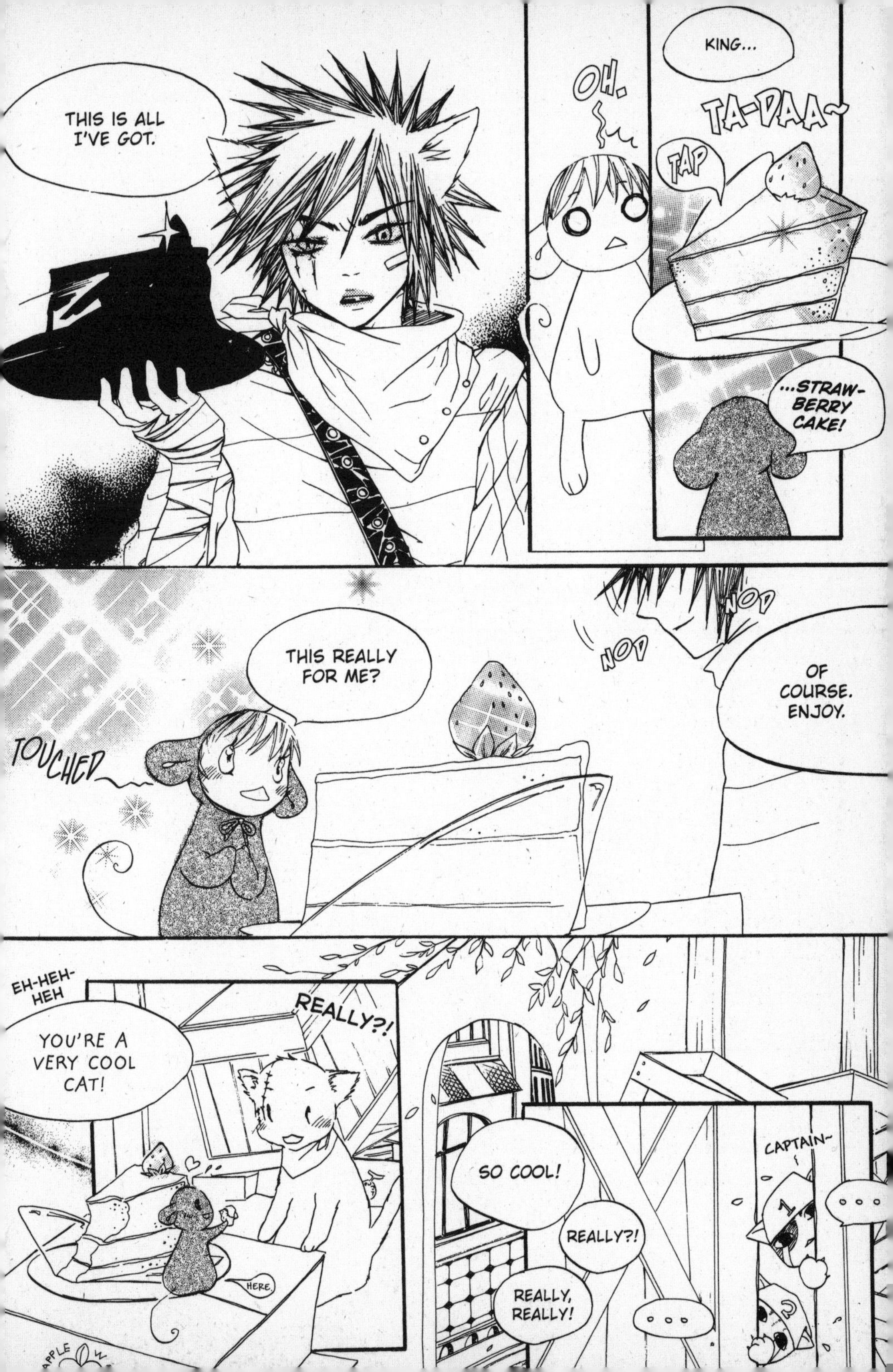
THIS IS ALL I'VE GOT.
OH.
KING...
TA-DAA~
TAP
...STRAW-BERRY CAKE!
TOUCHED~
THIS REALLY FOR ME?
NOD
NOD
OF COURSE. ENJOY.
EH-HEH-HEH
YOU'RE A VERY COOL CAT!
REALLY?!
HERE.
SO COOL!
REALLY?!
REALLY, REALLY!
...
CAPTAIN~
...

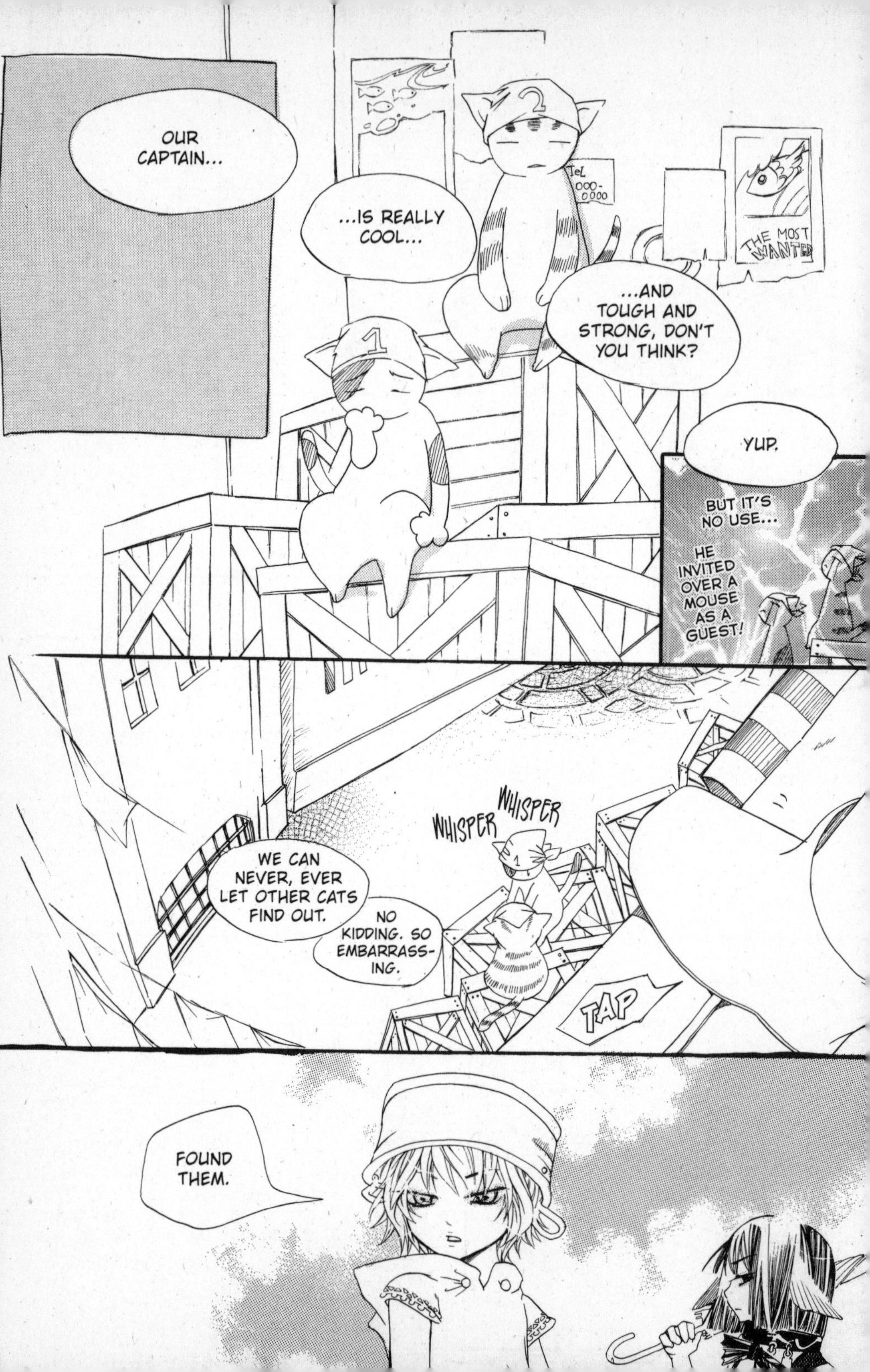
OUR CAPTAIN...
...IS REALLY COOL...
...AND TOUGH AND STRONG, DON'T YOU THINK?
TeL 000-0000
THE MOST WANTED
YUP.
BUT IT'S NO USE...
HE INVITED OVER A MOUSE AS A GUEST!
WHISPER
WHISPER
WE CAN NEVER, EVER LET OTHER CATS FIND OUT.
NO KIDDING. SO EMBARRASS-ING.
TAP
FOUND THEM.

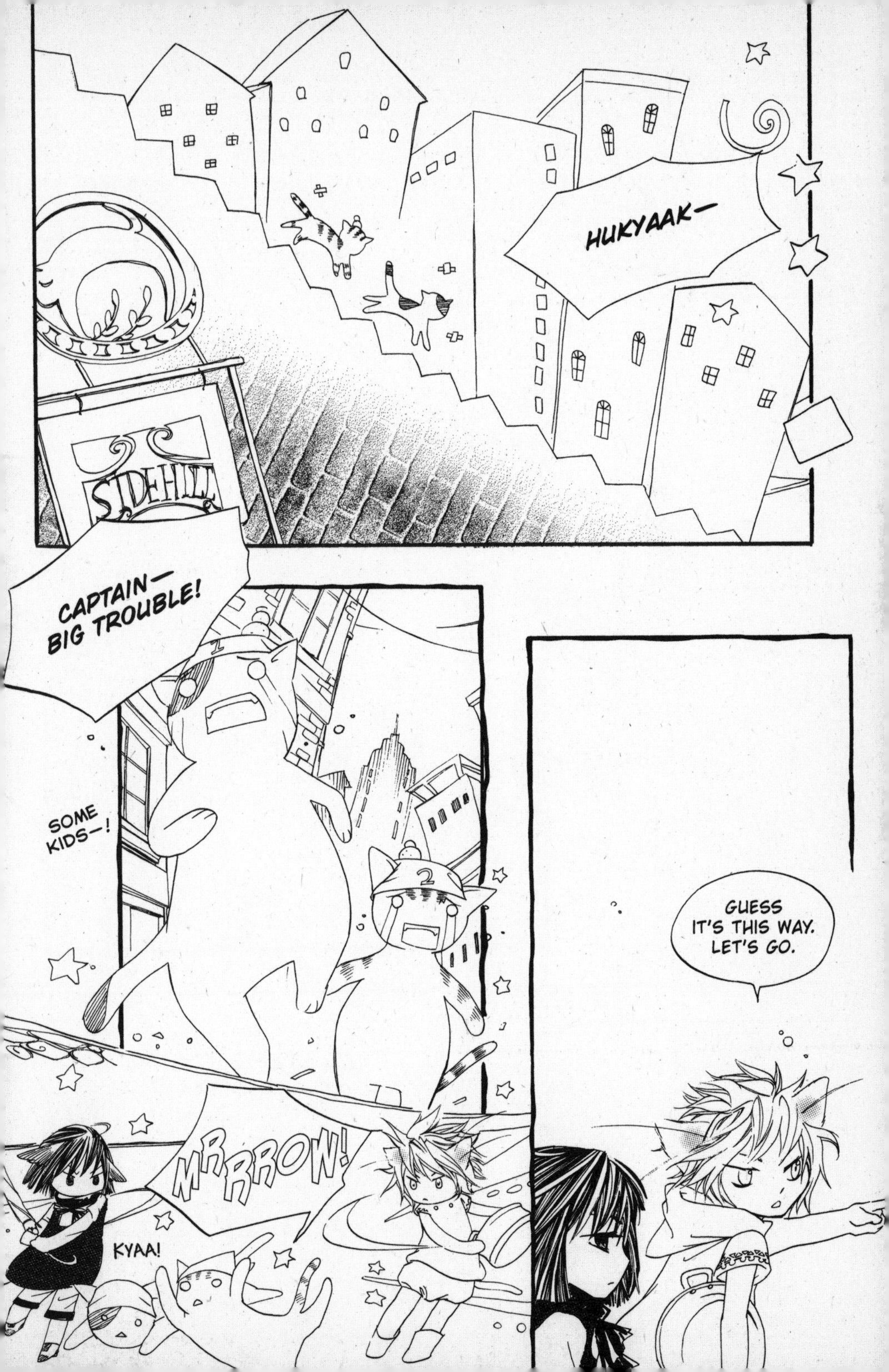
SIDEHILL
HUKYAAK—
CAPTAIN— BIG TROUBLE!
SOME KIDS—!
MRRROW!
KYAA!
GUESS IT'S THIS WAY. LET'S GO.

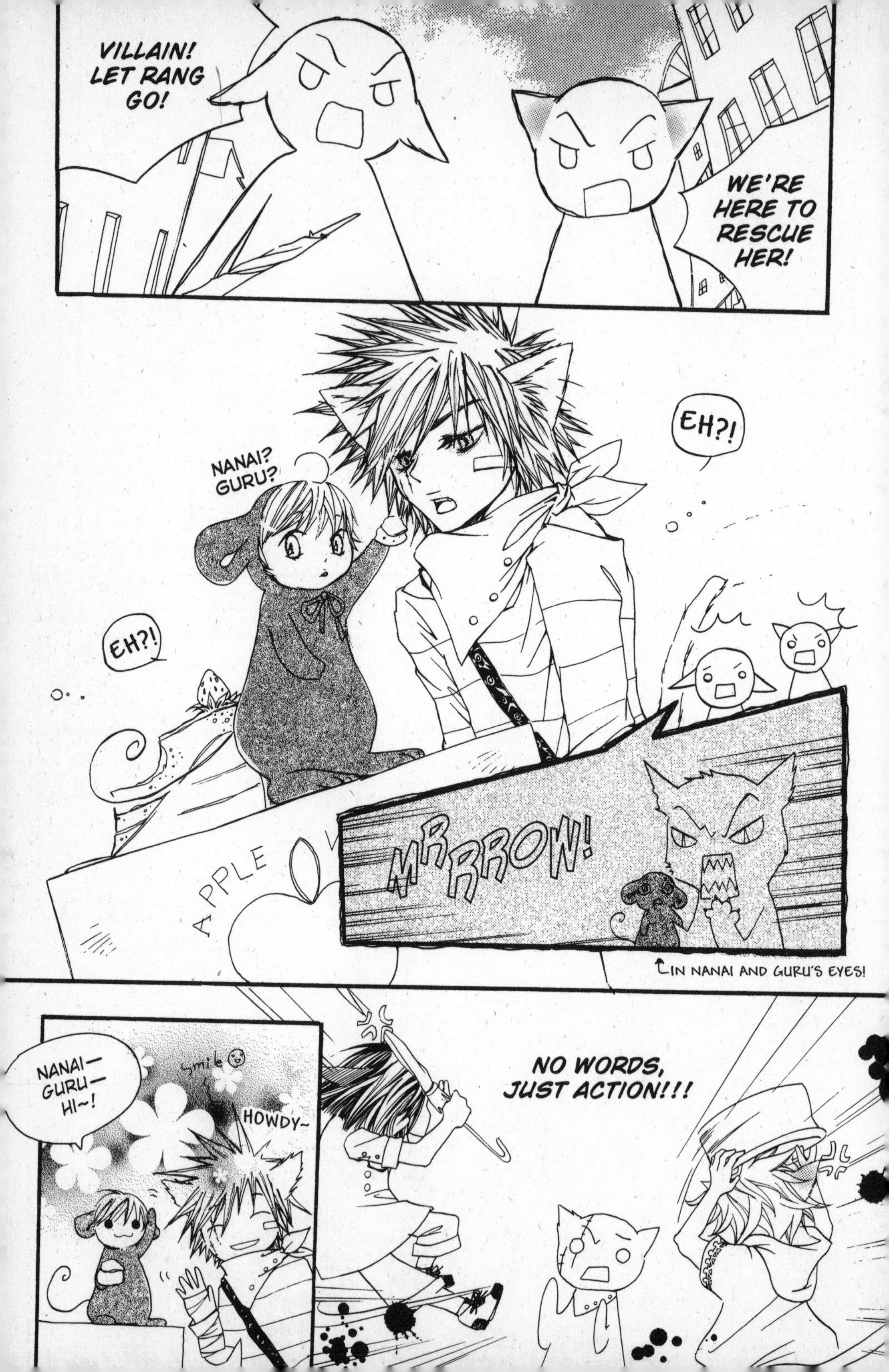
VILLAIN! LET RANG GO!
WE'RE HERE TO RESCUE HER!
EH?!
NANAI? GURU?
EH?!
APPLE
MRRROW!
IN NANAI AND GURU'S EYES!
NANAI— GURU— HI~!
Smile
HOWDY~
NO WORDS, JUST ACTION!!!

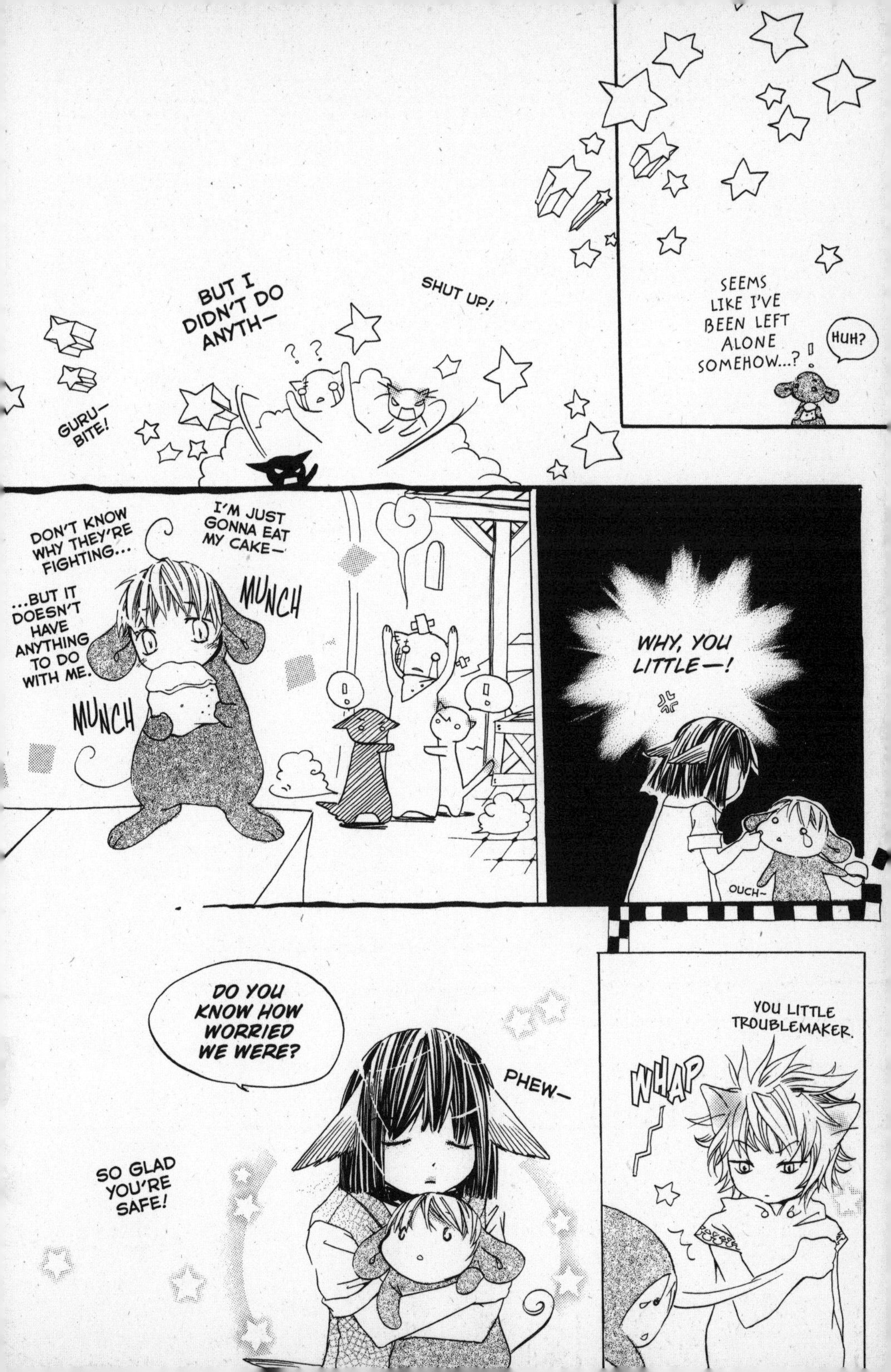
BUT I DIDN'T DO ANYTH—
SHUT UP!
GURU-BITE!
SEEMS LIKE I'VE BEEN LEFT ALONE SOMEHOW...?
HUH?
DON'T KNOW WHY THEY'RE FIGHTING...
I'M JUST GONNA EAT MY CAKE—
MUNCH
...BUT IT DOESN'T HAVE ANYTHING TO DO WITH ME.
MUNCH
WHY, YOU LITTLE—!
OUCH~
DO YOU KNOW HOW WORRIED WE WERE?
PHEW—
SO GLAD YOU'RE SAFE!
YOU LITTLE TROUBLEMAKER.
WHAP

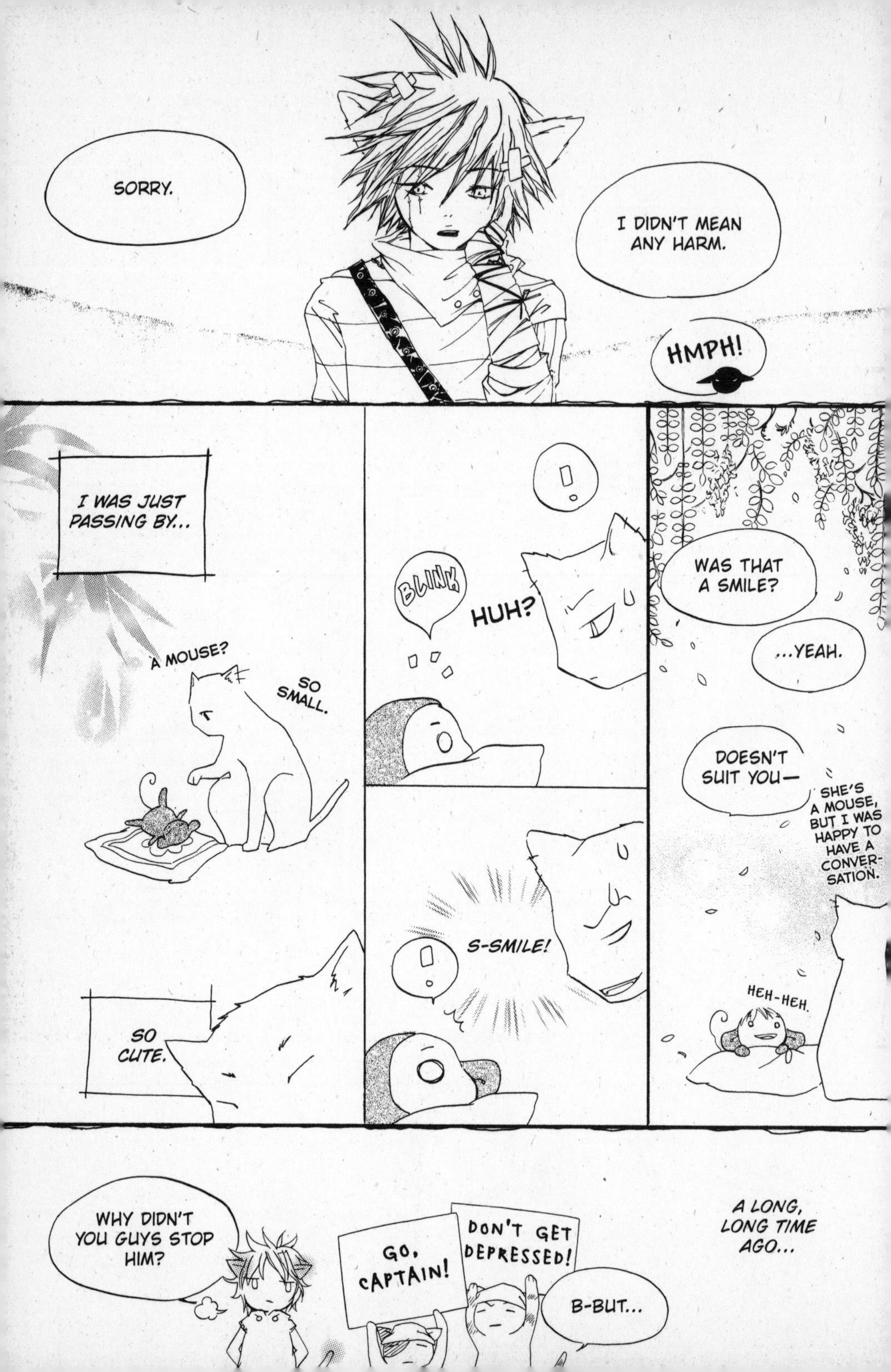
SORRY.
I DIDN'T MEAN ANY HARM.
HMPH!
I WAS JUST PASSING BY...
A MOUSE?
SO SMALL.
SO CUTE.
!
BLINK
HUH?
S-SMILE!
!
WAS THAT A SMILE?
...YEAH.
DOESN'T SUIT YOU—
SHE'S A MOUSE, BUT I WAS HAPPY TO HAVE A CONVERSATION.
HEH-HEH.
WHY DIDN'T YOU GUYS STOP HIM?
GO, CAPTAIN!
DON'T GET DEPRESSED!
B-BUT...
A LONG, LONG TIME AGO...

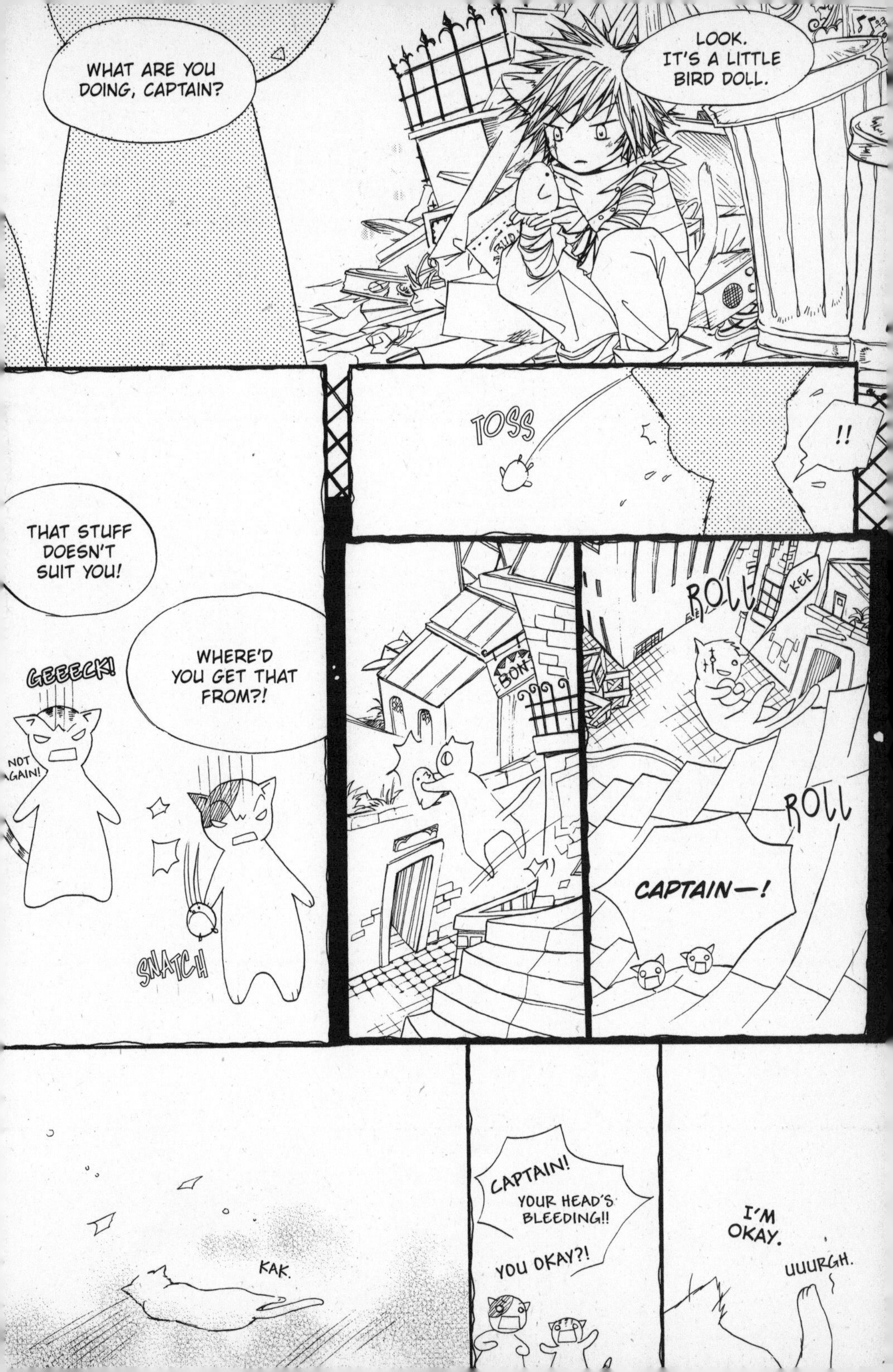

WHAT ARE YOU DOING, CAPTAIN?
LOOK. IT'S A LITTLE BIRD DOLL.
THAT STUFF DOESN'T SUIT YOU!
GEEECK!
NOT AGAIN!
WHERE'D YOU GET THAT FROM?!
SNATCH
TOSS
!!
BON
ROLL
KEK
ROLL
CAPTAIN—!
KAK.
CAPTAIN!
YOUR HEAD'S BLEEDING!!
YOU OKAY?!
I'M OKAY.
UUURGH.

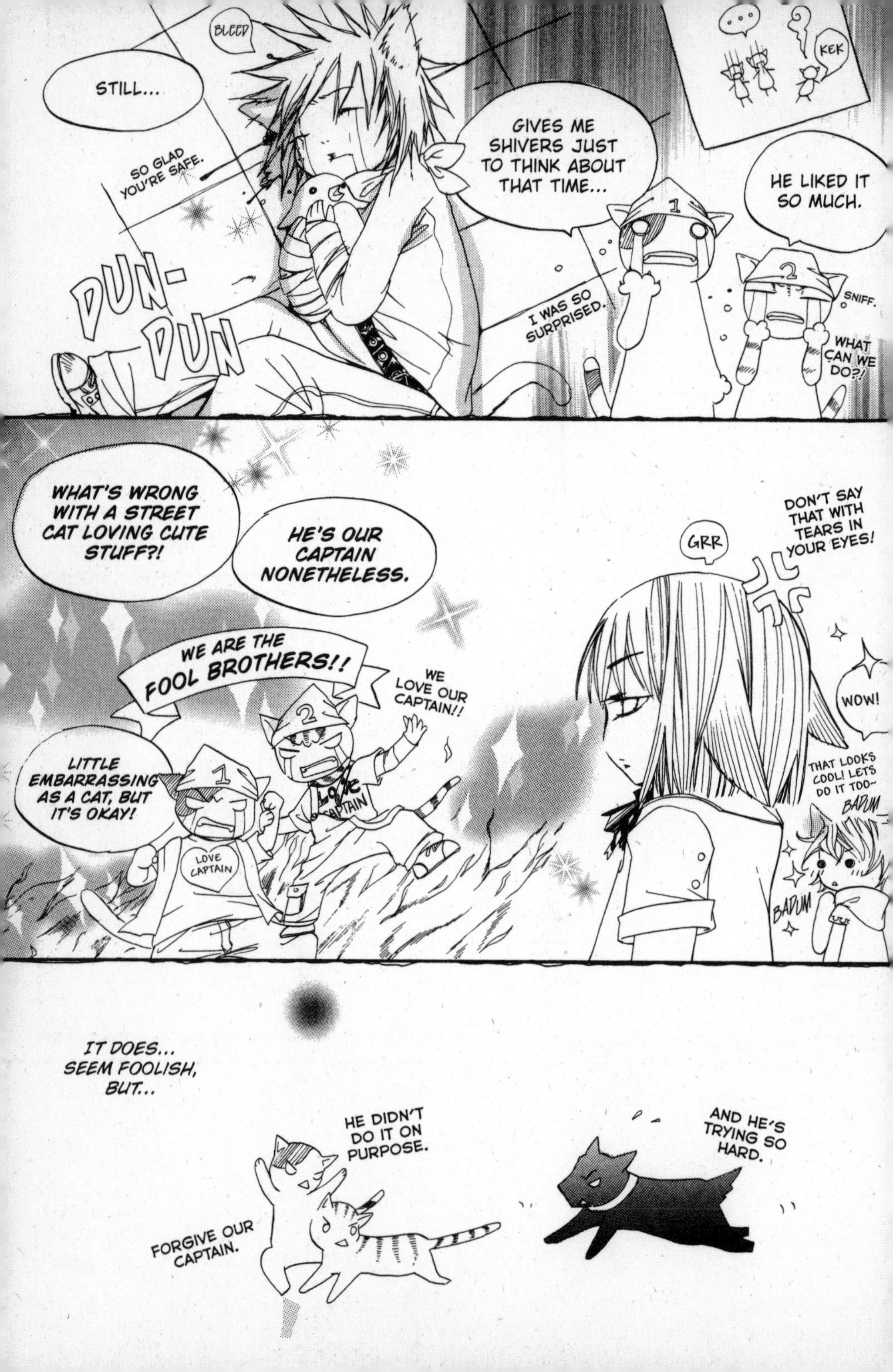

BLEED
STILL...
SO GLAD YOU'RE SAFE.
DUN-DUN
GIVES ME SHIVERS JUST TO THINK ABOUT THAT TIME...
KEK
I WAS SO SURPRISED.
HE LIKED IT SO MUCH.
SNIFF.
WHAT CAN WE DO?!
WHAT'S WRONG WITH A STREET CAT LOVING CUTE STUFF?!
HE'S OUR CAPTAIN NONETHELESS.
WE ARE THE FOOL BROTHERS!!
WE LOVE OUR CAPTAIN!!
LITTLE EMBARRASSING AS A CAT, BUT IT'S OKAY!
LOVE CAPTAIN
GRR
DON'T SAY THAT WITH TEARS IN YOUR EYES!
WOW!
THAT LOOKS COOL! LETS DO IT TOO~
BADUM
BADUM
IT DOES... SEEM FOOLISH, BUT...
HE DIDN'T DO IT ON PURPOSE.
FORGIVE OUR CAPTAIN.
AND HE'S TRYING SO HARD.

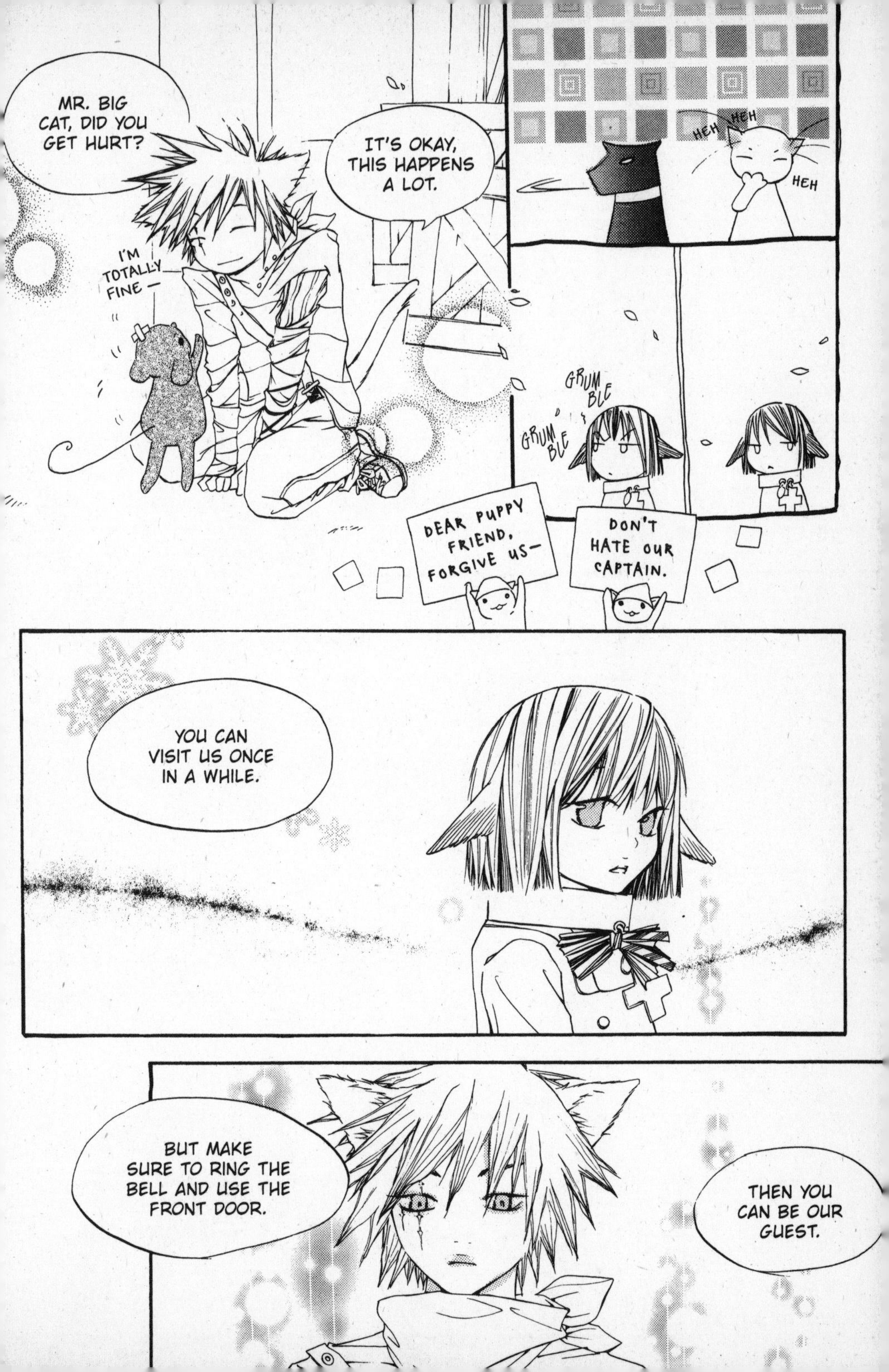
MR. BIG CAT, DID YOU GET HURT?
IT'S OKAY, THIS HAPPENS A LOT.
I'M TOTALLY FINE—
HEH HEH
HEH
GRUMBLE
GRUMBLE
DEAR PUPPY FRIEND, FORGIVE US—
DON'T HATE OUR CAPTAIN.
YOU CAN VISIT US ONCE IN A WHILE.
BUT MAKE SURE TO RING THE BELL AND USE THE FRONT DOOR.
THEN YOU CAN BE OUR GUEST.

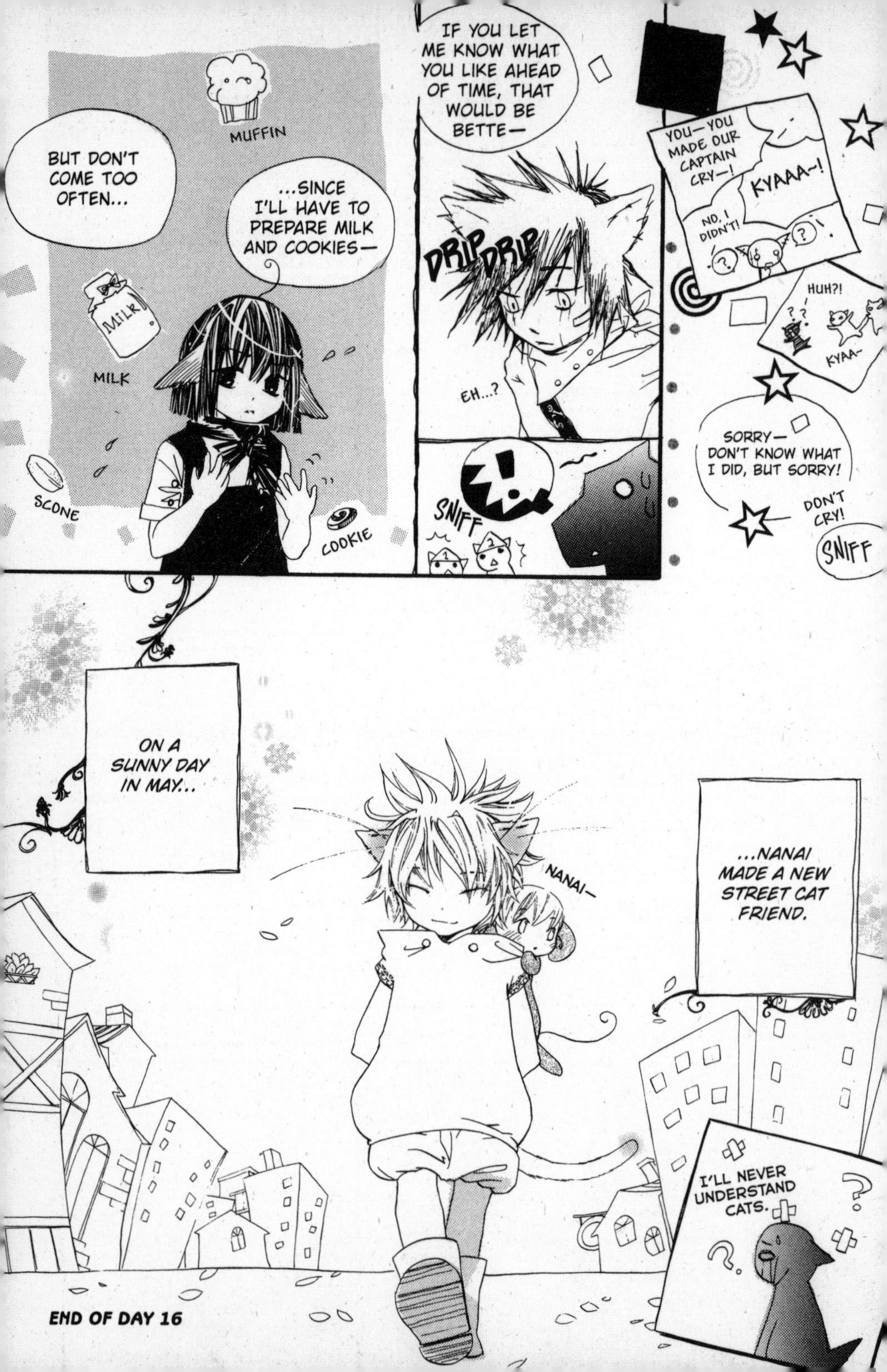
MUFFIN
BUT DON'T COME TOO OFTEN...
...SINCE I'LL HAVE TO PREPARE MILK AND COOKIES—
MILK
SCONE
COOKIE
IF YOU LET ME KNOW WHAT YOU LIKE AHEAD OF TIME, THAT WOULD BE BETTE—
DRIP DRIP
EH...?
SNIFF
YOU—YOU MADE OUR CAPTAIN CRY—!
KYAAA~!
NO, I DIDN'T!
HUH?!
KYAA~
SORRY— DON'T KNOW WHAT I DID, BUT SORRY!
DON'T CRY!
SNIFF
ON A SUNNY DAY IN MAY...
NANAI~
...NANAI MADE A NEW STREET CAT FRIEND.
I'LL NEVER UNDERSTAND CATS.
END OF DAY 16

DAY 17.
WORKING HOLIDAY

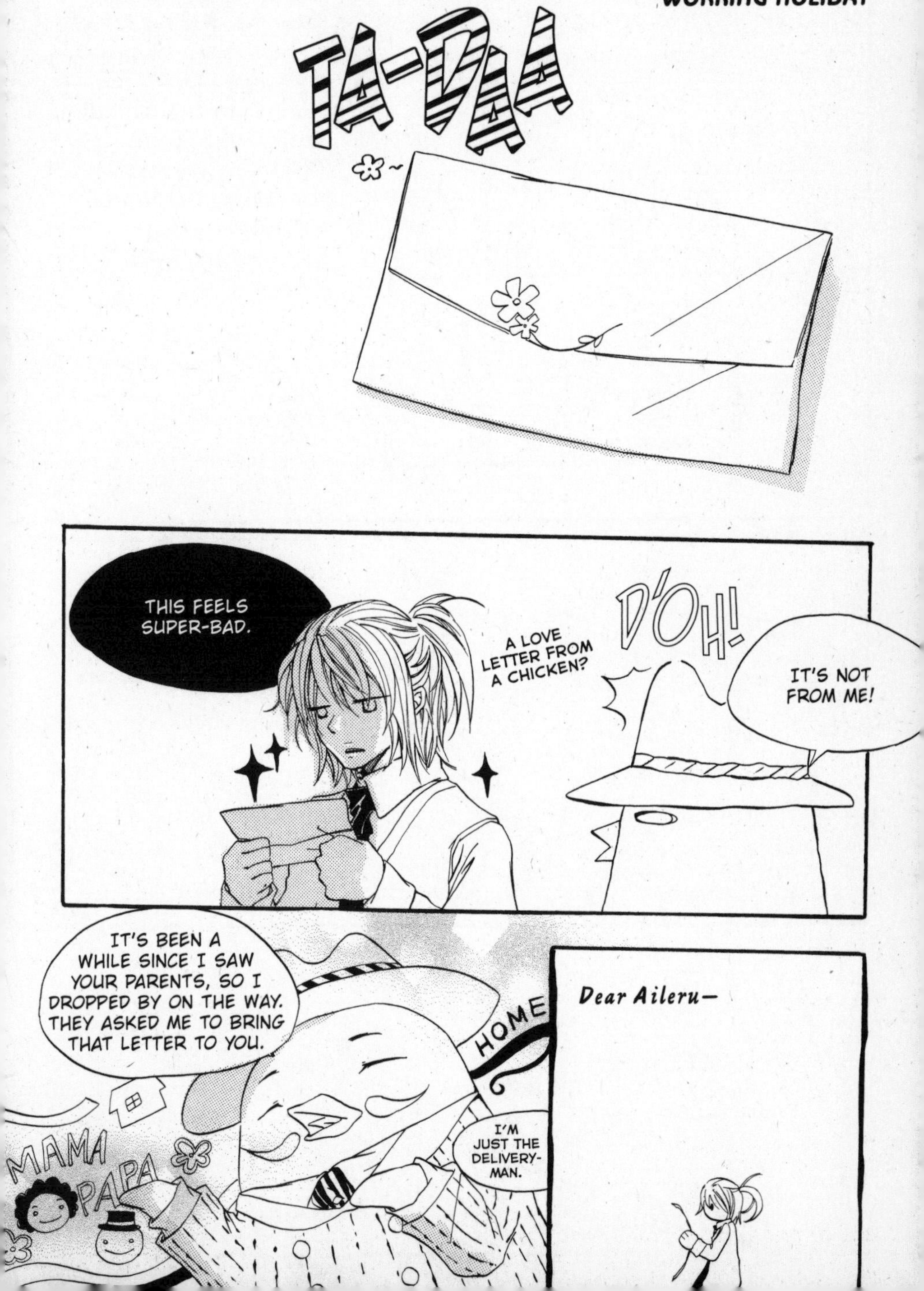
TA-DAA
THIS FEELS SUPER-BAD.
A LOVE LETTER FROM A CHICKEN?
D'OH!
IT'S NOT FROM ME!
IT'S BEEN A WHILE SINCE I SAW YOUR PARENTS, SO I DROPPED BY ON THE WAY. THEY ASKED ME TO BRING THAT LETTER TO YOU.
HOME
MAMA
PAPA
I'M JUST THE DELIVERY-MAN.
Dear Aileru—

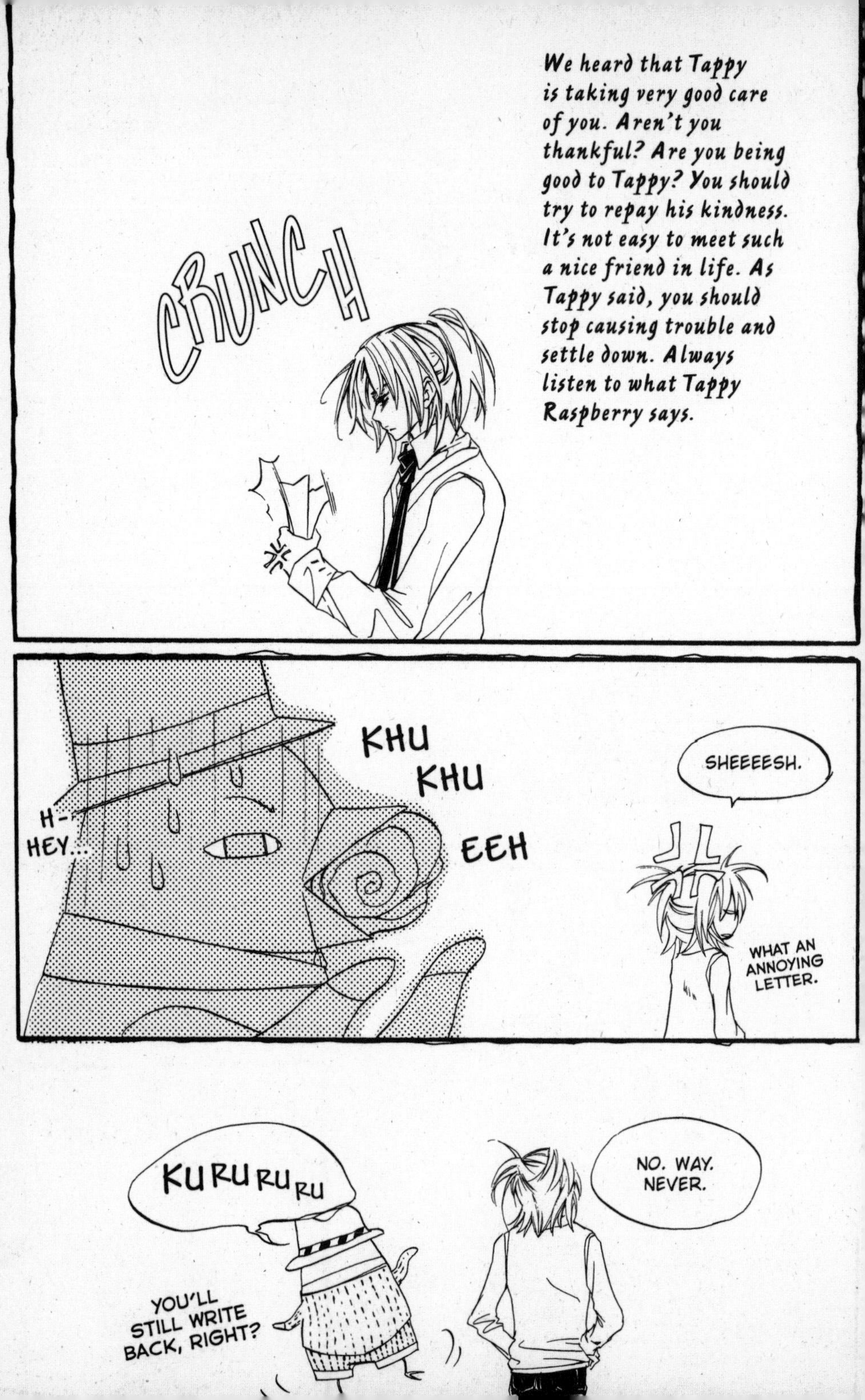
CRUNCH
We heard that Tappy is taking very good care of you. Aren't you thankful? Are you being good to Tappy? You should try to repay his kindness. It's not easy to meet such a nice friend in life. As Tappy said, you should stop causing trouble and settle down. Always listen to what Tappy Raspberry says.
H-HEY...
KHU KHU EEH
SHEEEEESH.
WHAT AN ANNOYING LETTER.
KURURURURU
YOU'LL STILL WRITE BACK, RIGHT?
NO. WAY. NEVER.

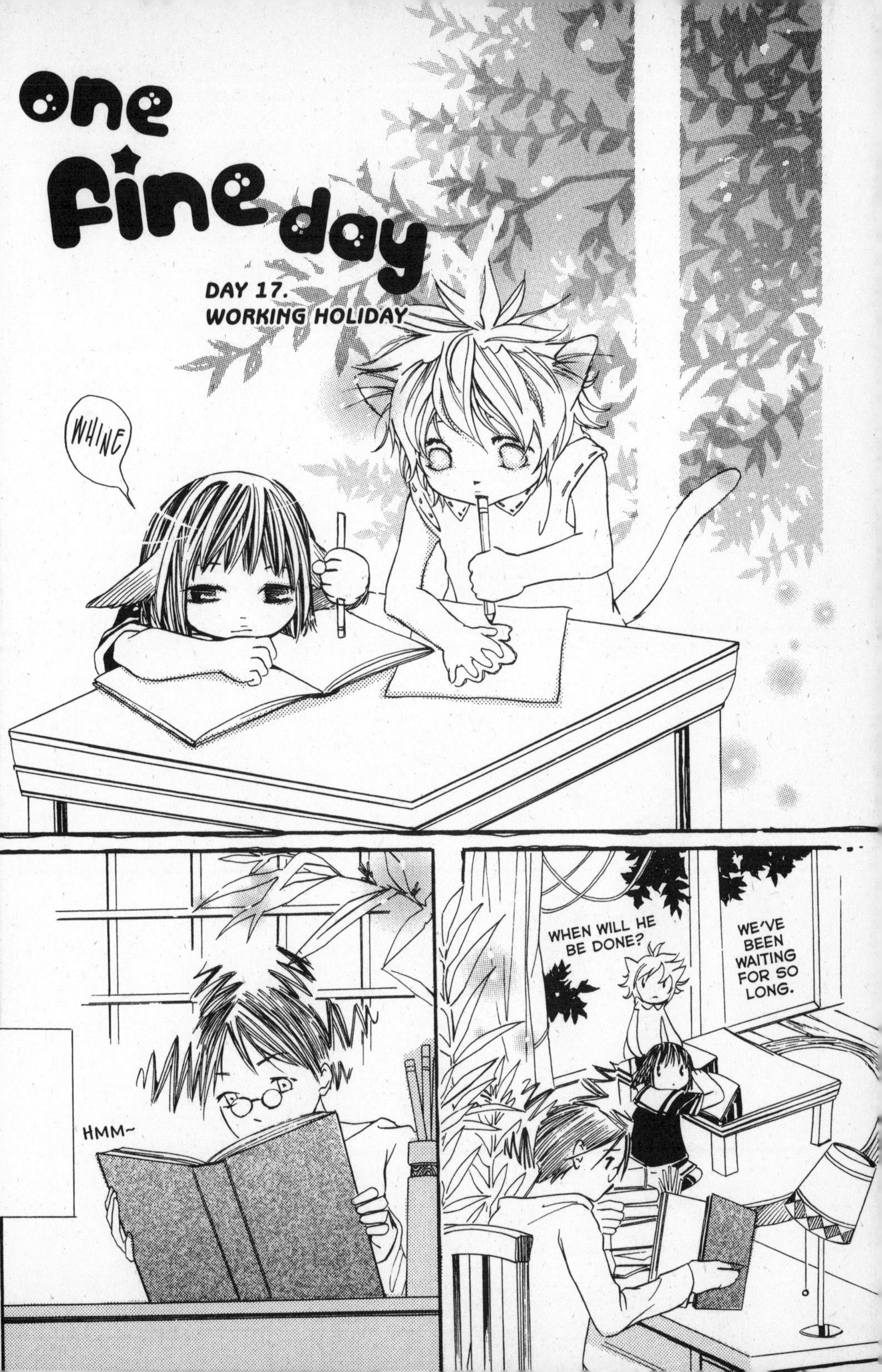
one fine day
DAY 17.
WORKING HOLIDAY
WHINE
HMM~
WHEN WILL HE BE DONE?
WE'VE BEEN WAITING FOR SO LONG.

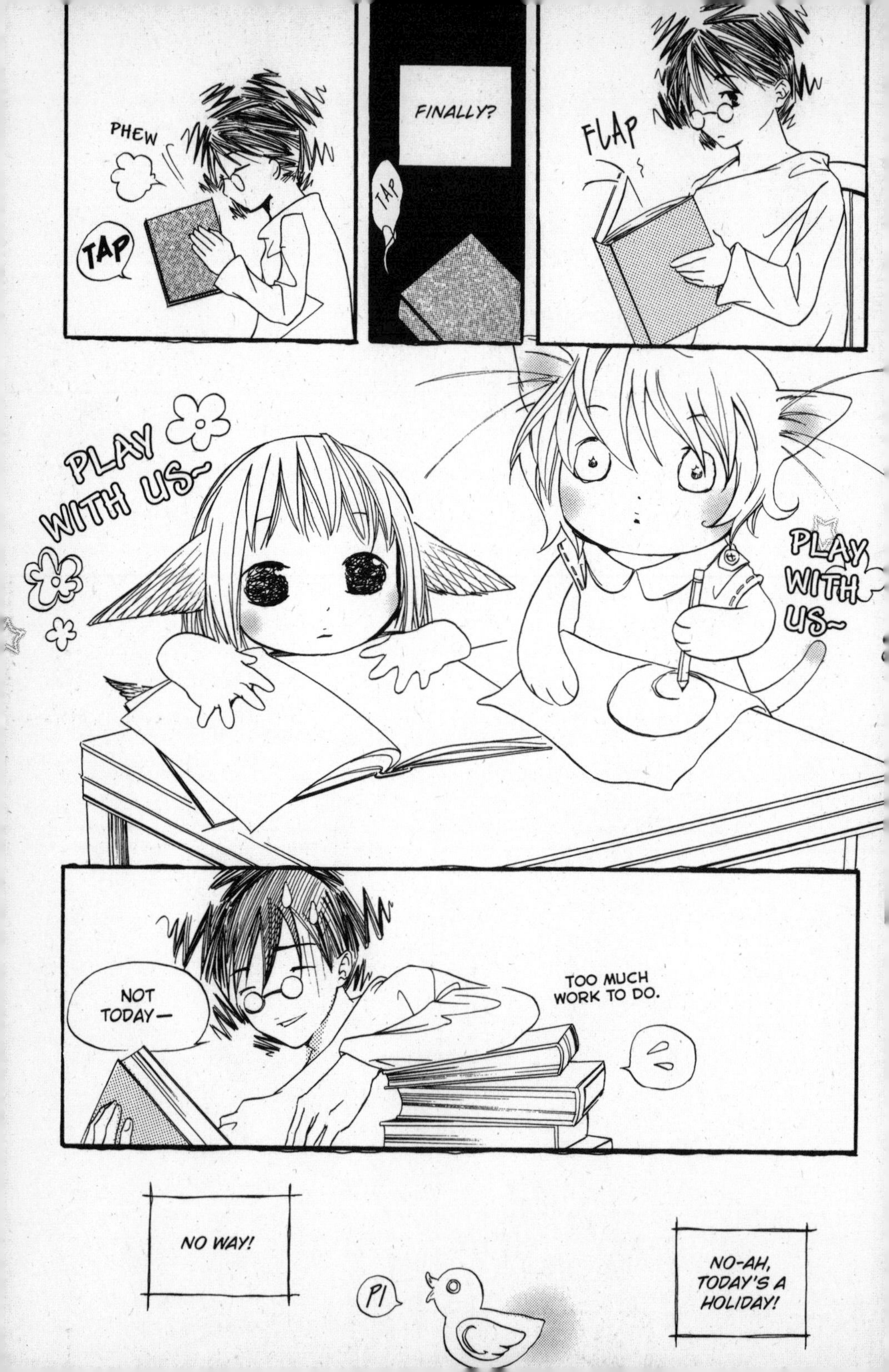
PHEW
TAP
FINALLY?
TAP
FLAP
PLAY WITH US~
PLAY WITH US~
NOT TODAY—
TOO MUCH WORK TO DO.
NO WAY!
PI
NO-AH, TODAY'S A HOLIDAY!

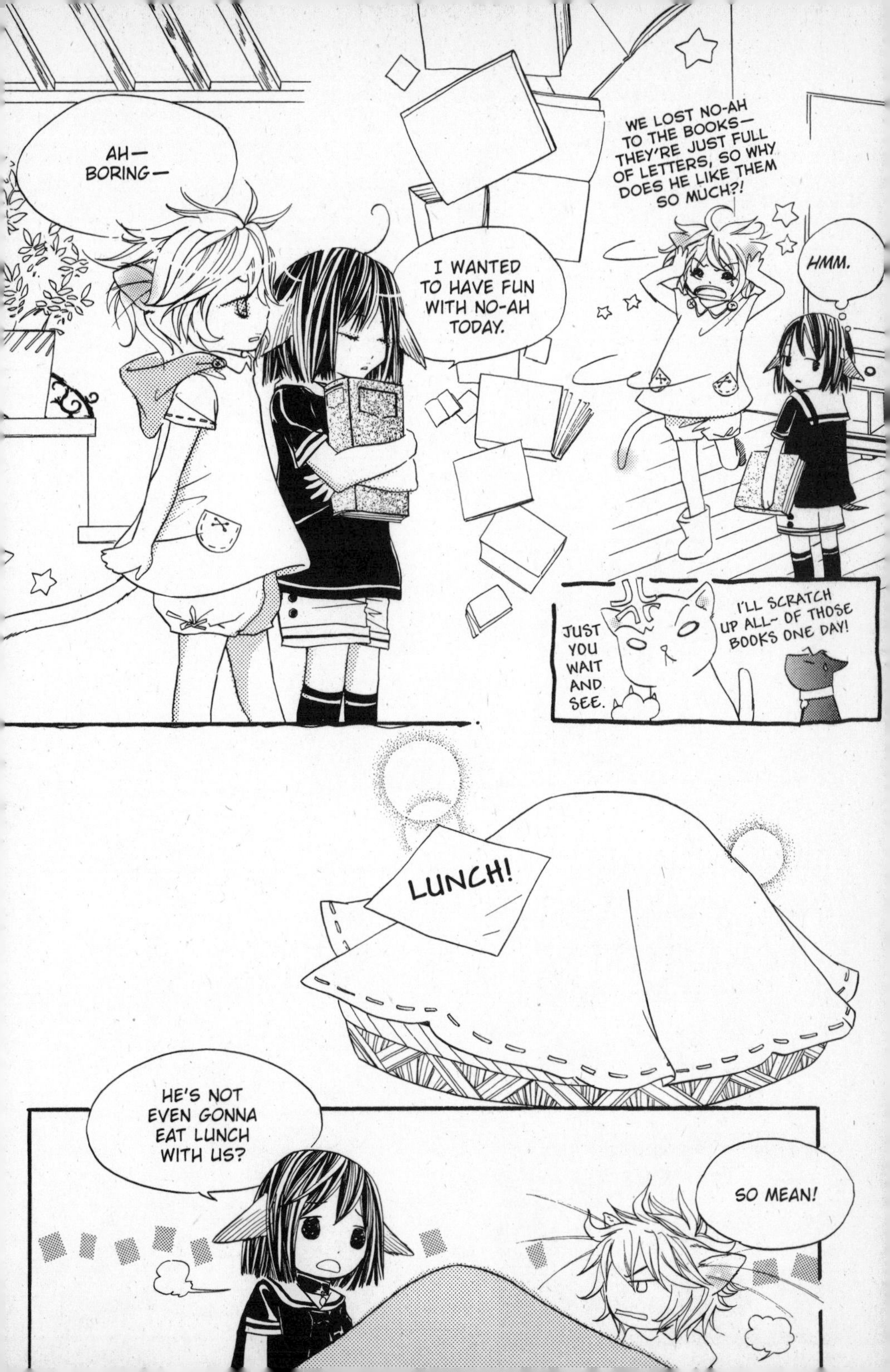
AH— BORING—
I WANTED TO HAVE FUN WITH NO-AH TODAY.
WE LOST NO-AH TO THE BOOKS— THEY'RE JUST FULL OF LETTERS, SO WHY DOES HE LIKE THEM SO MUCH?!
HMM.
JUST YOU WAIT AND SEE.
I'LL SCRATCH UP ALL~ OF THOSE BOOKS ONE DAY!
LUNCH!
HE'S NOT EVEN GONNA EAT LUNCH WITH US?
SO MEAN!

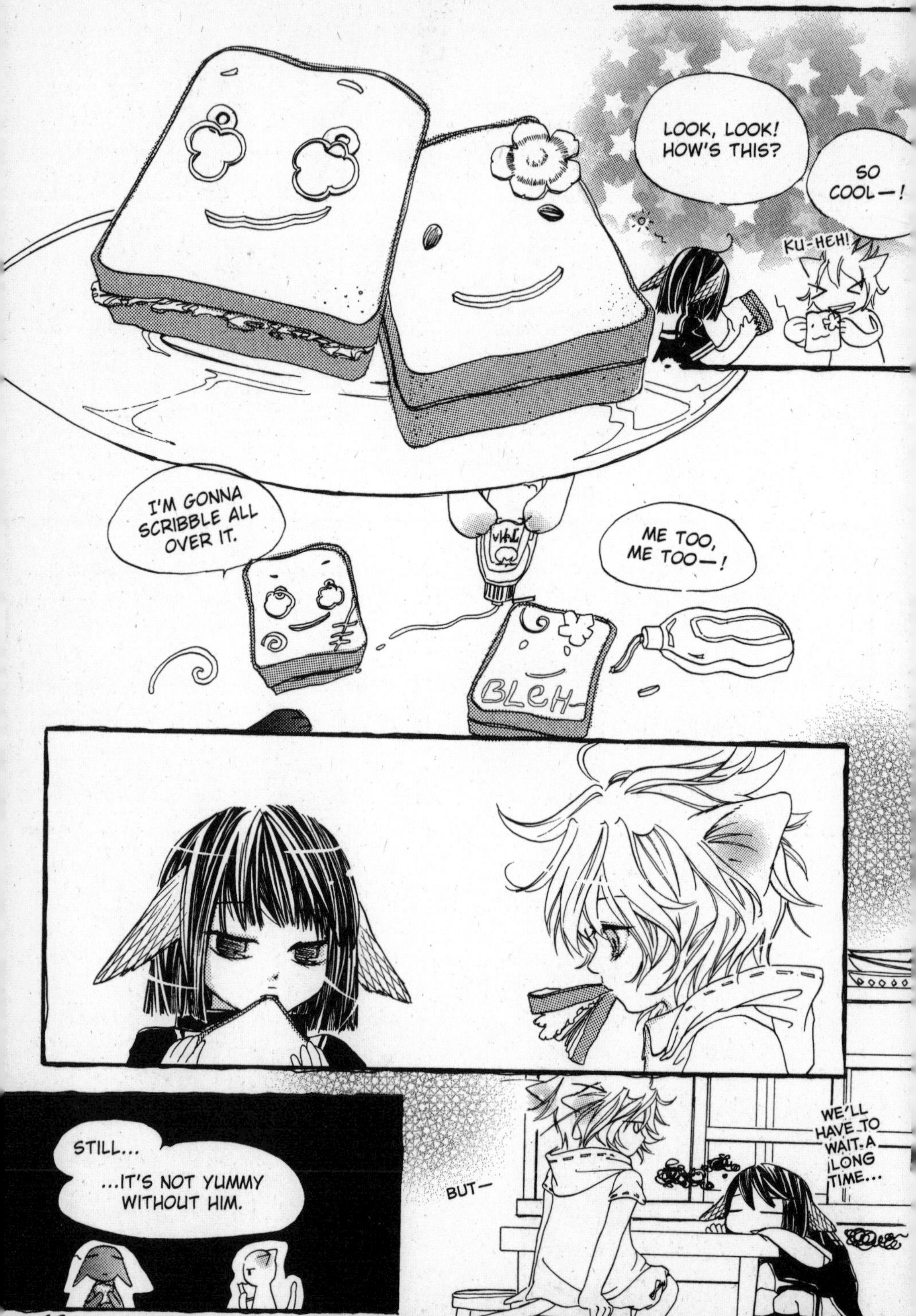
LOOK, LOOK! HOW'S THIS?
SO COOL—!
KU-HEH!
I'M GONNA SCRIBBLE ALL OVER IT.
ME TOO, ME TOO—!
BLCH—
STILL...
...IT'S NOT YUMMY WITHOUT HIM.
BUT—
WE'LL HAVE TO WAIT A LONG TIME...

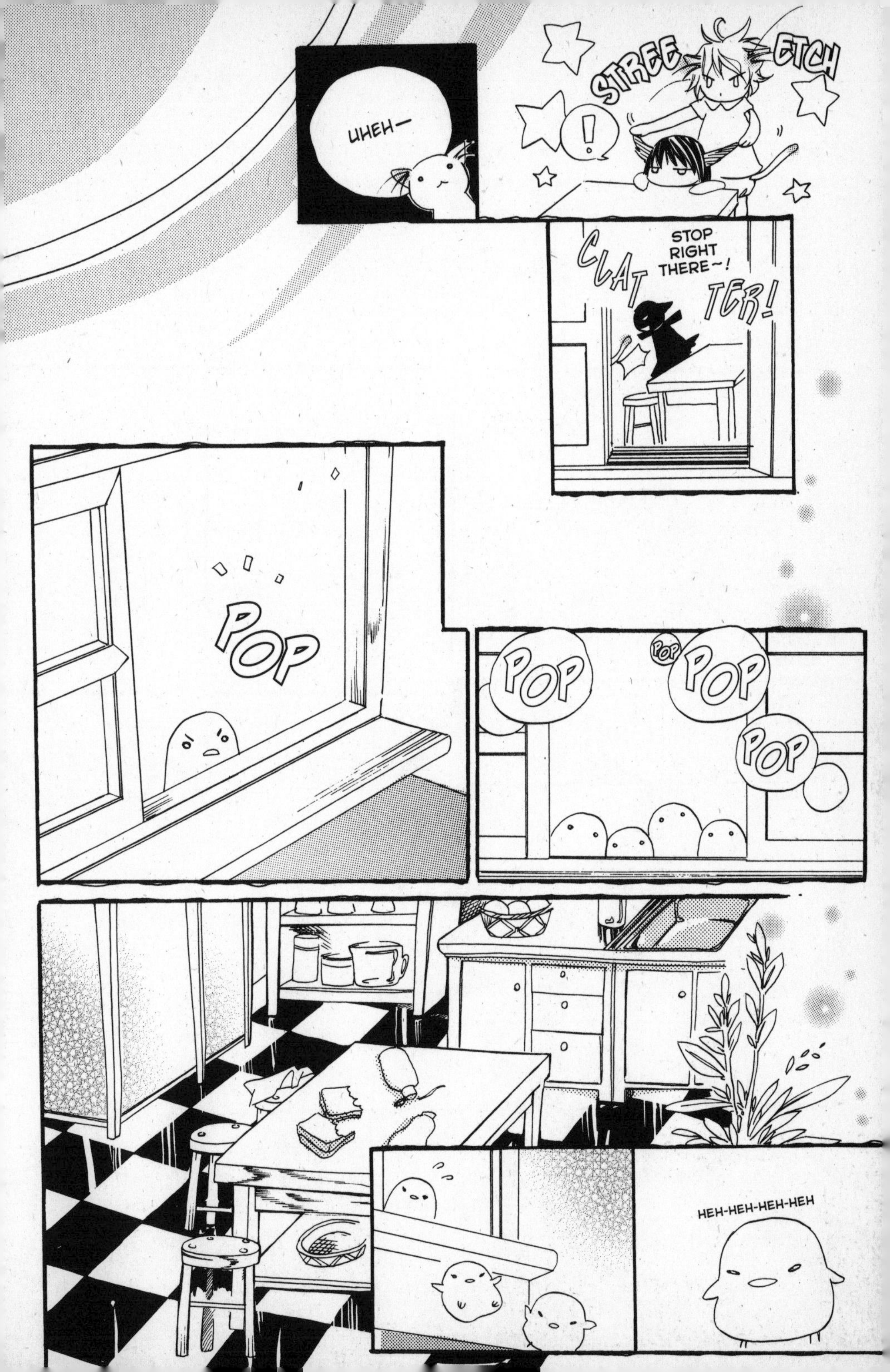
UHEH—
STREE-ETCH
!
CLAT TER!
STOP RIGHT THERE~!
POP
POP
POP
POP POP
POP
HEH-HEH-HEH-HEH

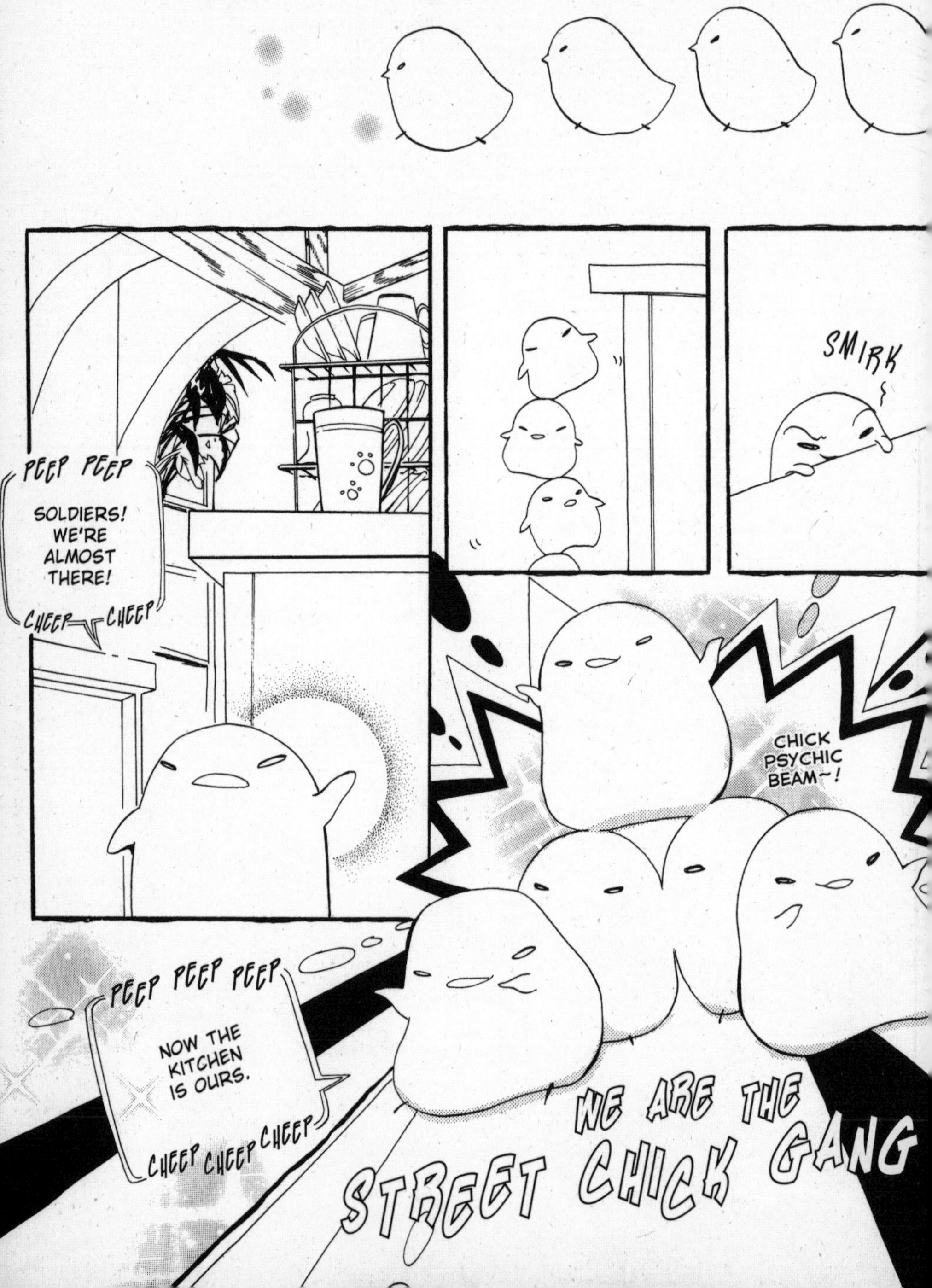
PEEP PEEP
SOLDIERS! WE'RE ALMOST THERE!
CHEEP CHEEP
SMIRK
CHICK PSYCHIC BEAM~!
PEEP PEEP PEEP
NOW THE KITCHEN IS OURS.
CHEEP CHEEP CHEEP
WE ARE THE STREET CHICK GANG

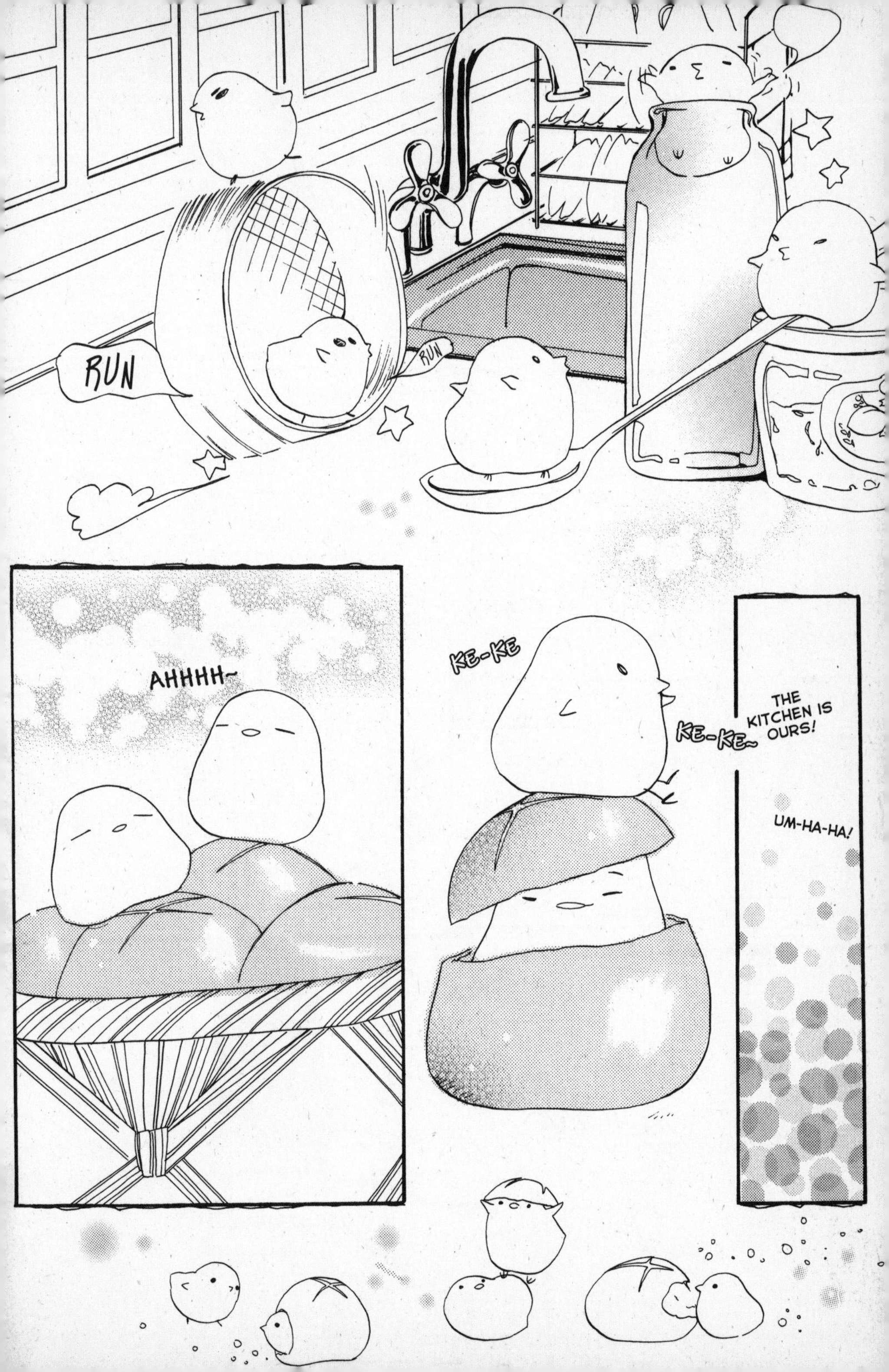
RUN
RUN
AHHHH~
KE-KE
KE-KE~
THE KITCHEN IS OURS!
UM-HA-HA!

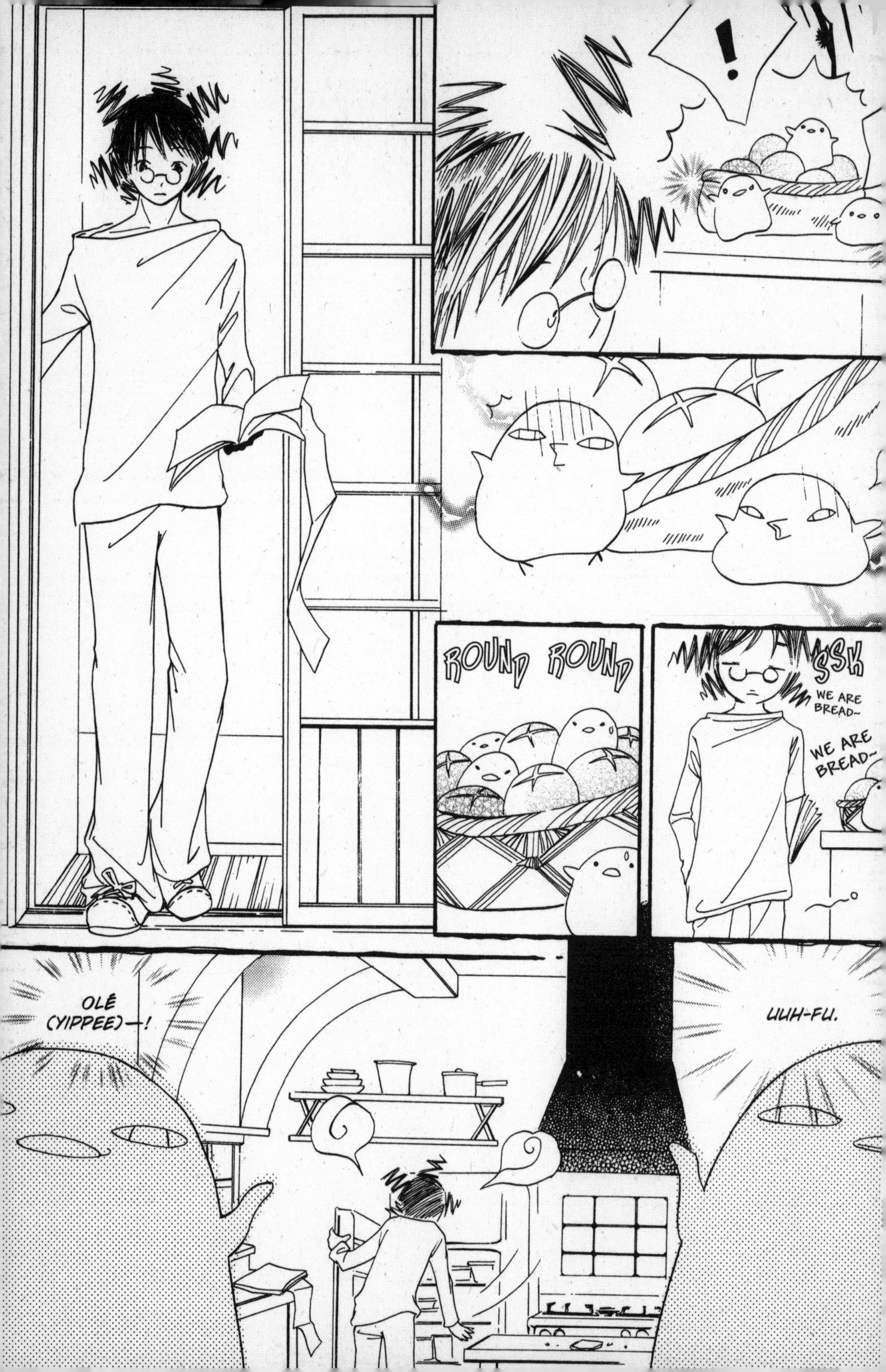
!
ROUND ROUND
SSK
WE ARE BREAD~
WE ARE BREAD~
OLÉ (YIPPEE)—!
UUH-FU.

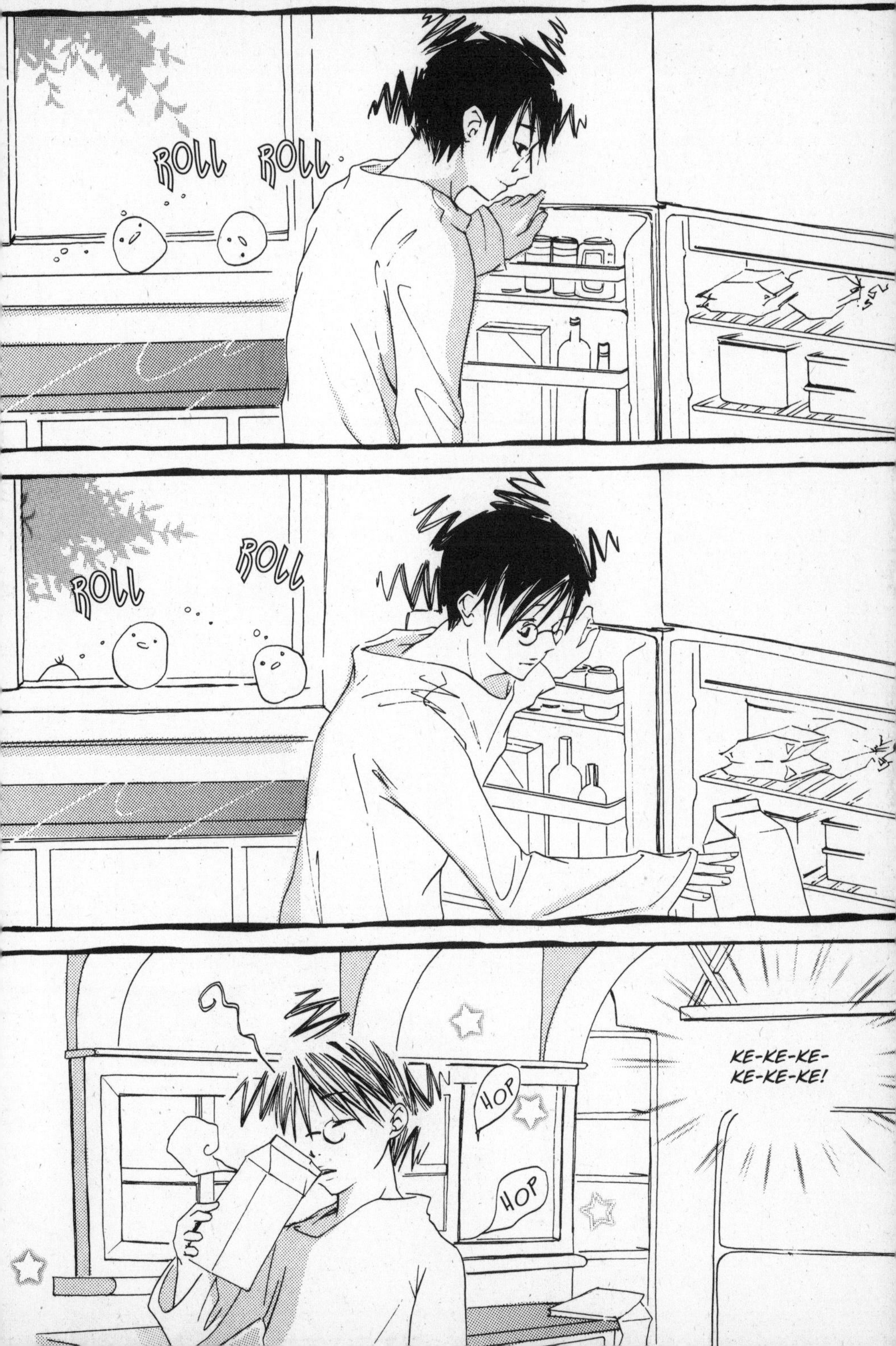
ROLL ROLL
ROLL
ROLL
HOP
HOP
KE-KE-KE-
KE-KE-KE!

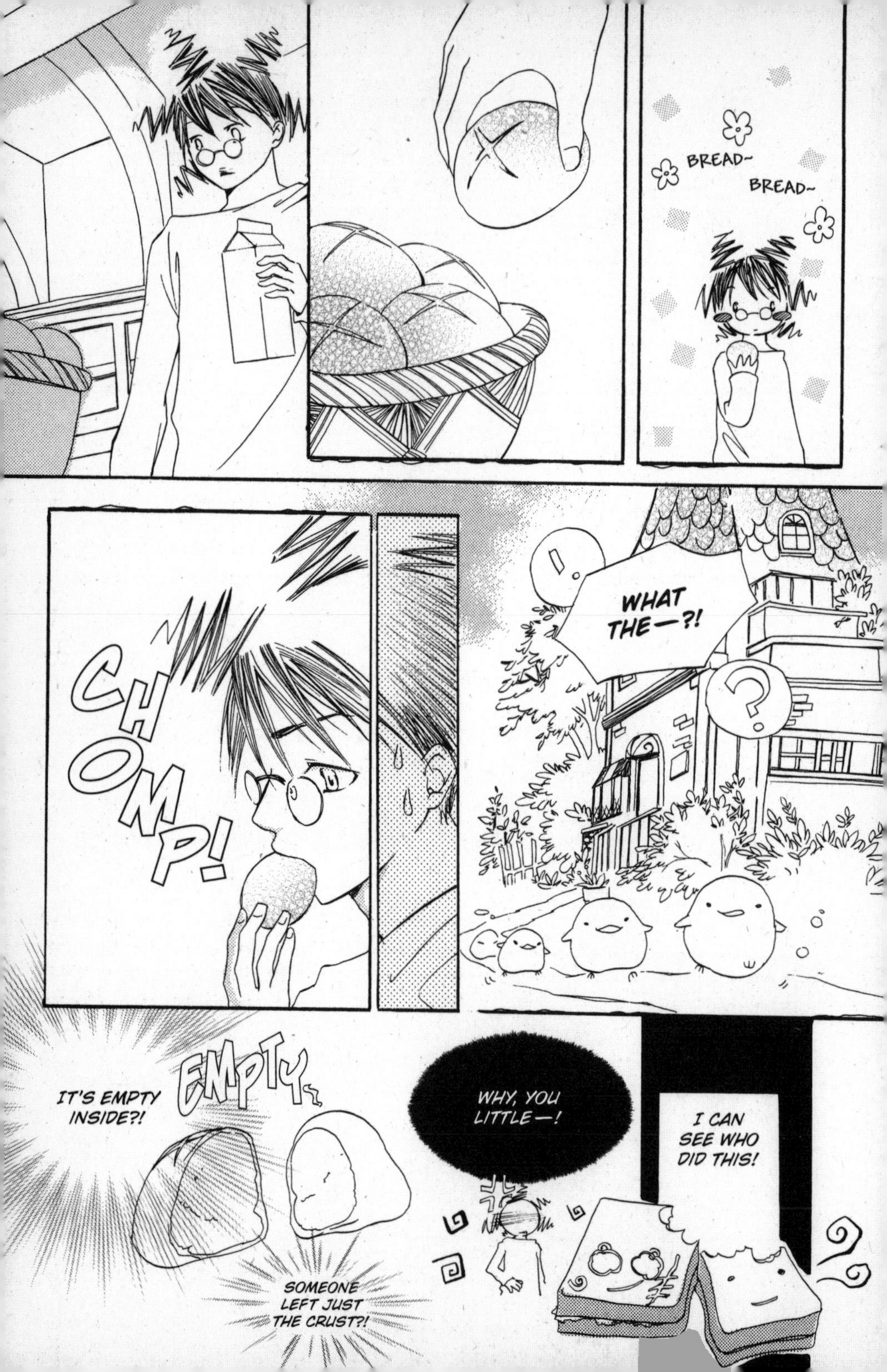
BREAD~
BREAD~
CHOMP!
!
WHAT THE—?!
?
IT'S EMPTY INSIDE?!
EMPTY
SOMEONE LEFT JUST THE CRUST?!
WHY, YOU LITTLE—!
I CAN SEE WHO DID THIS!

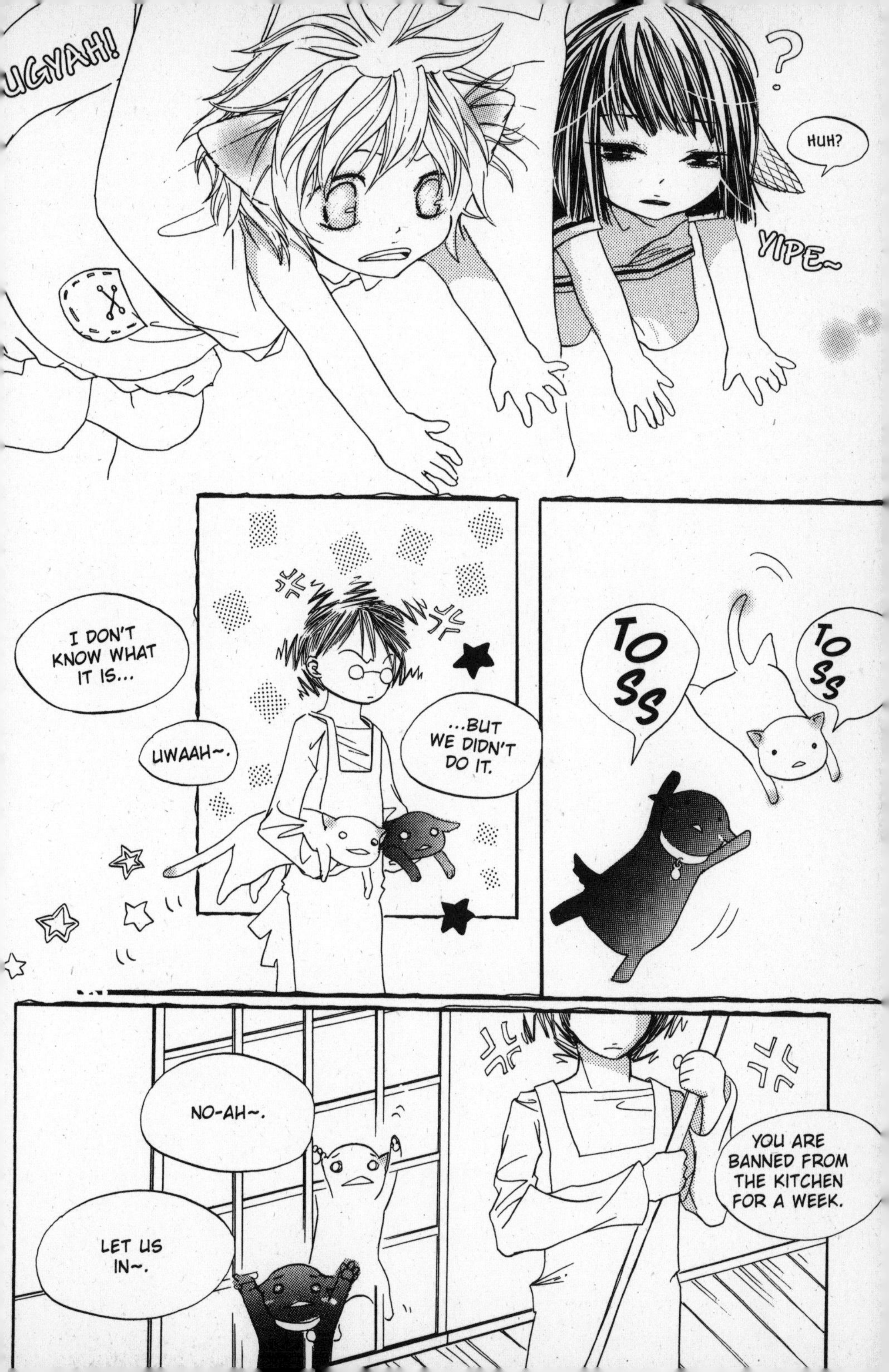
UGYAH!
?
HUH?
YIPE~
I DON'T KNOW WHAT IT IS...
UWAAH~.
...BUT WE DIDN'T DO IT.
TOSS
TOSS
NO-AH~.
LET US IN~.
YOU ARE BANNED FROM THE KITCHEN FOR A WEEK.

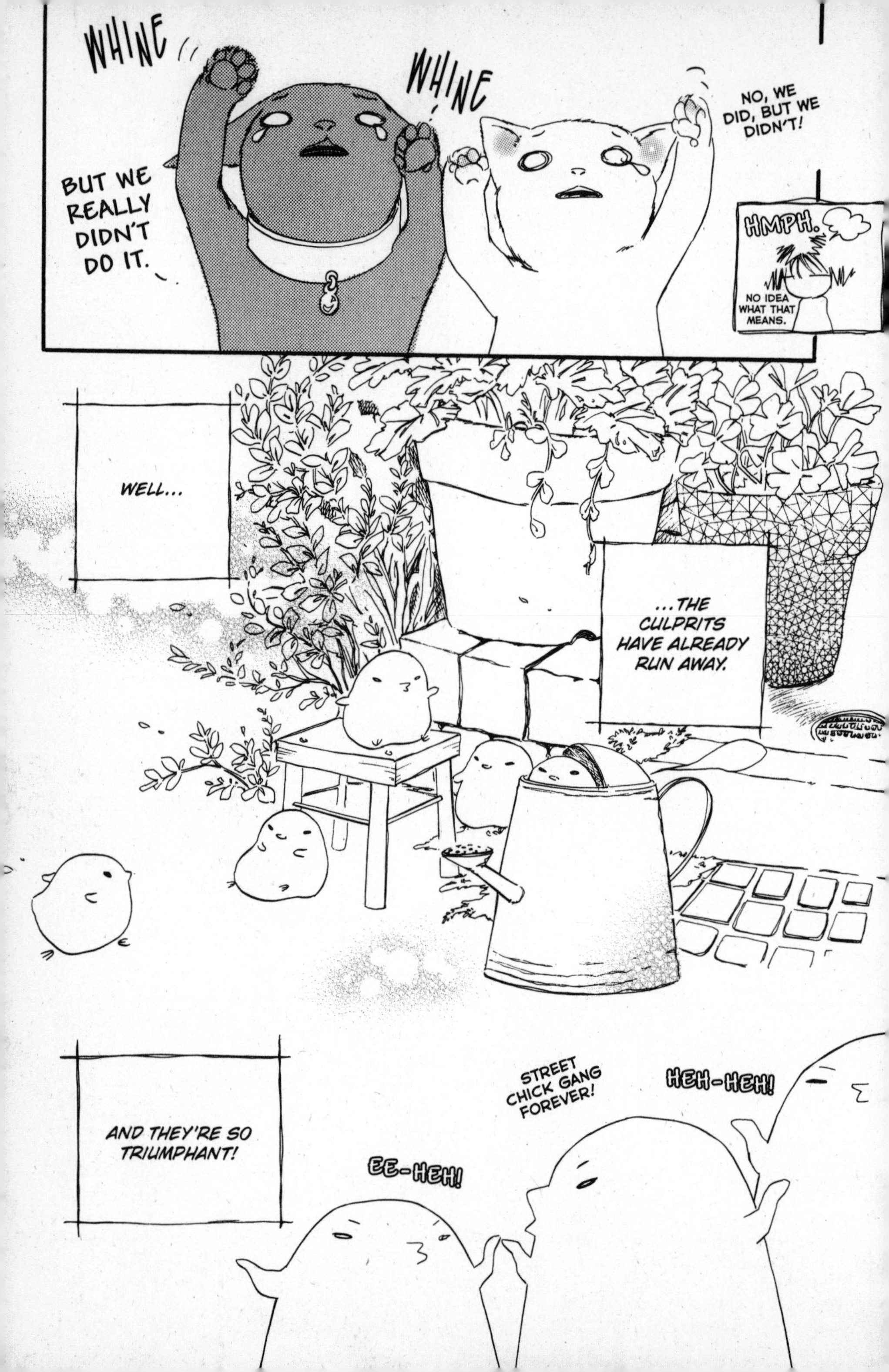
WHINE
BUT WE REALLY DIDN'T DO IT.
WHINE
NO, WE DID, BUT WE DIDN'T!
HMPH.
NO IDEA WHAT THAT MEANS.
WELL...
...THE CULPRITS HAVE ALREADY RUN AWAY.
AND THEY'RE SO TRIUMPHANT!
EE-HEH!
STREET CHICK GANG FOREVER!
HEH-HEH!

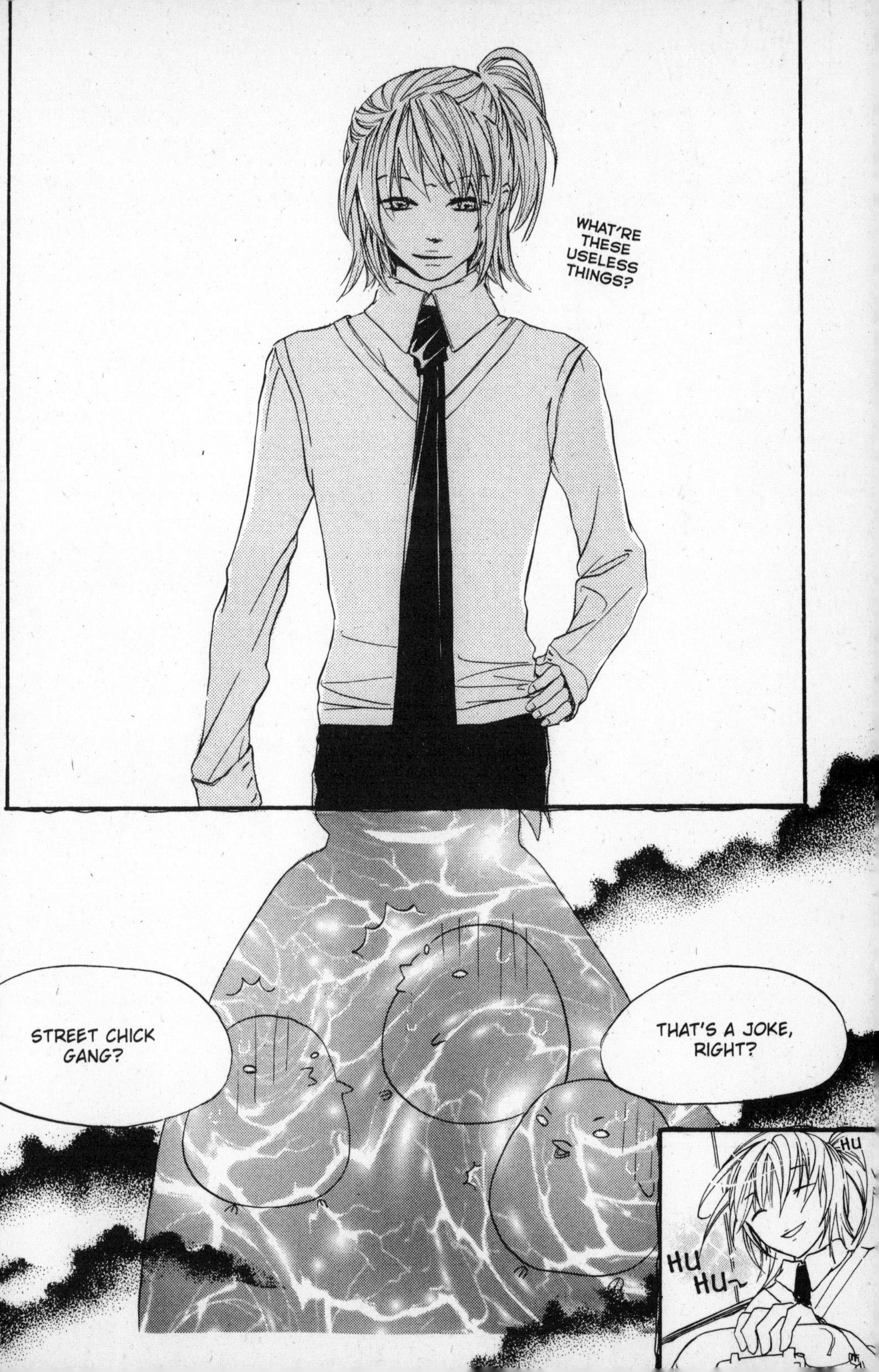
WHAT'RE THESE USELESS THINGS?
STREET CHICK GANG?
THAT'S A JOKE, RIGHT?
HU
HU HU~

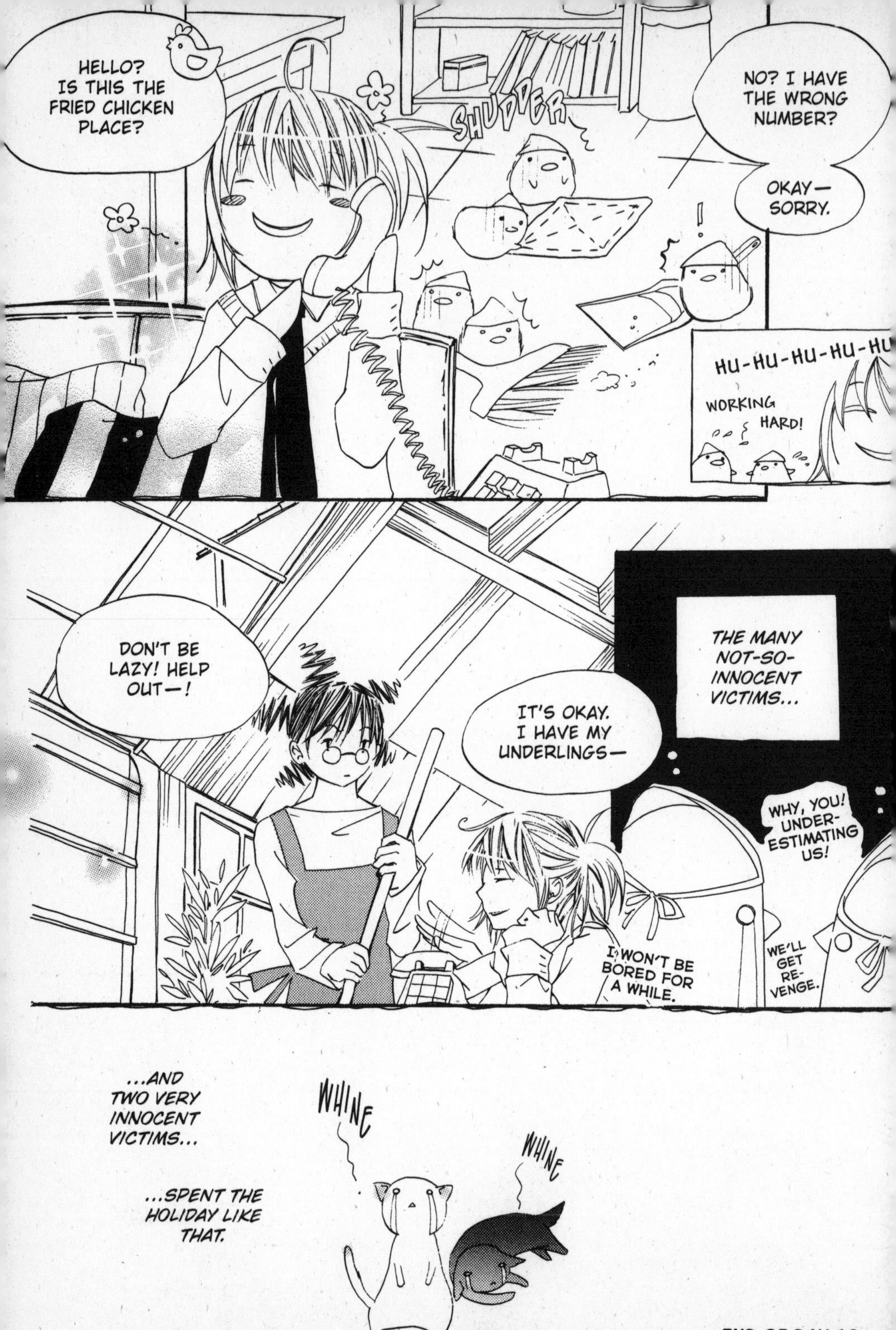
HELLO? IS THIS THE FRIED CHICKEN PLACE?
SHUDDER
NO? I HAVE THE WRONG NUMBER?
OKAY— SORRY.
HU-HU-HU-HU-HU
WORKING HARD!
DON'T BE LAZY! HELP OUT—!
IT'S OKAY. I HAVE MY UNDERLINGS—
THE MANY NOT-SO-INNOCENT VICTIMS...
WHY, YOU! UNDER-ESTIMATING US!
I WON'T BE BORED FOR A WHILE.
WE'LL GET RE-VENGE.
...AND TWO VERY INNOCENT VICTIMS...
WHINE
...SPENT THE HOLIDAY LIKE THAT.
WHINE

END OF DAY 18

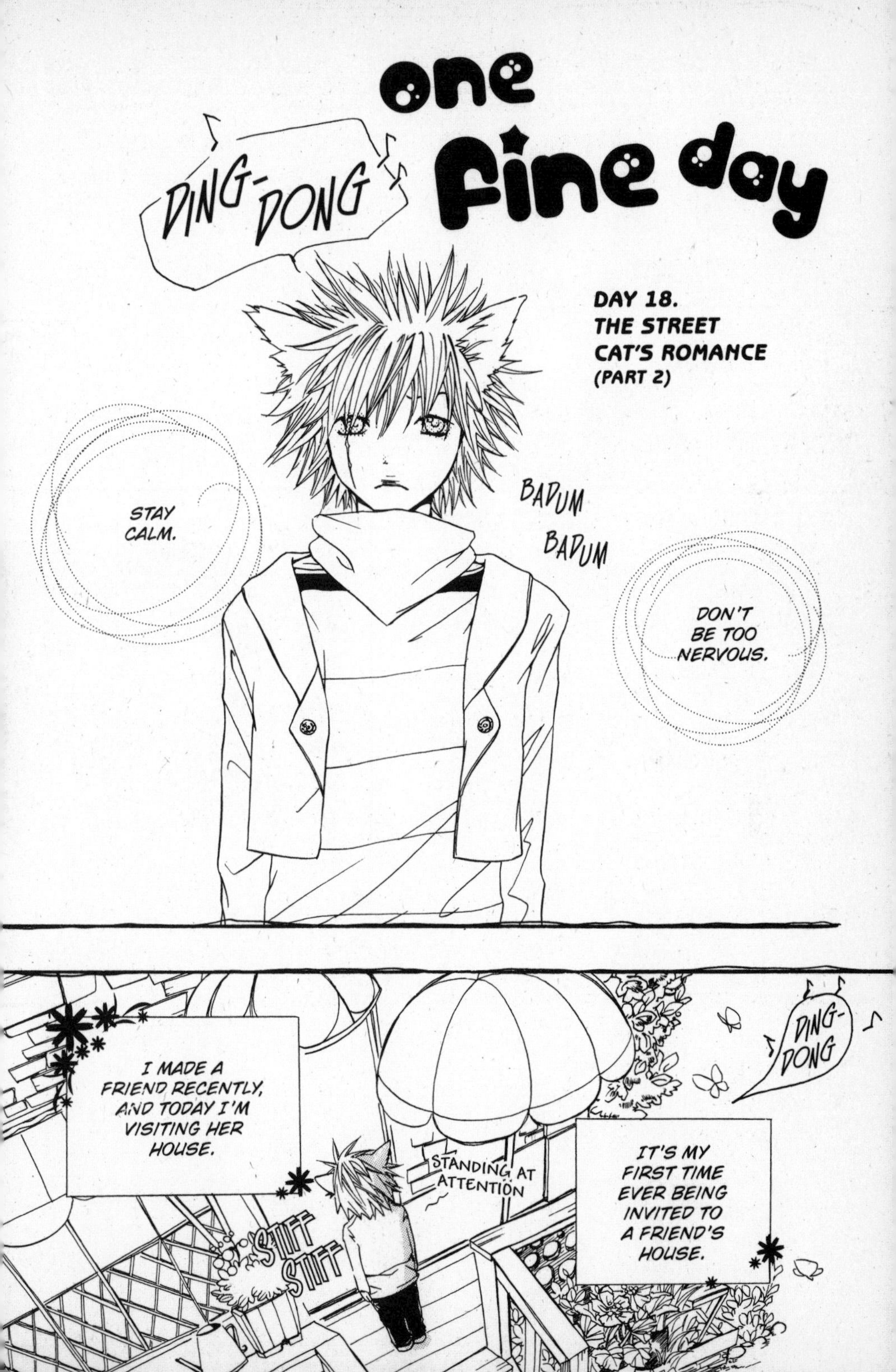
DING-DONG
one Fine day
DAY 18.
THE STREET
CAT'S ROMANCE
(PART 2)
STAY CALM.
BADUM
BADUM
DON'T BE TOO NERVOUS.
I MADE A FRIEND RECENTLY, AND TODAY I'M VISITING HER HOUSE.
STANDING AT ATTENTION
STIFF STIFF
DING-DONG
IT'S MY FIRST TIME EVER BEING INVITED TO A FRIEND'S HOUSE.

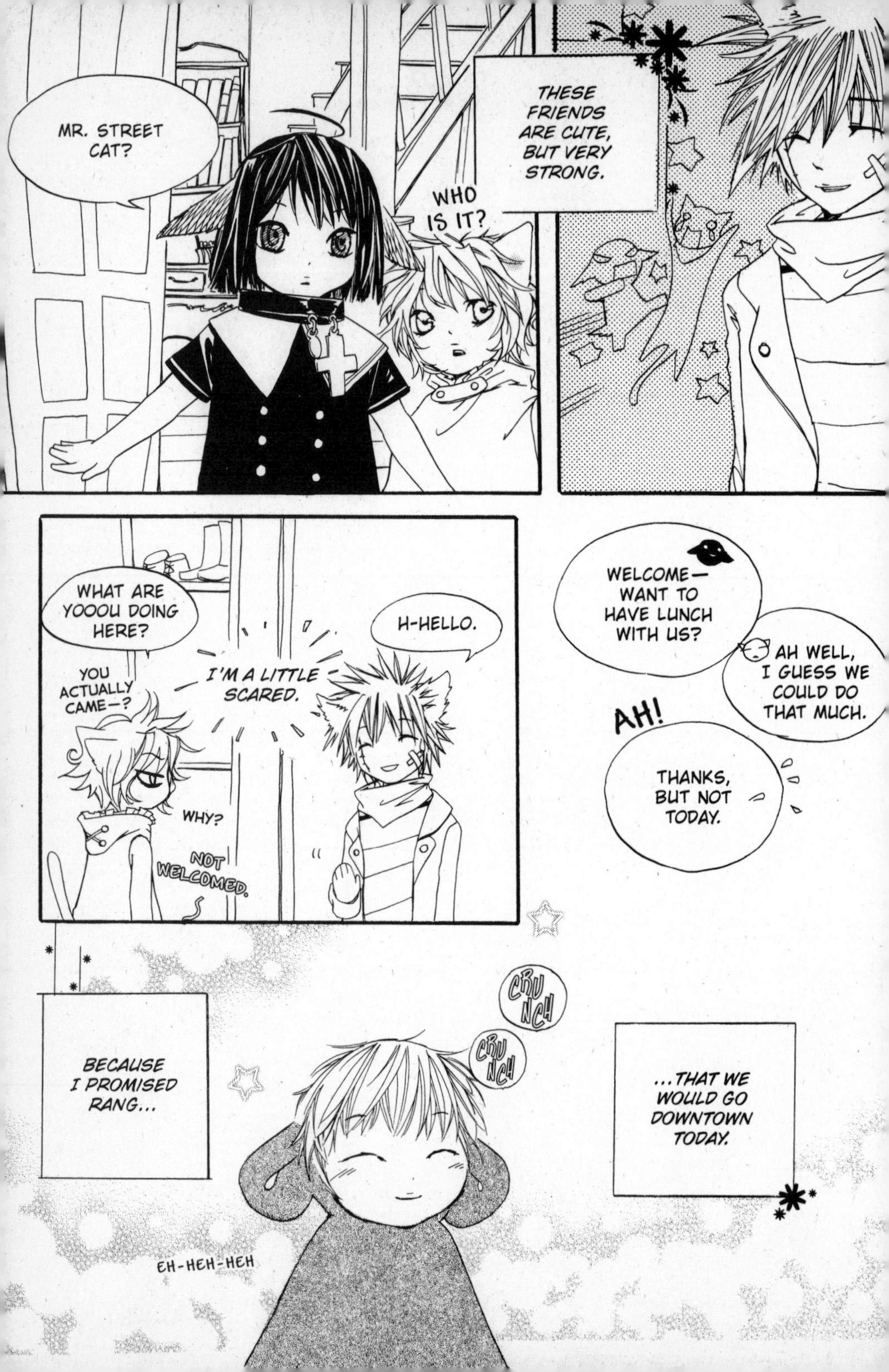
MR. STREET CAT?
WHO IS IT?
THESE FRIENDS ARE CUTE, BUT VERY STRONG.
WHAT ARE YOOOU DOING HERE?
YOU ACTUALLY CAME—?
I'M A LITTLE SCARED.
H-HELLO.
WHY?
NOT WELCOMED.
WELCOME—WANT TO HAVE LUNCH WITH US?
AH WELL, I GUESS WE COULD DO THAT MUCH.
AH!
THANKS, BUT NOT TODAY.
BECAUSE I PROMISED RANG...
CRUNCH
CRUNCH
EH-HEH-HEH
...THAT WE WOULD GO DOWNTOWN TODAY.

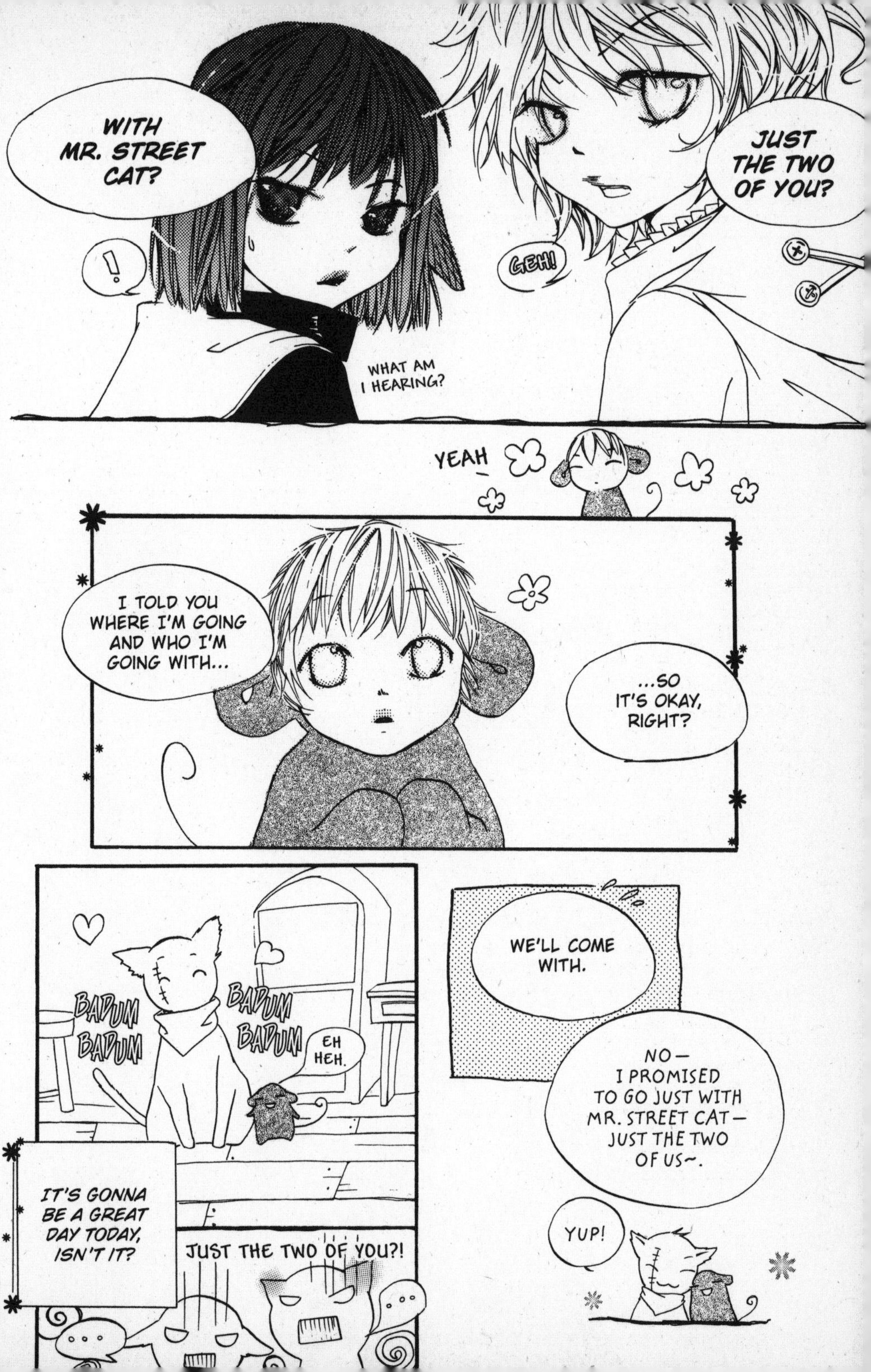
WITH MR. STREET CAT?
!
WHAT AM I HEARING?
GEH!
JUST THE TWO OF YOU?
YEAH
I TOLD YOU WHERE I'M GOING AND WHO I'M GOING WITH...
...SO IT'S OKAY, RIGHT?
BADUM BADUM
BADUM BADUM
EH HEH.
IT'S GONNA BE A GREAT DAY TODAY, ISN'T IT?
JUST THE TWO OF YOU?!
WE'LL COME WITH.
NO— I PROMISED TO GO JUST WITH MR. STREET CAT— JUST THE TWO OF US~.
YUP!

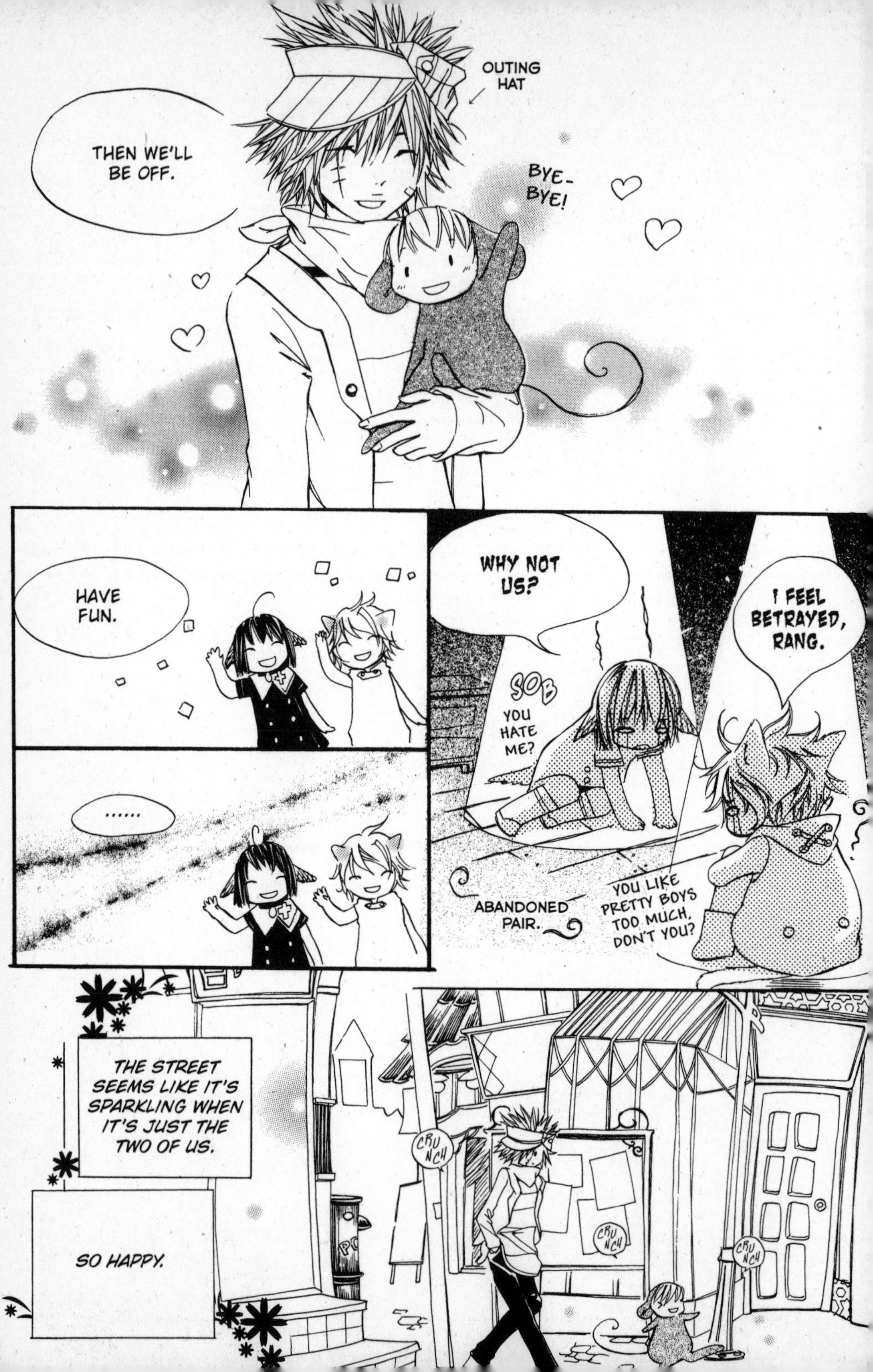
THEN WE'LL BE OFF.
OUTING HAT
BYE-BYE!
HAVE FUN.
......
WHY NOT US?
SOB
YOU HATE ME?
I FEEL BETRAYED, RANG.
ABANDONED PAIR.
YOU LIKE PRETTY BOYS TOO MUCH, DON'T YOU?
THE STREET SEEMS LIKE IT'S SPARKLING WHEN IT'S JUST THE TWO OF US.
SO HAPPY.
CRUNCH
CRUNCH
CRUNCH

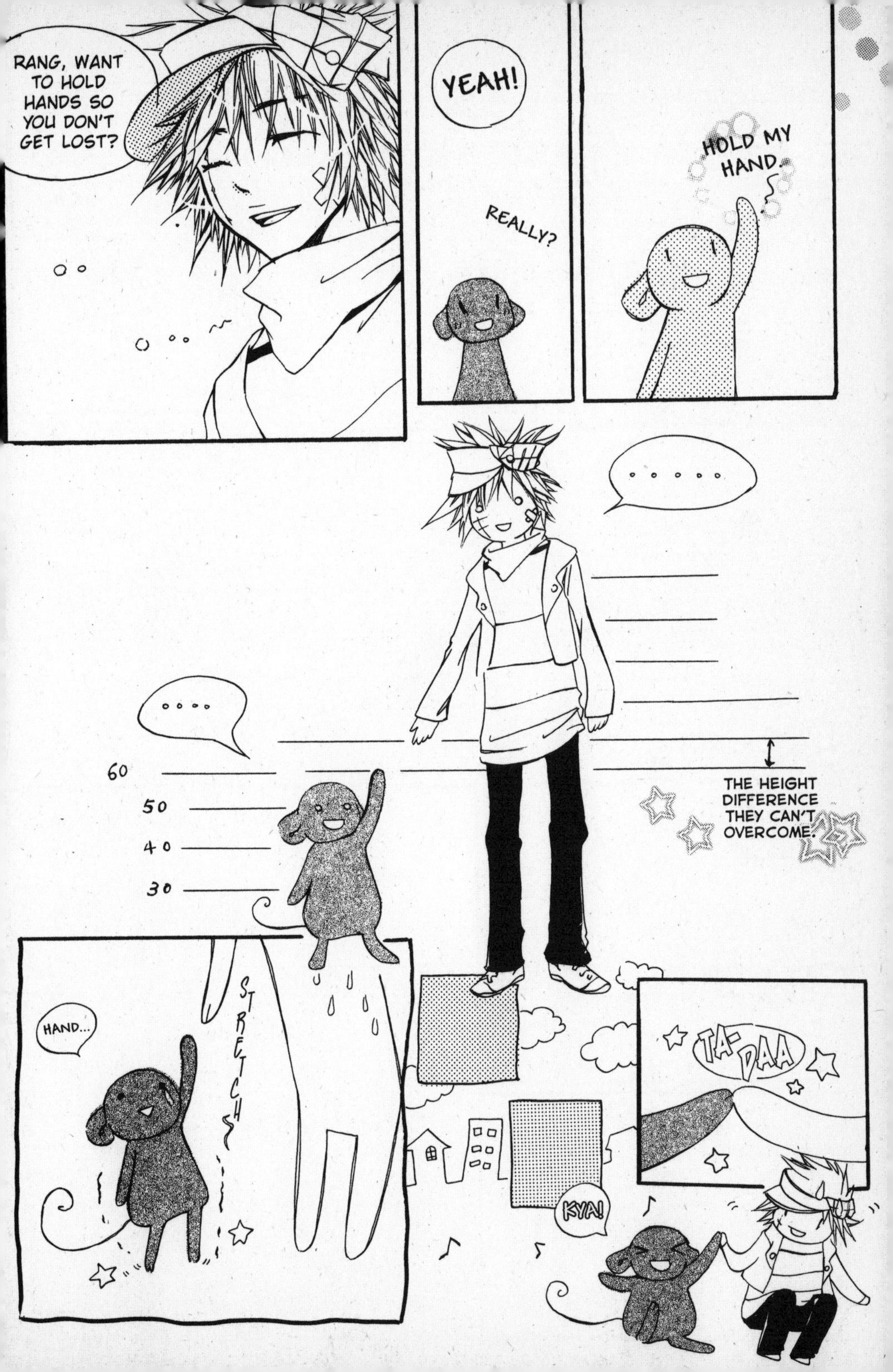
RANG, WANT TO HOLD HANDS SO YOU DON'T GET LOST?
YEAH!
REALLY?
HOLD MY HAND.
.....
....
60
50
40
30
THE HEIGHT DIFFERENCE THEY CAN'T OVERCOME.
HAND...
STRETCH
TA-DAA
KYA!

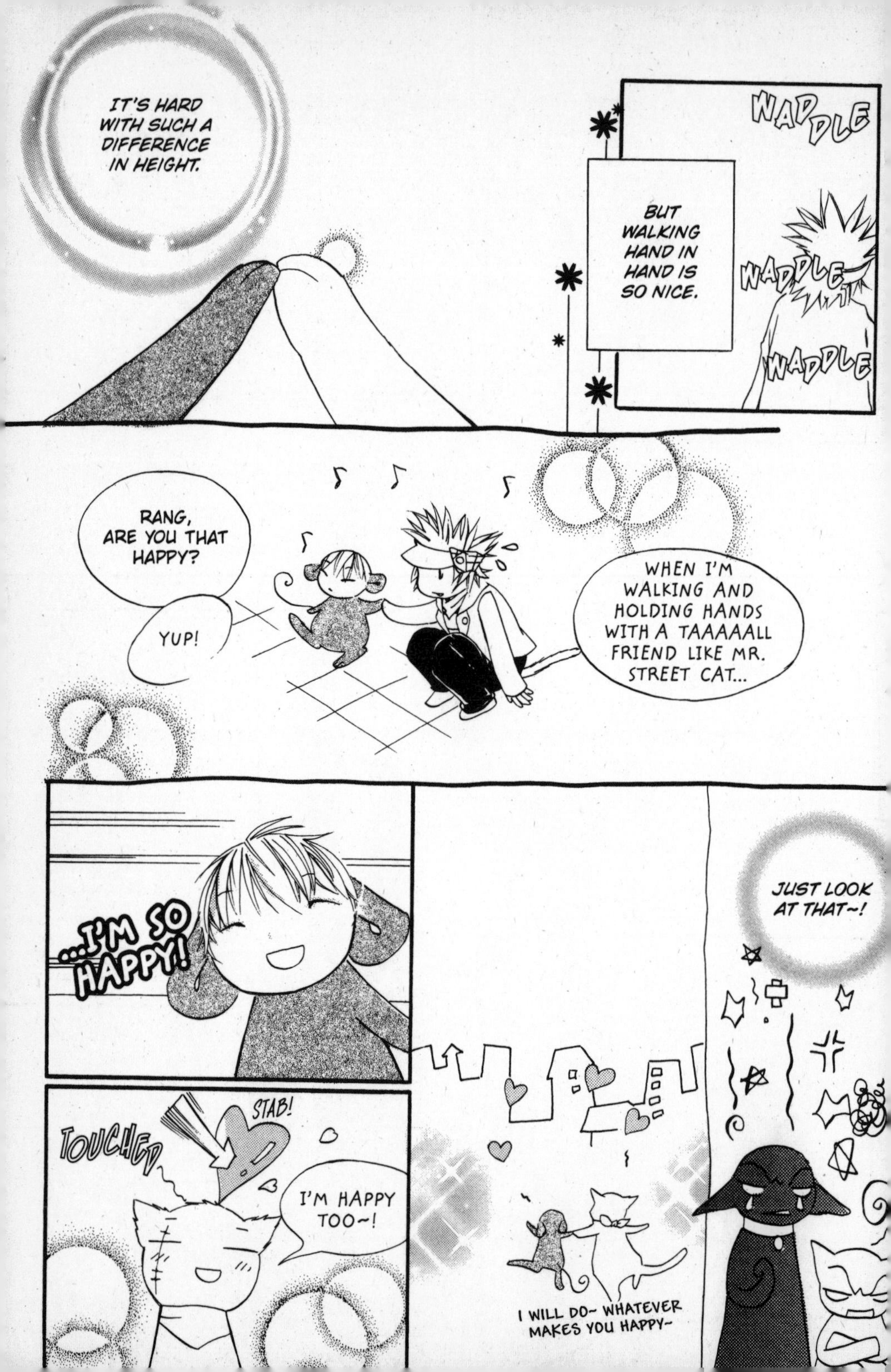
IT'S HARD WITH SUCH A DIFFERENCE IN HEIGHT.
WADDLE
BUT WALKING HAND IN HAND IS SO NICE.
WADDLE
WADDLE
RANG, ARE YOU THAT HAPPY?
YUP!
WHEN I'M WALKING AND HOLDING HANDS WITH A TAAAAALL FRIEND LIKE MR. STREET CAT...
...I'M SO HAPPY!
TOUCHED
STAB!
I'M HAPPY TOO~!
JUST LOOK AT THAT~!
I WILL DO~ WHATEVER MAKES YOU HAPPY~

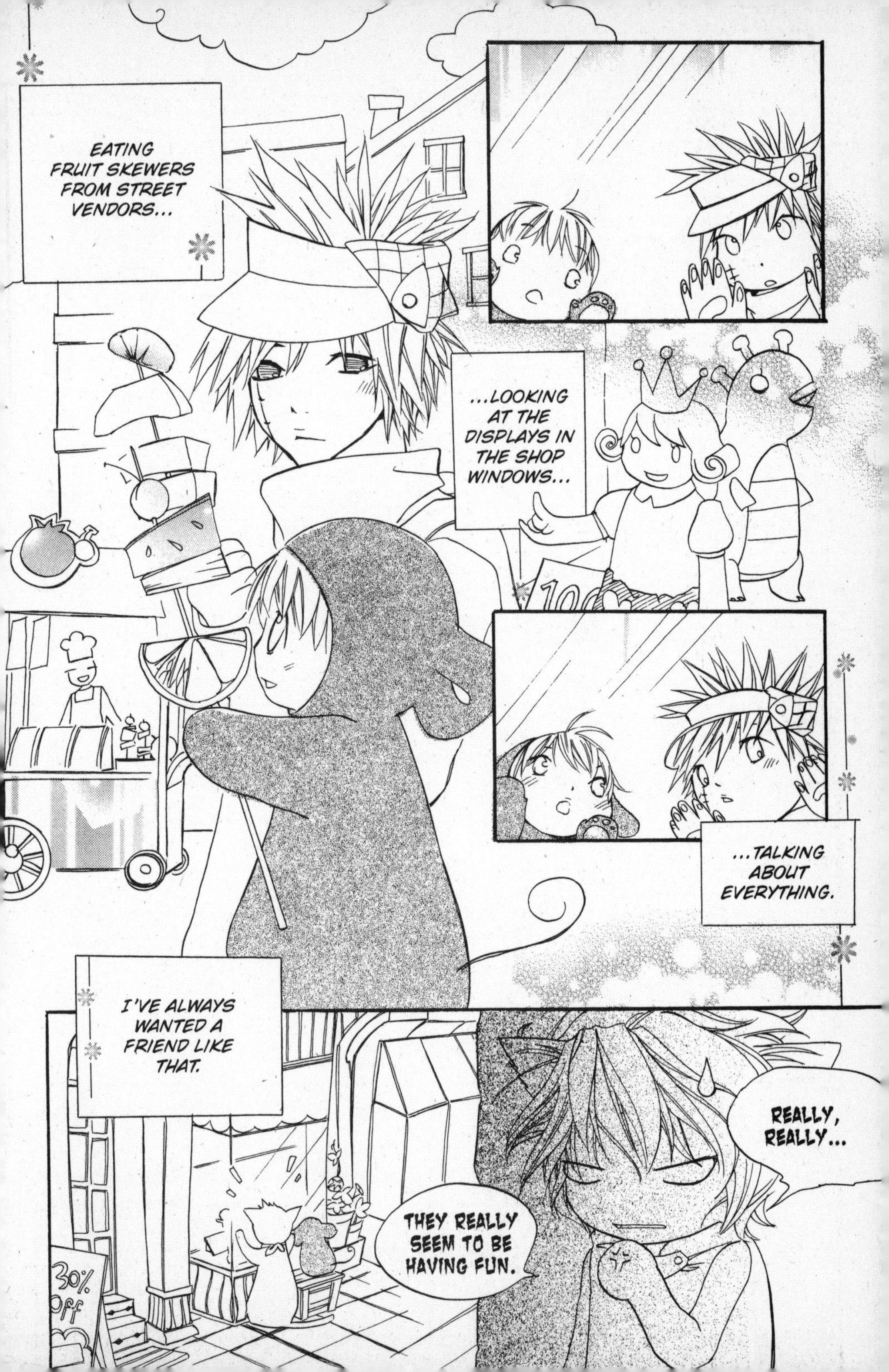
EATING FRUIT SKEWERS FROM STREET VENDORS...
...LOOKING AT THE DISPLAYS IN THE SHOP WINDOWS...
...TALKING ABOUT EVERYTHING.
I'VE ALWAYS WANTED A FRIEND LIKE THAT.
30% Off
THEY REALLY SEEM TO BE HAVING FUN.
REALLY, REALLY...

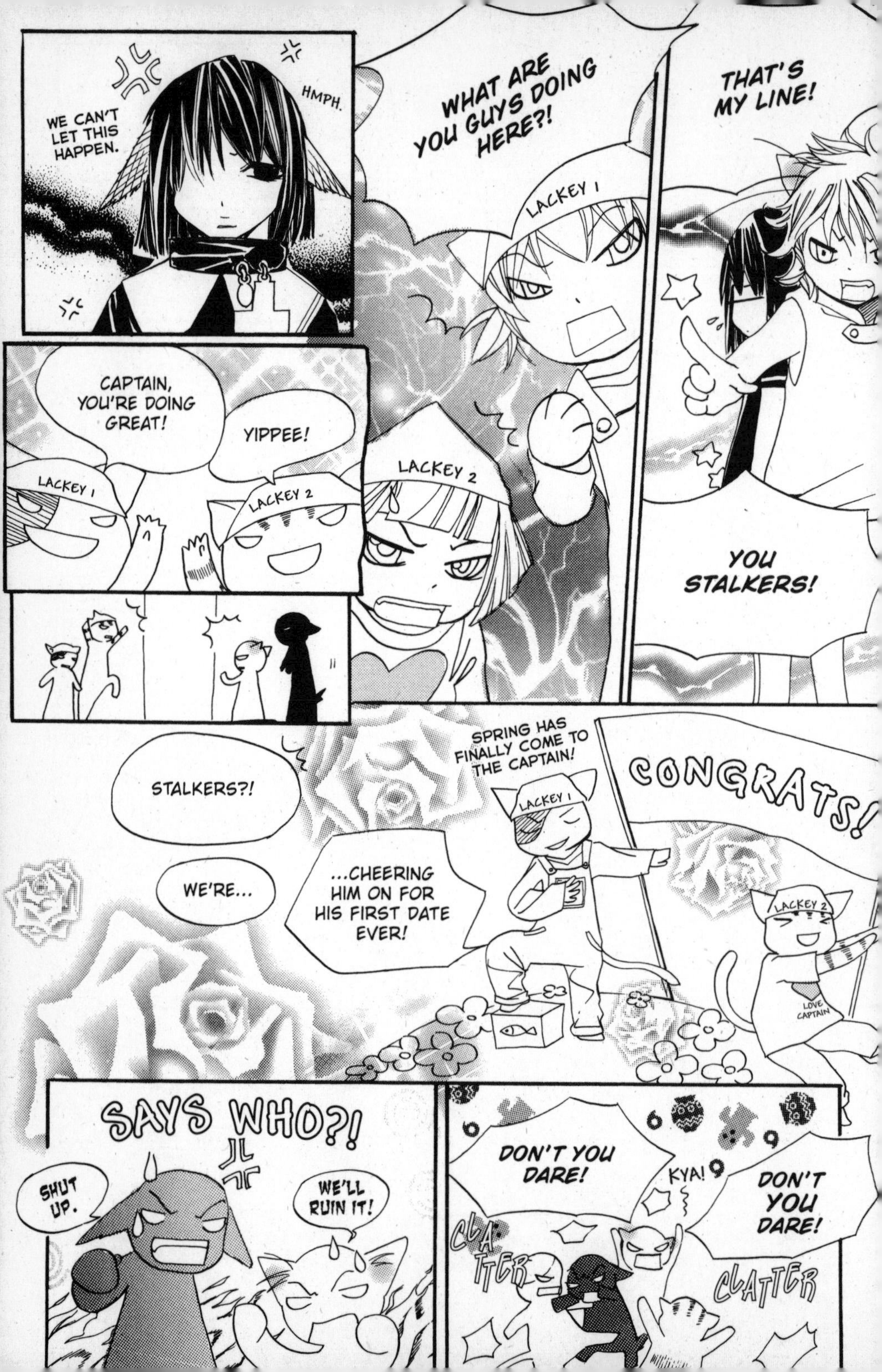

WE CAN'T LET THIS HAPPEN.
HMPH.
CAPTAIN, YOU'RE DOING GREAT!
YIPPEE!
LACKEY 1
LACKEY 2
WHAT ARE YOU GUYS DOING HERE?!
LACKEY 1
LACKEY 2
THAT'S MY LINE!
YOU STALKERS!
STALKERS?!
WE'RE...
...CHEERING HIM ON FOR HIS FIRST DATE EVER!
SPRING HAS FINALLY COME TO THE CAPTAIN!
LACKEY 1
CONGRATS!
LACKEY 2
LOVE CAPTAIN
SAYS WHO?!
SHUT UP.
WE'LL RUIN IT!
DON'T YOU DARE!
KYA!
DON'T YOU DARE!
CLATTER
CLATTER

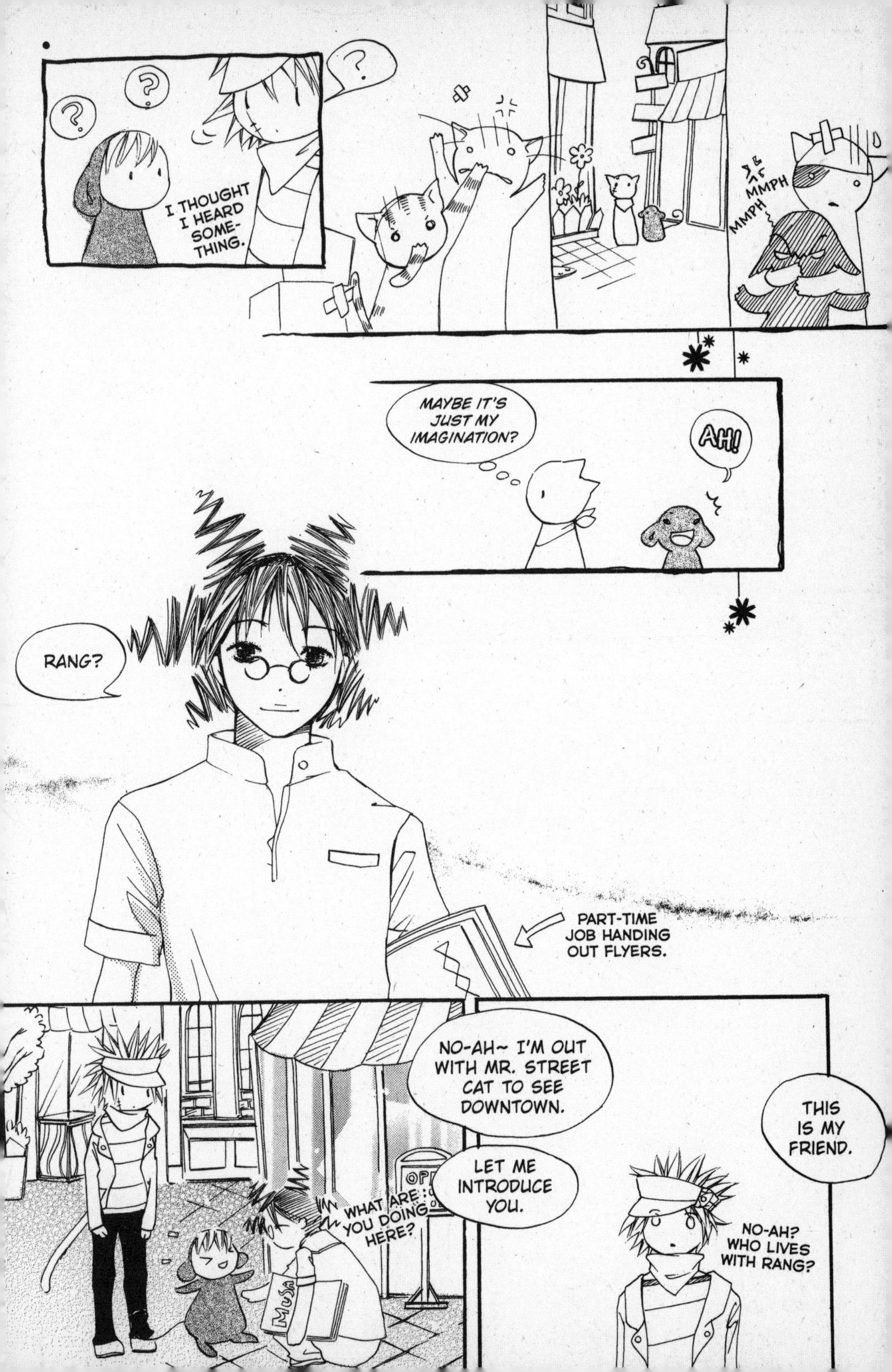
I THOUGHT I HEARD SOME-THING.
MMPH MMPH
MAYBE IT'S JUST MY IMAGINATION?
AH!
RANG?
PART-TIME JOB HANDING OUT FLYERS.
WHAT ARE YOU DOING HERE?
NO-AH~ I'M OUT WITH MR. STREET CAT TO SEE DOWNTOWN.
LET ME INTRODUCE YOU.
THIS IS MY FRIEND.
NO-AH? WHO LIVES WITH RANG?

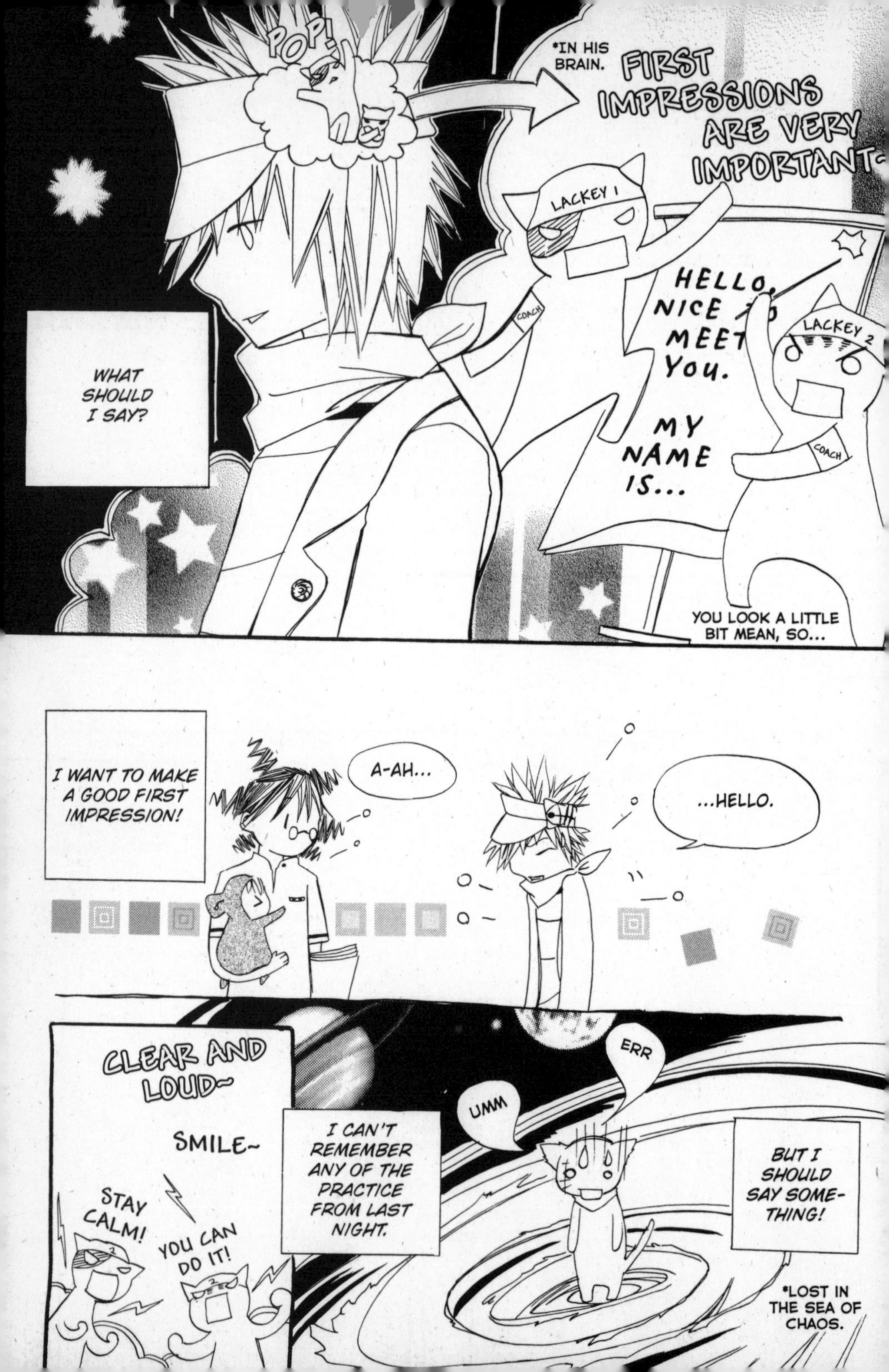
POP!
*IN HIS BRAIN.
FIRST IMPRESSIONS ARE VERY IMPORTANT~
WHAT SHOULD I SAY?
LACKEY 1
COACH
HELLO, NICE TO MEET YOU.
MY NAME IS...
LACKEY 2
COACH
YOU LOOK A LITTLE BIT MEAN, SO...
I WANT TO MAKE A GOOD FIRST IMPRESSION!
A-AH...
...HELLO.
CLEAR AND LOUD~
SMILE~
STAY CALM!
YOU CAN DO IT!
I CAN'T REMEMBER ANY OF THE PRACTICE FROM LAST NIGHT.
UMM
ERR
BUT I SHOULD SAY SOME-THING!
*LOST IN THE SEA OF CHAOS.

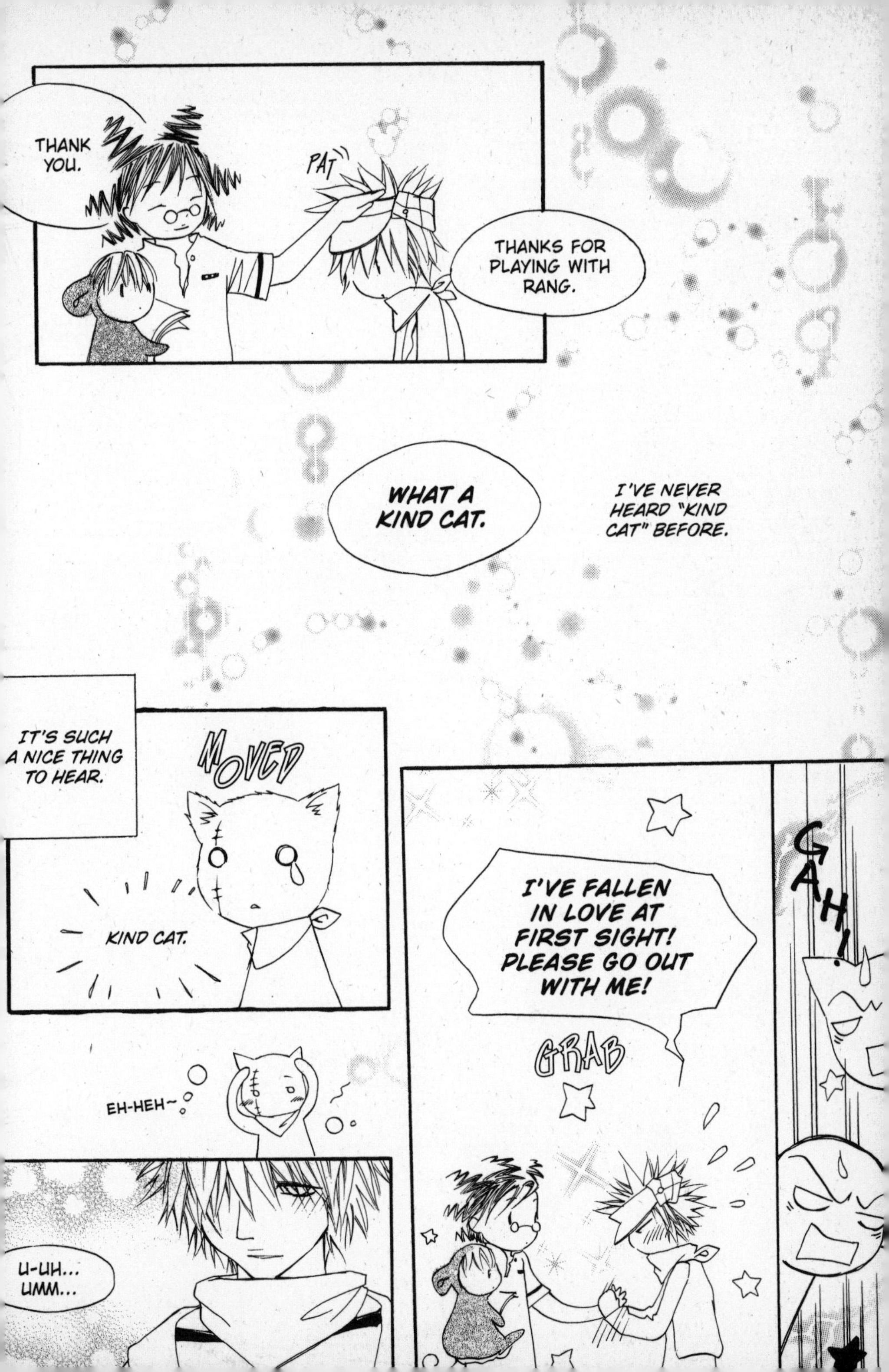
THANK YOU.
PAT
THANKS FOR PLAYING WITH RANG.
WHAT A KIND CAT.
I'VE NEVER HEARD "KIND CAT" BEFORE.
IT'S SUCH A NICE THING TO HEAR.
MOVED
KIND CAT.
EH-HEH~
U-UH... UMM...
I'VE FALLEN IN LOVE AT FIRST SIGHT! PLEASE GO OUT WITH ME!
GRAB
GAH!

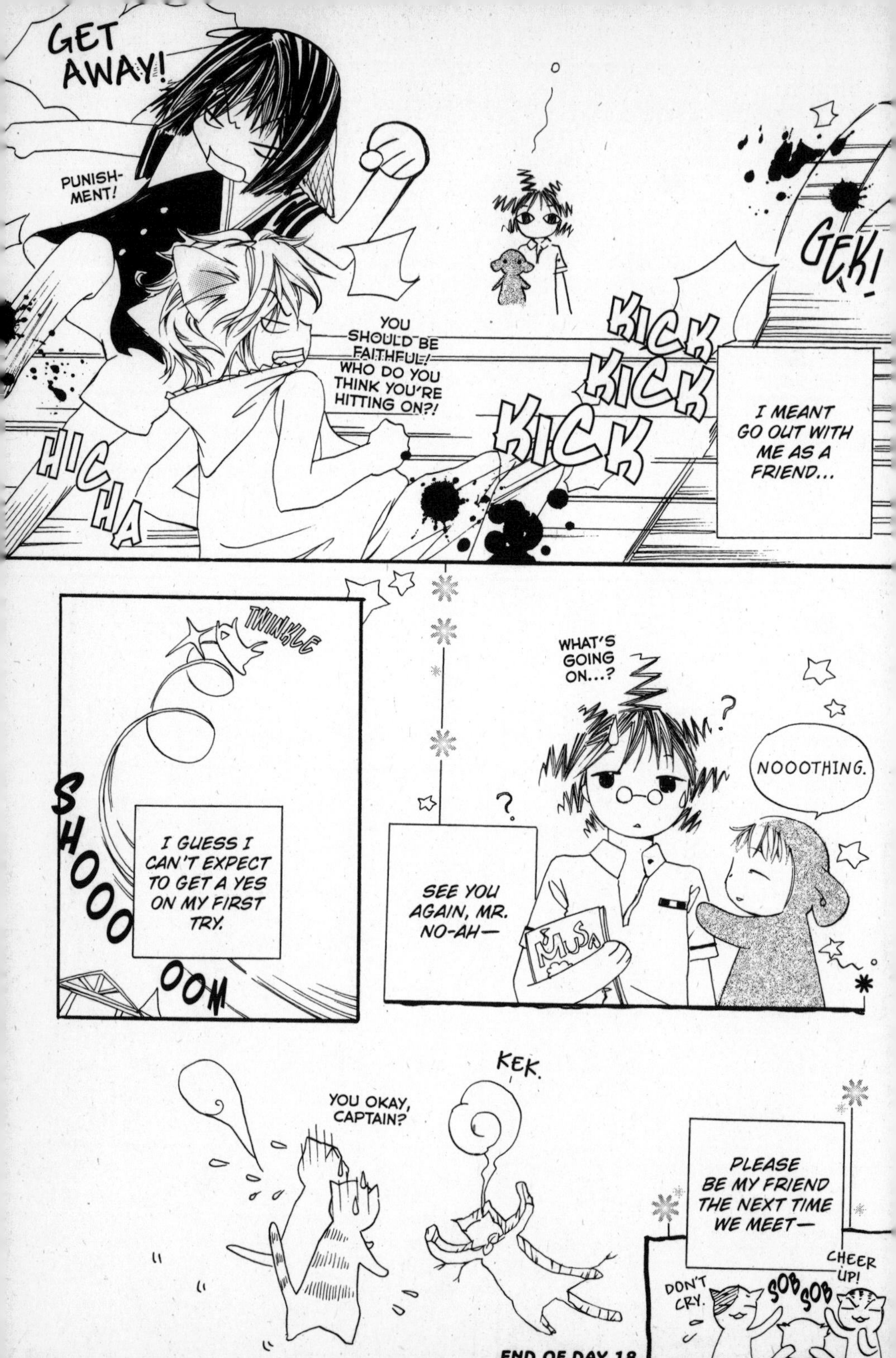
GET AWAY!
PUNISH-MENT!
YOU SHOULD BE FAITHFUL! WHO DO YOU THINK YOU'RE HITTING ON?!
HICHA
KICK KICK KICK
GEK!
I MEANT GO OUT WITH ME AS A FRIEND...
TWINKLE
SHOOOOOOM
I GUESS I CAN'T EXPECT TO GET A YES ON MY FIRST TRY.
WHAT'S GOING ON...?
NOOOTHING.
SEE YOU AGAIN, MR. NO-AH—
YOU OKAY, CAPTAIN?
KEK.
PLEASE BE MY FRIEND THE NEXT TIME WE MEET—
DON'T CRY.
SOB SOB
CHEER UP!
END OF DAY 18

DAY 19.
TALKING ABOUT YOU

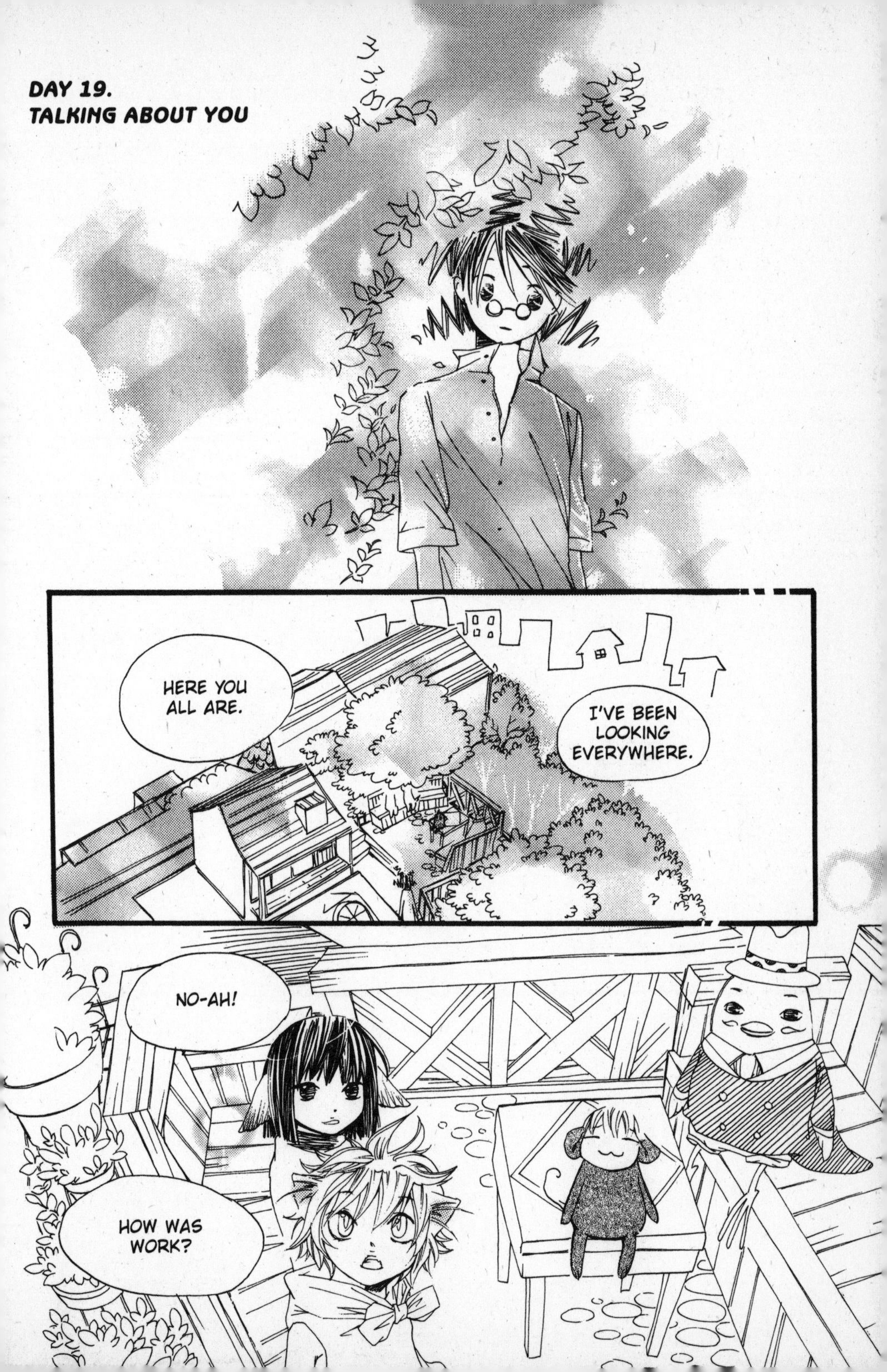
HERE YOU ALL ARE.
I'VE BEEN LOOKING EVERYWHERE.
NO-AH!
HOW WAS WORK?

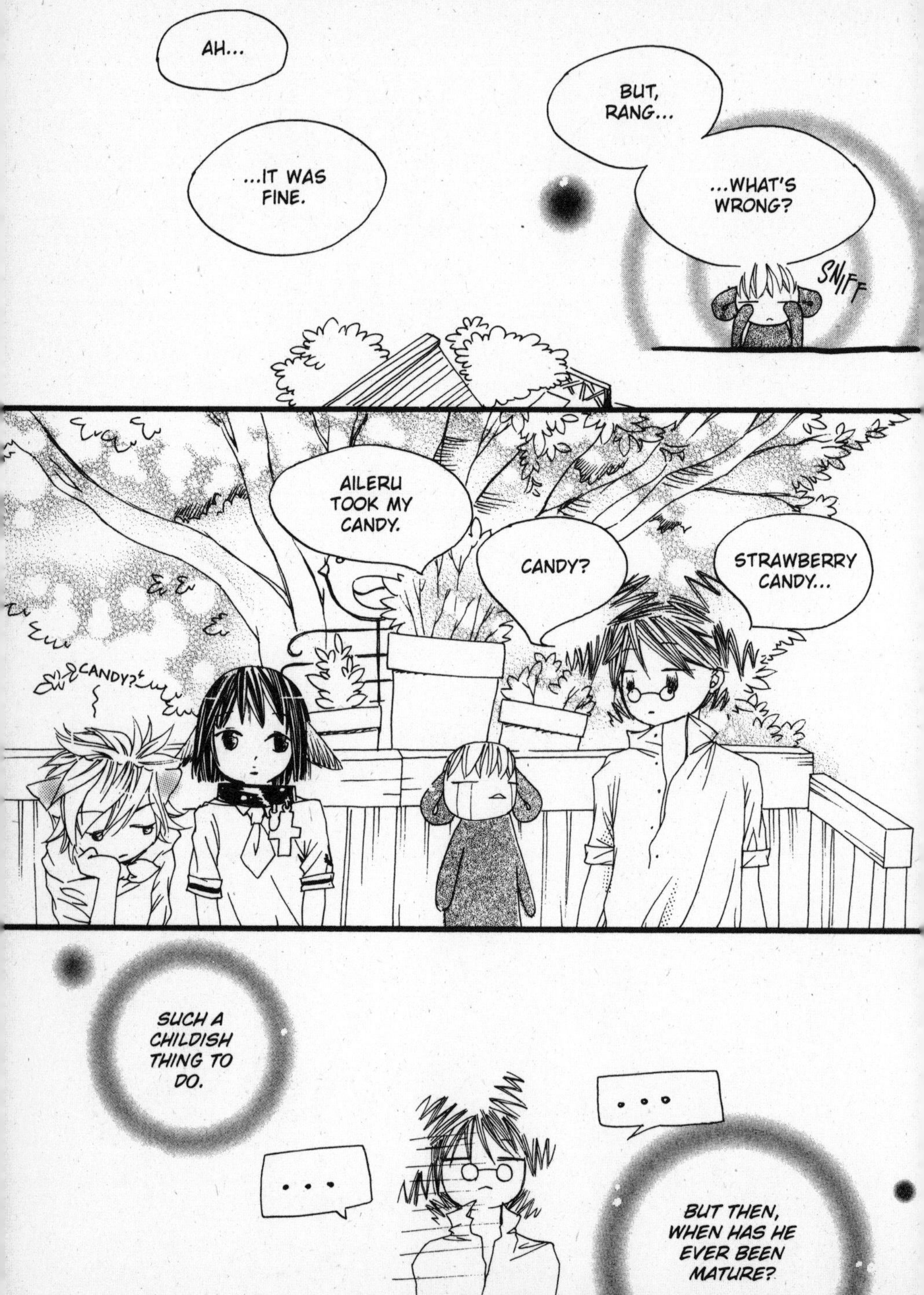
AH...
...IT WAS FINE.
BUT, RANG...
...WHAT'S WRONG?
SNIFF
AILERU TOOK MY CANDY.
CANDY?
STRAWBERRY CANDY...
CANDY?
SUCH A CHILDISH THING TO DO.
...
...
BUT THEN, WHEN HAS HE EVER BEEN MATURE?

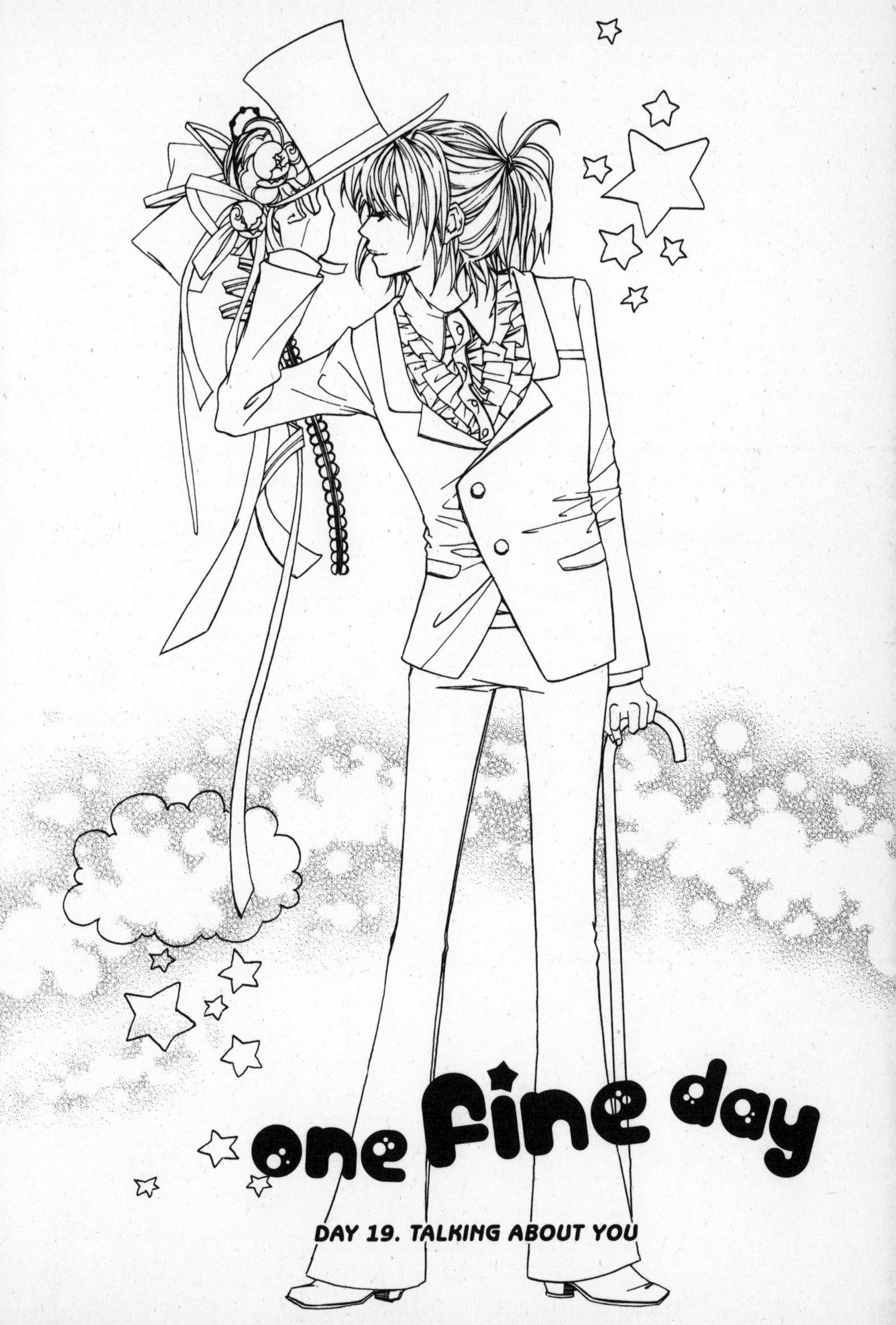
one fine day
DAY 19. TALKING ABOUT YOU

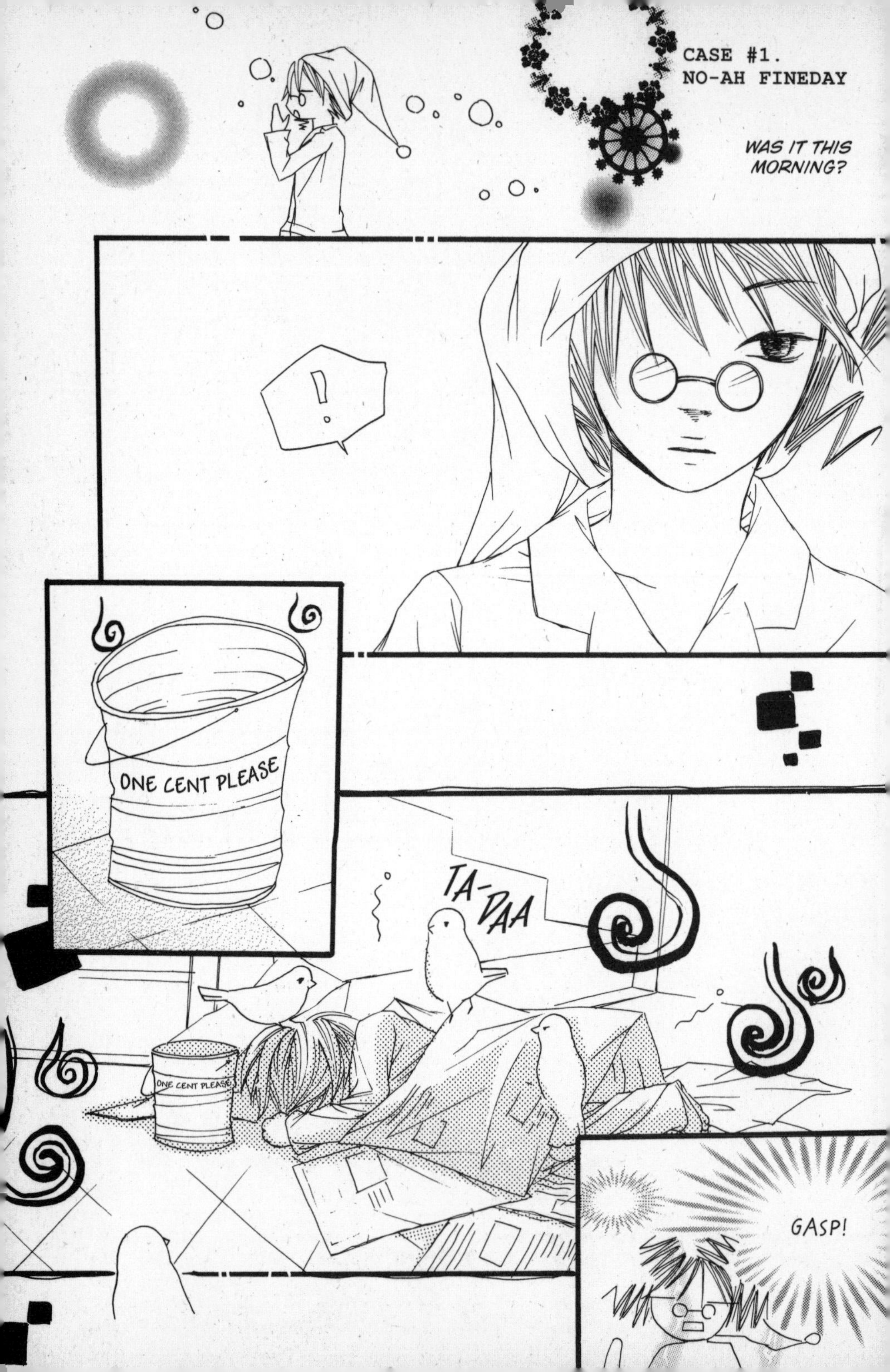
CASE #1.
NO-AH FINEDAY
WAS IT THIS MORNING?
!
ONE CENT PLEASE
TA-DAA
ONE CENT PLEASE
GASP!

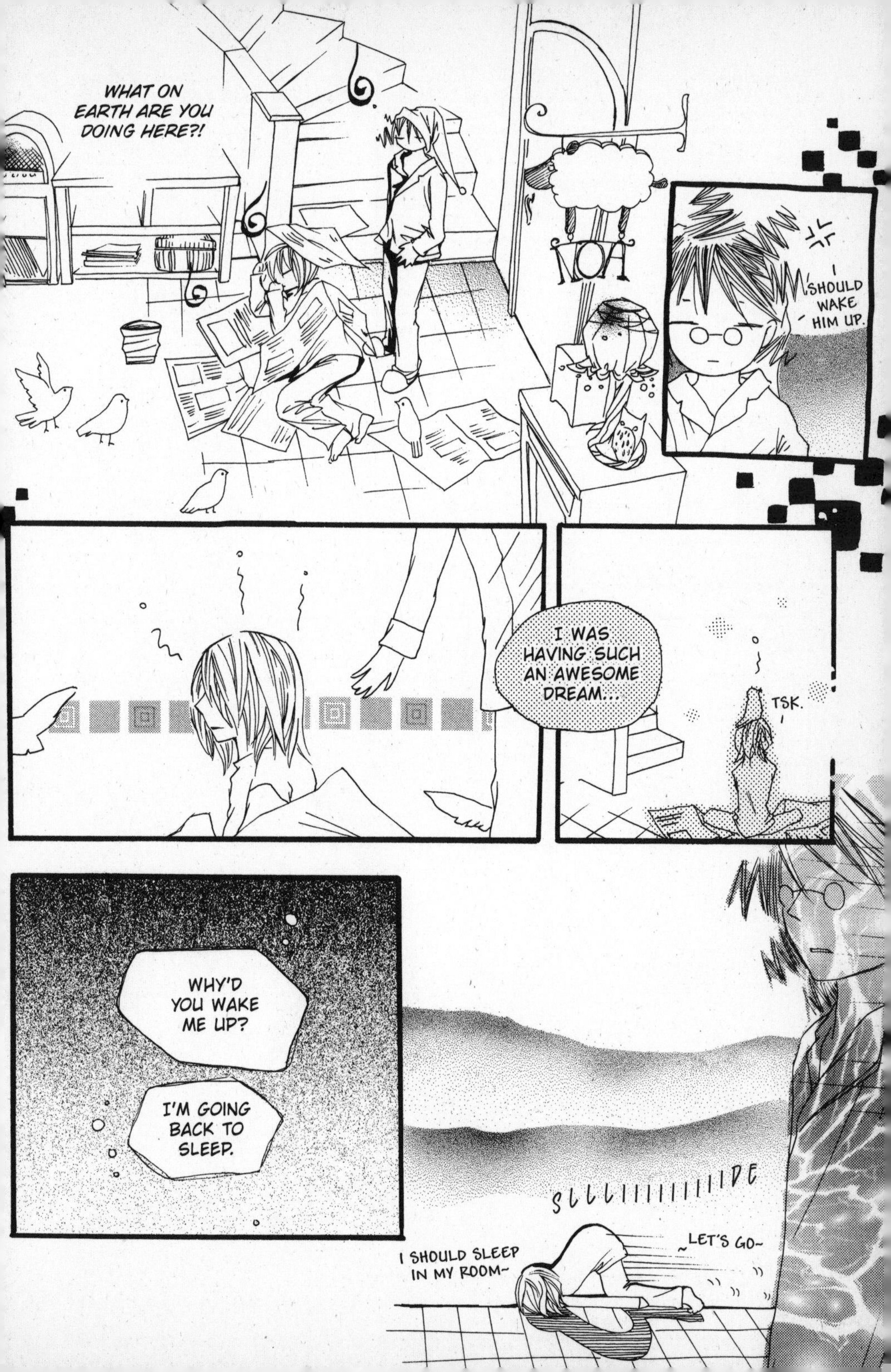
WHAT ON EARTH ARE YOU DOING HERE?!
NOA
I SHOULD WAKE HIM UP.
I WAS HAVING SUCH AN AWESOME DREAM...
TSK.
WHY'D YOU WAKE ME UP?
I'M GOING BACK TO SLEEP.
SLLLIIIIIIIIIIDE
I SHOULD SLEEP IN MY ROOM~
~LET'S GO~

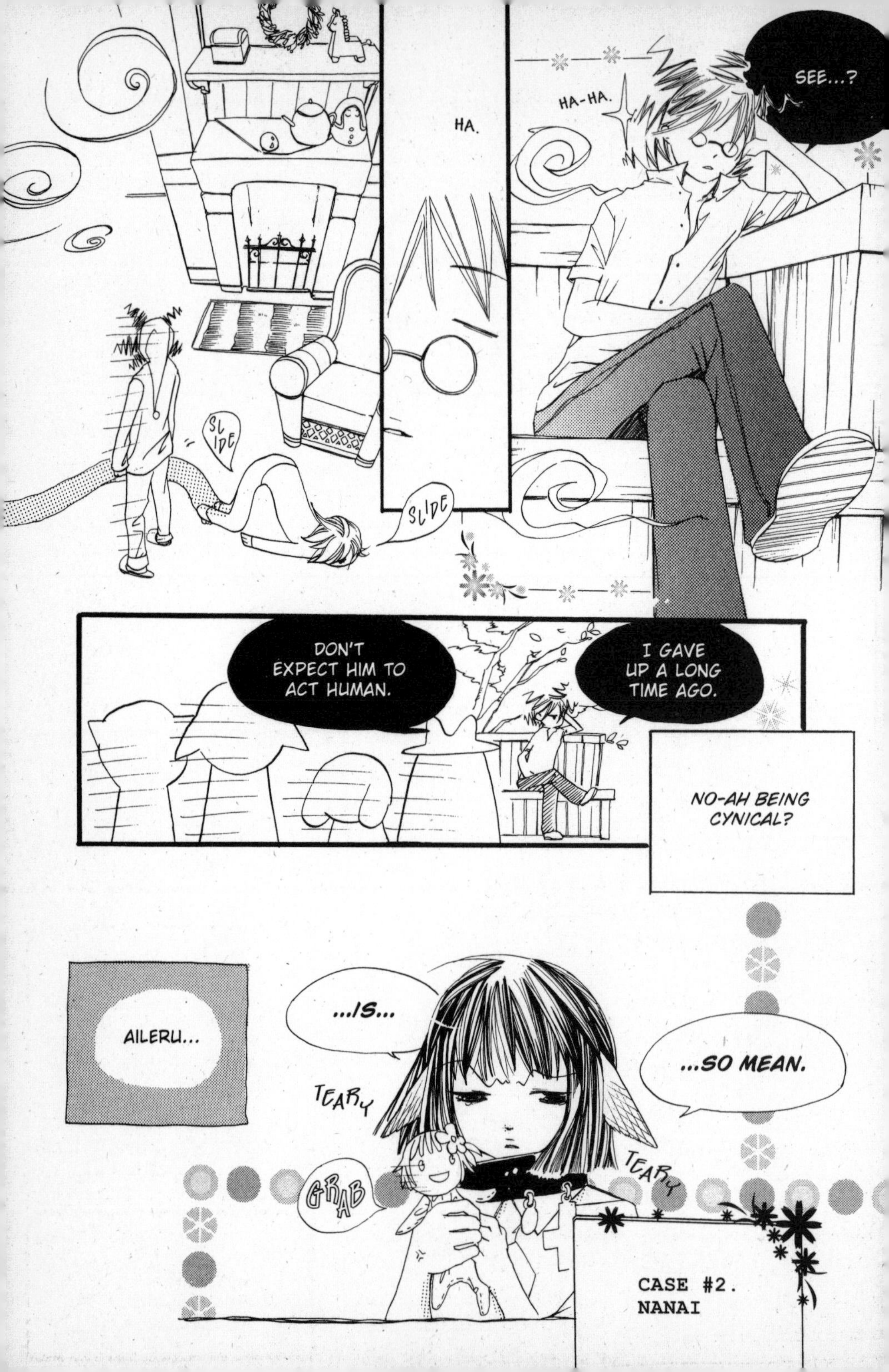
SLIDE
SLIDE
HA.
HA-HA.
SEE...?
DON'T EXPECT HIM TO ACT HUMAN.
I GAVE UP A LONG TIME AGO.
NO-AH BEING CYNICAL?
AILERU...
...IS...
...SO MEAN.
TEARY
TEARY
GRAB
CASE #2.
NANAI

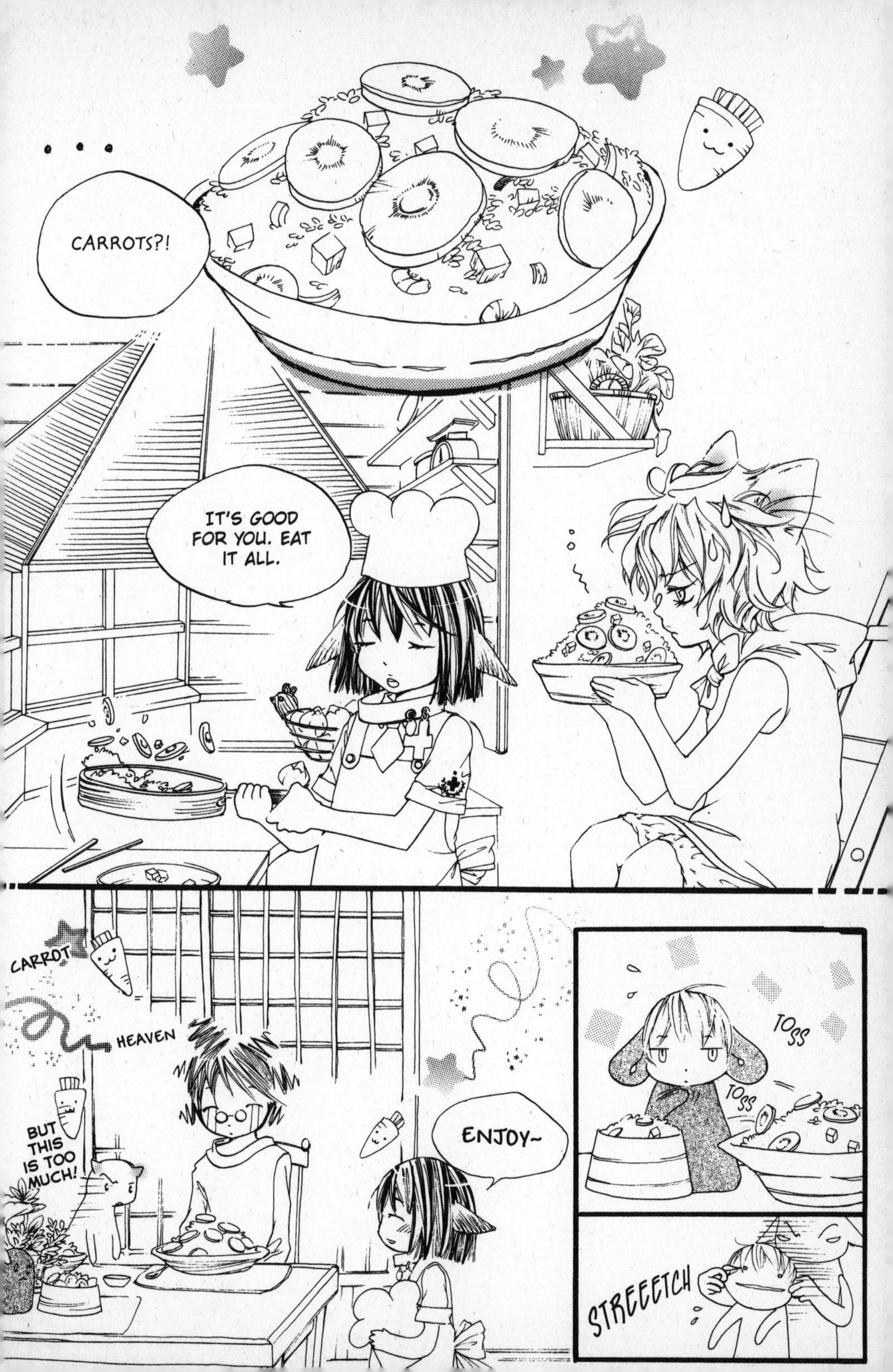

. . .
CARROTS?!
IT'S GOOD FOR YOU. EAT IT ALL.
CARROT
HEAVEN
BUT THIS IS TOO MUCH!
ENJOY~
TOSS
TOSS
STREEETCH

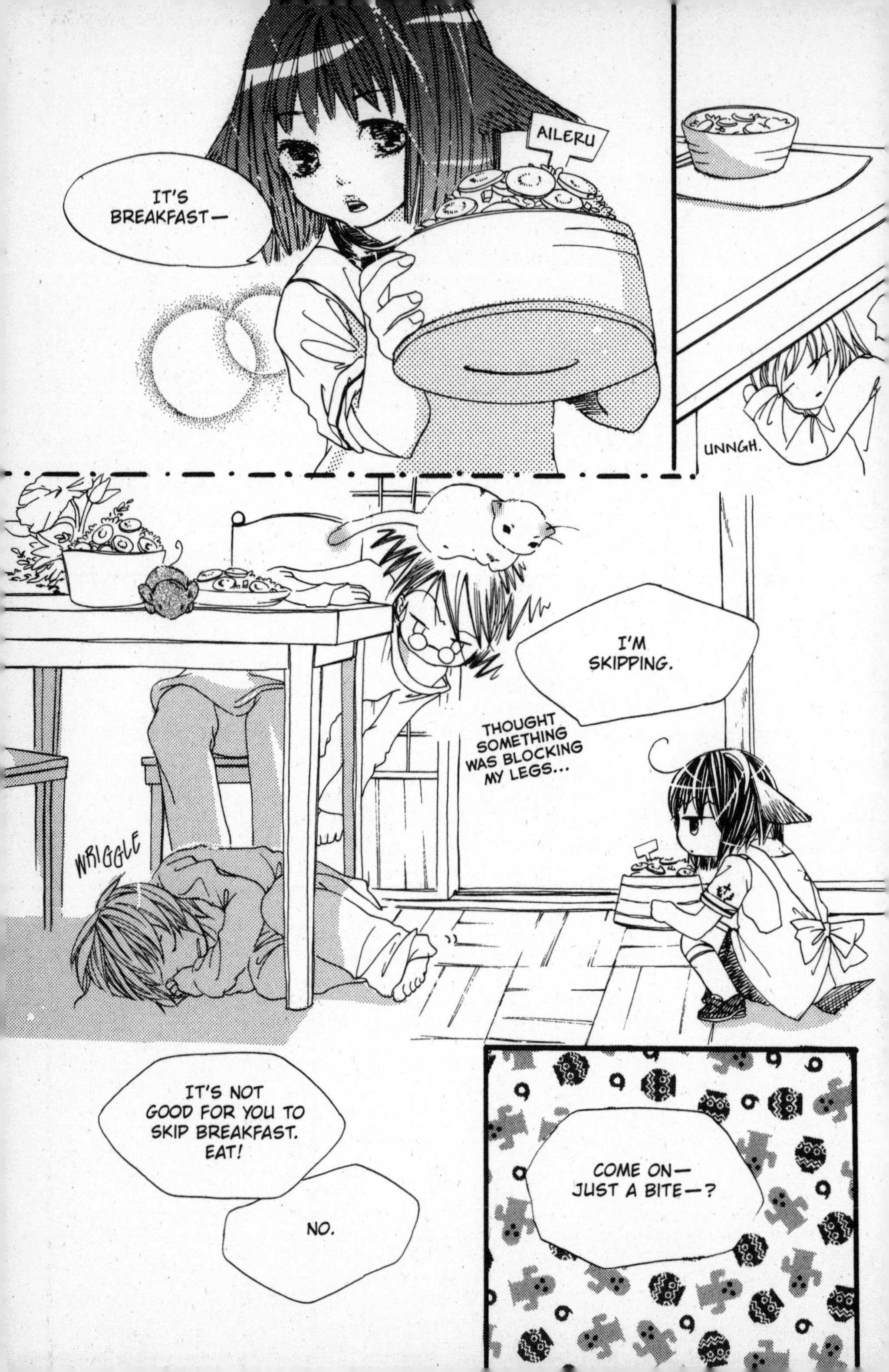
IT'S BREAKFAST—
AILERU
UNNGH.
WRIGGLE
I'M SKIPPING.
THOUGHT SOMETHING WAS BLOCKING MY LEGS...
IT'S NOT GOOD FOR YOU TO SKIP BREAKFAST. EAT!
NO.
COME ON— JUST A BITE—?

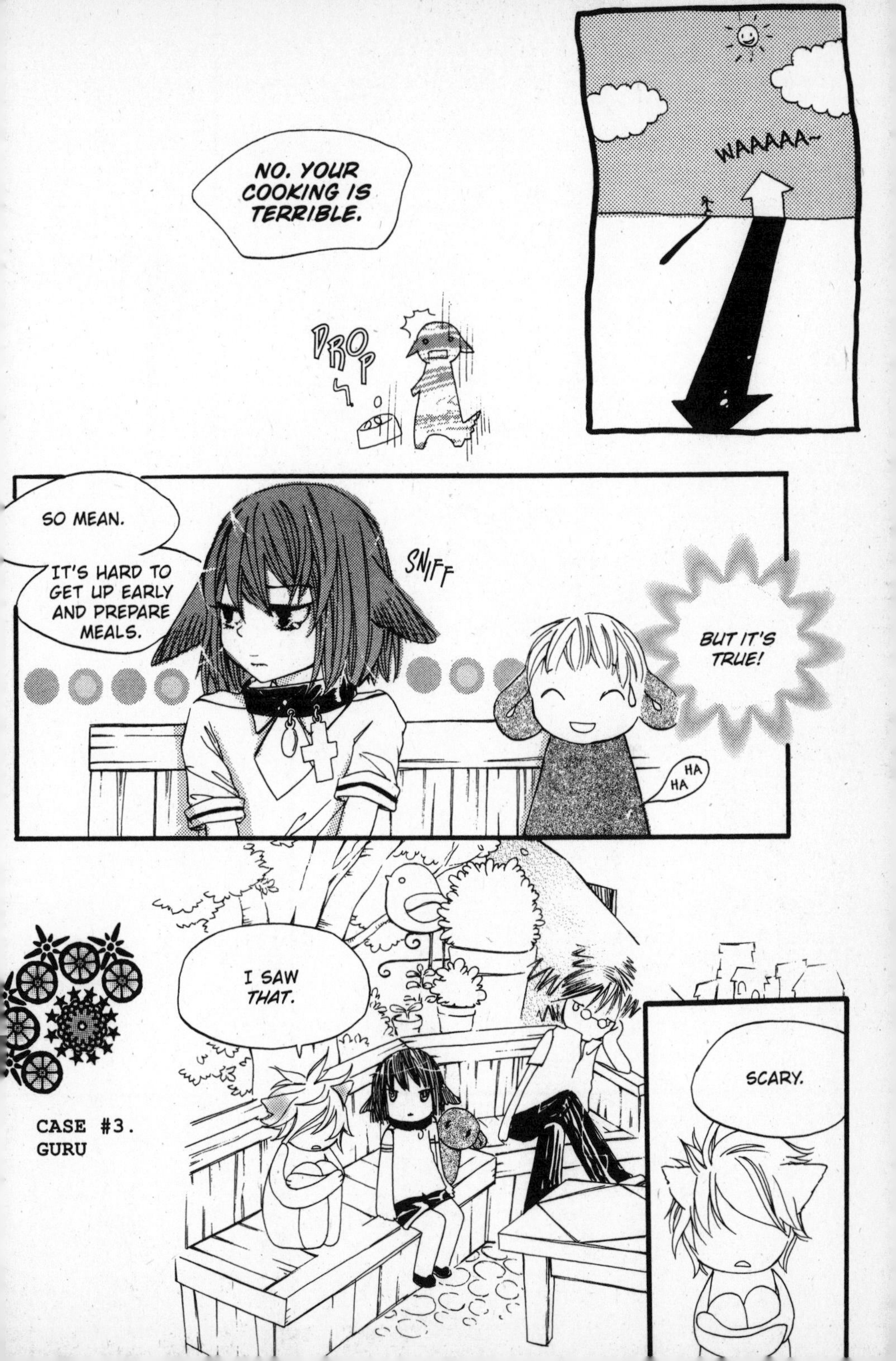
NO. YOUR COOKING IS TERRIBLE.
DROP
WAAAAA-
SO MEAN.
IT'S HARD TO GET UP EARLY AND PREPARE MEALS.
SNIFF
BUT IT'S TRUE!
HA HA
I SAW THAT.
SCARY.
CASE #3.
GURU

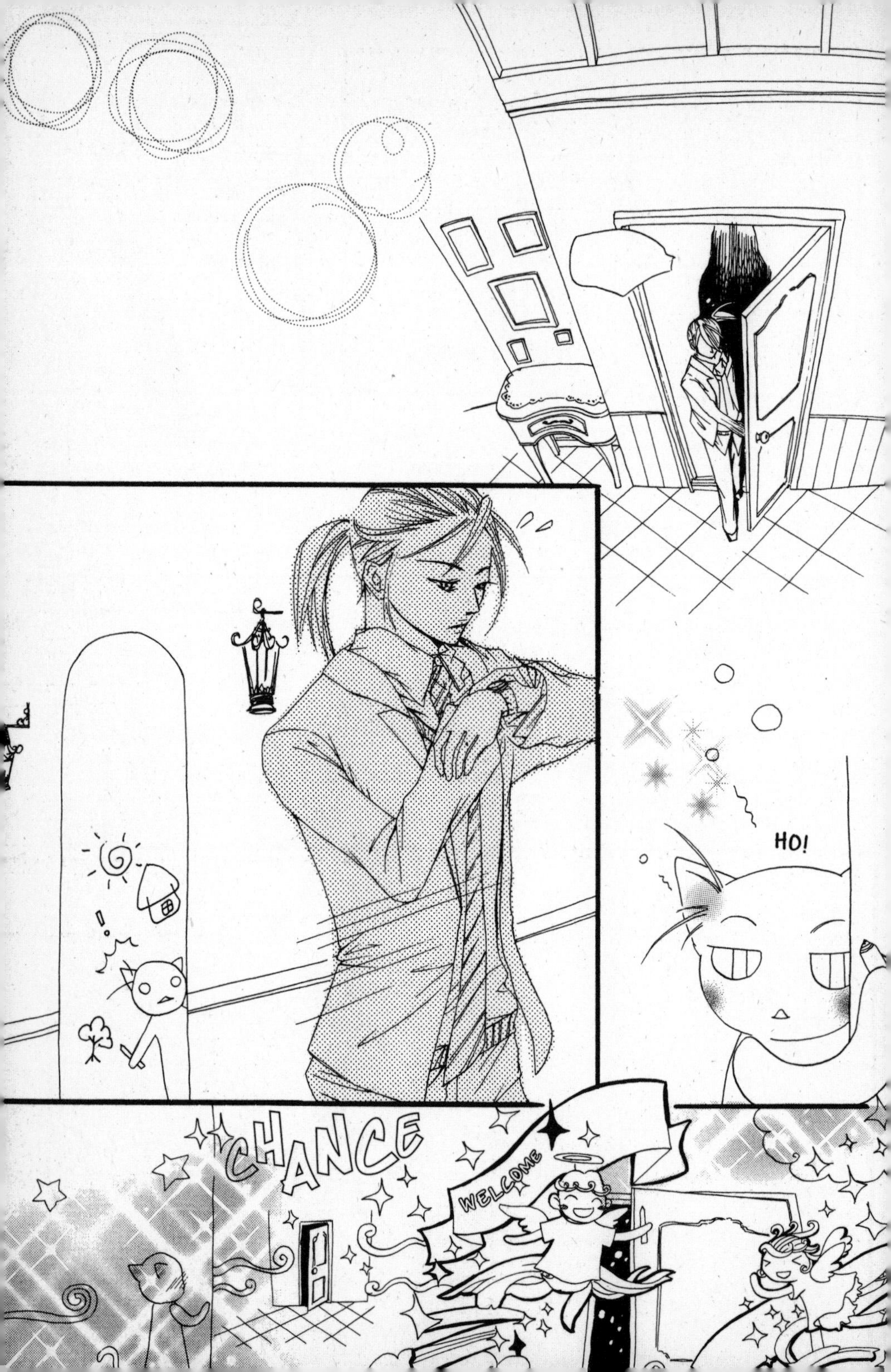
HO!
CHANCE
WELCOME

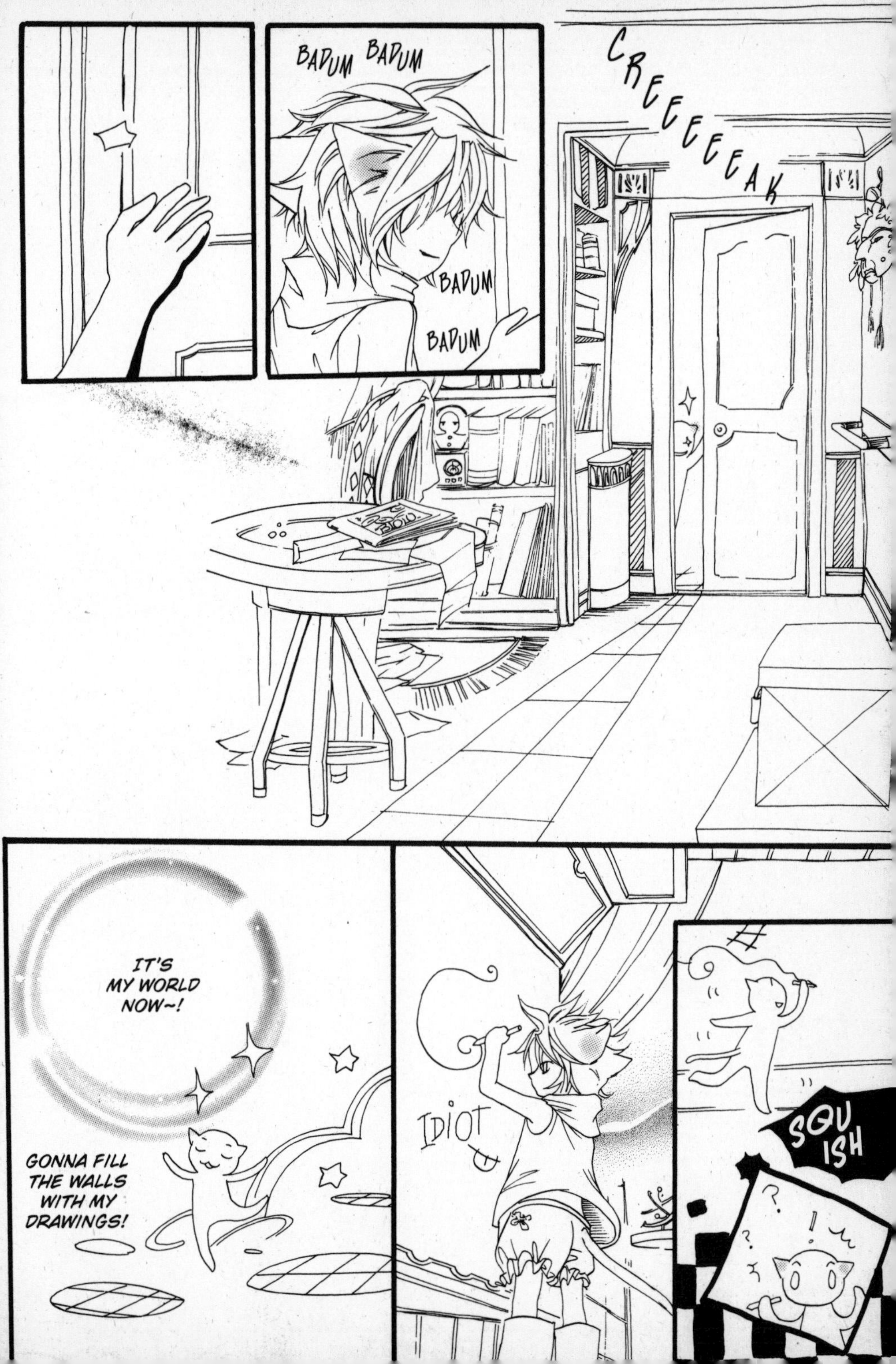
BADUM BADUM
BADUM
BADUM
CREEEEEAK
IT'S MY WORLD NOW~!
GONNA FILL THE WALLS WITH MY DRAWINGS!
IDIOT
SQUISH

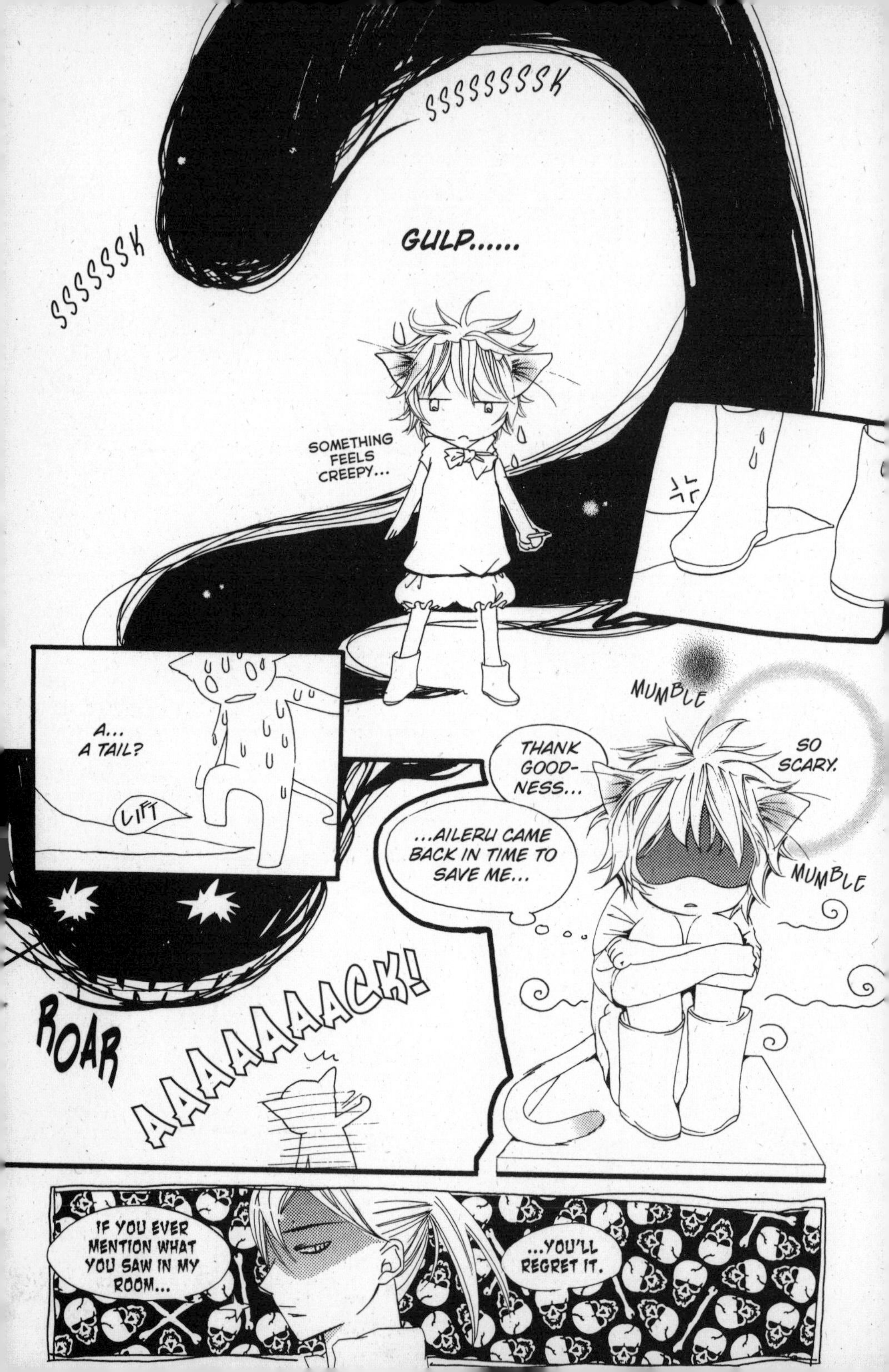
SSSSSSSSK
SSSSSSK
GULP......
SOMETHING FEELS CREEPY...
A... A TAIL?
LIFT
ROAR
AAAAAAACK!
MUMBLE
THANK GOODNESS...
...AILERU CAME BACK IN TIME TO SAVE ME...
SO SCARY.
MUMBLE
IF YOU EVER MENTION WHAT YOU SAW IN MY ROOM...
...YOU'LL REGRET IT.

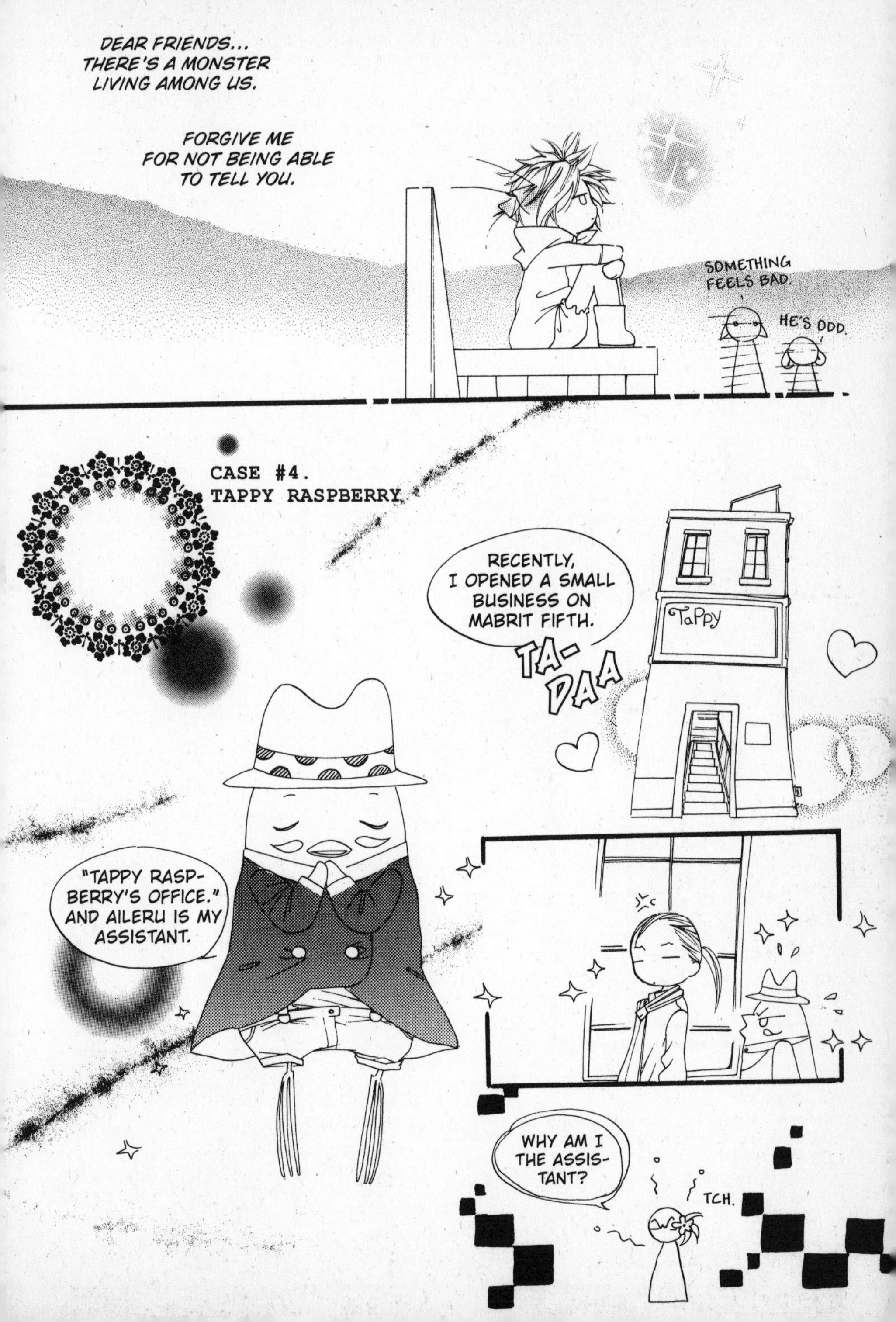
DEAR FRIENDS... THERE'S A MONSTER LIVING AMONG US.
FORGIVE ME FOR NOT BEING ABLE TO TELL YOU.
SOMETHING FEELS BAD.
HE'S ODD.
CASE #4. TAPPY RASPBERRY
RECENTLY, I OPENED A SMALL BUSINESS ON MABRIT FIFTH.
TA-DAA
TaPPy
"TAPPY RASPBERRY'S OFFICE." AND AILERU IS MY ASSISTANT.
WHY AM I THE ASSISTANT?
TCH.

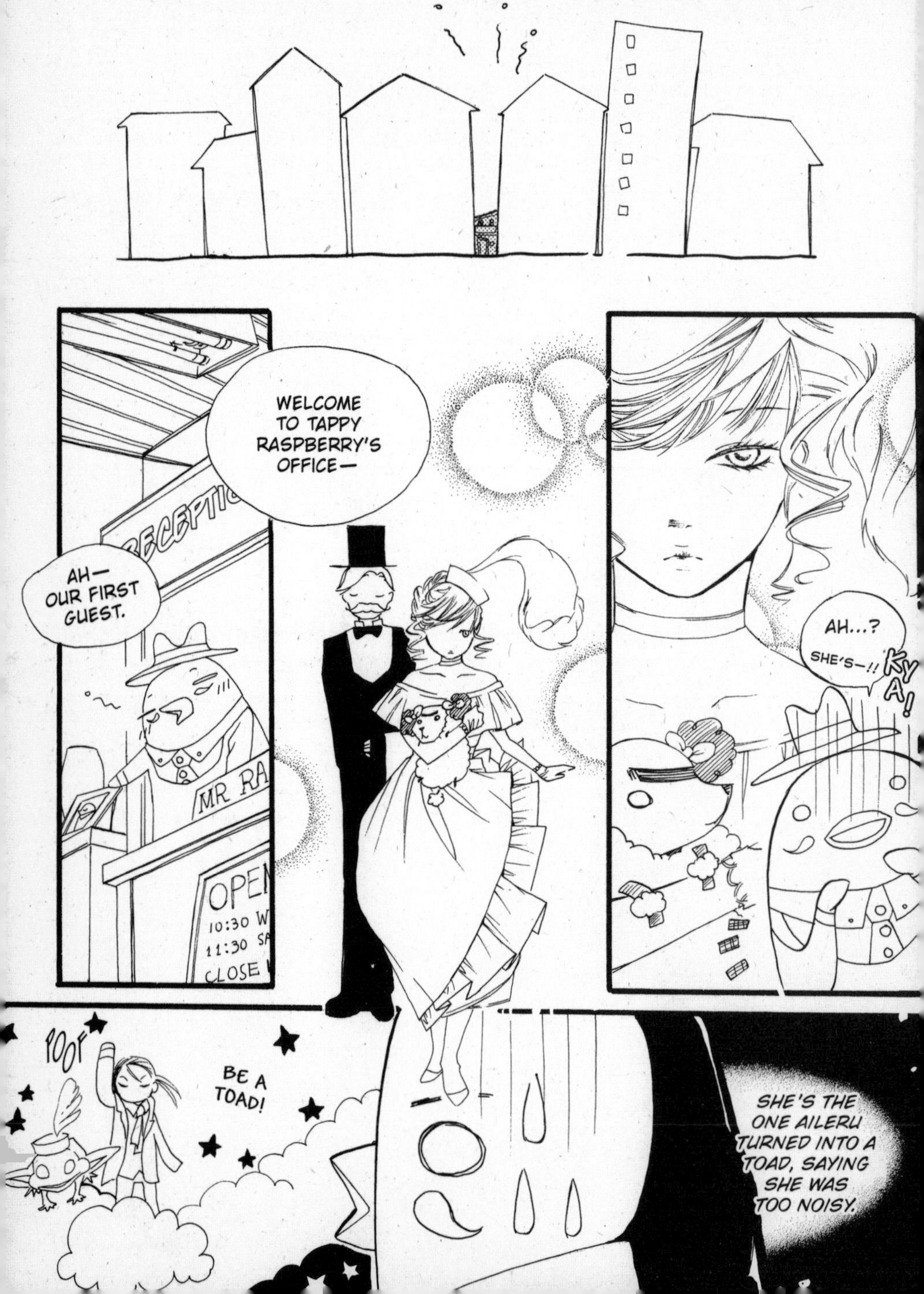
WELCOME TO TAPPY RASPBERRY'S OFFICE—
RECEPTIO
AH— OUR FIRST GUEST.
MR RA
OPEN
10:30 W
11:30 SA
CLOSE
AH...?
SHE'S—!!
KYA!
POOF
BE A TOAD!
SHE'S THE ONE AILERU TURNED INTO A TOAD, SAYING SHE WAS TOO NOISY.

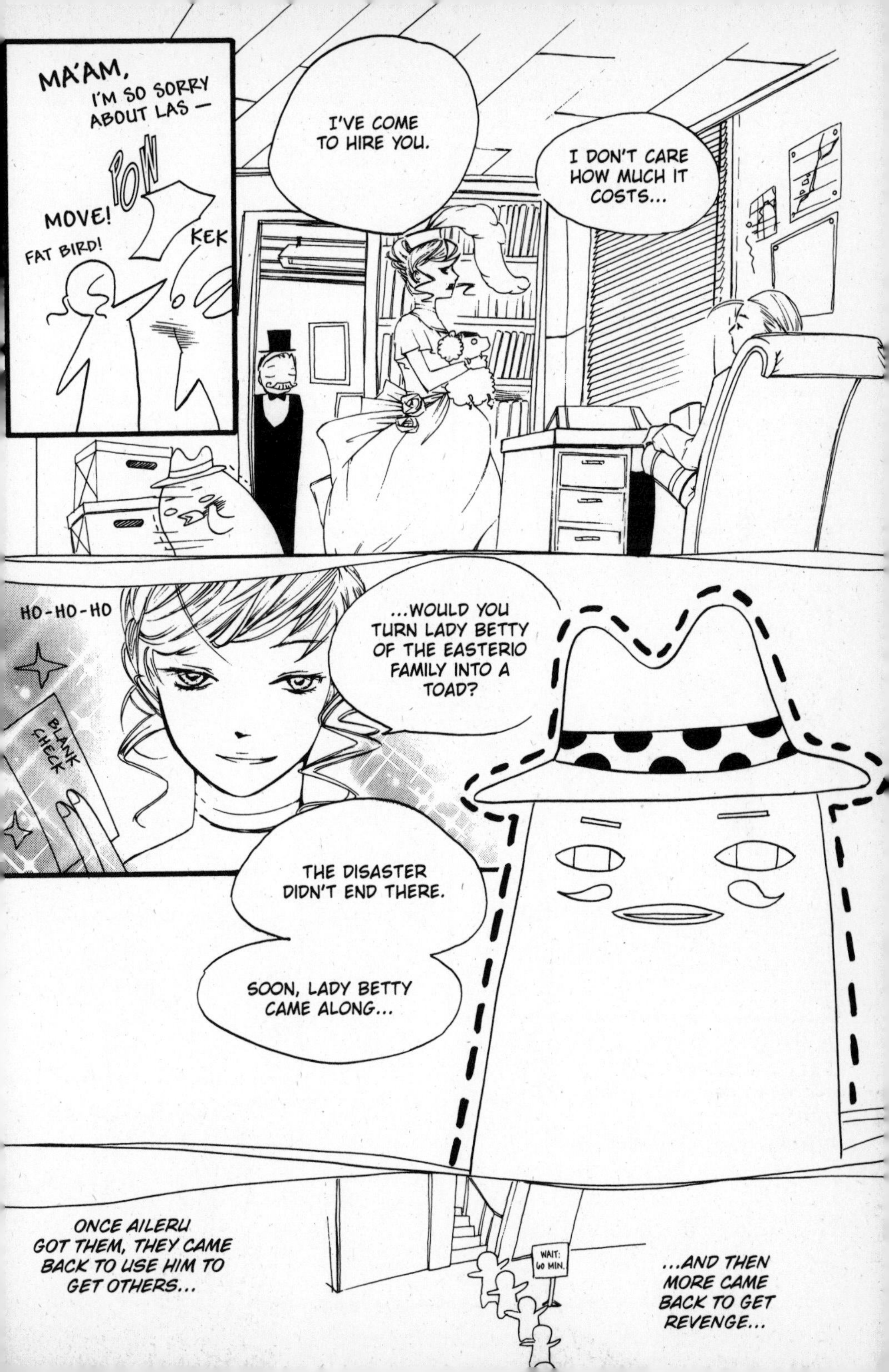
MA'AM, I'M SO SORRY ABOUT LAS—
POW
MOVE!
FAT BIRD!
KEK
I'VE COME TO HIRE YOU.
I DON'T CARE HOW MUCH IT COSTS...
HO-HO-HO
BLANK CHECK
...WOULD YOU TURN LADY BETTY OF THE EASTERIO FAMILY INTO A TOAD?
THE DISASTER DIDN'T END THERE.
SOON, LADY BETTY CAME ALONG...
ONCE AILERU GOT THEM, THEY CAME BACK TO USE HIM TO GET OTHERS...
WAIT: 60 MIN.
...AND THEN MORE CAME BACK TO GET REVENGE...

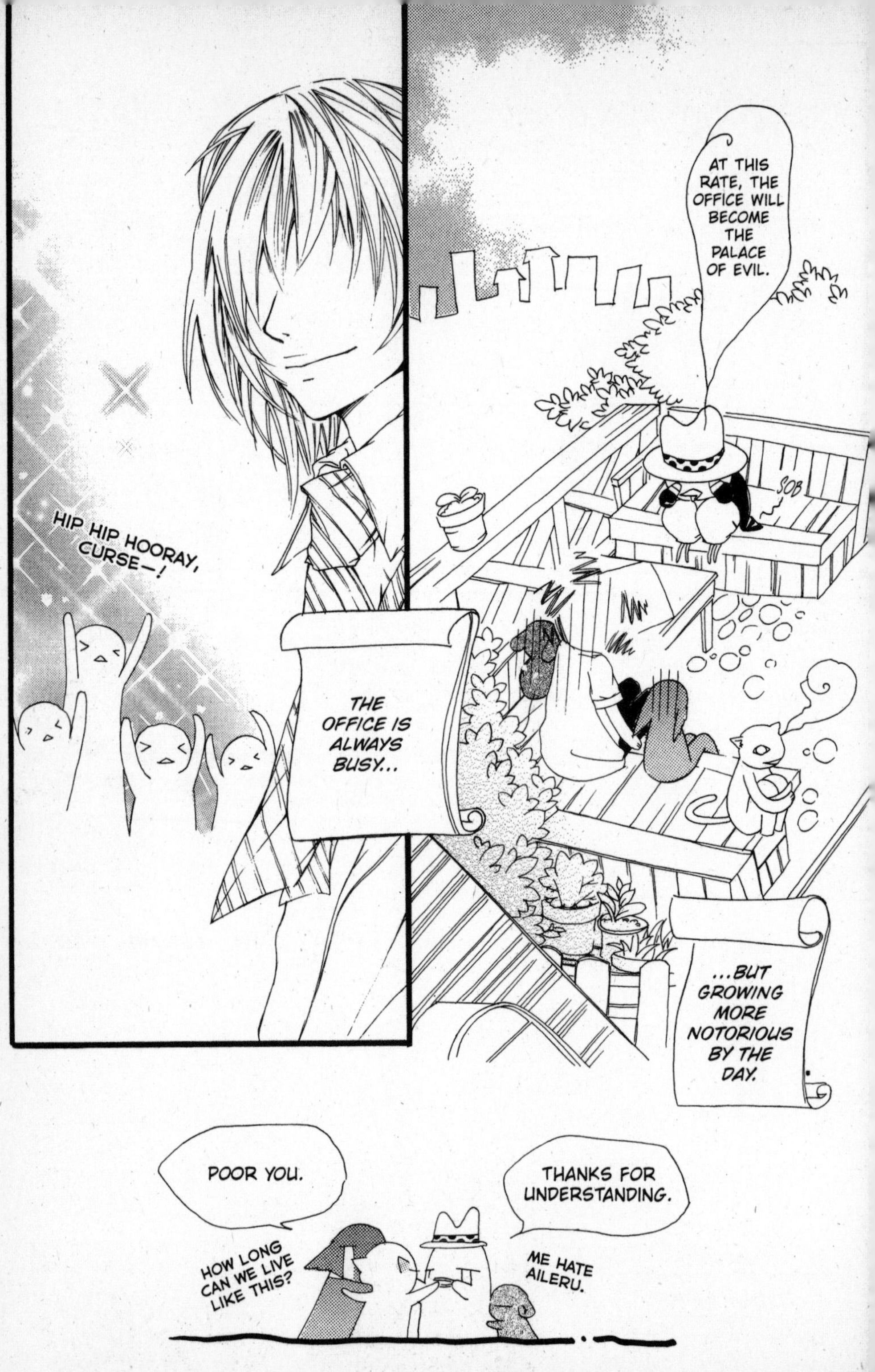
HIP HIP HOORAY, CURSE—!
THE OFFICE IS ALWAYS BUSY...
AT THIS RATE, THE OFFICE WILL BECOME THE PALACE OF EVIL.
SOB
...BUT GROWING MORE NOTORIOUS BY THE DAY.
POOR YOU.
HOW LONG CAN WE LIVE LIKE THIS?
THANKS FOR UNDERSTANDING.
ME HATE AILERU.

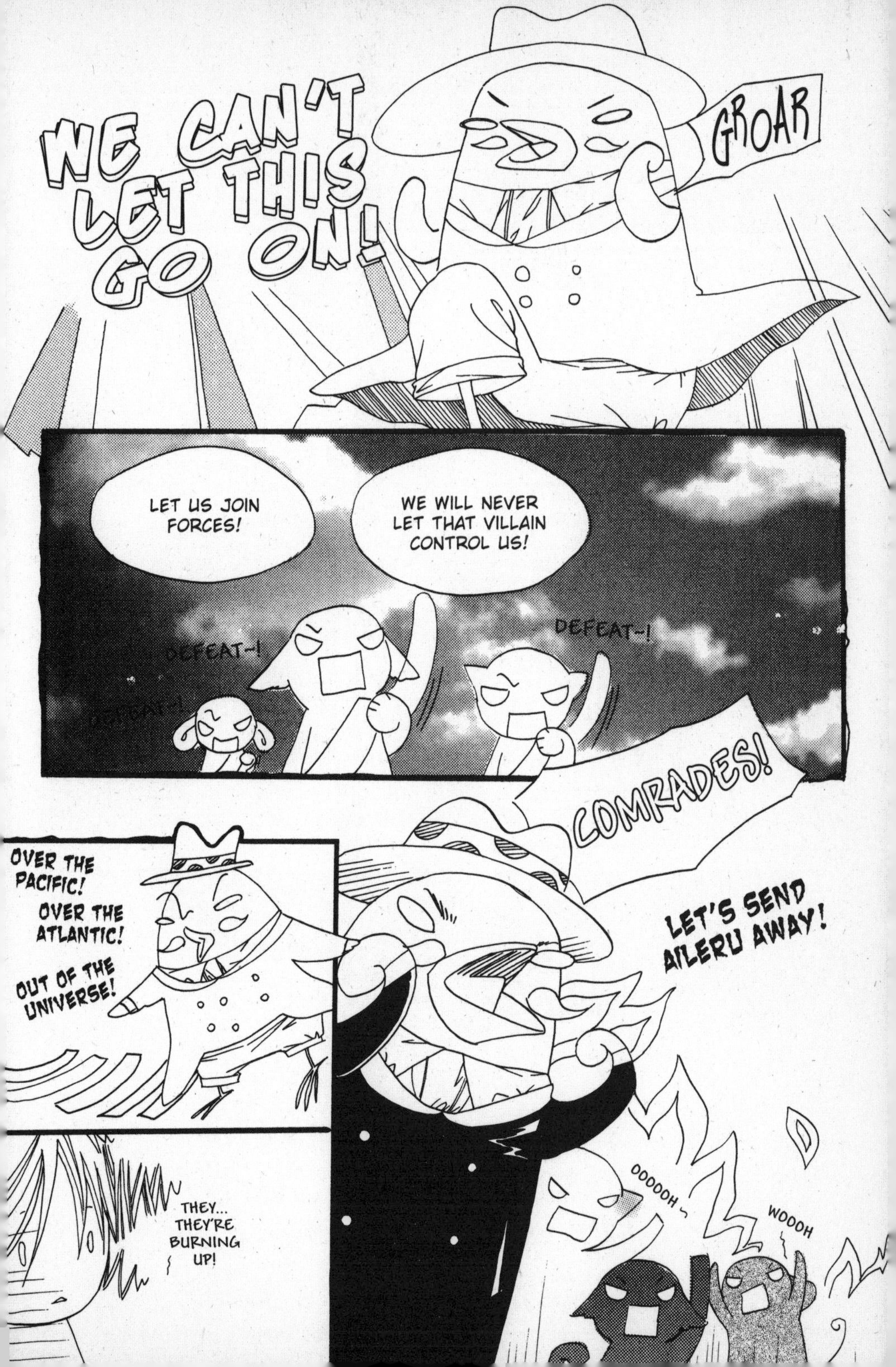
WE CAN'T LET THIS GO ON!
GROAR
LET US JOIN FORCES!
WE WILL NEVER LET THAT VILLAIN CONTROL US!
DEFEAT-!
DEFEAT-!
OVER THE PACIFIC!
OVER THE ATLANTIC!
OUT OF THE UNIVERSE!
THEY... THEY'RE BURNING UP!
COMRADES!
LET'S SEND AILERU AWAY!
OOOOOH~
WOOOH

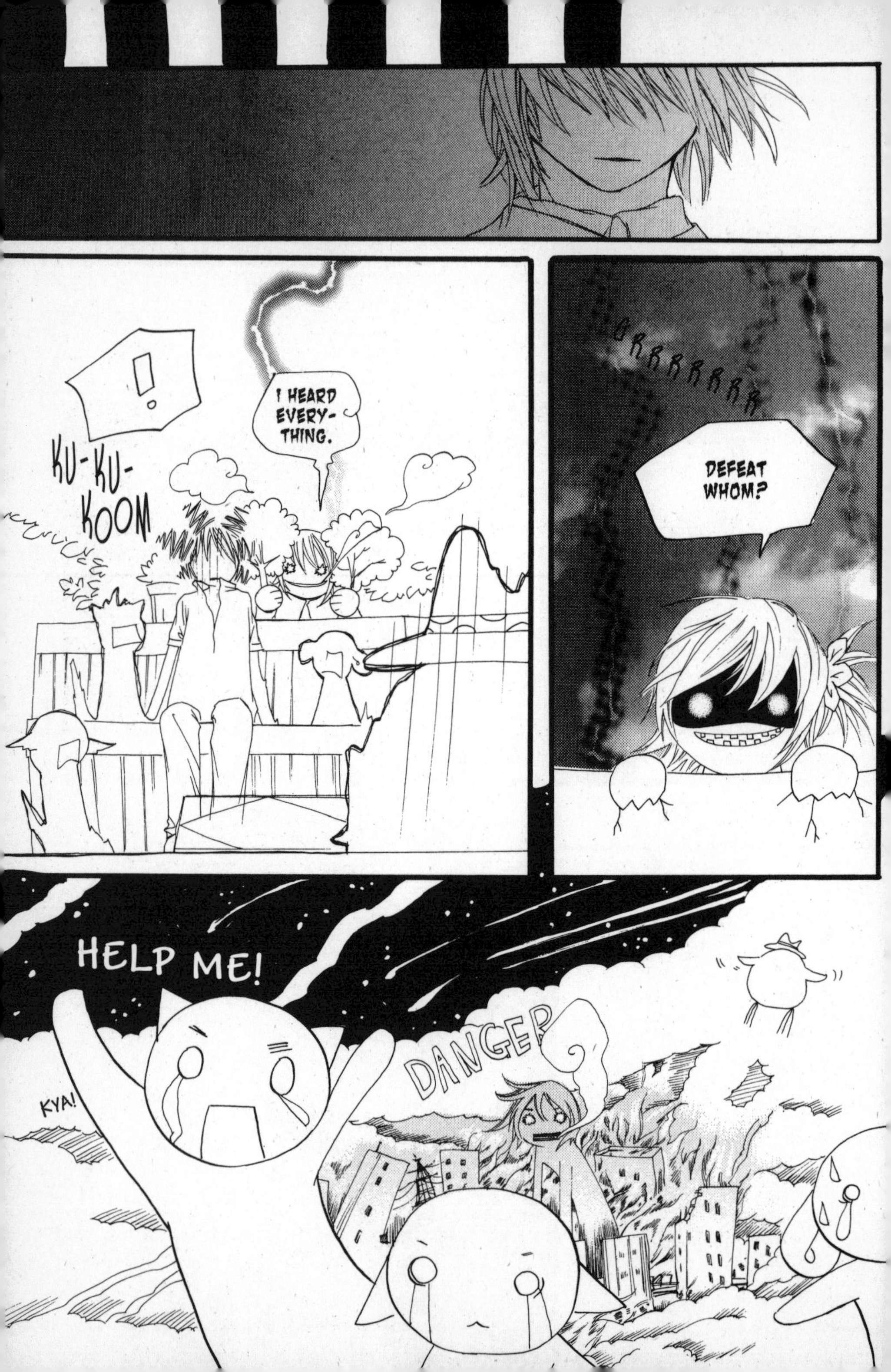
!
KU-KU-KOOM
I HEARD EVERY-THING.
GRRRRRRRRR
DEFEAT WHOM?
HELP ME!
KYA!
DANGER

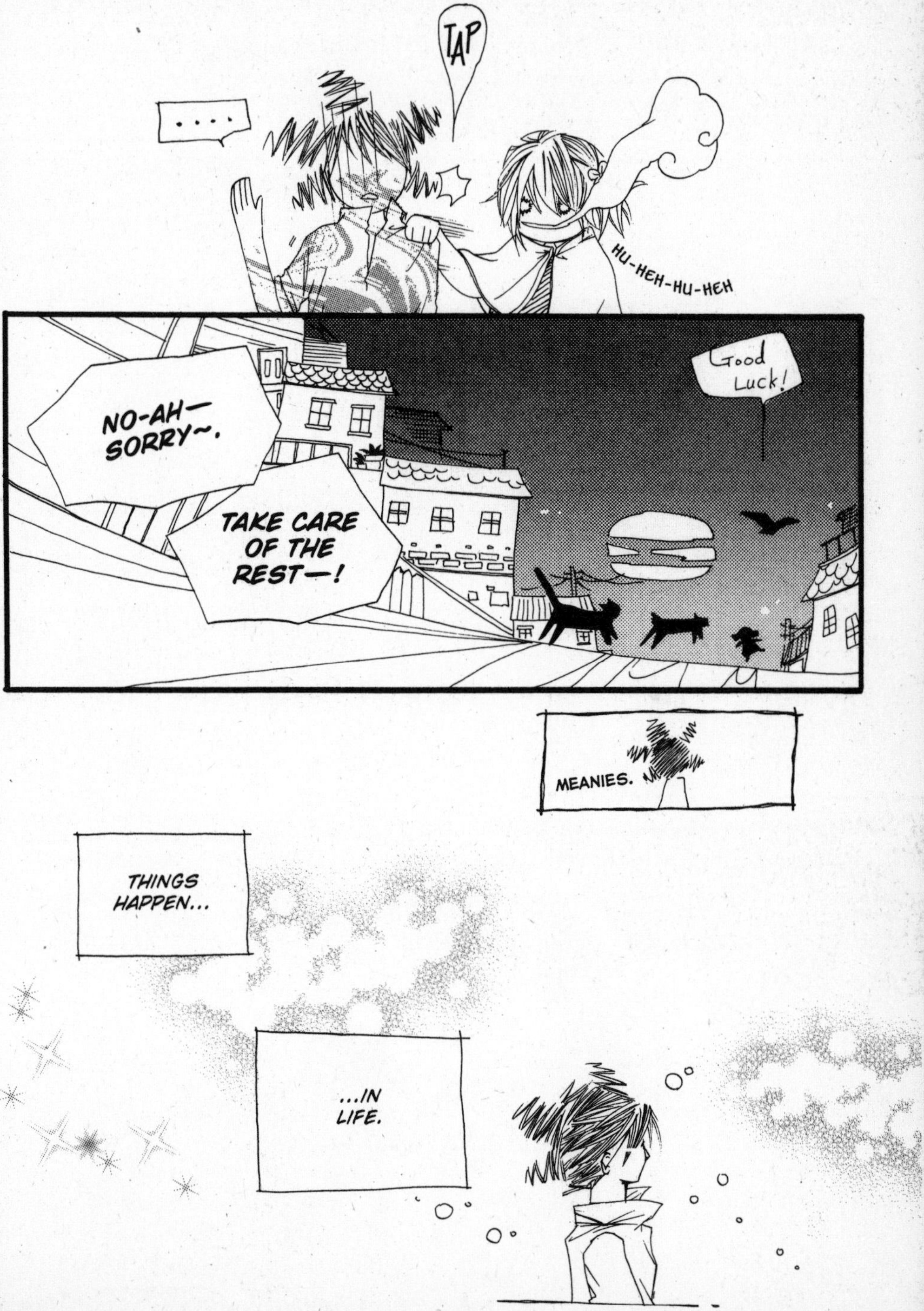
....
TAP
HU-HEH-HU-HEH
NO-AH— SORRY~.
TAKE CARE OF THE REST—!
Good Luck!
MEANIES.
THINGS HAPPEN...
...IN LIFE.

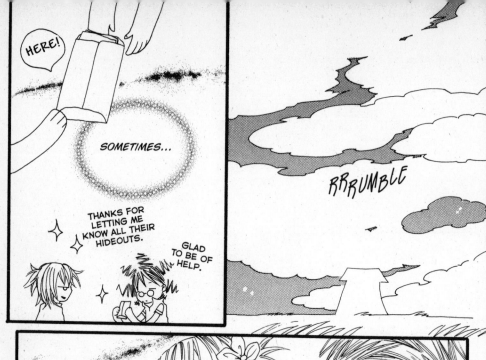

HERE!

SOMETIMES...

THANKS FOR LETTING ME KNOW ALL THEIR HIDEOUTS.

GLAD TO BE OF HELP.

RRRUMBLE

...UNEXPECTED HARDSHIPS COME YOUR WAY.

KE-KE-KE

TOMORROW WILL BE A FUN DAY.

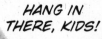

HANG IN THERE, KIDS!

END OF DAY 19

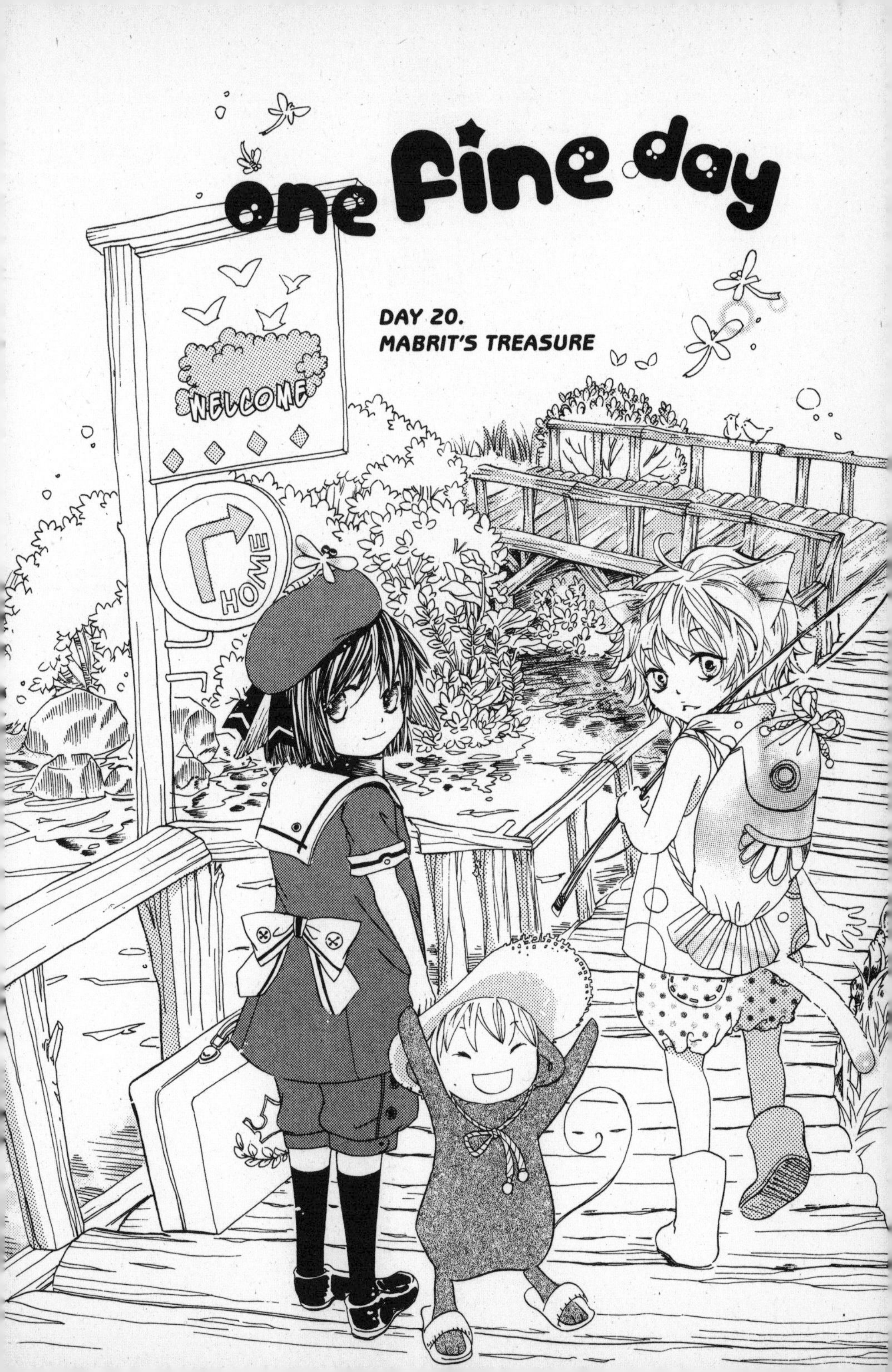
one fine day
DAY 20.
MABRIT'S TREASURE
WELCOME
HOME

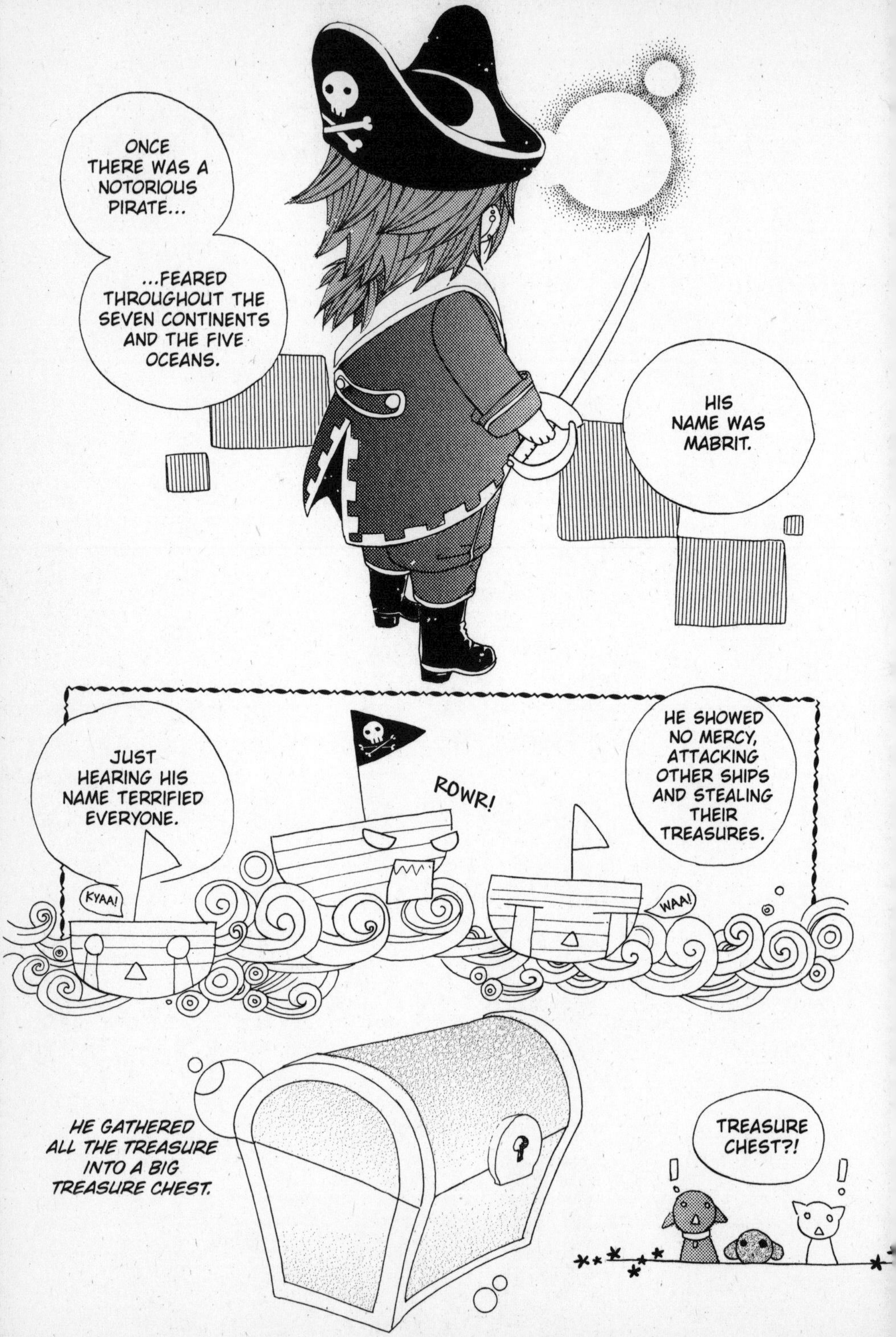

ONCE THERE WAS A NOTORIOUS PIRATE...
...FEARED THROUGHOUT THE SEVEN CONTINENTS AND THE FIVE OCEANS.
HIS NAME WAS MABRIT.
JUST HEARING HIS NAME TERRIFIED EVERYONE.
KYAA!
ROWR!
WAA!
HE SHOWED NO MERCY, ATTACKING OTHER SHIPS AND STEALING THEIR TREASURES.
HE GATHERED ALL THE TREASURE INTO A BIG TREASURE CHEST.
TREASURE CHEST?!

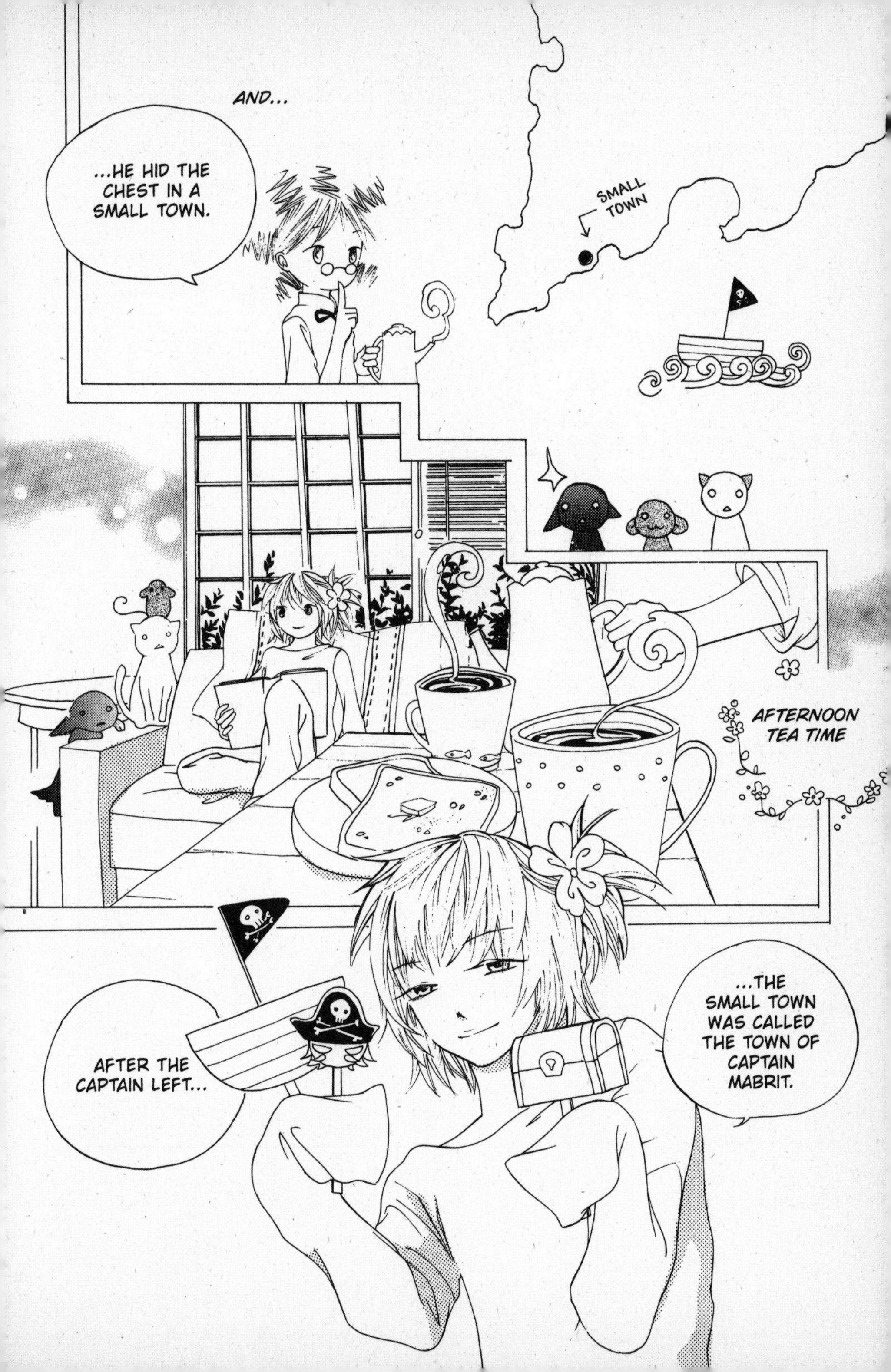
AND...
...HE HID THE CHEST IN A SMALL TOWN.
SMALL TOWN
AFTERNOON TEA TIME
AFTER THE CAPTAIN LEFT...
...THE SMALL TOWN WAS CALLED THE TOWN OF CAPTAIN MABRIT.

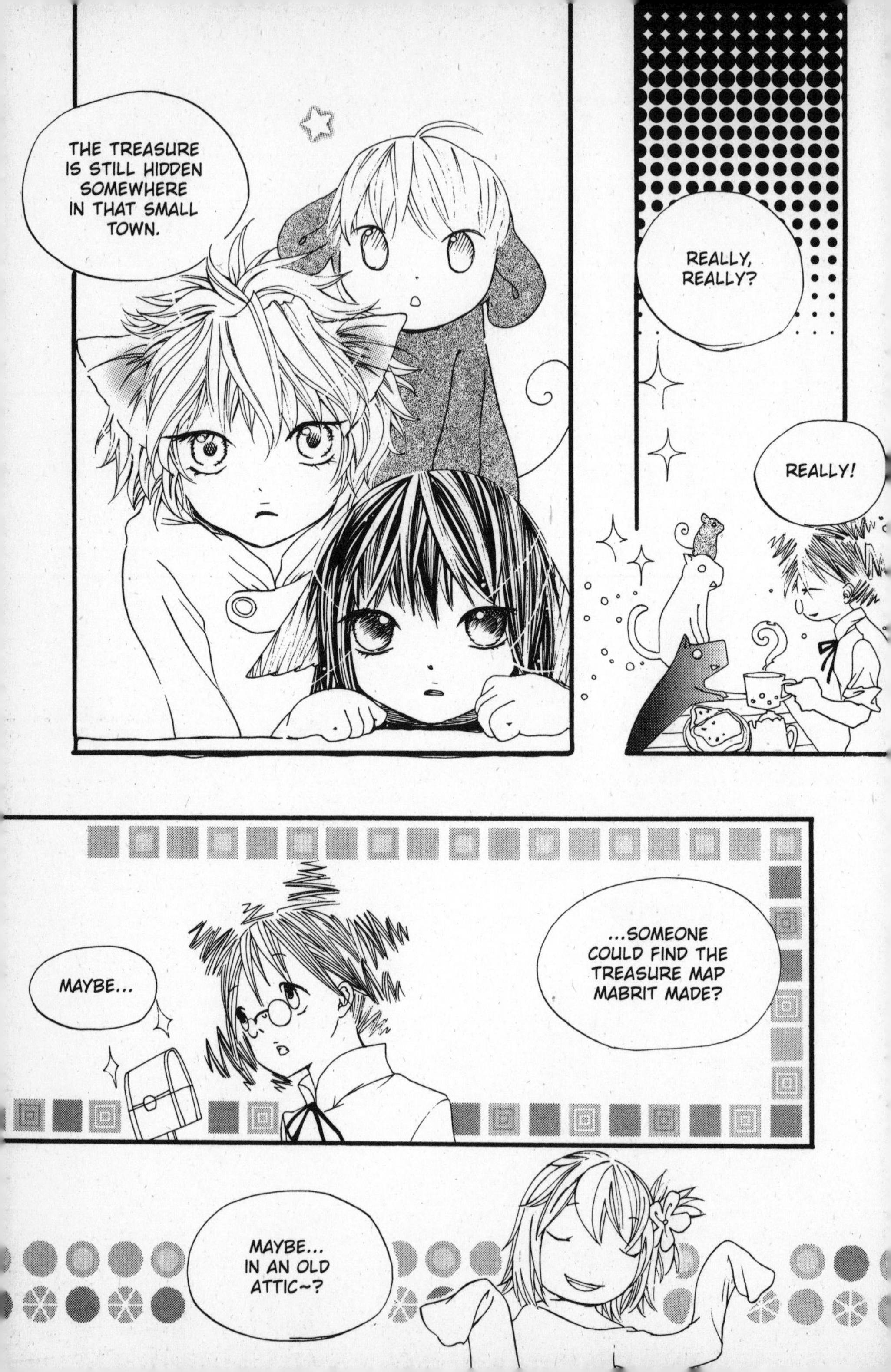
THE TREASURE IS STILL HIDDEN SOMEWHERE IN THAT SMALL TOWN.
REALLY, REALLY?
REALLY!
MAYBE...
...SOMEONE COULD FIND THE TREASURE MAP MABRIT MADE?
MAYBE... IN AN OLD ATTIC~?

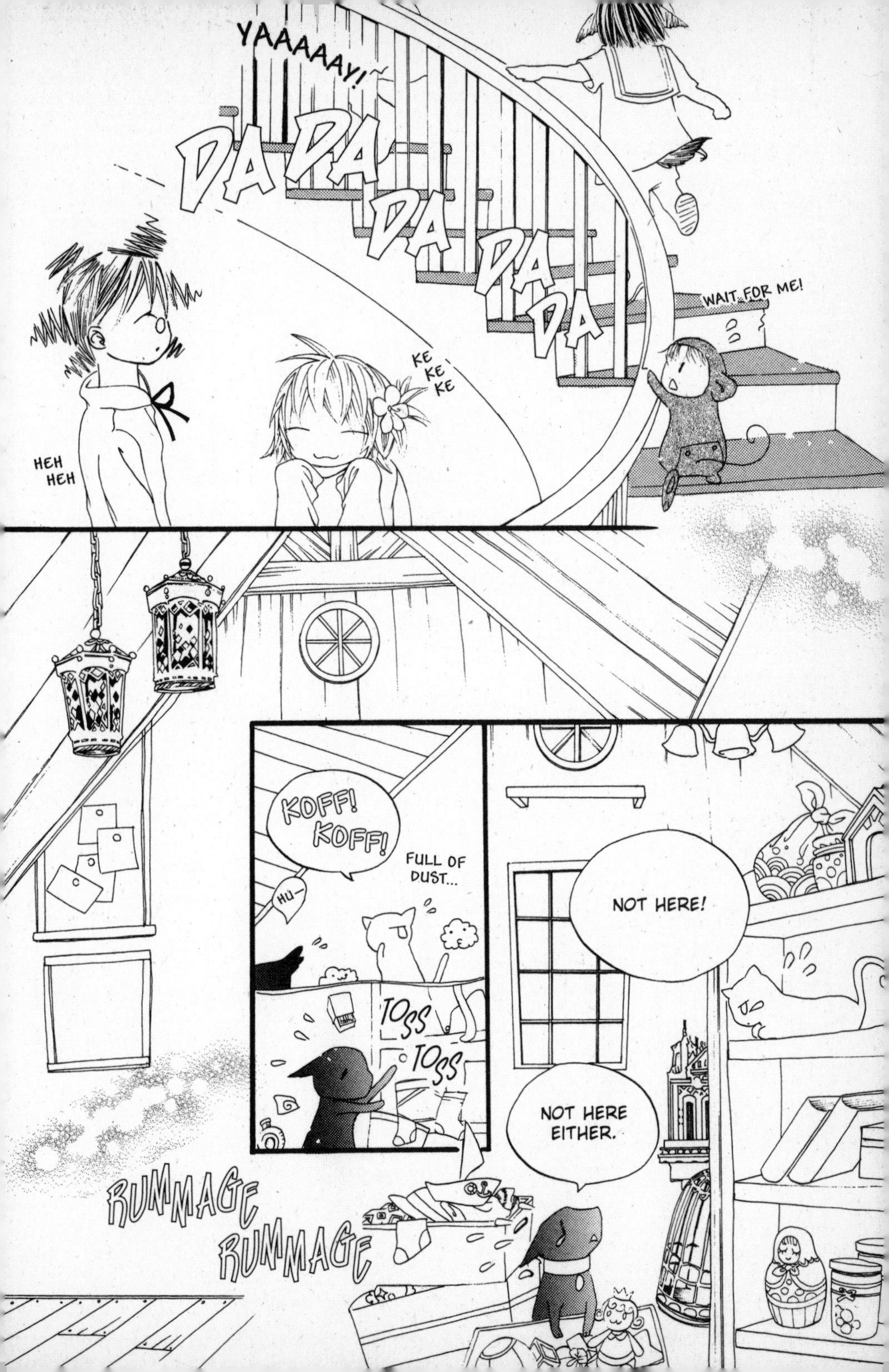

YAAAAAY!~
DA DA DA DA DA DA
WAIT FOR ME!
KE KE KE
HEH HEH
RUMMAGE RUMMAGE
KOFF! KOFF!
FULL OF DUST...
HU-
TOSS TOSS
NOT HERE!
NOT HERE EITHER.

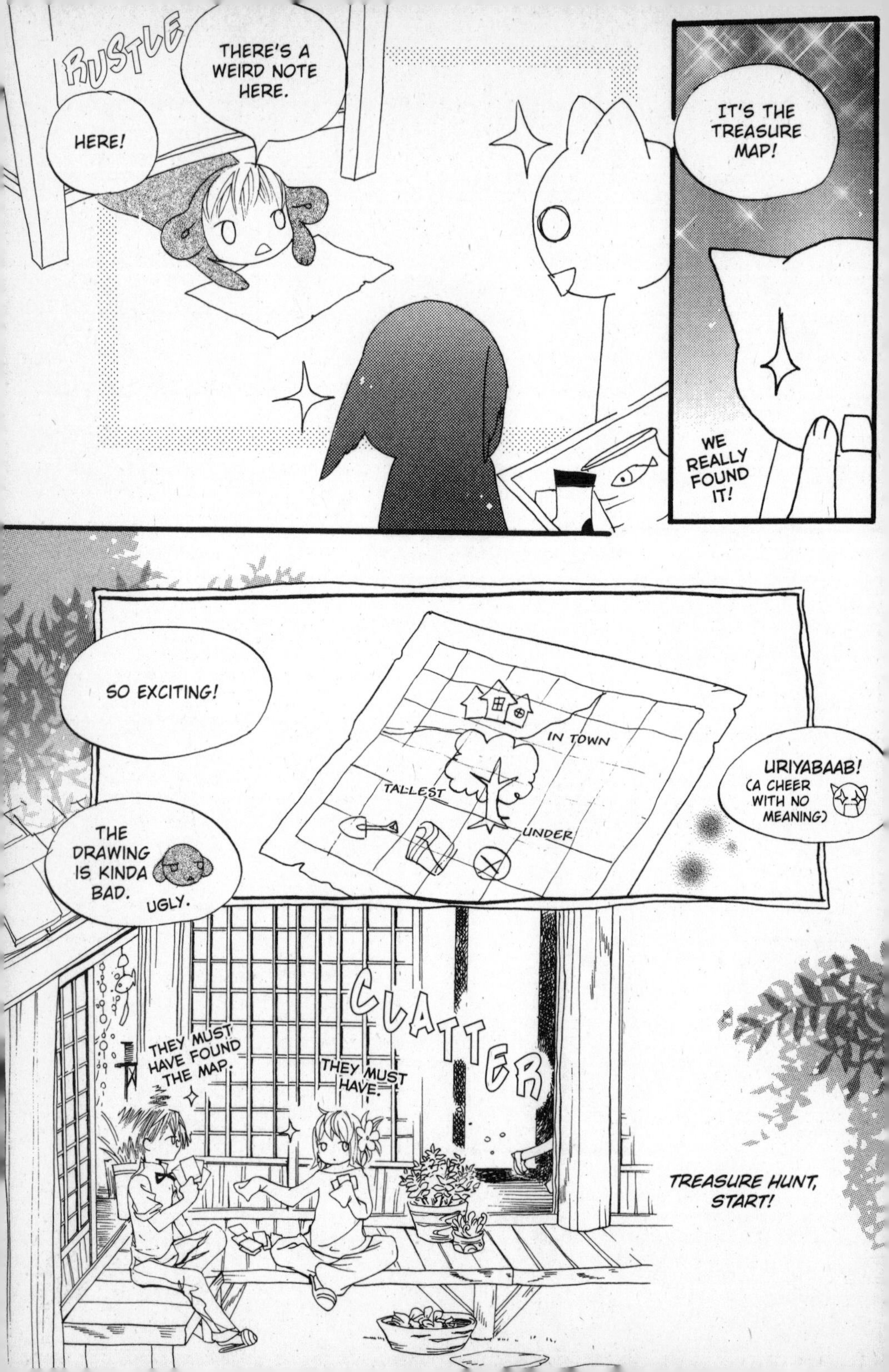
RUSTLE
THERE'S A WEIRD NOTE HERE.
HERE!
IT'S THE TREASURE MAP!
WE REALLY FOUND IT!
SO EXCITING!
IN TOWN
TALLEST
UNDER
URIYABAAB! (A CHEER WITH NO MEANING)
THE DRAWING IS KINDA BAD.
UGLY.
CLATTER
THEY MUST HAVE FOUND THE MAP.
THEY MUST HAVE.
TREASURE HUNT, START!

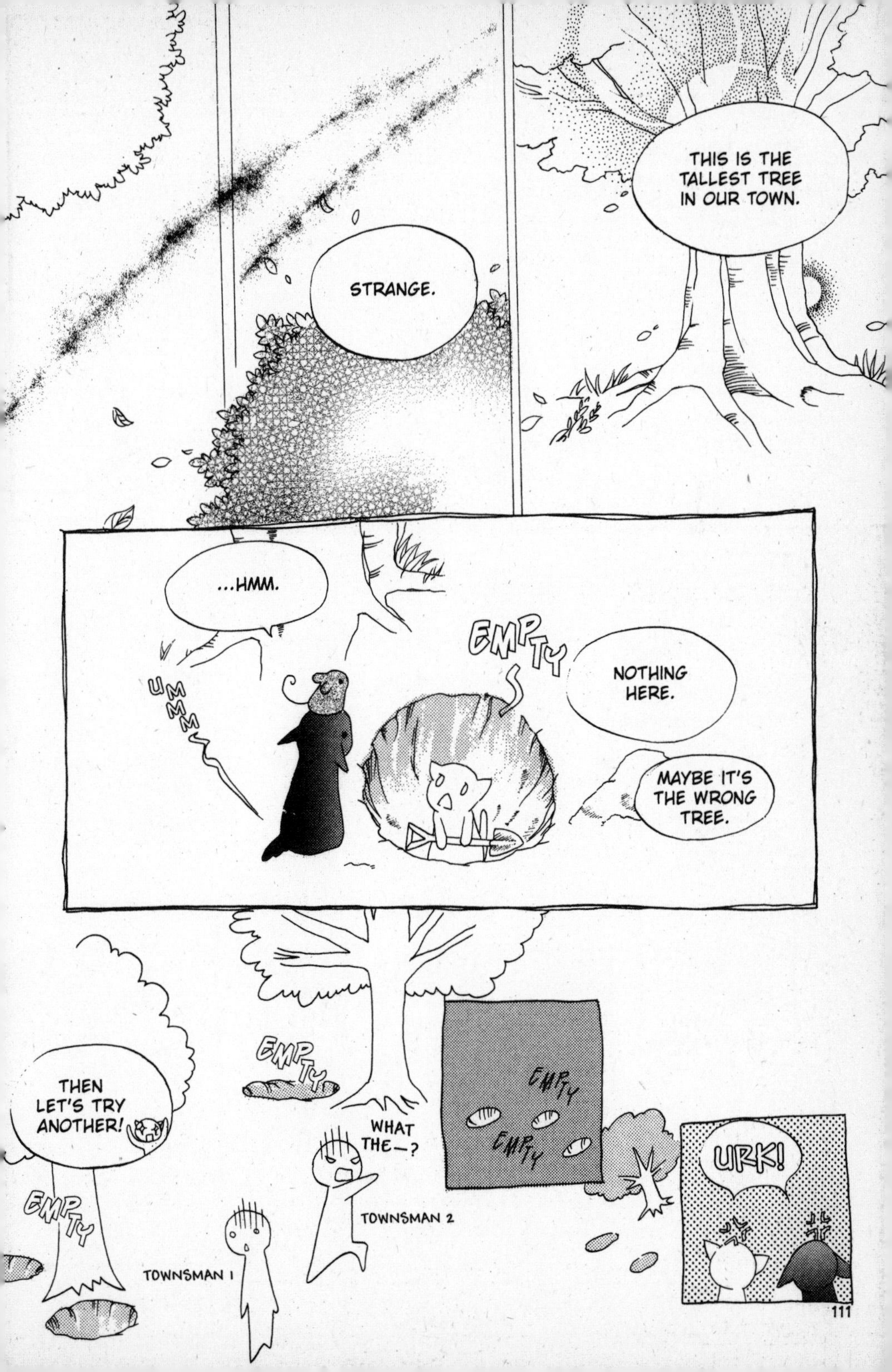
STRANGE.
THIS IS THE TALLEST TREE IN OUR TOWN.
...HMM.
UMMM
EMPTY
NOTHING HERE.
MAYBE IT'S THE WRONG TREE.
THEN LET'S TRY ANOTHER!
EMPTY
EMPTY
WHAT THE—?
TOWNSMAN 2
TOWNSMAN 1
EMPTY
EMPTY
URK!

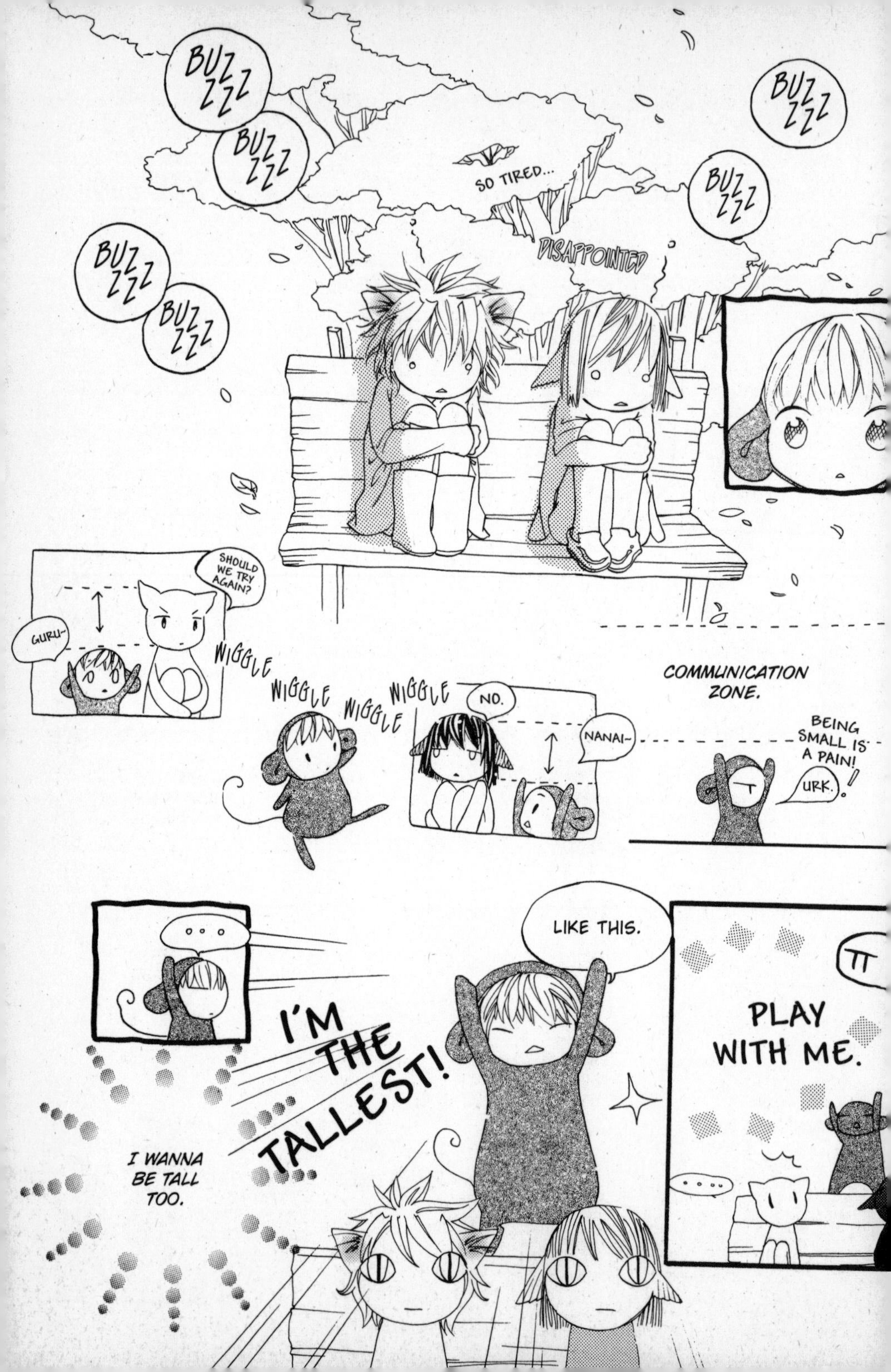

BUZZZ
BUZZZ
BUZZZ
BUZZZ
BUZZZ
BUZZZ
SO TIRED...
DISAPPOINTED
GURU-
SHOULD WE TRY AGAIN?
WIGGLE
WIGGLE
WIGGLE
WIGGLE
NO.
NANAI-
COMMUNICATION ZONE.
BEING SMALL IS A PAIN!
URK.
...
I'M THE TALLEST!
I WANNA BE TALL TOO.
LIKE THIS.
PLAY WITH ME.
....

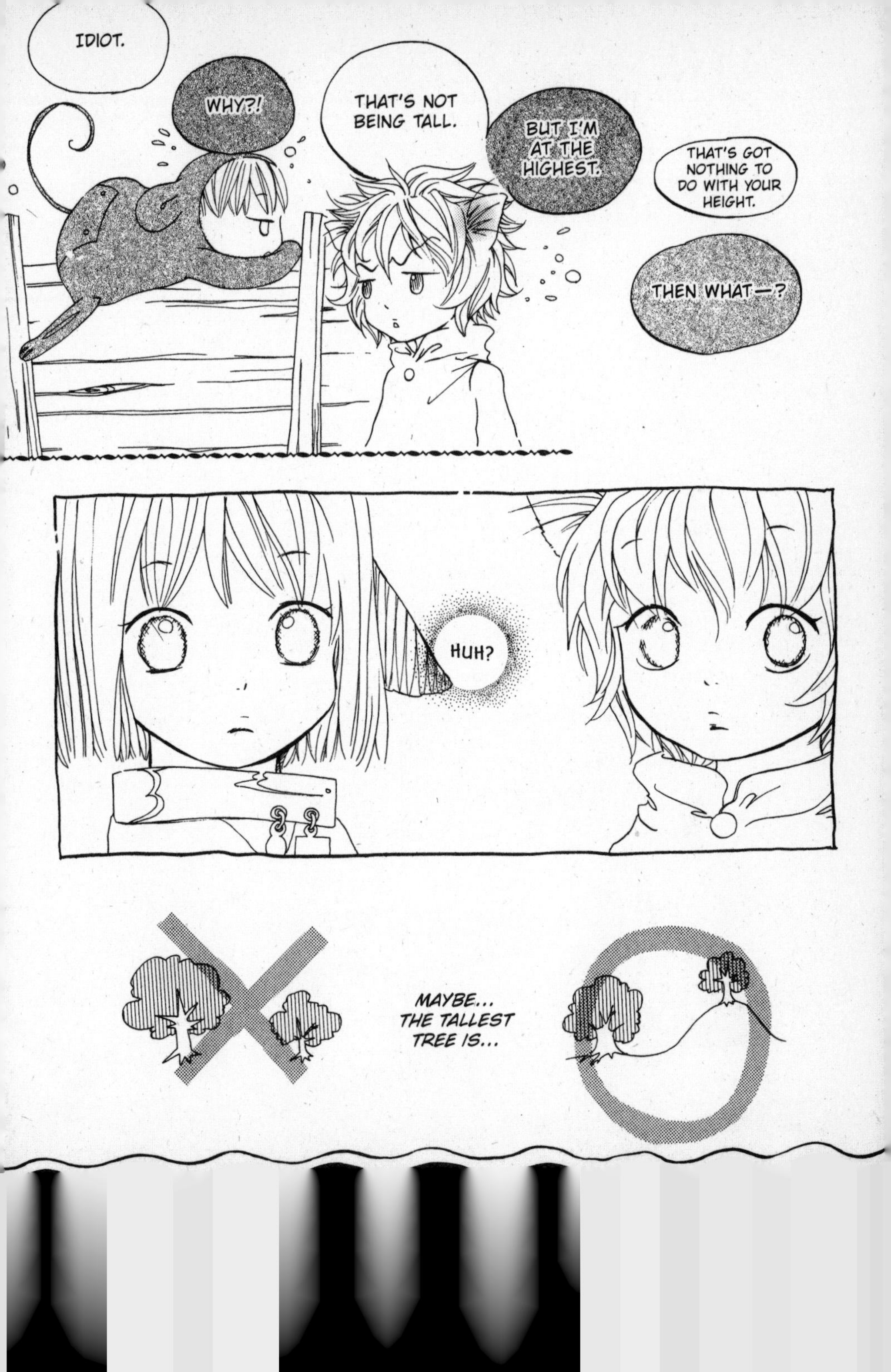
IDIOT.
WHY?!
THAT'S NOT BEING TALL.
BUT I'M AT THE HIGHEST.
THAT'S GOT NOTHING TO DO WITH YOUR HEIGHT.
THEN WHAT—?
HUH?
MAYBE... THE TALLEST TREE IS...

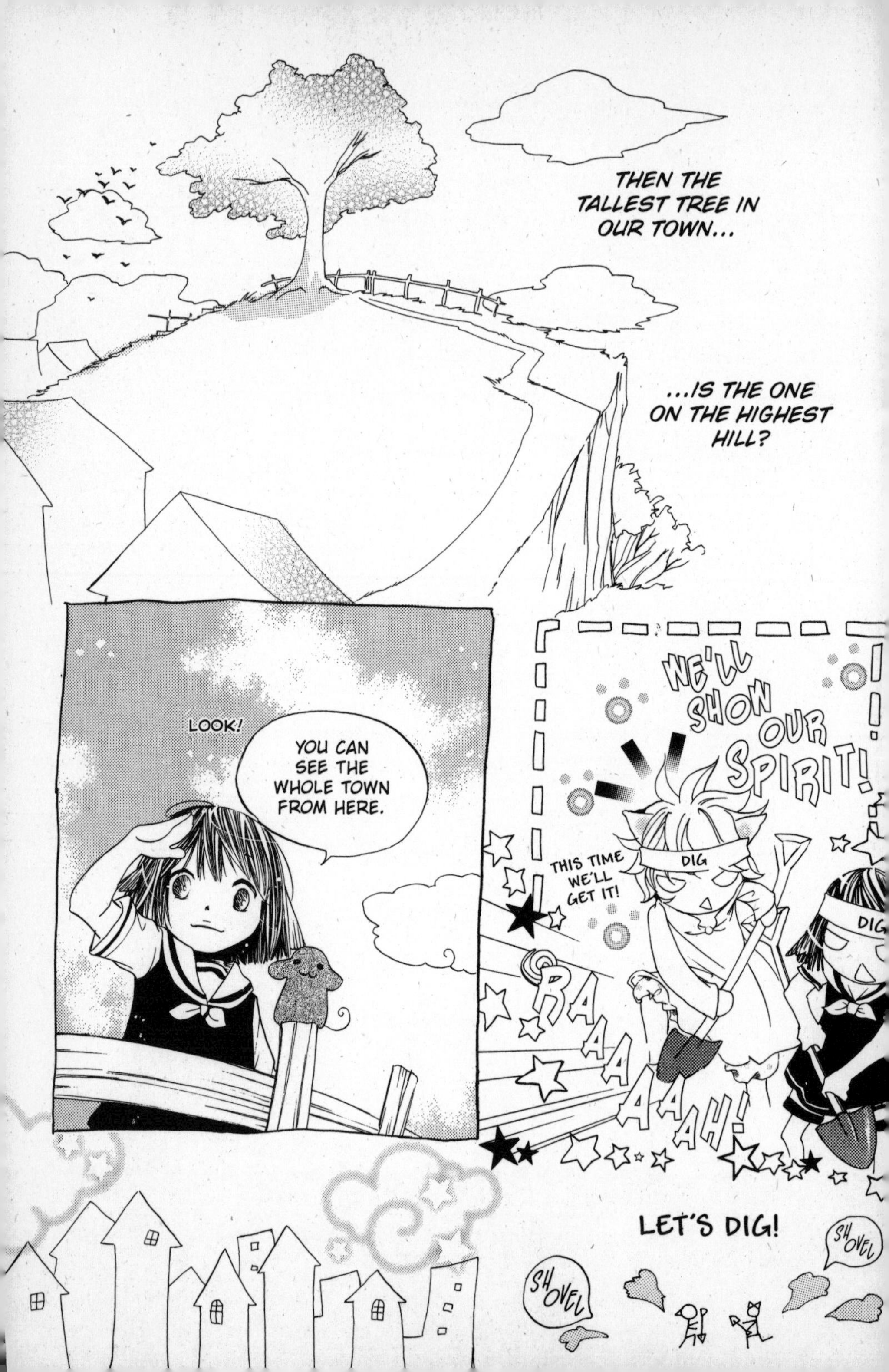
THEN THE TALLEST TREE IN OUR TOWN...
...IS THE ONE ON THE HIGHEST HILL?
LOOK!
YOU CAN SEE THE WHOLE TOWN FROM HERE.
WE'LL SHOW OUR SPIRIT!
THIS TIME WE'LL GET IT!
DIG
RAAAAAAH!
LET'S DIG!
SHOVEL
SHOVEL

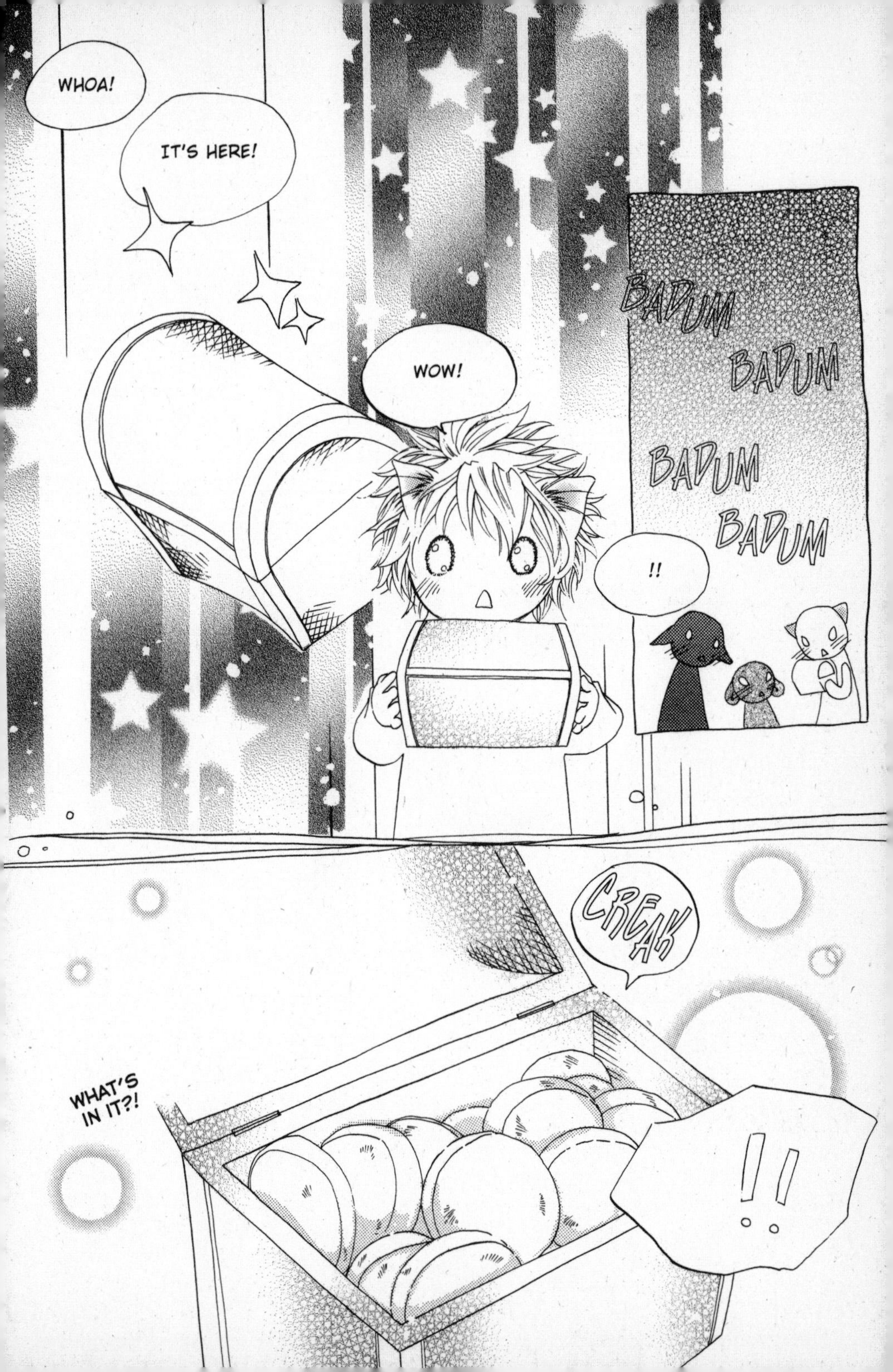
WHOA!
IT'S HERE!
WOW!
!!
BADUM
BADUM
BADUM
BADUM
CREAK
WHAT'S IN IT?!
!!

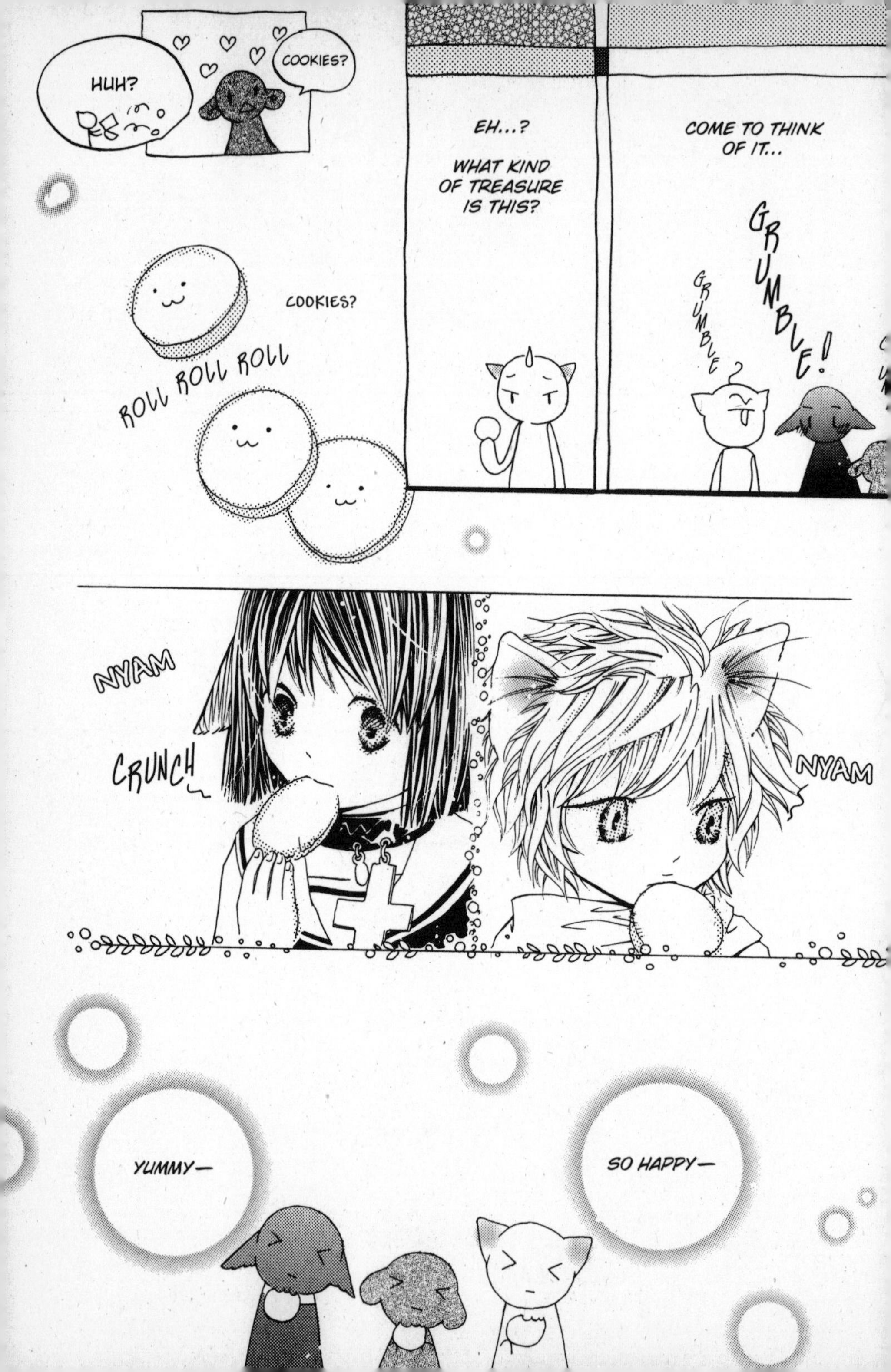
COME TO THINK OF IT...
GRUMBLE
GRUMBLE!
EH...?
WHAT KIND OF TREASURE IS THIS?
COOKIES?
HUH?
COOKIES?
ROLL ROLL ROLL
NYAM
NYAM
CRUNCH
SO HAPPY—
YUMMY—

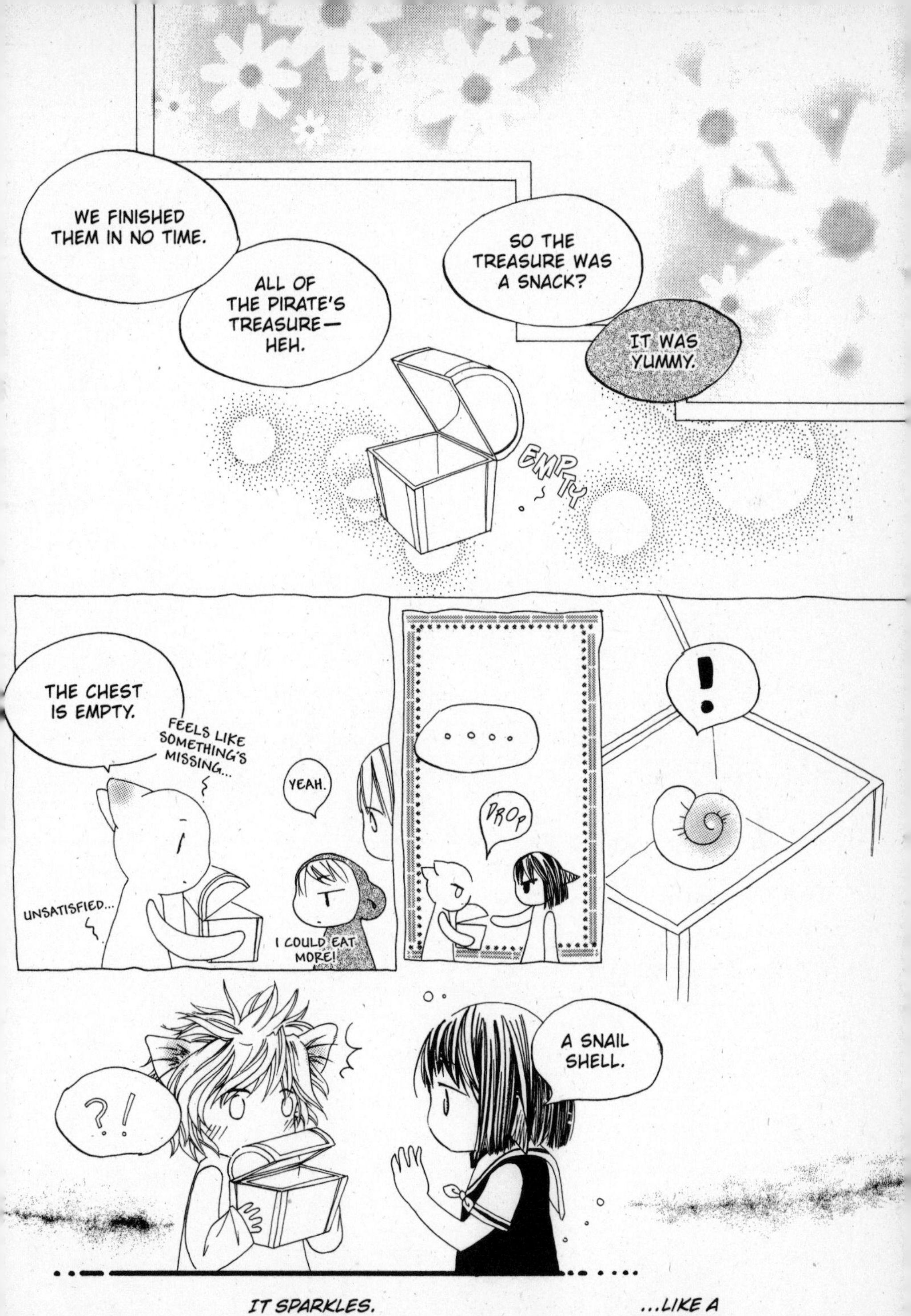
WE FINISHED THEM IN NO TIME.
ALL OF THE PIRATE'S TREASURE—HEH.
SO THE TREASURE WAS A SNACK?
IT WAS YUMMY.
EMPTY
THE CHEST IS EMPTY.
FEELS LIKE SOMETHING'S MISSING...
UNSATISFIED...
YEAH.
I COULD EAT MORE!
....
DROP
!
?!
A SNAIL SHELL.
IT SPARKLES. VERY PRETTY...
...LIKE A TREASURE.

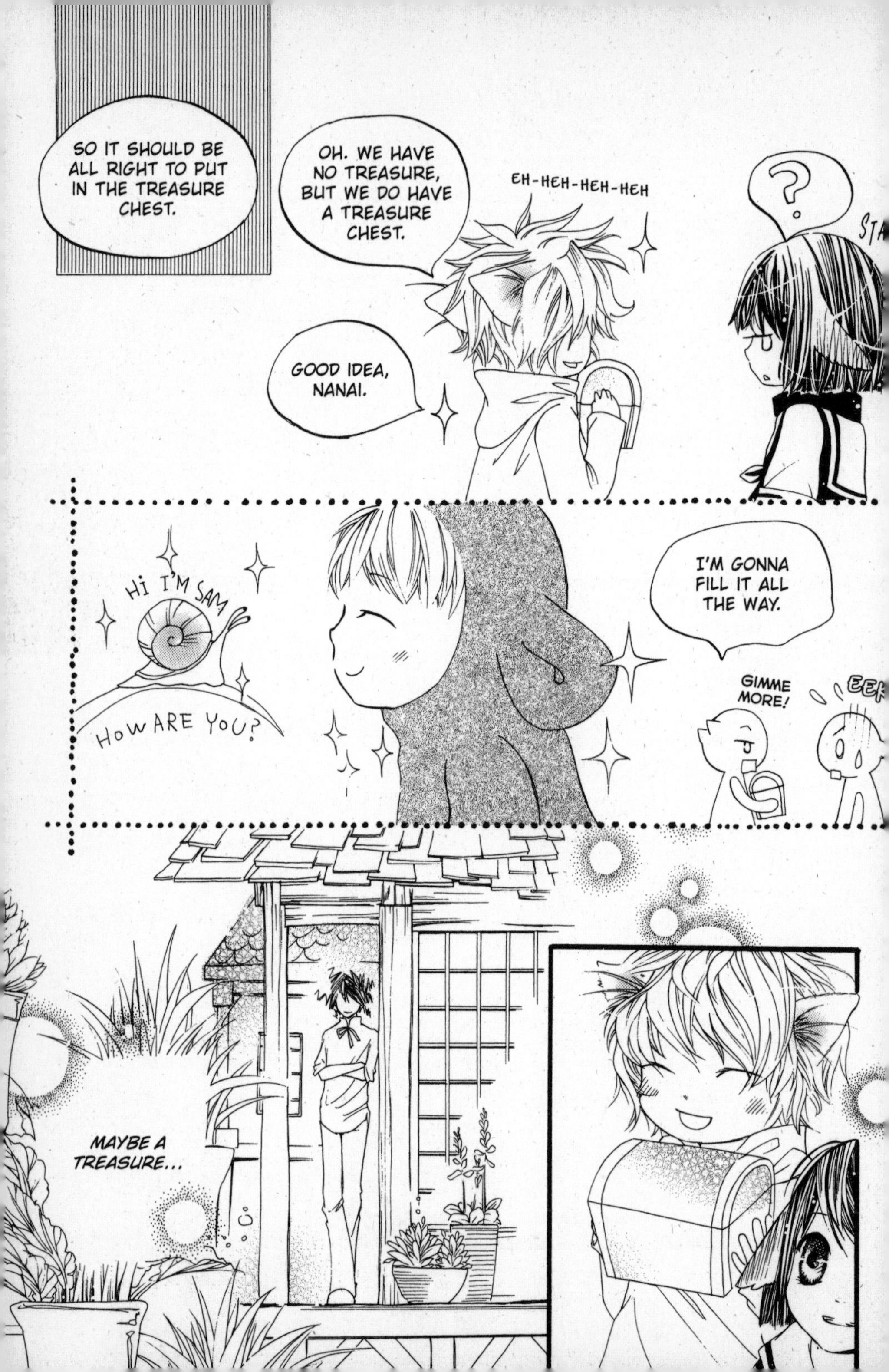
SO IT SHOULD BE ALL RIGHT TO PUT IN THE TREASURE CHEST.
OH. WE HAVE NO TREASURE, BUT WE DO HAVE A TREASURE CHEST.
EH-HEH-HEH-HEH
?
GOOD IDEA, NANAI.
HI I'M SAM
HOW ARE YOU?
I'M GONNA FILL IT ALL THE WAY.
GIMME MORE!
MAYBE A TREASURE...

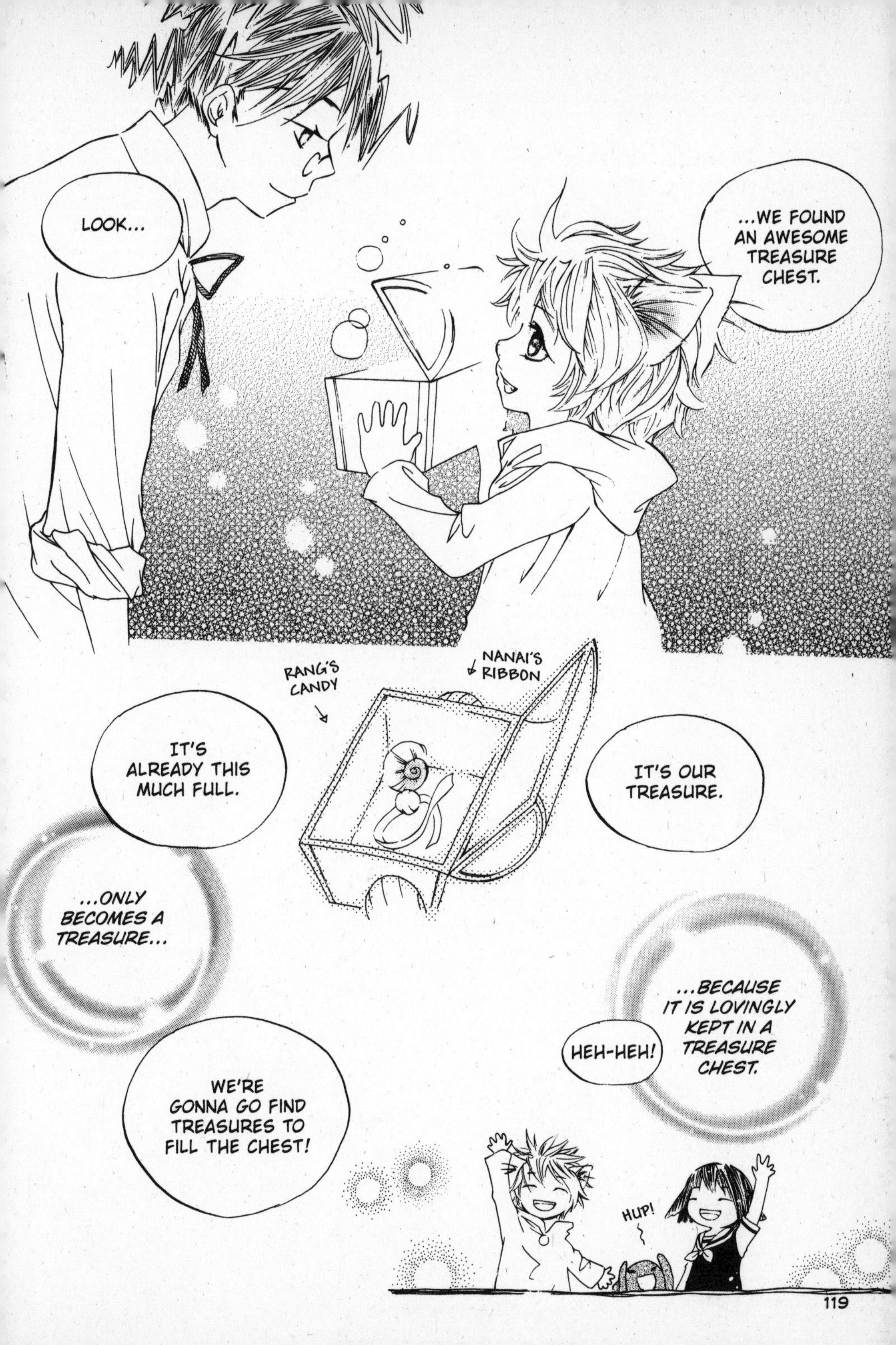
LOOK...
...WE FOUND AN AWESOME TREASURE CHEST.
RANG'S CANDY
NANAI'S RIBBON
IT'S ALREADY THIS MUCH FULL.
IT'S OUR TREASURE.
...ONLY BECOMES A TREASURE...
...BECAUSE IT IS LOVINGLY KEPT IN A TREASURE CHEST.
HEH-HEH!
WE'RE GONNA GO FIND TREASURES TO FILL THE CHEST!
HUP!

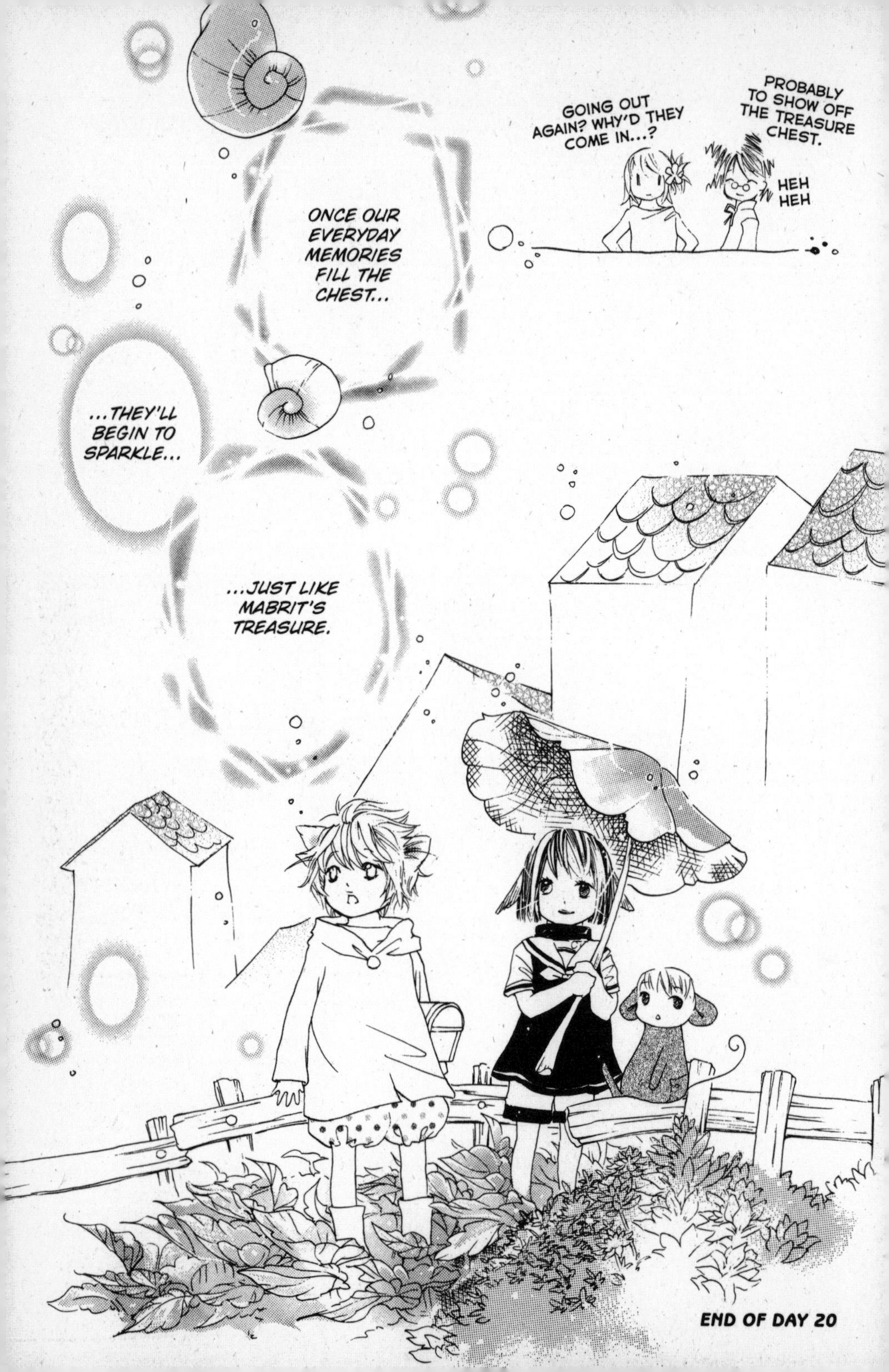
ONCE OUR EVERYDAY MEMORIES FILL THE CHEST...
GOING OUT AGAIN? WHY'D THEY COME IN...?
PROBABLY TO SHOW OFF THE TREASURE CHEST.
HEH HEH
...THEY'LL BEGIN TO SPARKLE...
...JUST LIKE MABRIT'S TREASURE.
END OF DAY 20

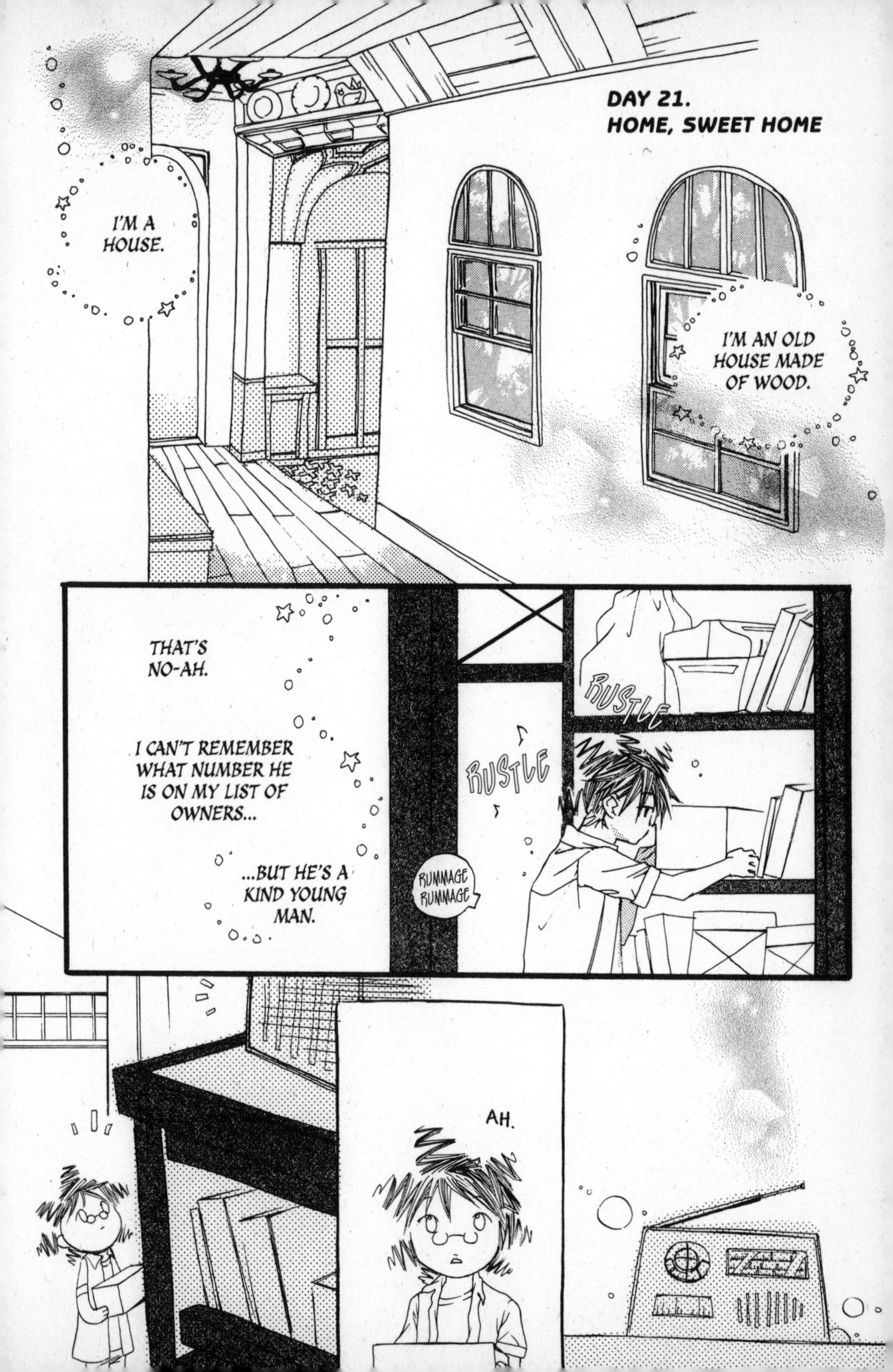
DAY 21.
HOME, SWEET HOME
I'M A HOUSE.
I'M AN OLD HOUSE MADE OF WOOD.
THAT'S NO-AH.
I CAN'T REMEMBER WHAT NUMBER HE IS ON MY LIST OF OWNERS...
...BUT HE'S A KIND YOUNG MAN.
RUSTLE
RUSTLE
RUMMAGE RUMMAGE
AH.

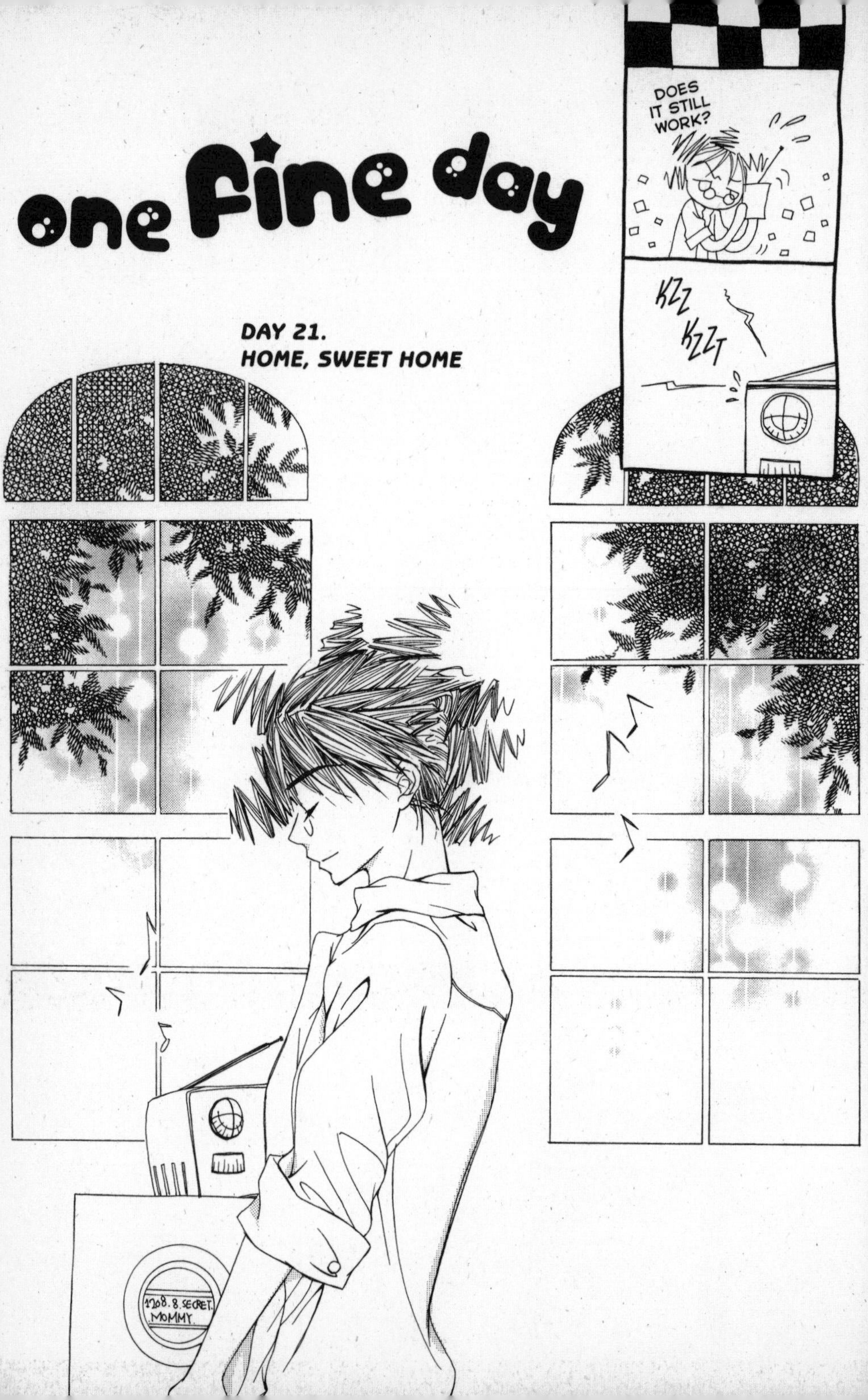
one fine day
DAY 21.
HOME, SWEET HOME
DOES IT STILL WORK?
KZZ KZZT
1208.8.SECRET.
MOMMY.

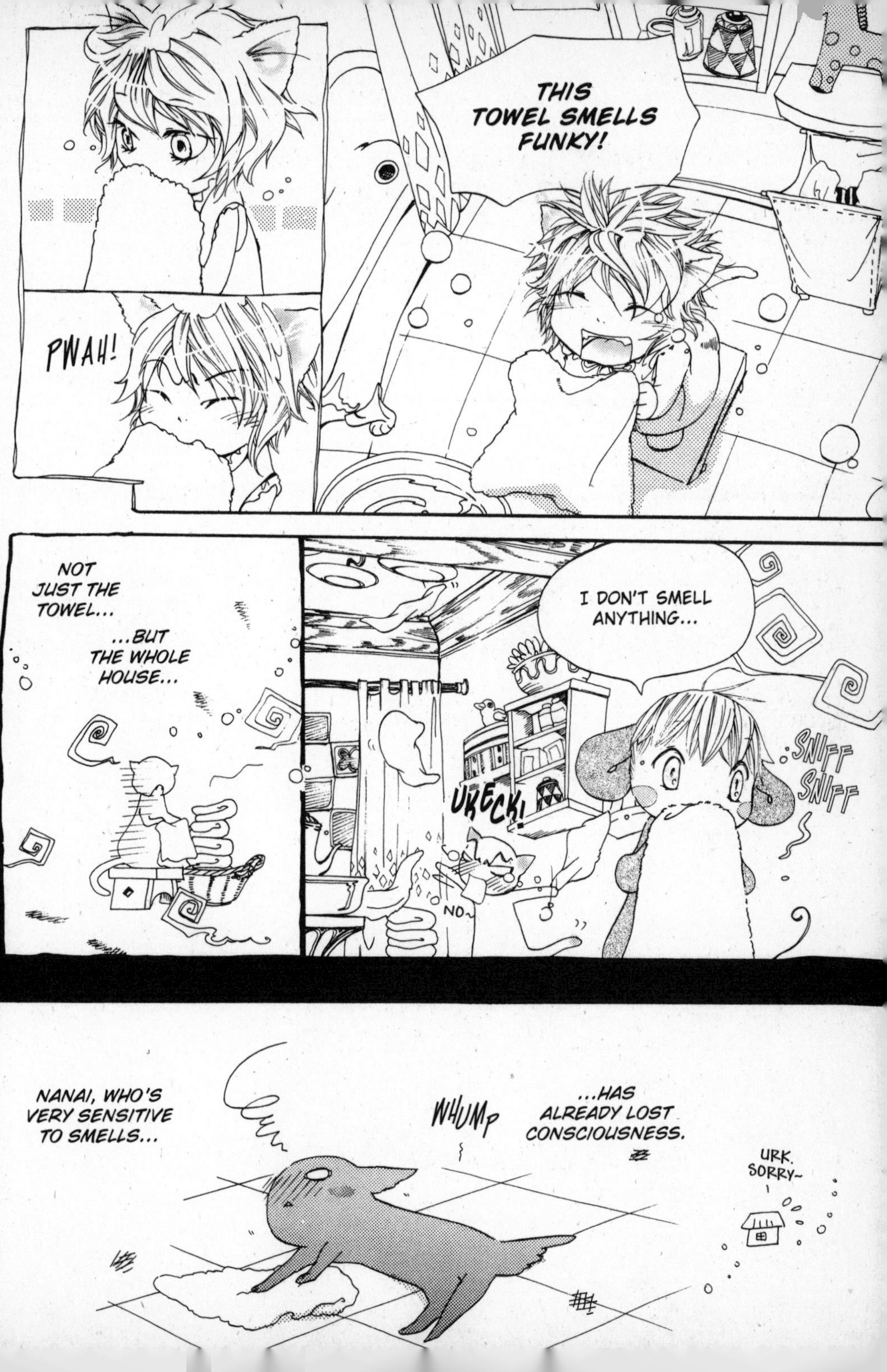
PWAH!
THIS TOWEL SMELLS FUNKY!
NOT JUST THE TOWEL...
...BUT THE WHOLE HOUSE...
I DON'T SMELL ANYTHING...
UKECK!
NO
SNIFF SNIFF
NANAI, WHO'S VERY SENSITIVE TO SMELLS...
WHUMP
...HAS ALREADY LOST CONSCIOUSNESS.
URK. SORRY~

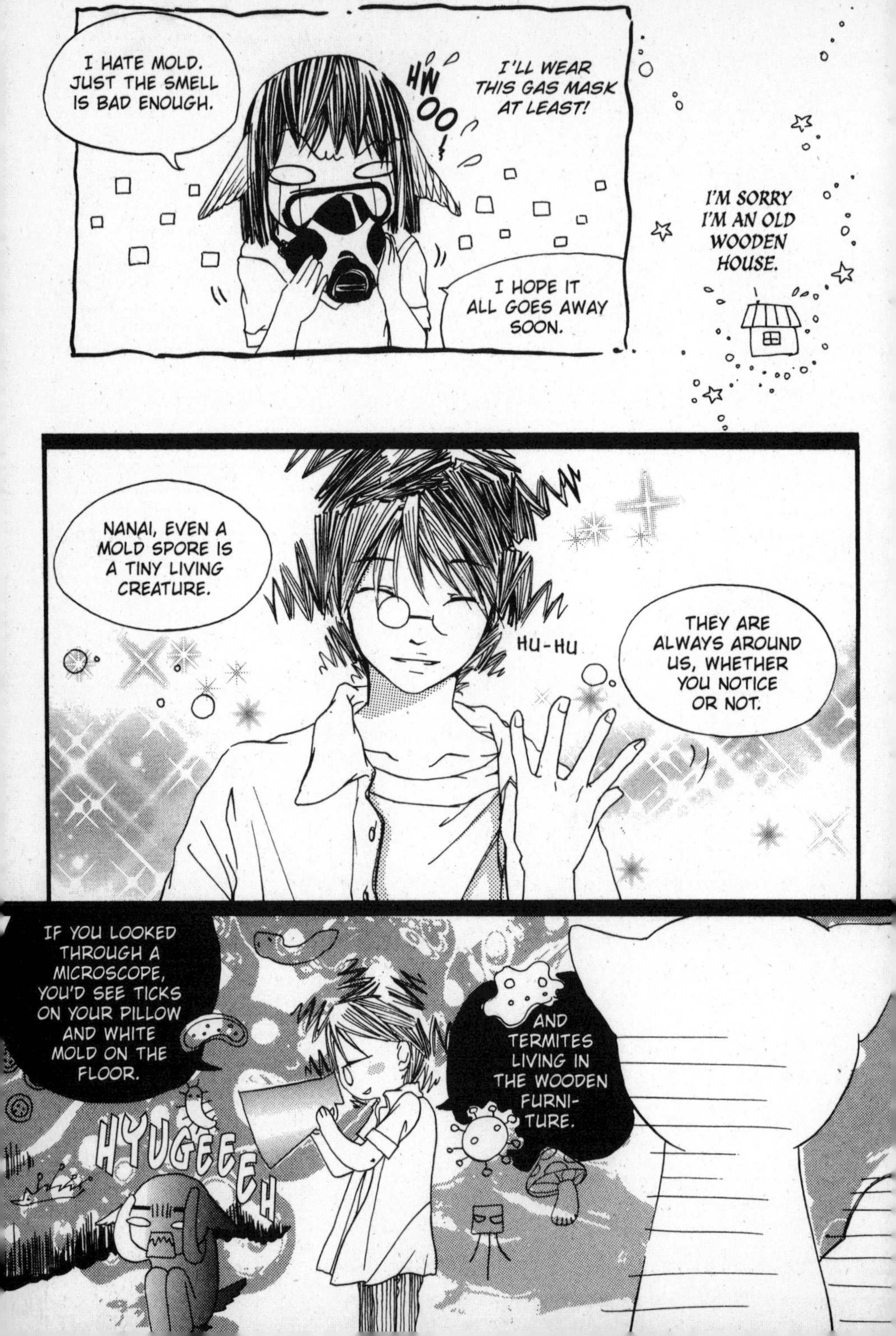
I HATE MOLD. JUST THE SMELL IS BAD ENOUGH.
HWOO
I'LL WEAR THIS GAS MASK AT LEAST!
I HOPE IT ALL GOES AWAY SOON.
I'M SORRY I'M AN OLD WOODEN HOUSE.
NANAI, EVEN A MOLD SPORE IS A TINY LIVING CREATURE.
HU-HU
THEY ARE ALWAYS AROUND US, WHETHER YOU NOTICE OR NOT.
IF YOU LOOKED THROUGH A MICROSCOPE, YOU'D SEE TICKS ON YOUR PILLOW AND WHITE MOLD ON THE FLOOR.
HYUGEEEEH
AND TERMITES LIVING IN THE WOODEN FURNI-TURE.

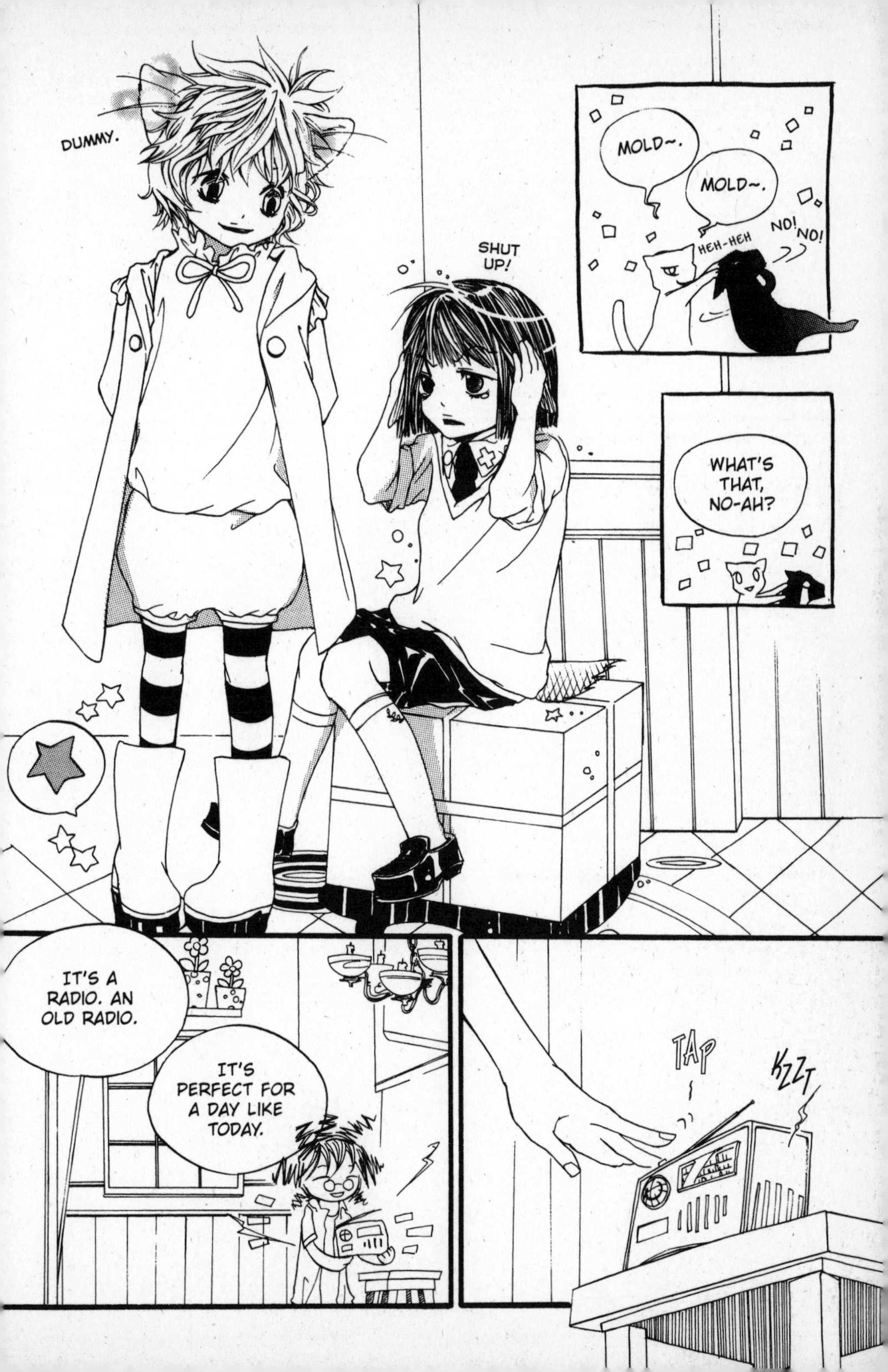

DUMMY.
SHUT UP!
MOLD~.
MOLD~.
HEH-HEH
NO! NO!
WHAT'S THAT, NO-AH?
IT'S A RADIO. AN OLD RADIO.
IT'S PERFECT FOR A DAY LIKE TODAY.
TAP
KZZT

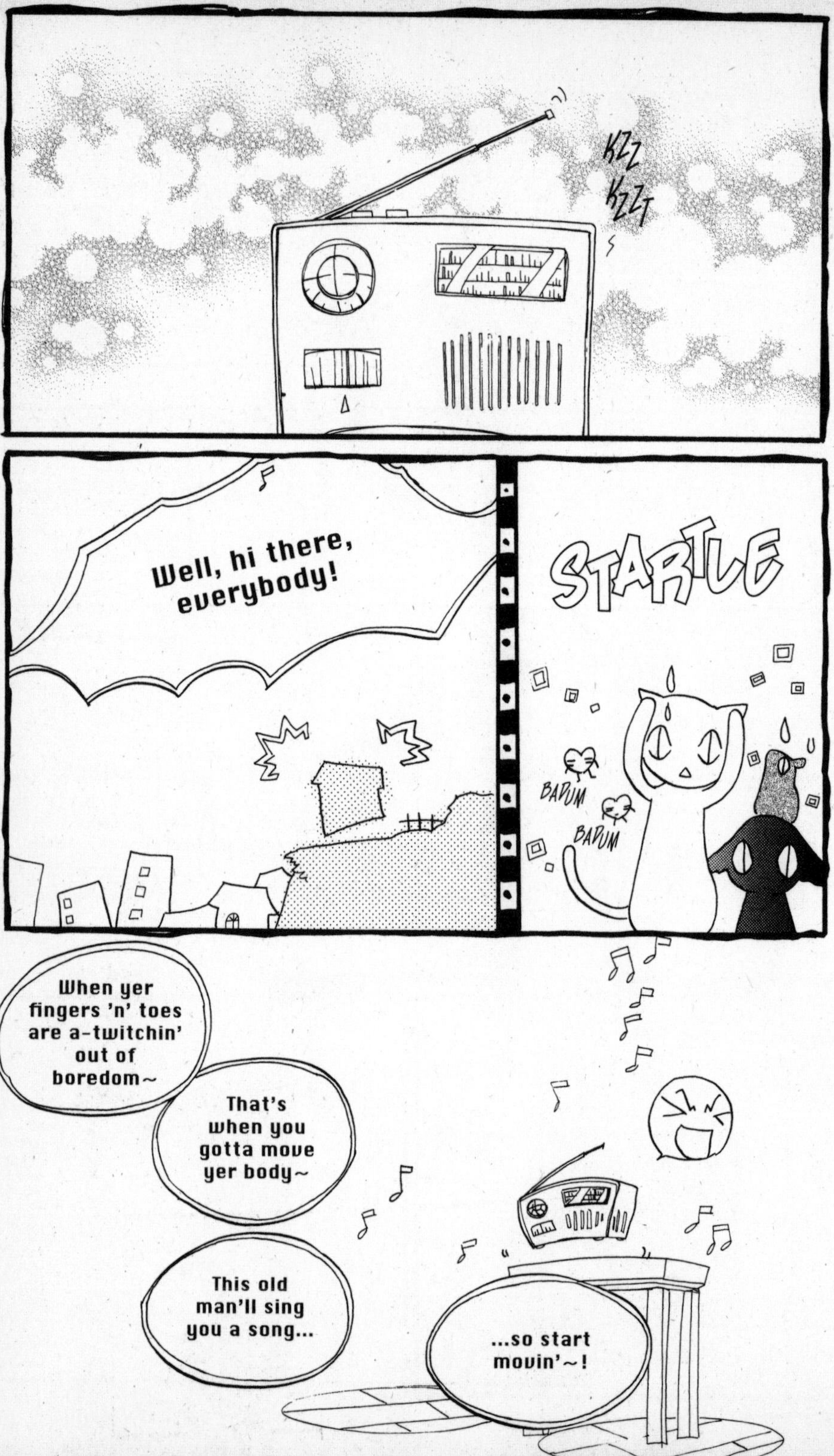
KZZ KZZT
Well, hi there, everybody!
STARTLE
BADUM
BADUM
When yer fingers 'n' toes are a-twitchin' out of boredom~
That's when you gotta move yer body~
This old man'll sing you a song...
...so start movin'~!

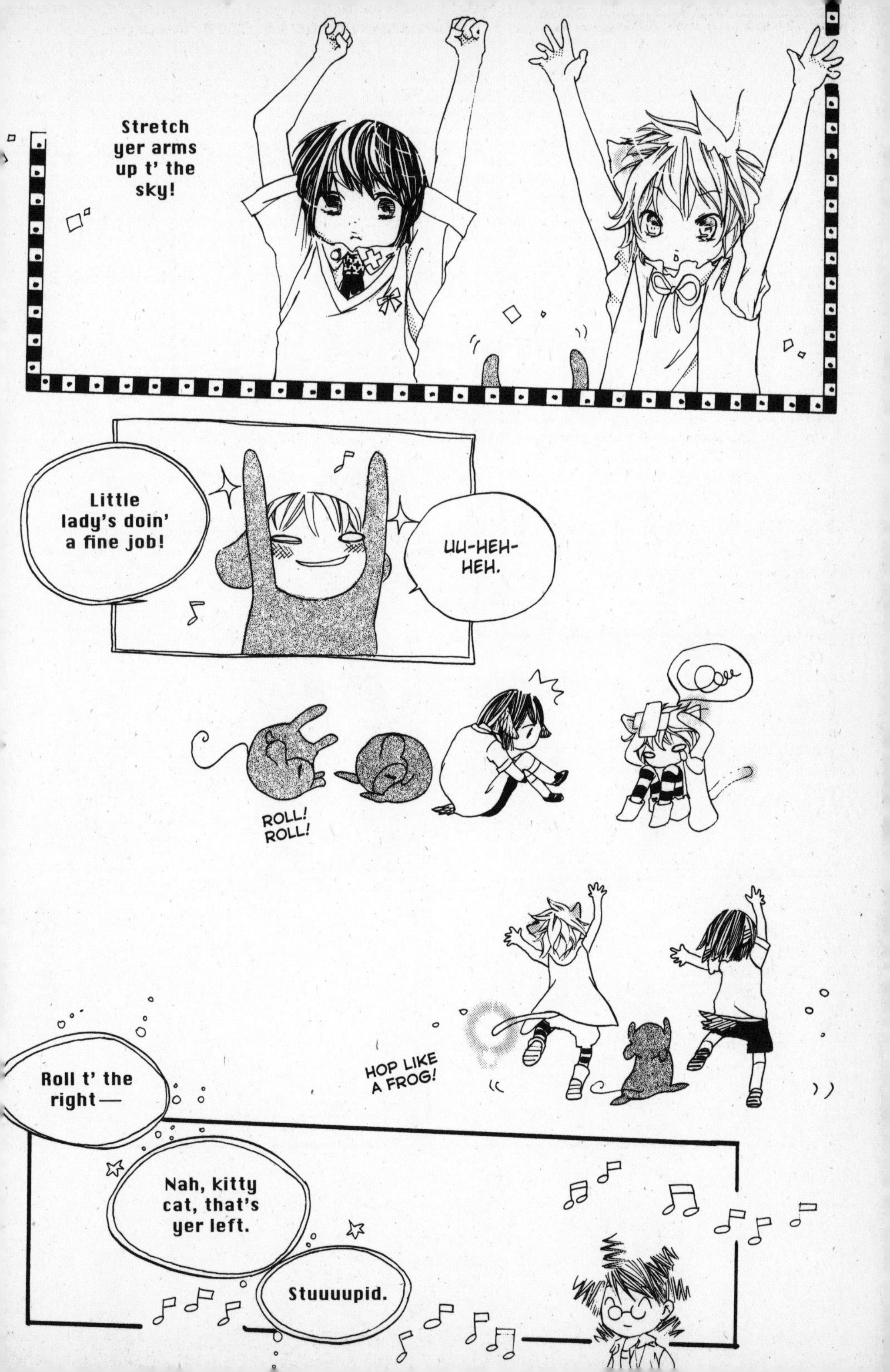

Stretch yer arms up t' the sky!
Little lady's doin' a fine job!
UU-HEH-HEH.
ROLL! ROLL!
HOP LIKE A FROG!
Roll t' the right—
Nah, kitty cat, that's yer left.
Stuuuupid.

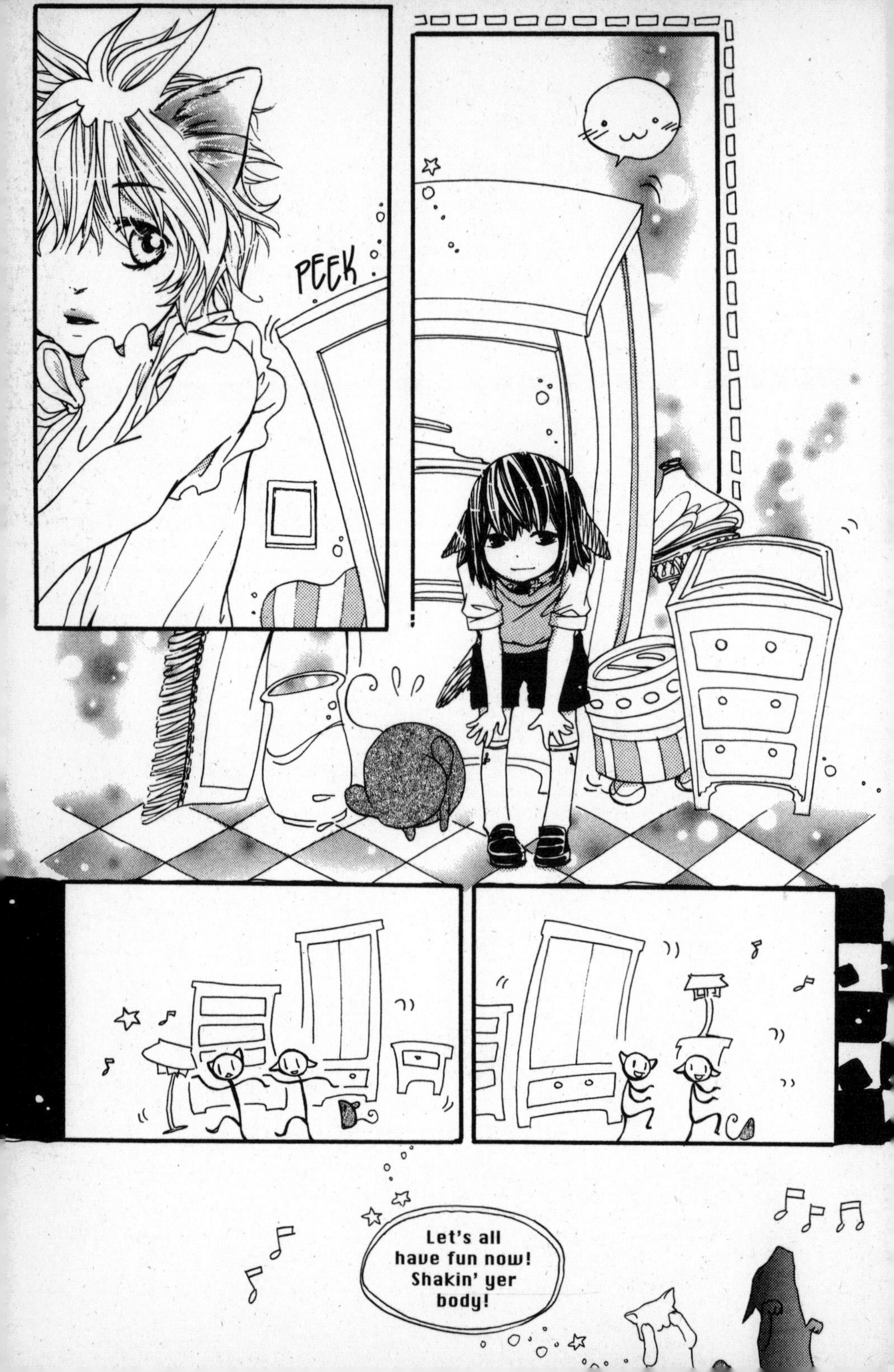
PEEK
Let's all have fun now! Shakin' yer body!

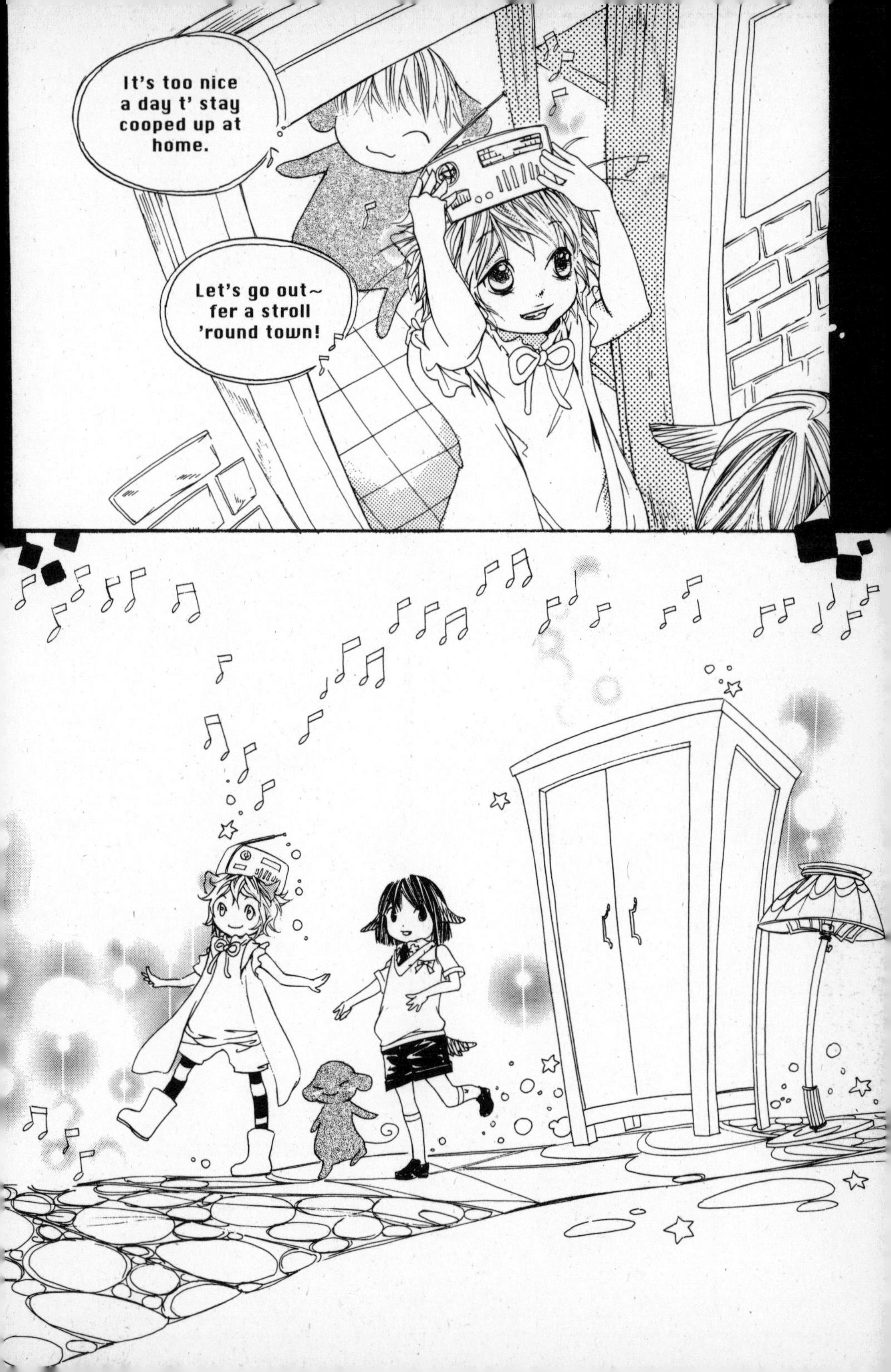
It's too nice a day t' stay cooped up at home.
Let's go out~ fer a stroll 'round town!

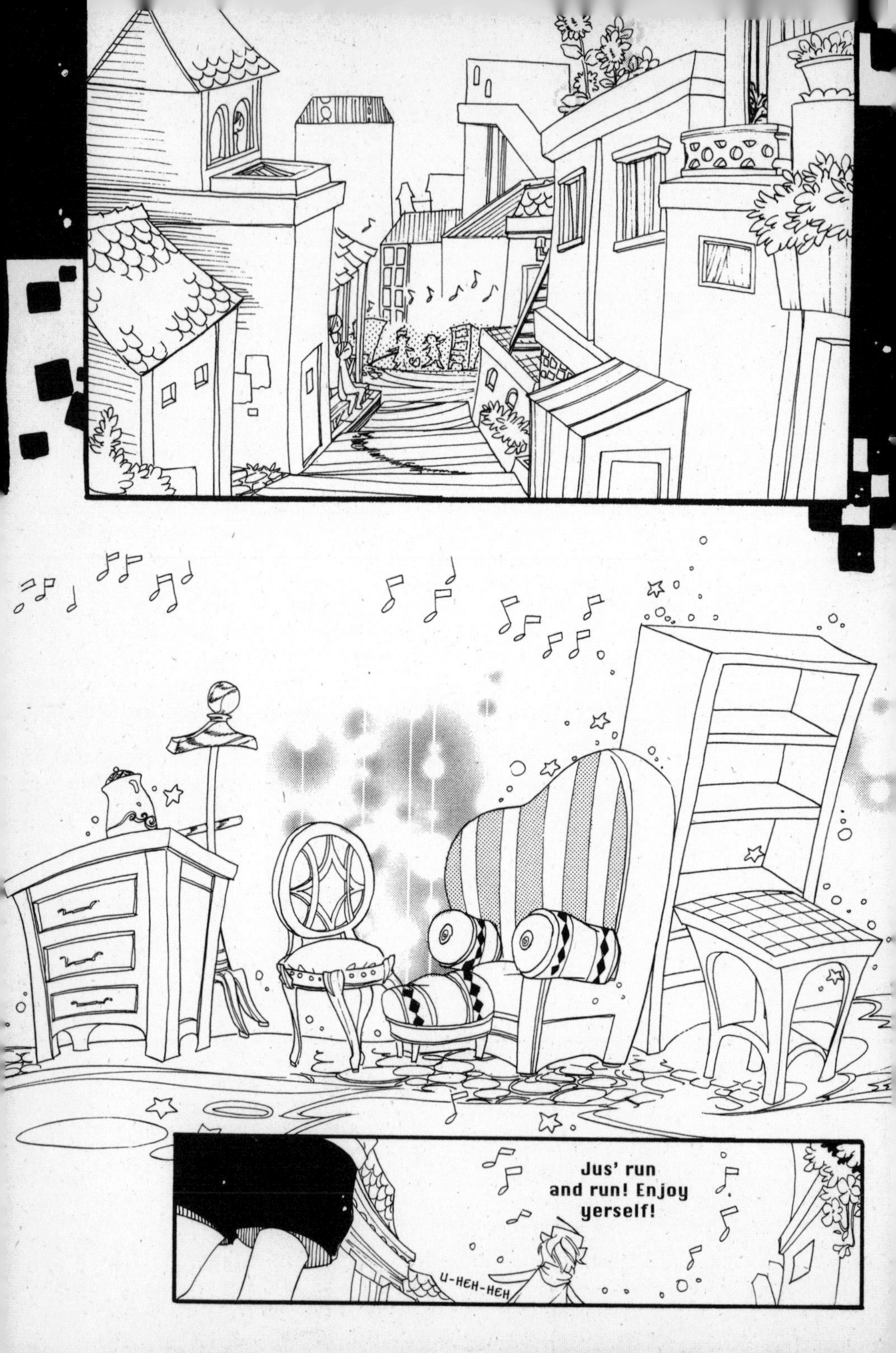
Jus' run and run! Enjoy yerself!
U-HEH-HEH

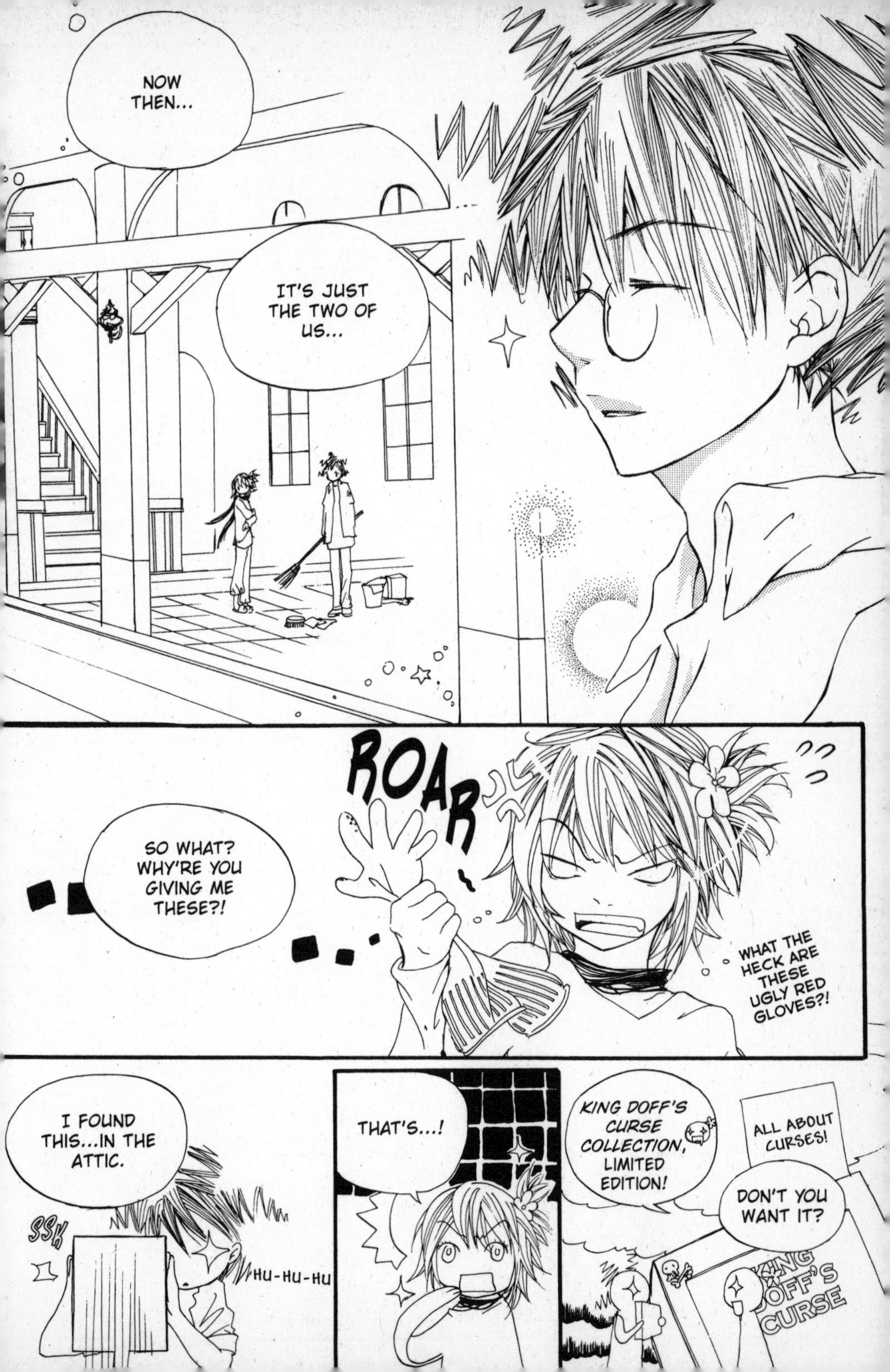
NOW THEN...
IT'S JUST THE TWO OF US...
ROAR
SO WHAT? WHY'RE YOU GIVING ME THESE?!
WHAT THE HECK ARE THESE UGLY RED GLOVES?!
I FOUND THIS...IN THE ATTIC.
SSK
HU-HU-HU
THAT'S...!
KING DOFF'S CURSE COLLECTION, LIMITED EDITION!
ALL ABOUT CURSES!
DON'T YOU WANT IT?
KING DOFF'S CURSE

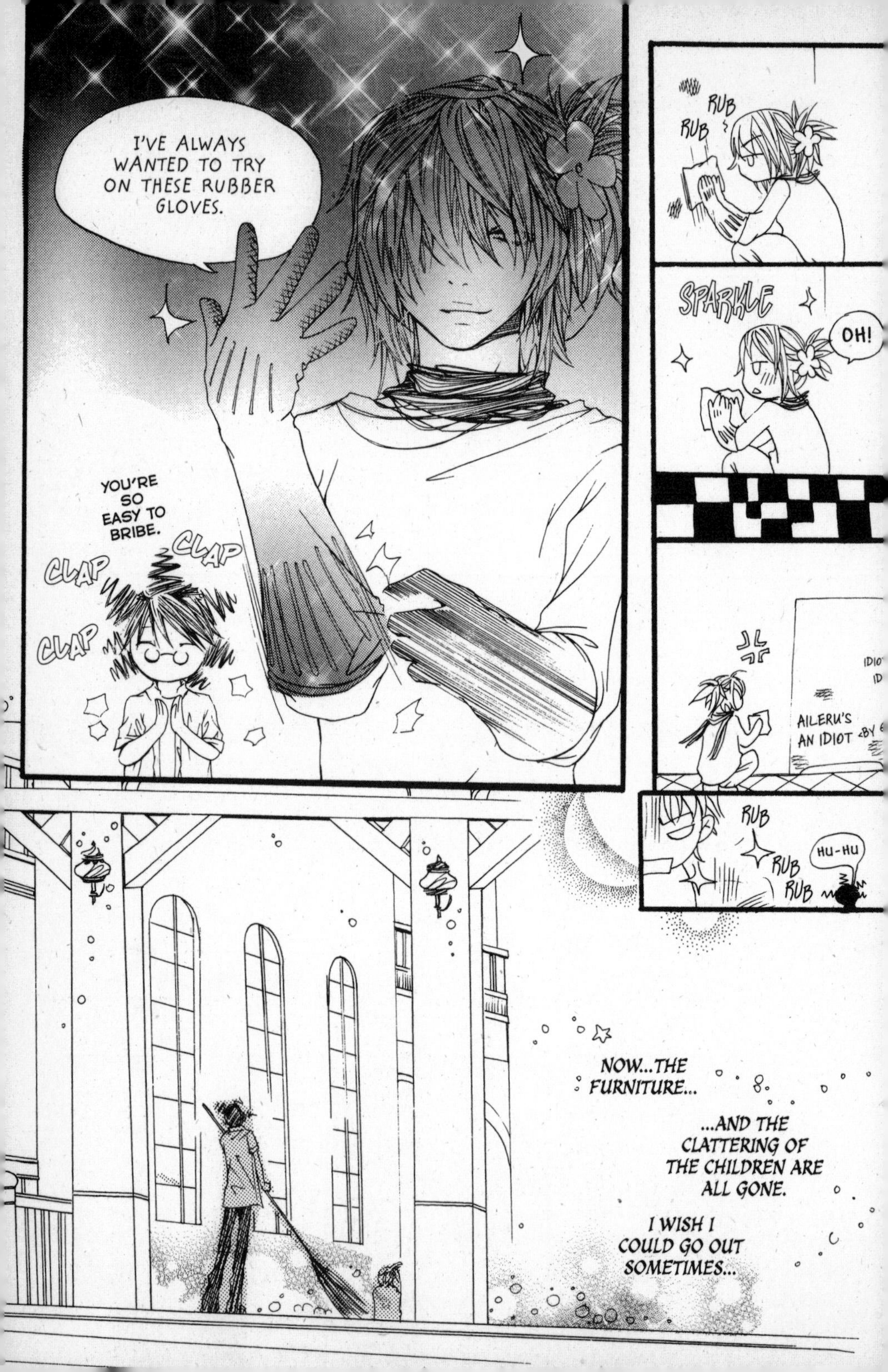
RUB
RUB
SPARKLE
OH!
AILERU'S AN IDIOT
RUB
RUB
RUB
HU-HU
I'VE ALWAYS WANTED TO TRY ON THESE RUBBER GLOVES.
YOU'RE SO EASY TO BRIBE.
CLAP
CLAP
CLAP
NOW...THE FURNITURE...
...AND THE CLATTERING OF THE CHILDREN ARE ALL GONE.
I WISH I COULD GO OUT SOMETIMES...

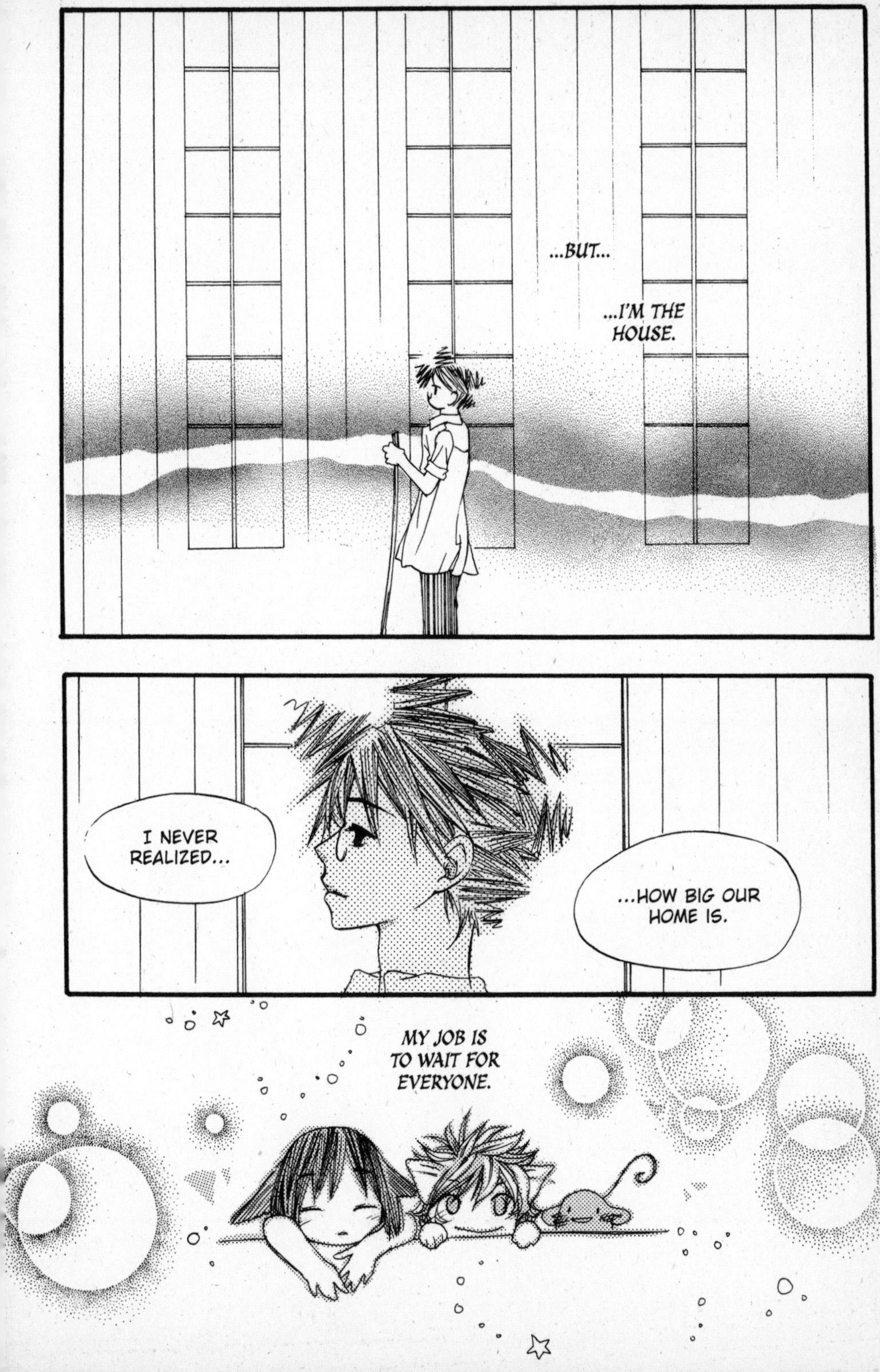
...BUT...
...I'M THE HOUSE.
I NEVER REALIZED...
...HOW BIG OUR HOME IS.
MY JOB IS TO WAIT FOR EVERYONE.

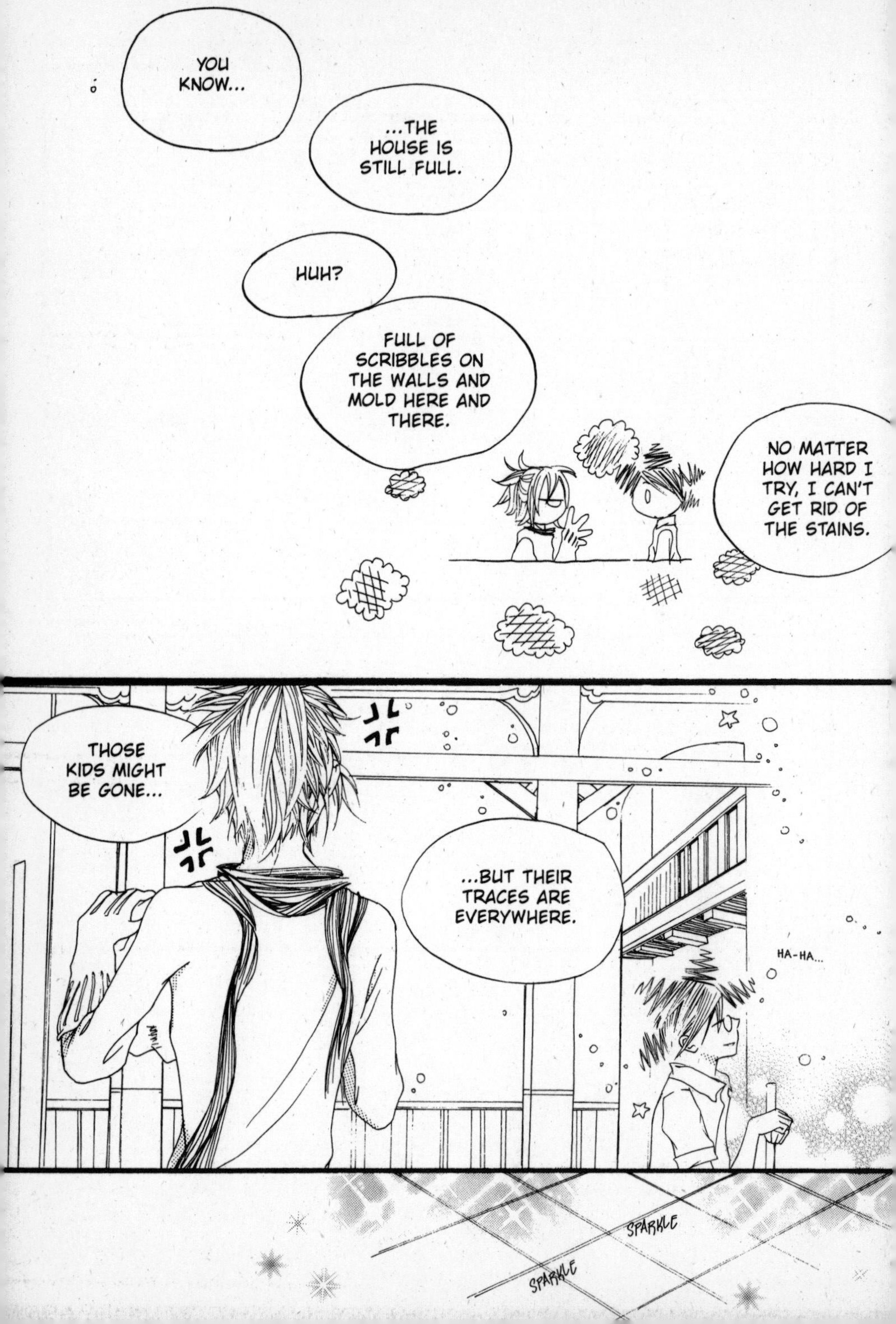
YOU KNOW...
...THE HOUSE IS STILL FULL.
HUH?
FULL OF SCRIBBLES ON THE WALLS AND MOLD HERE AND THERE.
NO MATTER HOW HARD I TRY, I CAN'T GET RID OF THE STAINS.
THOSE KIDS MIGHT BE GONE...
...BUT THEIR TRACES ARE EVERYWHERE.
HA-HA...
SPARKLE
SPARKLE

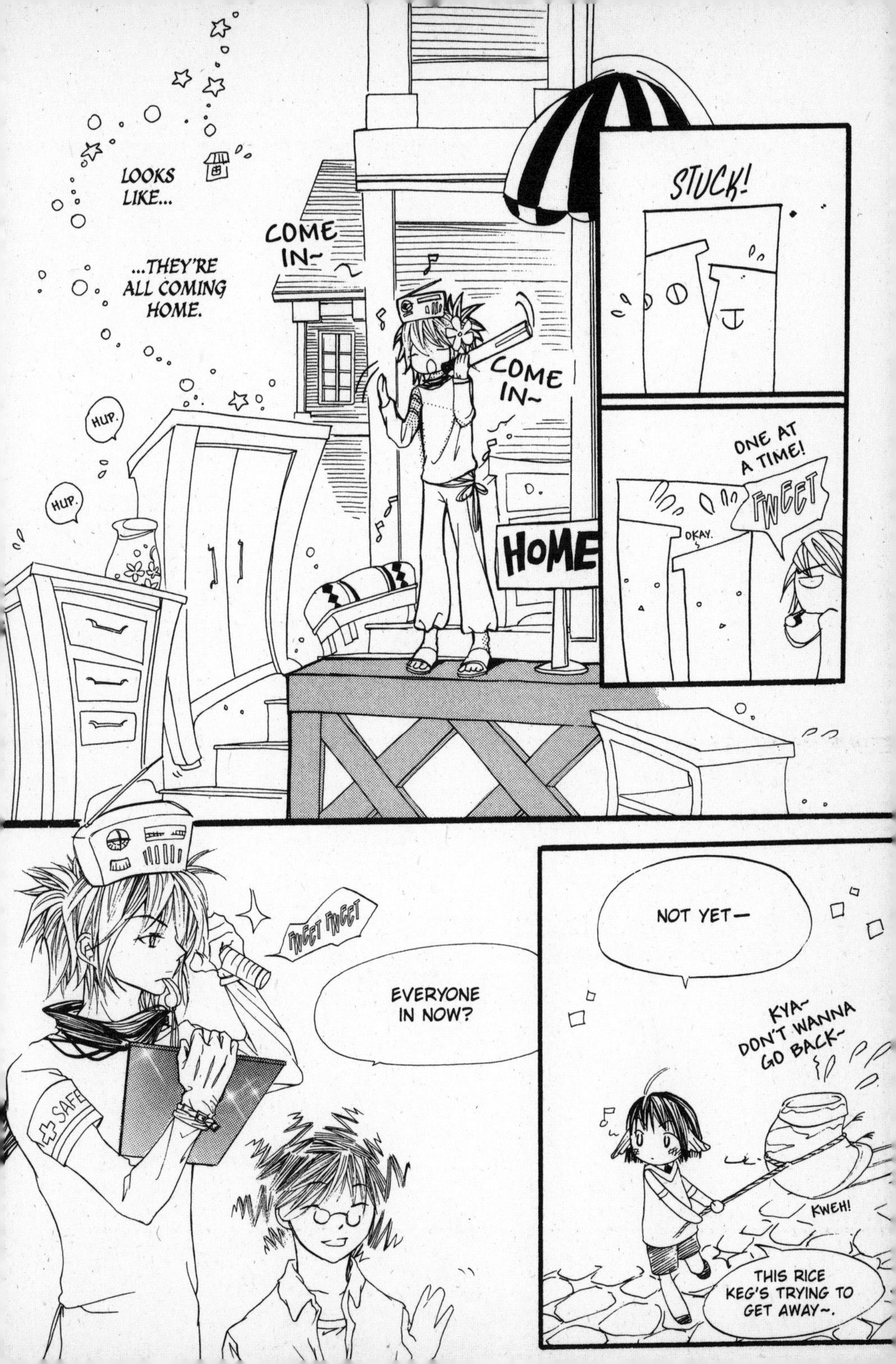
LOOKS LIKE...
...THEY'RE ALL COMING HOME.
HUP.
HUP.
COME IN~
COME IN~
HOME
STUCK!
ONE AT A TIME!
FWEET
OKAY.
FWEET FWEET
EVERYONE IN NOW?
SAFE
NOT YET—
KYA~ DON'T WANNA GO BACK~
KWEH!
THIS RICE KEG'S TRYING TO GET AWAY~.

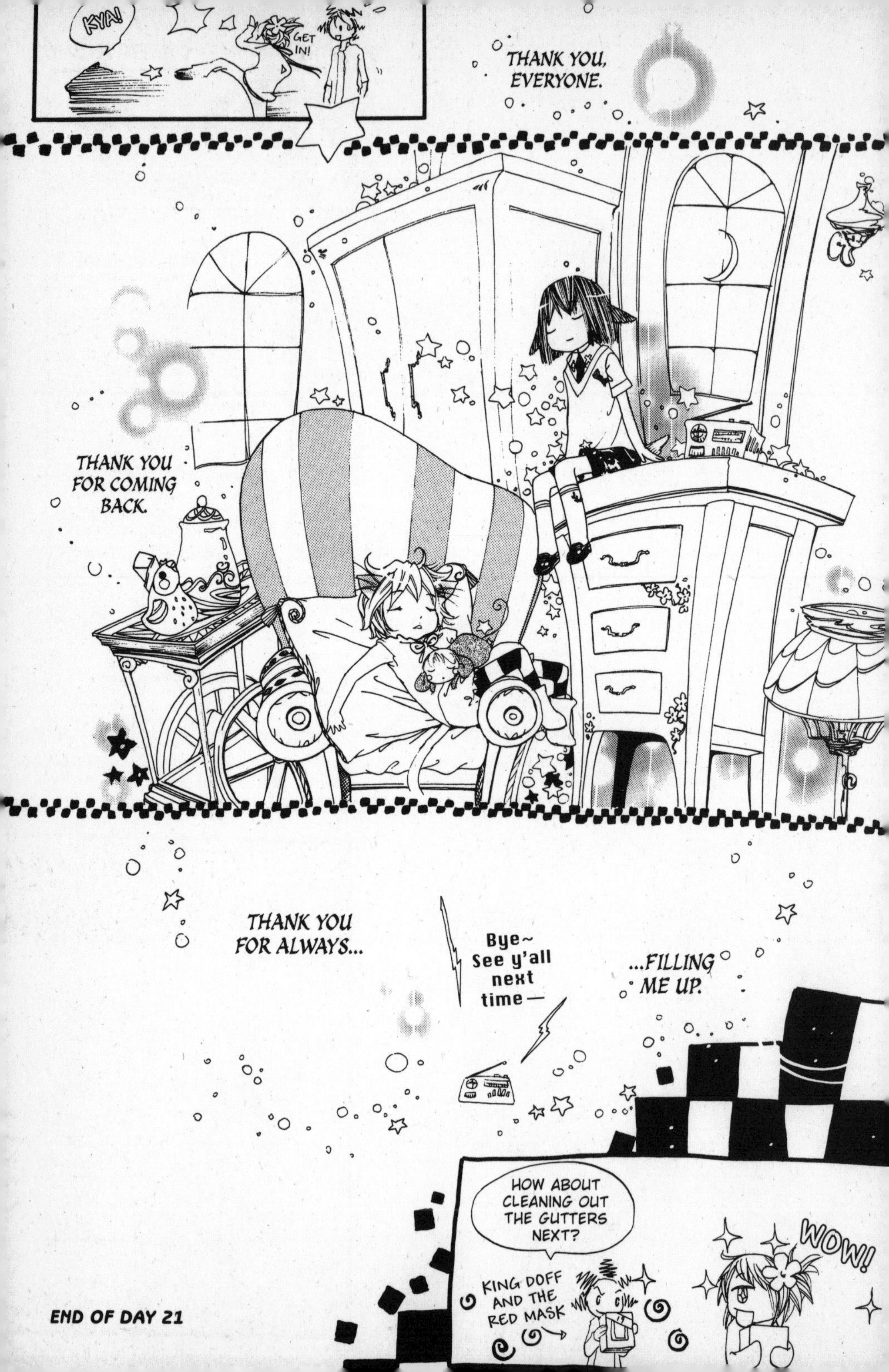
KYA!
GET IN!
THANK YOU, EVERYONE.
THANK YOU FOR COMING BACK.
THANK YOU FOR ALWAYS...
Bye~ See y'all next time—
...FILLING ME UP.
HOW ABOUT CLEANING OUT THE GUTTERS NEXT?
KING DOFF AND THE RED MASK
WOW!

END OF DAY 21

DAY 22. NO-AH WITH A GREEN THUMB

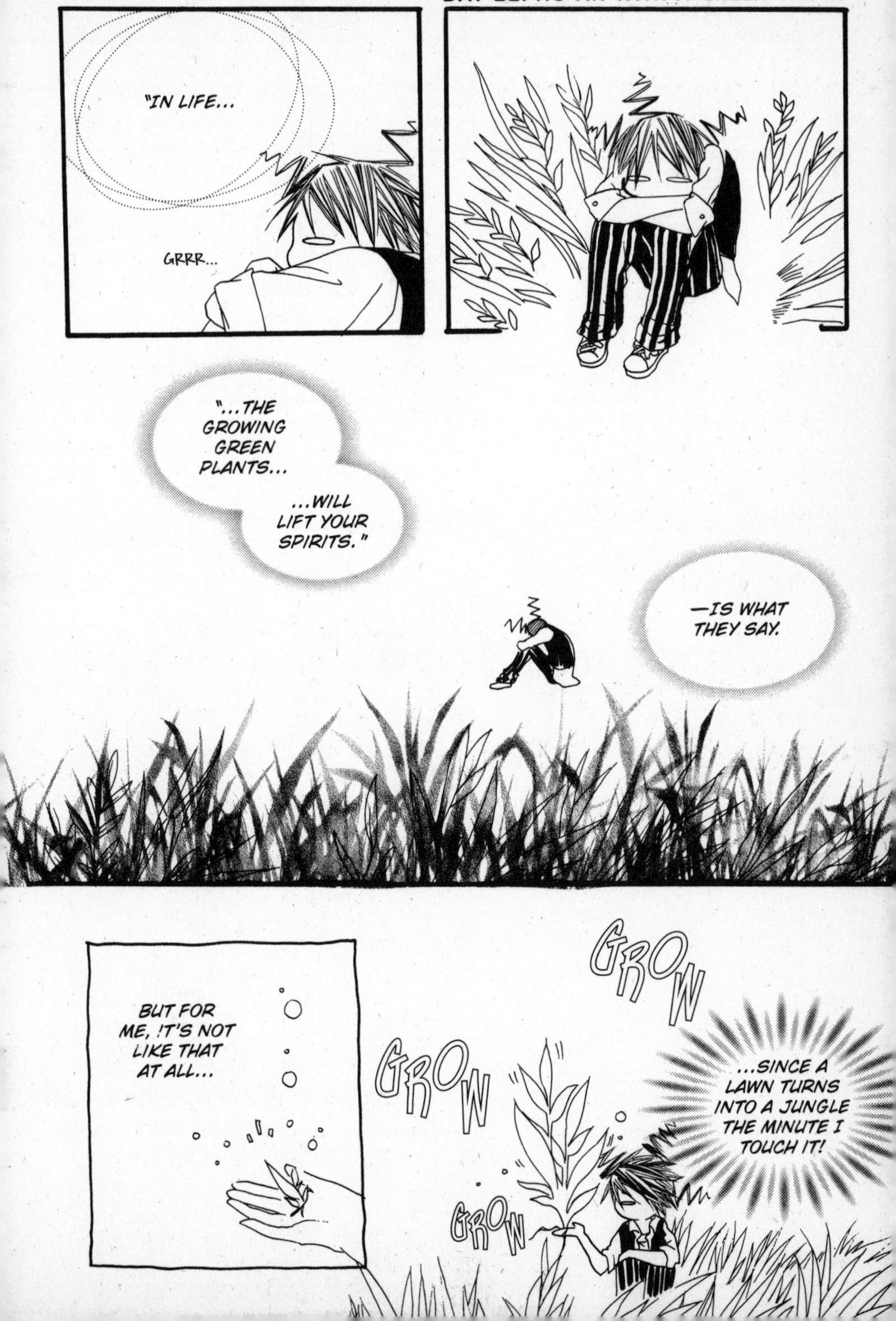

"IN LIFE...
GRRR...
"...THE GROWING GREEN PLANTS...
...WILL LIFT YOUR SPIRITS."
—IS WHAT THEY SAY.
BUT FOR ME, IT'S NOT LIKE THAT AT ALL...
GROW
GROW
GROW
...SINCE A LAWN TURNS INTO A JUNGLE THE MINUTE I TOUCH IT!

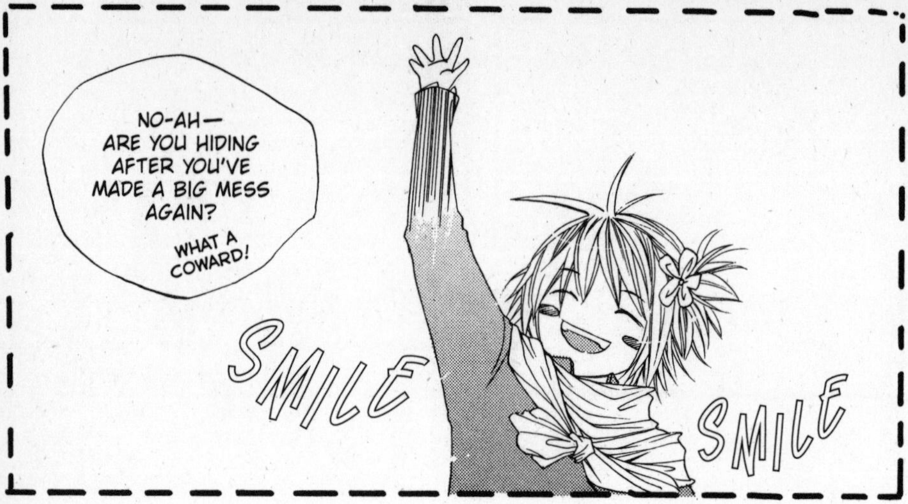
NO-AH— ARE YOU HIDING AFTER YOU'VE MADE A BIG MESS AGAIN?
WHAT A COWARD!
SMILE
SMILE

one fine day

DAY 22.
NO-AH WITH A GREEN THUMB

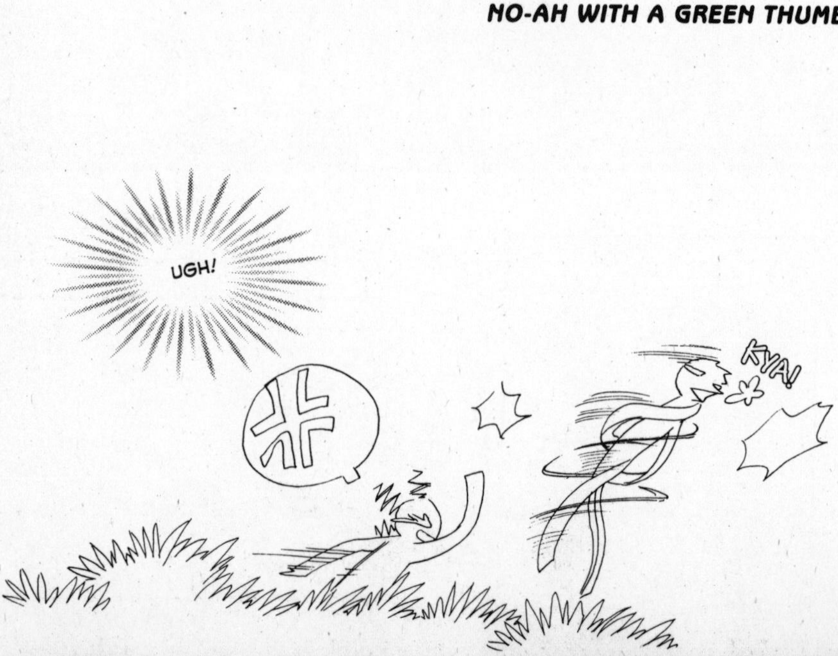
UGH!
KYA!

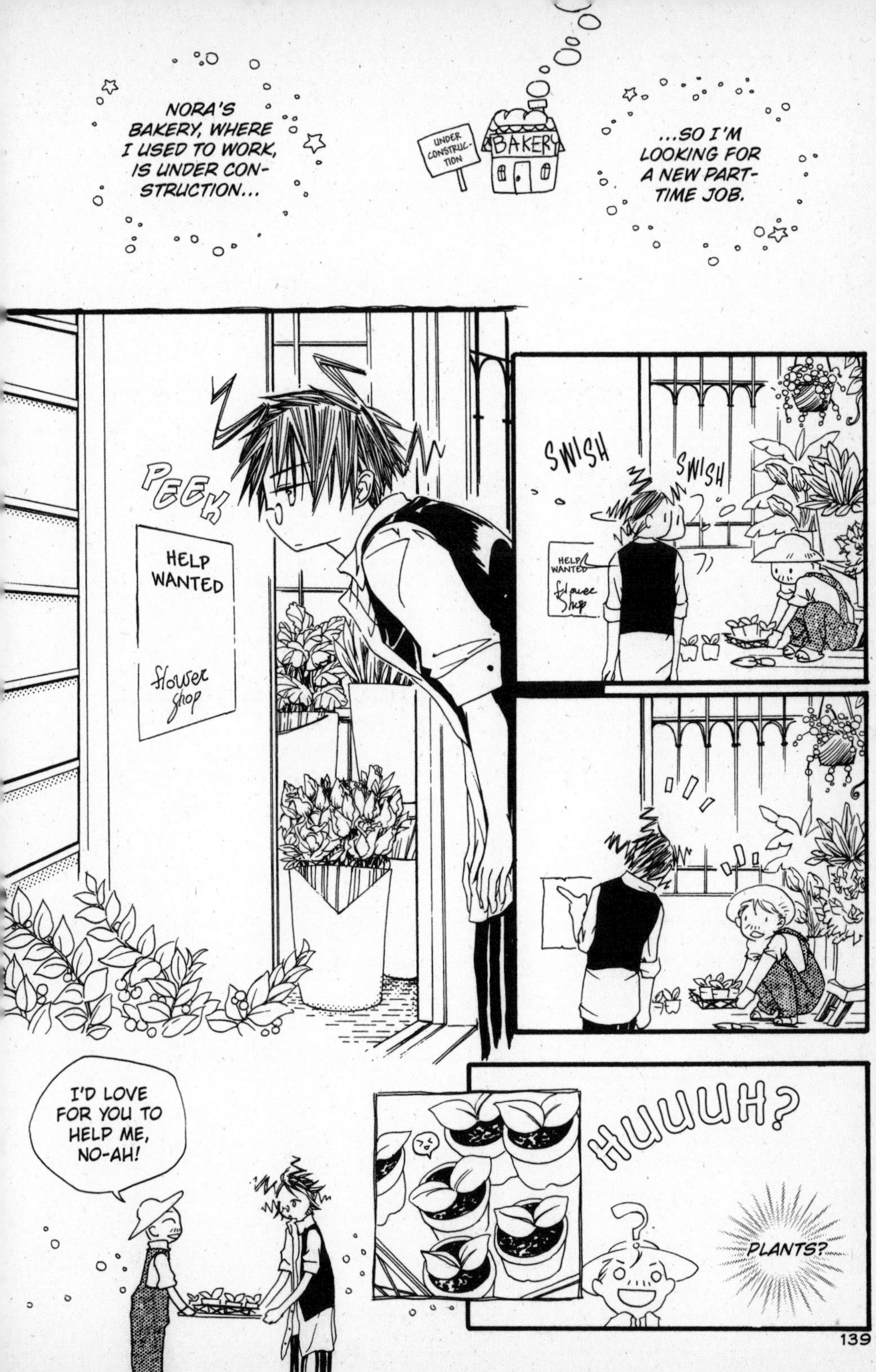
NORA'S BAKERY, WHERE I USED TO WORK, IS UNDER CONSTRUCTION...
UNDER CONSTRUCTION
BAKERY
...SO I'M LOOKING FOR A NEW PART-TIME JOB.
PEEK
HELP WANTED
flower shop
SWISH
SWISH
HELP WANTED
flower shop
I'D LOVE FOR YOU TO HELP ME, NO-AH!
HUUUUH?
PLANTS?

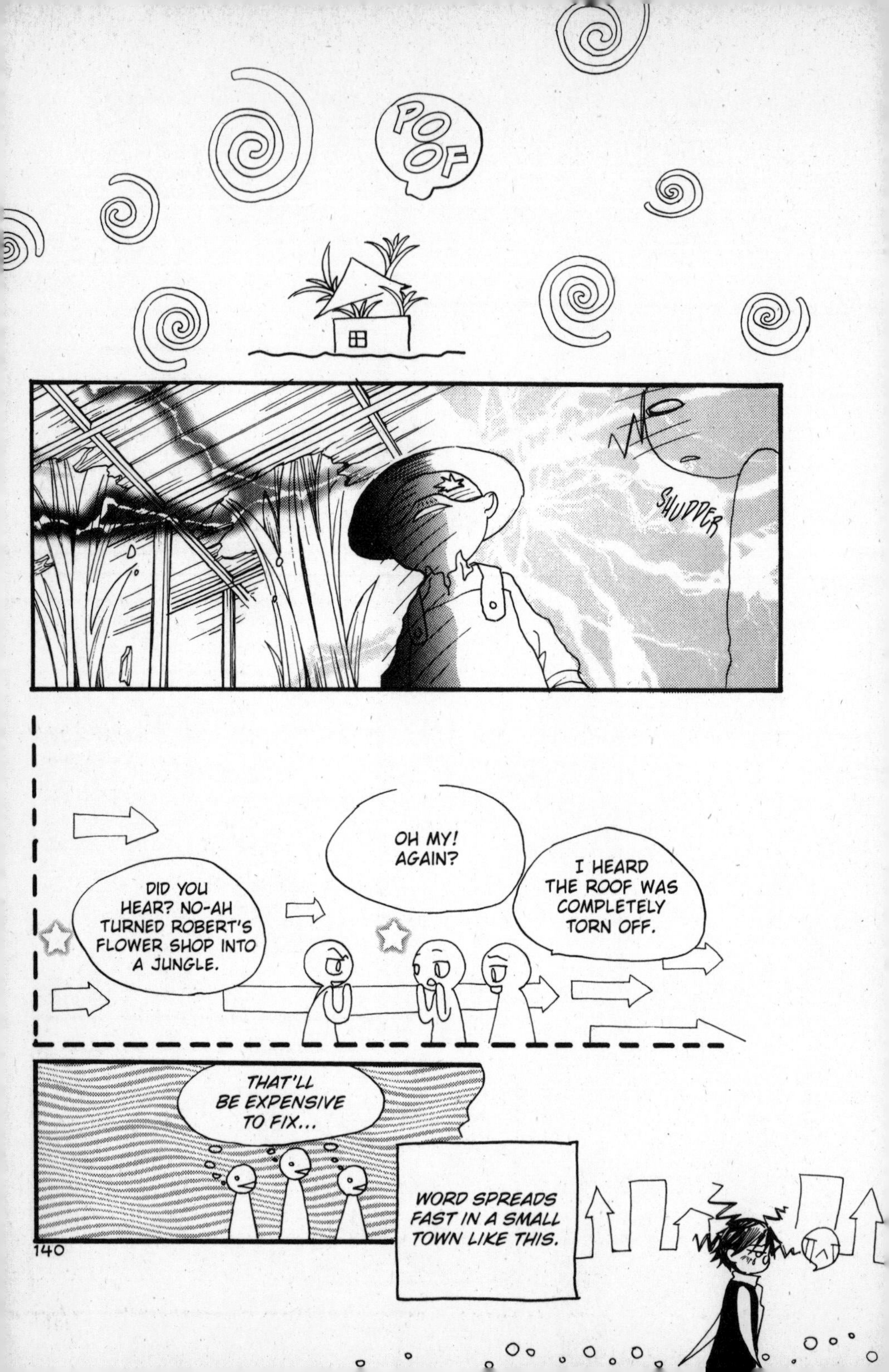
POOF
SHUDDER
DID YOU HEAR? NO-AH TURNED ROBERT'S FLOWER SHOP INTO A JUNGLE.
OH MY! AGAIN?
I HEARD THE ROOF WAS COMPLETELY TORN OFF.
THAT'LL BE EXPENSIVE TO FIX...
WORD SPREADS FAST IN A SMALL TOWN LIKE THIS.

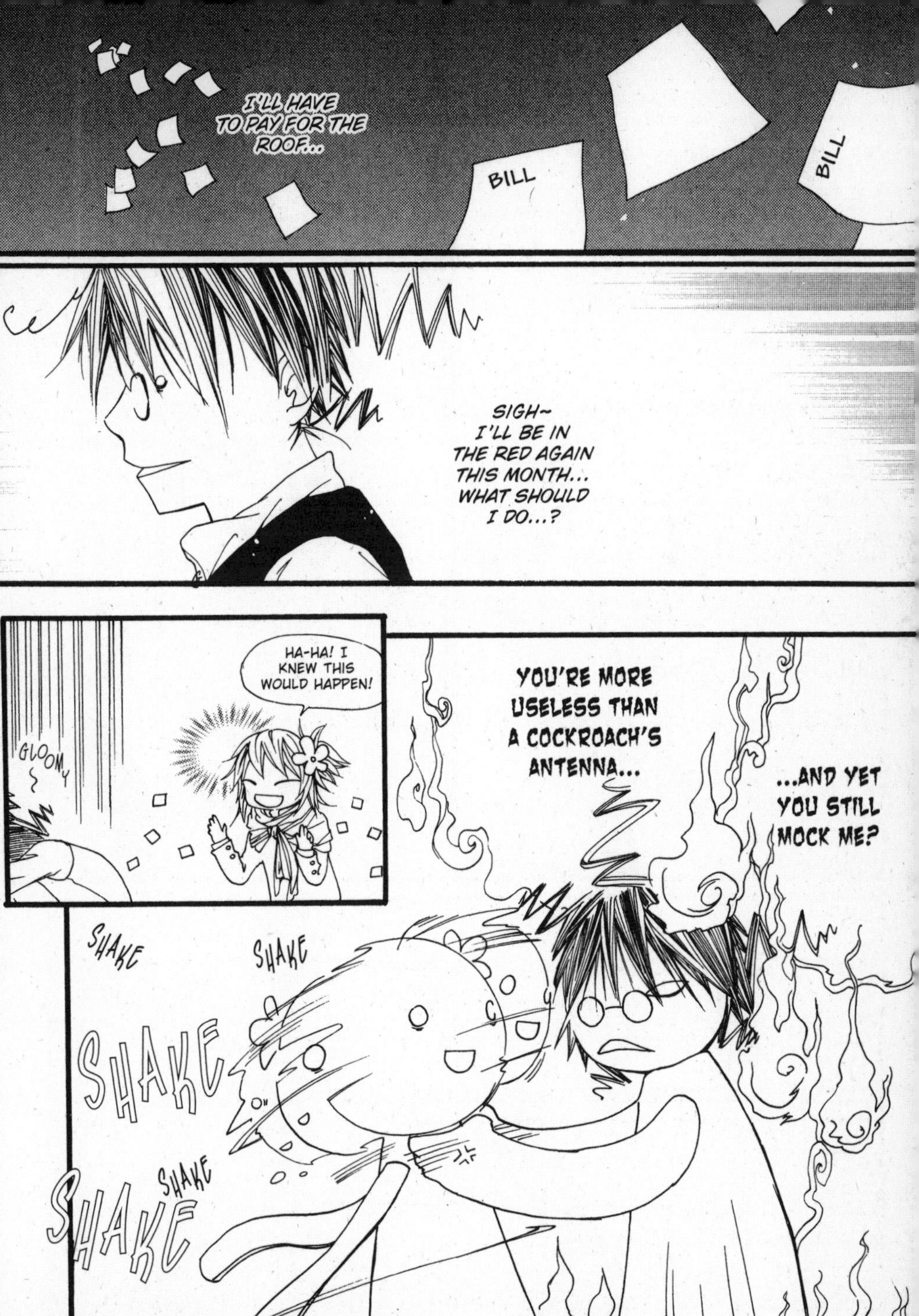

I'LL HAVE TO PAY FOR THE ROOF...
BILL
BILL
SIGH~ I'LL BE IN THE RED AGAIN THIS MONTH... WHAT SHOULD I DO...?
GLOOMY
HA-HA! I KNEW THIS WOULD HAPPEN!
YOU'RE MORE USELESS THAN A COCKROACH'S ANTENNA...
...AND YET YOU STILL MOCK ME?
SHAKE
SHAKE
SHAKE
SHAKE
SHAKE
SHAKE
SHAKE

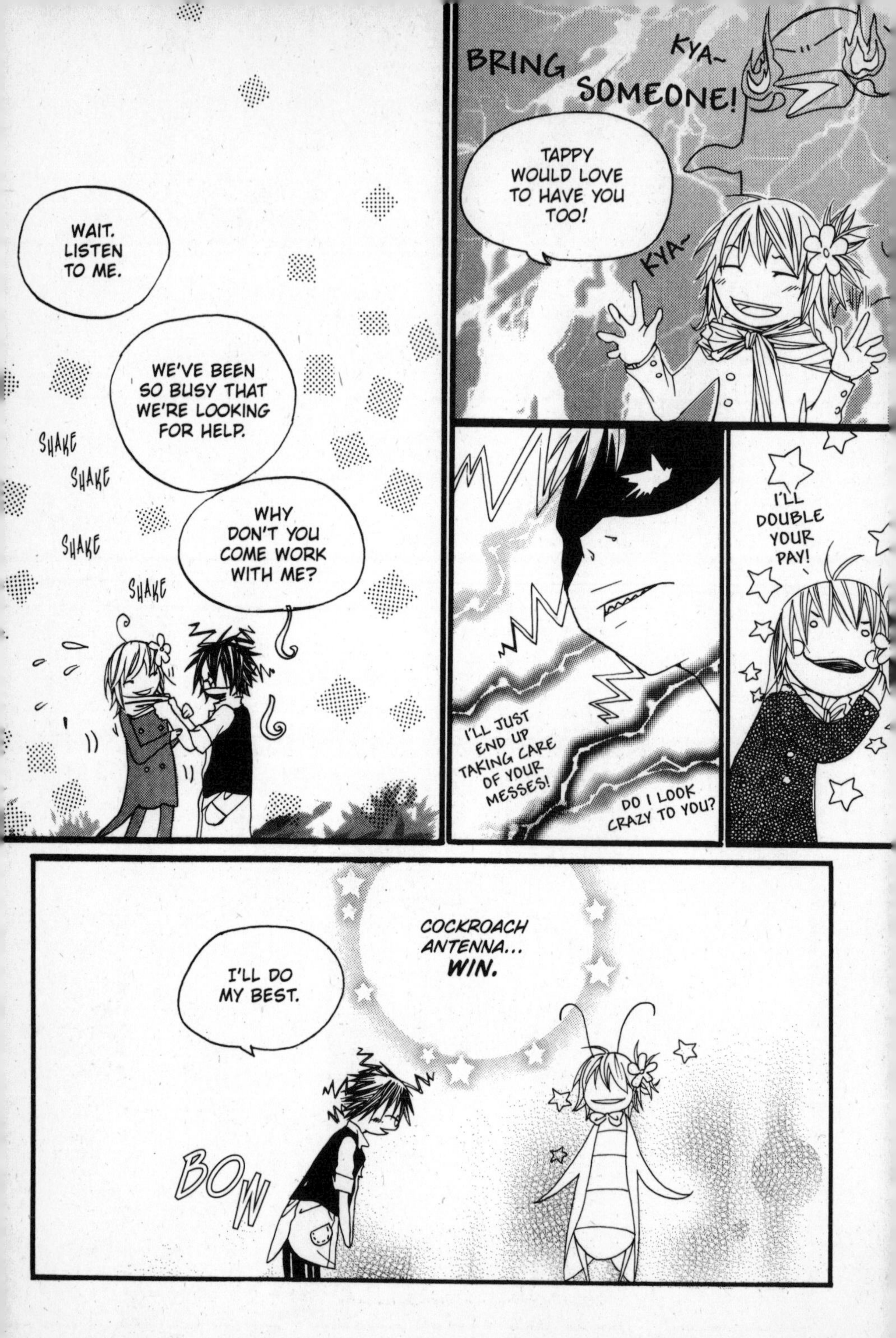
WAIT. LISTEN TO ME.
WE'VE BEEN SO BUSY THAT WE'RE LOOKING FOR HELP.
SHAKE
SHAKE
SHAKE
SHAKE
WHY DON'T YOU COME WORK WITH ME?
BRING
KYA~
SOMEONE!
TAPPY WOULD LOVE TO HAVE YOU TOO!
KYA~
I'LL JUST END UP TAKING CARE OF YOUR MESSES!
DO I LOOK CRAZY TO YOU?
I'LL DOUBLE YOUR PAY!
I'LL DO MY BEST.
COCKROACH ANTENNA... WIN.
BOW

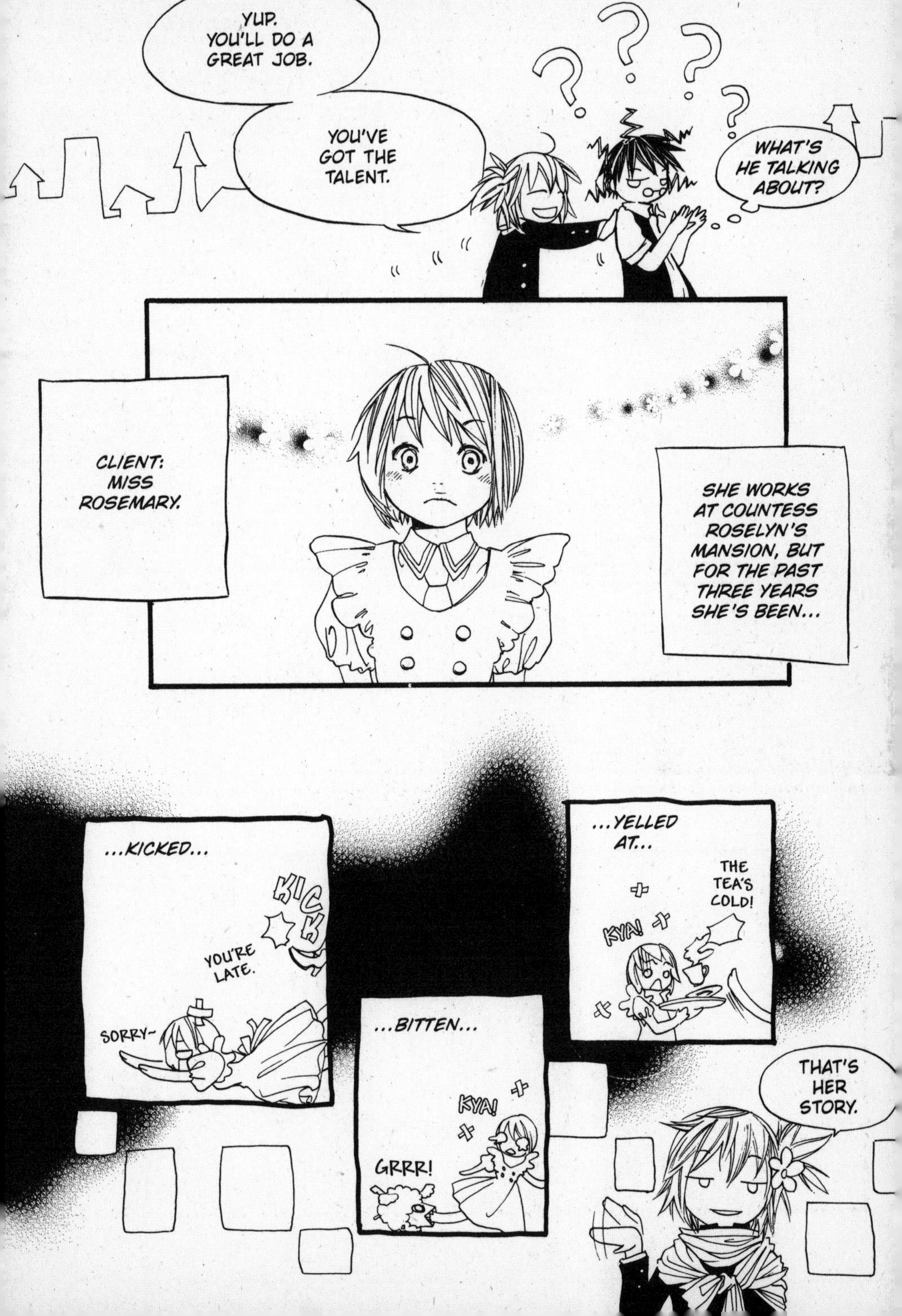
YUP. YOU'LL DO A GREAT JOB.
YOU'VE GOT THE TALENT.
WHAT'S HE TALKING ABOUT?
CLIENT: MISS ROSEMARY.
SHE WORKS AT COUNTESS ROSELYN'S MANSION, BUT FOR THE PAST THREE YEARS SHE'S BEEN...
...KICKED...
KICK
YOU'RE LATE.
SORRY~
...YELLED AT...
THE TEA'S COLD!
KYA!
...BITTEN...
KYA!
GRRR!
THAT'S HER STORY.

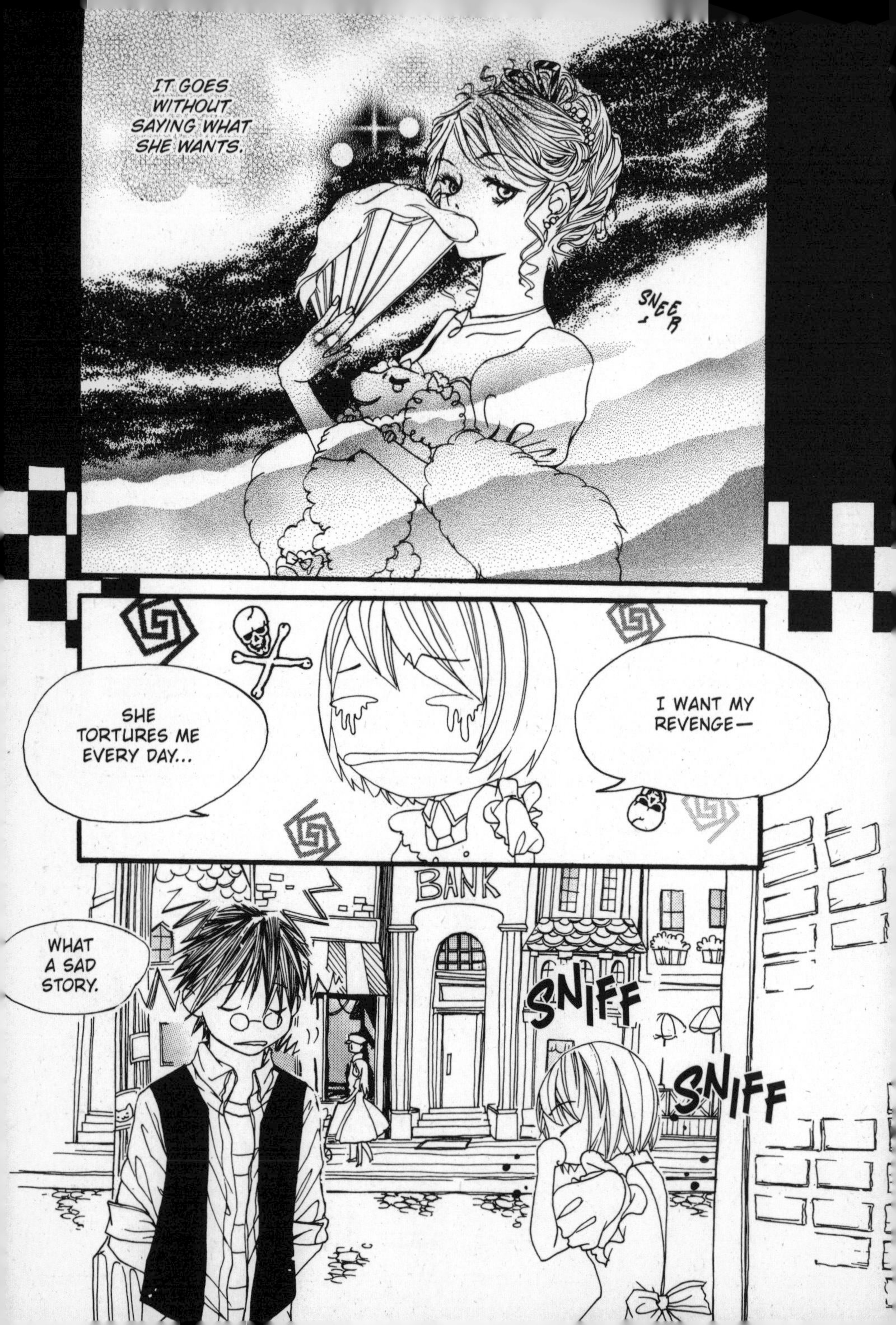
IT GOES WITHOUT SAYING WHAT SHE WANTS.
SNEER
SHE TORTURES ME EVERY DAY...
I WANT MY REVENGE—
BANK
WHAT A SAD STORY.
SNIFF
SNIFF

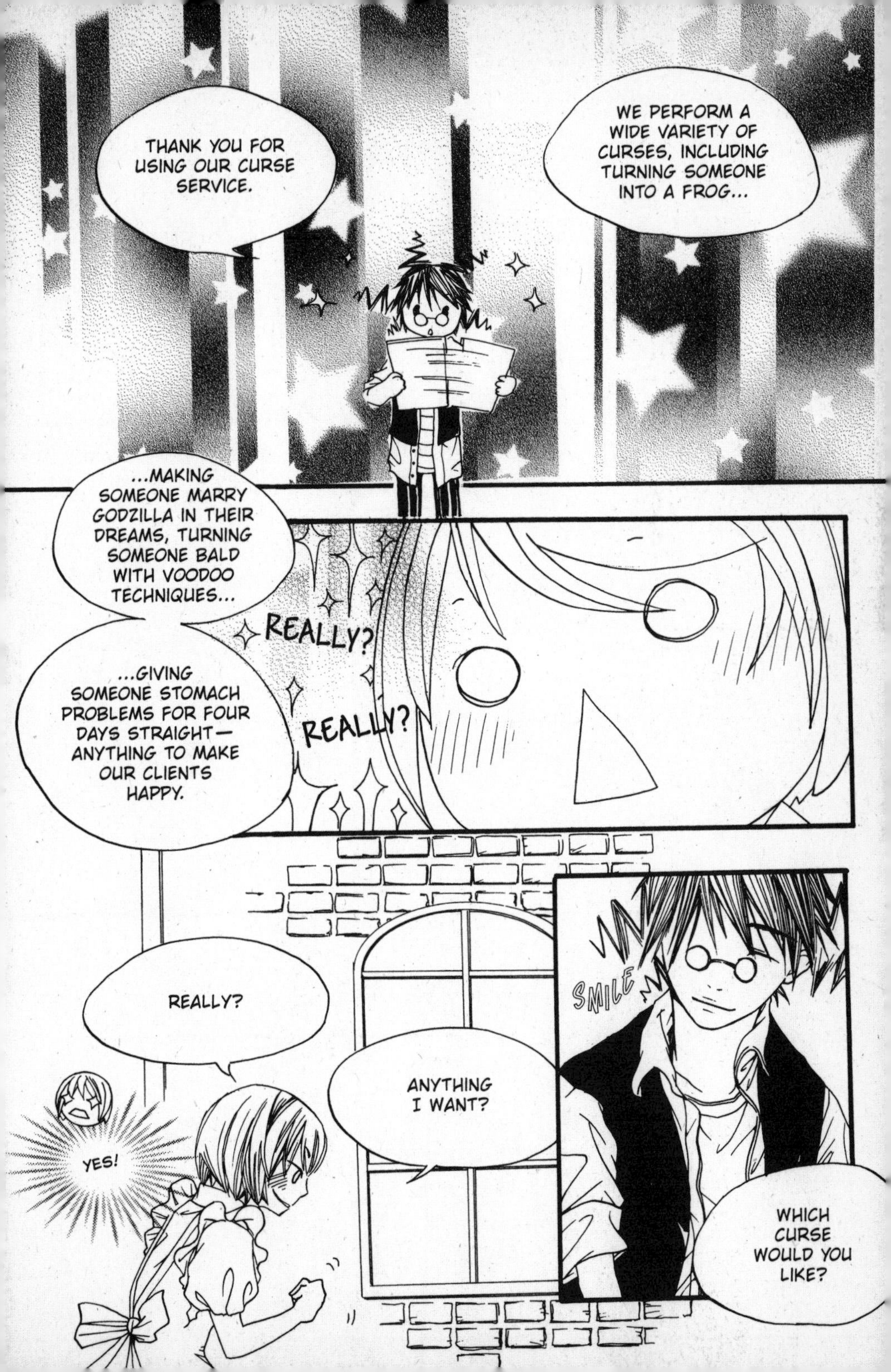
THANK YOU FOR USING OUR CURSE SERVICE.
WE PERFORM A WIDE VARIETY OF CURSES, INCLUDING TURNING SOMEONE INTO A FROG...
...MAKING SOMEONE MARRY GODZILLA IN THEIR DREAMS, TURNING SOMEONE BALD WITH VOODOO TECHNIQUES...
...GIVING SOMEONE STOMACH PROBLEMS FOR FOUR DAYS STRAIGHT— ANYTHING TO MAKE OUR CLIENTS HAPPY.
REALLY?
REALLY?
REALLY?
YES!
ANYTHING I WANT?
SMILE
WHICH CURSE WOULD YOU LIKE?

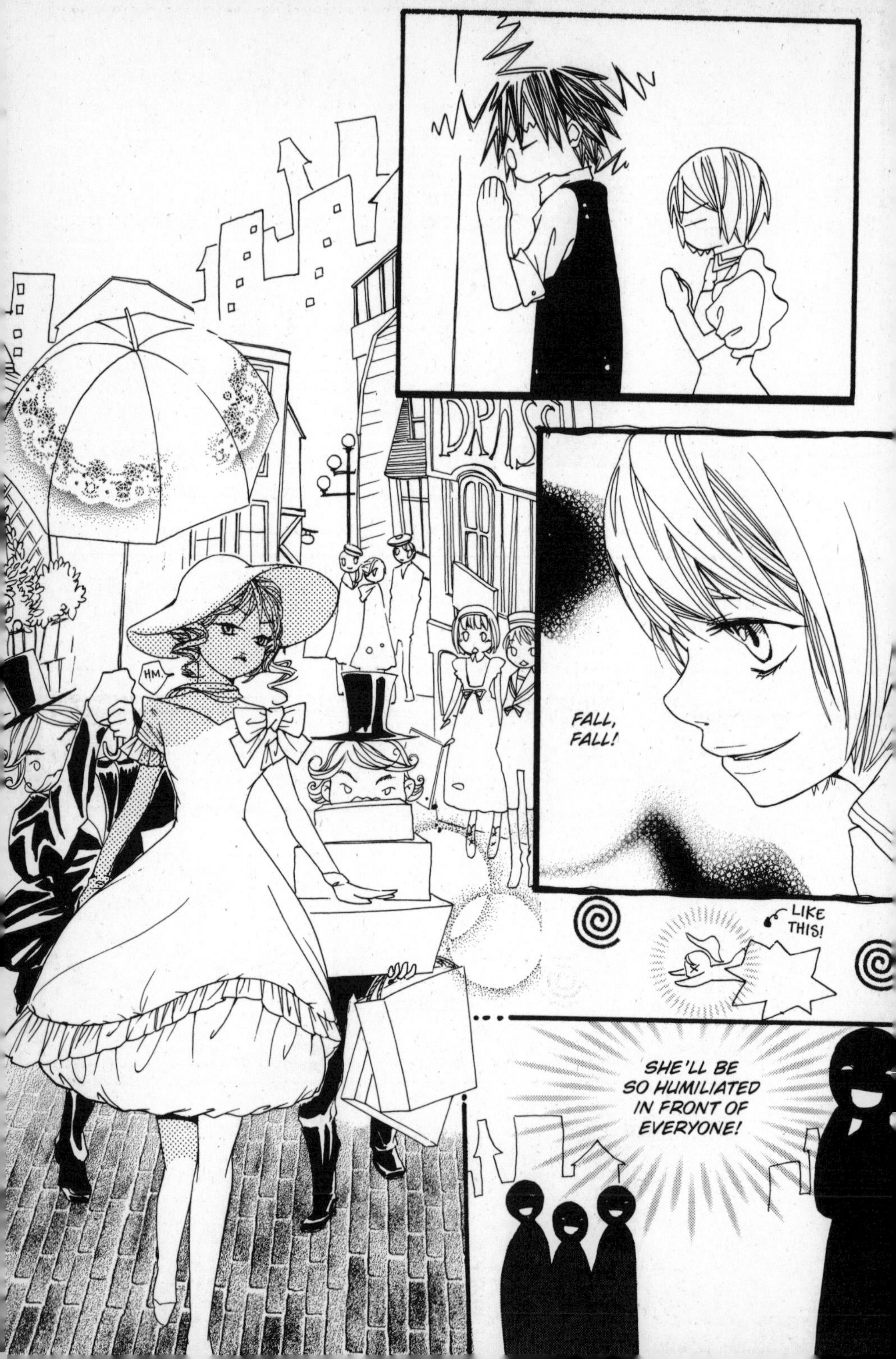
HM.
FALL, FALL!
LIKE THIS!
SHE'LL BE SO HUMILIATED IN FRONT OF EVERYONE!

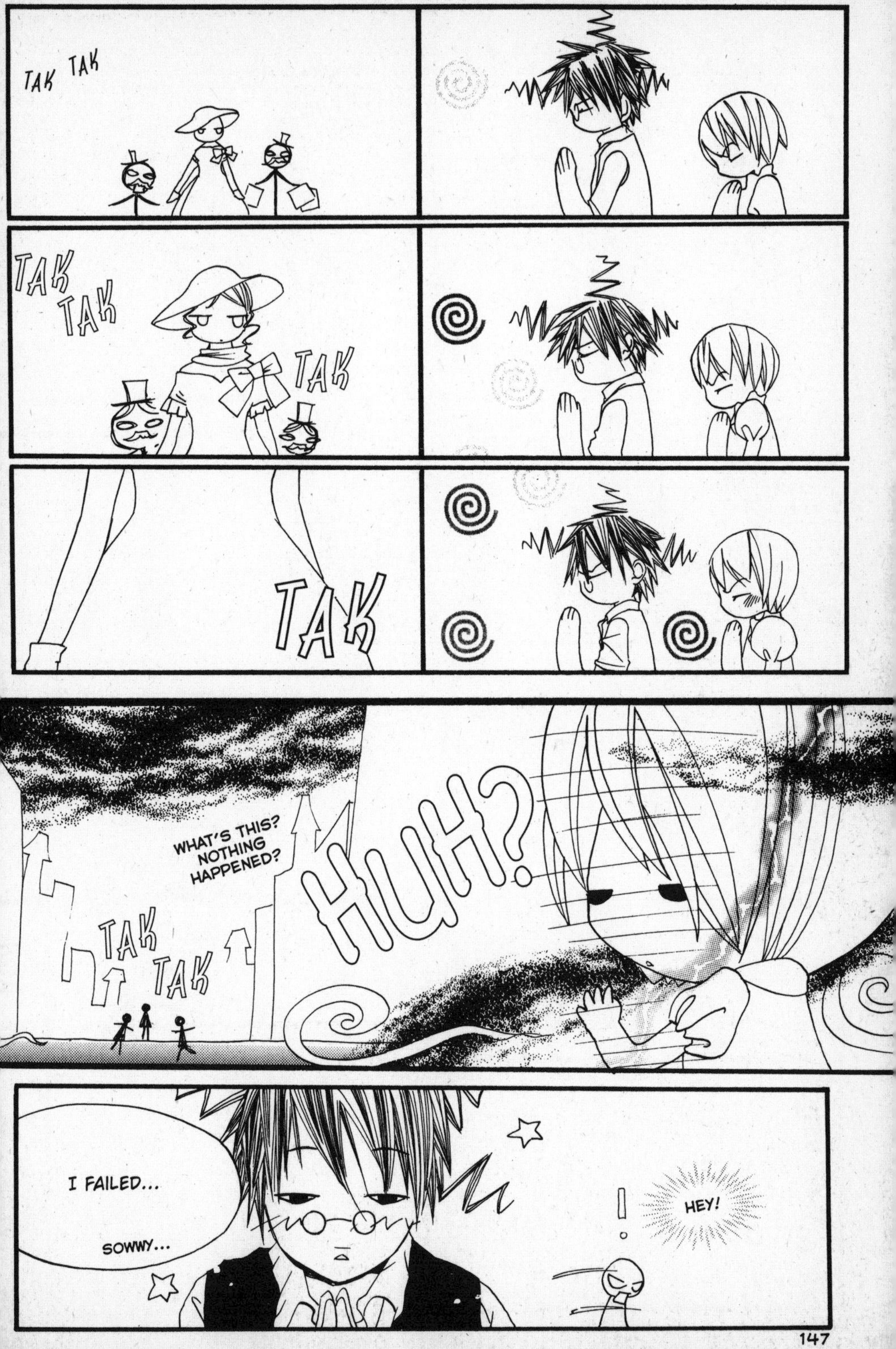
TAK TAK
TAK
TAK
TAK
TAK
WHAT'S THIS? NOTHING HAPPENED?
TAK
TAK
HUH?
I FAILED...
SOWWY...
!
HEY!

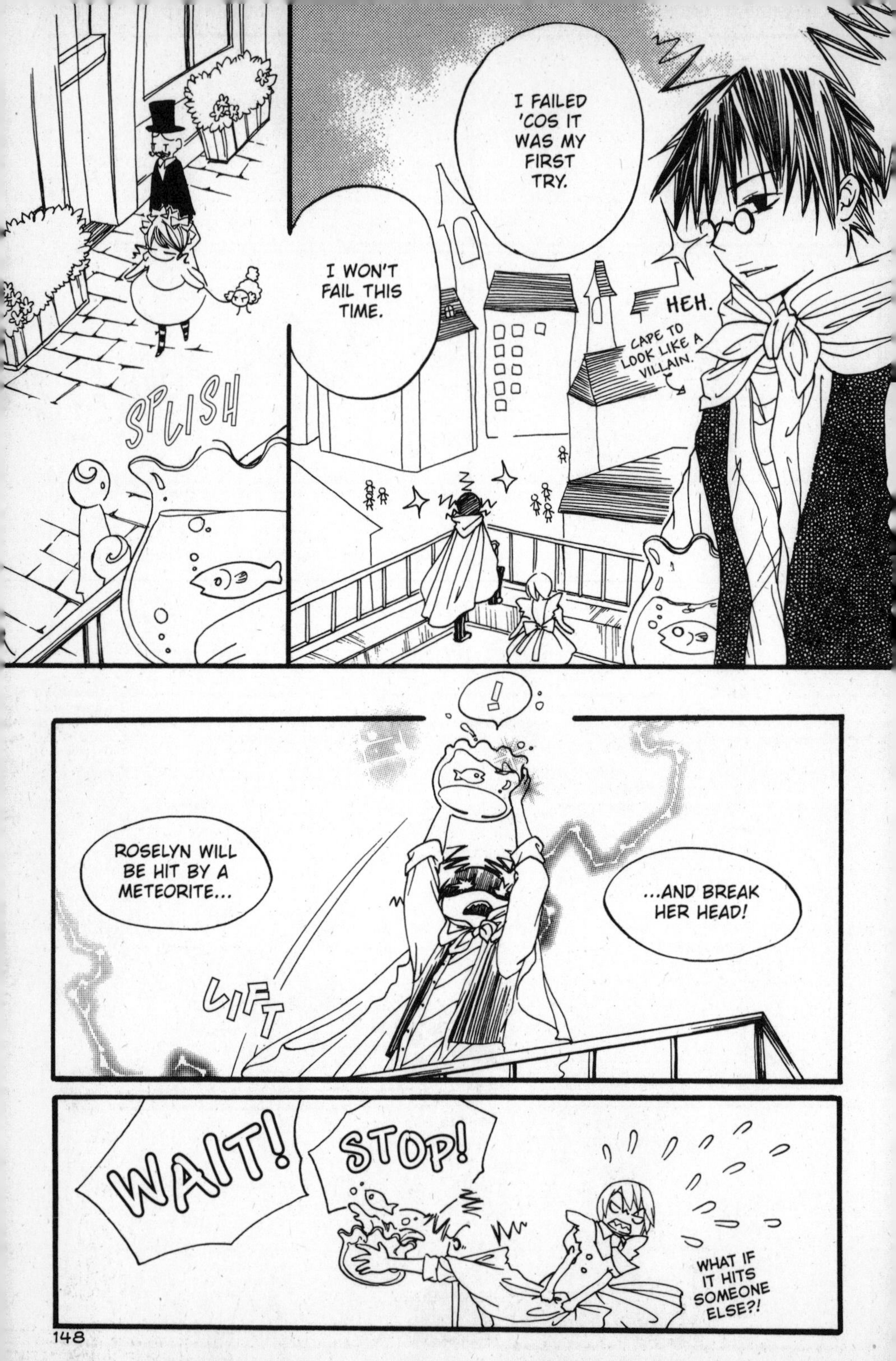
SPLISH
I FAILED 'COS IT WAS MY FIRST TRY.
I WON'T FAIL THIS TIME.
HEH.
CAPE TO LOOK LIKE A VILLAIN.
!
ROSELYN WILL BE HIT BY A METEORITE...
...AND BREAK HER HEAD!
LIFT
WAIT!
STOP!
WHAT IF IT HITS SOMEONE ELSE?!

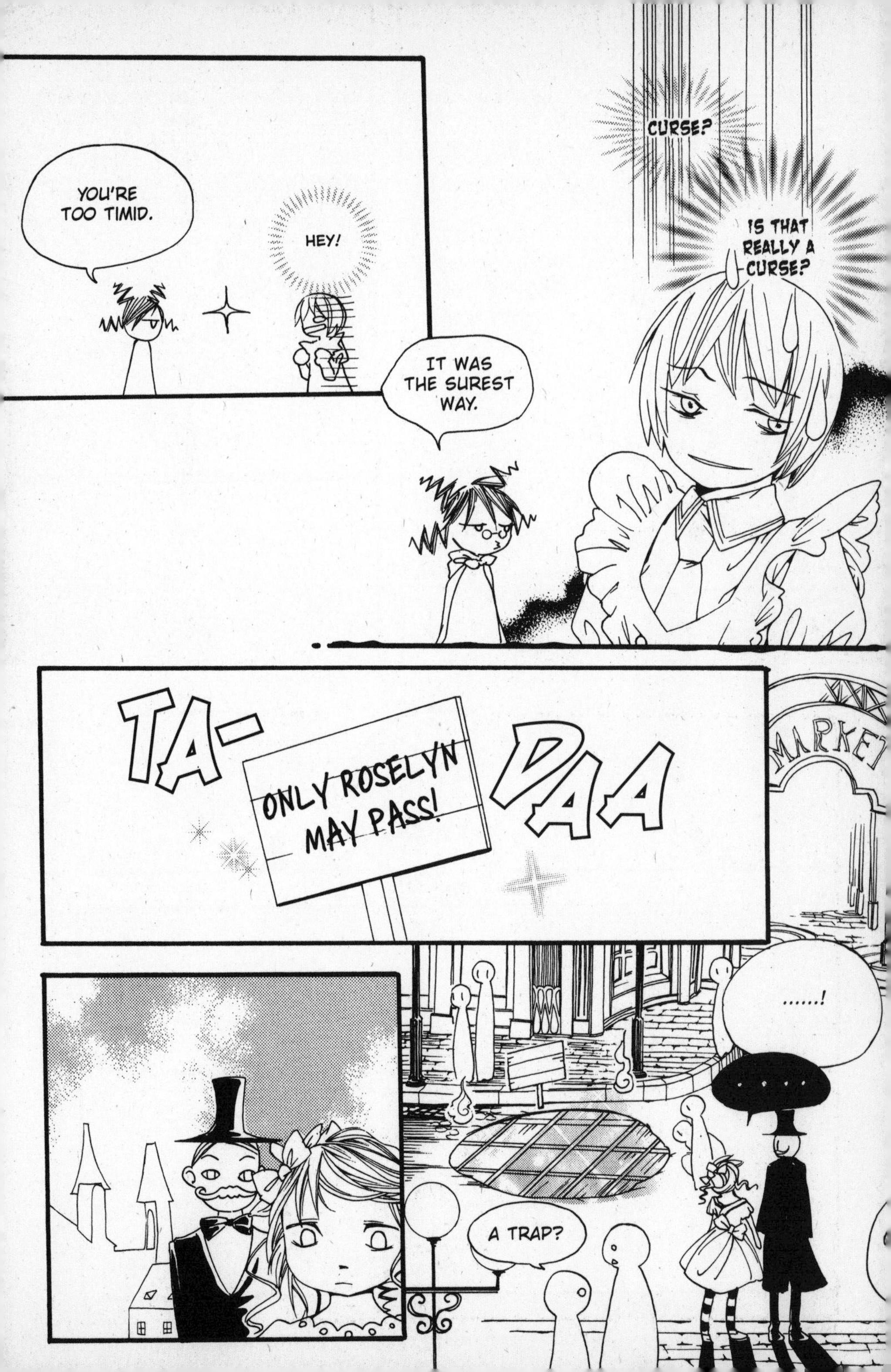
YOU'RE TOO TIMID.
HEY!
CURSE?
IS THAT REALLY A CURSE?
IT WAS THE SUREST WAY.
TA-DAA
ONLY ROSELYN MAY PASS!
MARKET
......!
A TRAP?

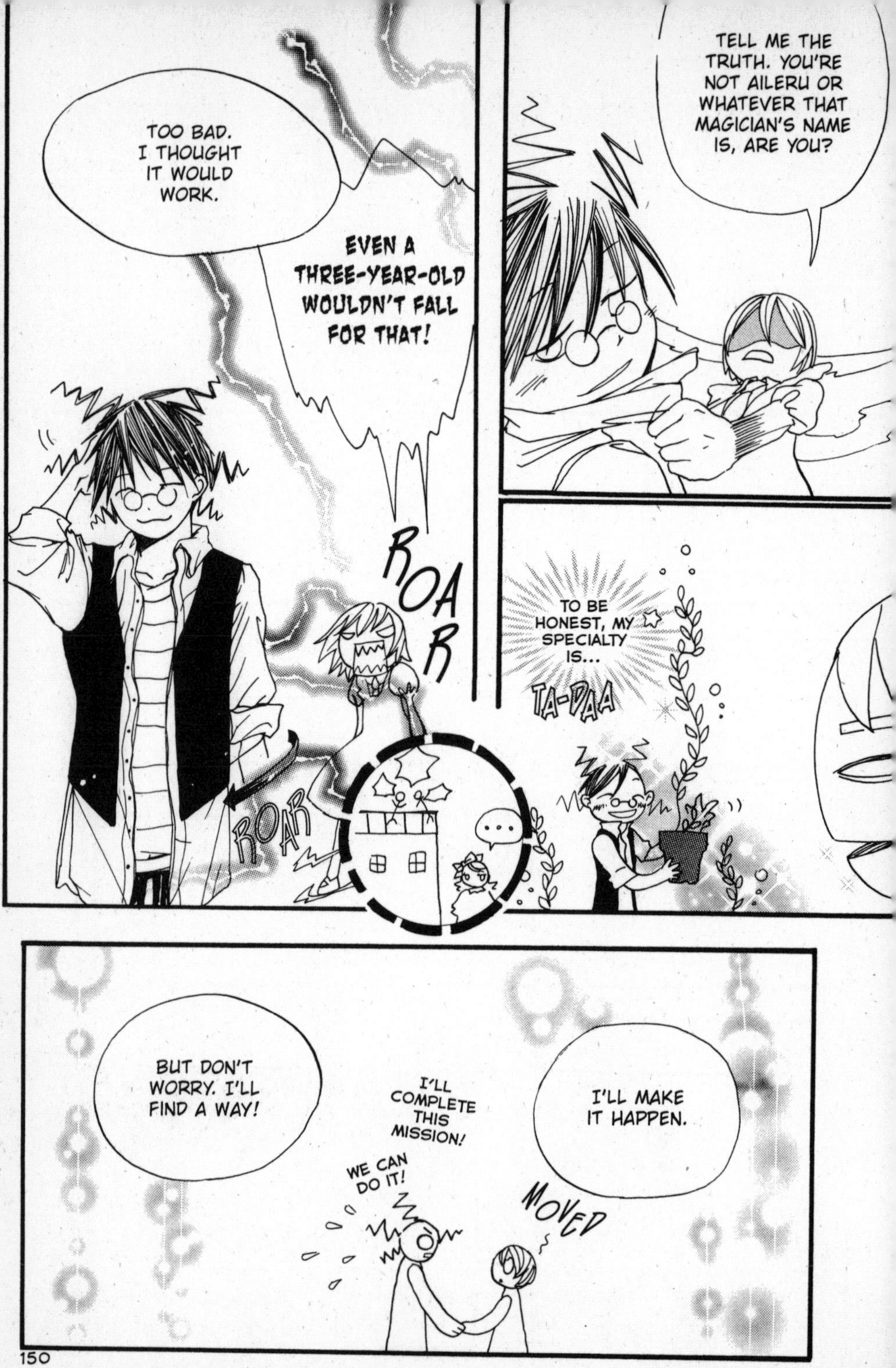
TOO BAD. I THOUGHT IT WOULD WORK.
EVEN A THREE-YEAR-OLD WOULDN'T FALL FOR THAT!
ROAR
ROAR
...
TELL ME THE TRUTH. YOU'RE NOT AILERU OR WHATEVER THAT MAGICIAN'S NAME IS, ARE YOU?
TO BE HONEST, MY SPECIALTY IS...
TA-DAA
BUT DON'T WORRY. I'LL FIND A WAY!
I'LL COMPLETE THIS MISSION!
WE CAN DO IT!
I'LL MAKE IT HAPPEN.
MOVED

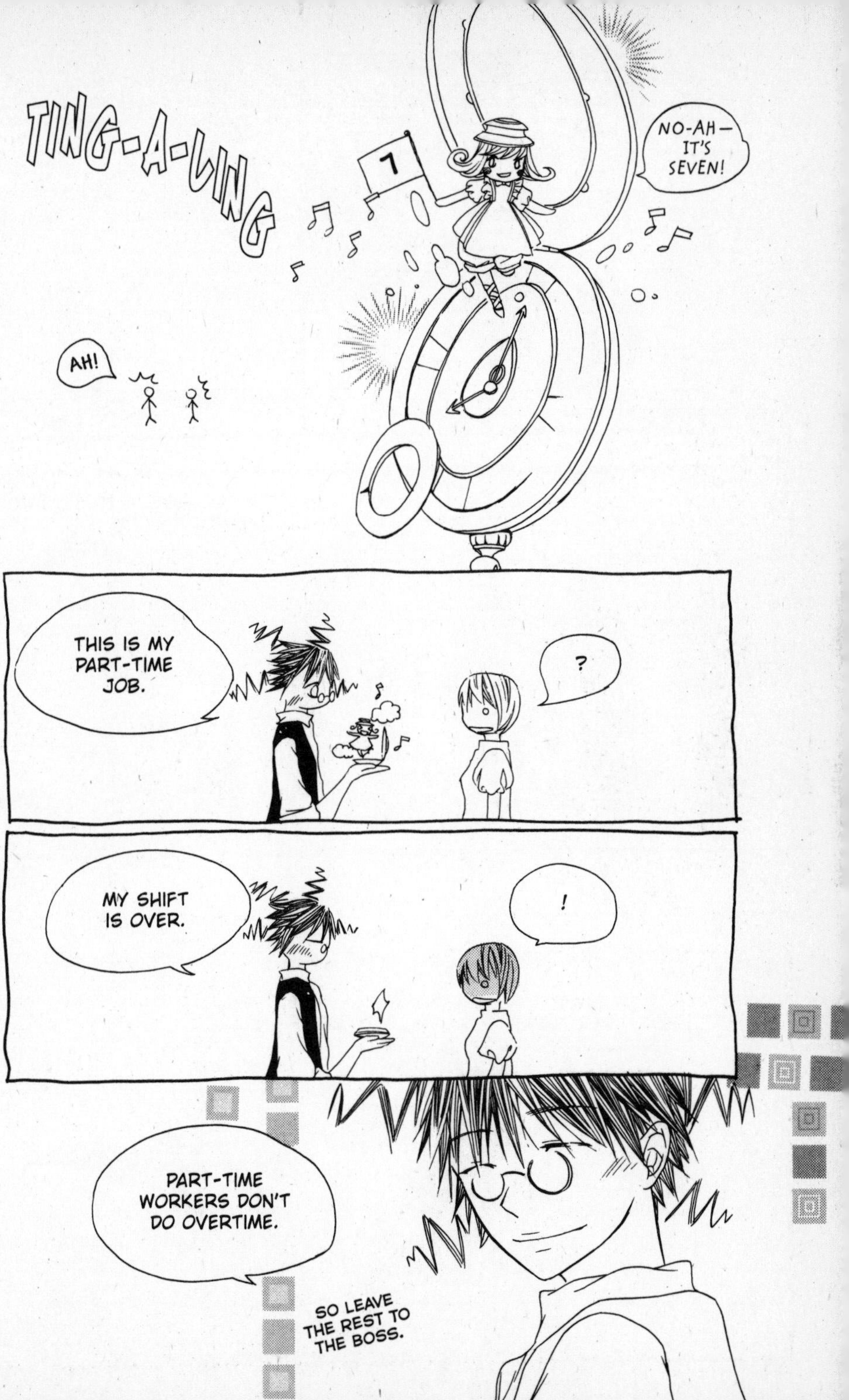
TING-A-LING
7
NO-AH— IT'S SEVEN!
AH!
THIS IS MY PART-TIME JOB.
?
MY SHIFT IS OVER.
!
PART-TIME WORKERS DON'T DO OVERTIME.
SO LEAVE THE REST TO THE BOSS.

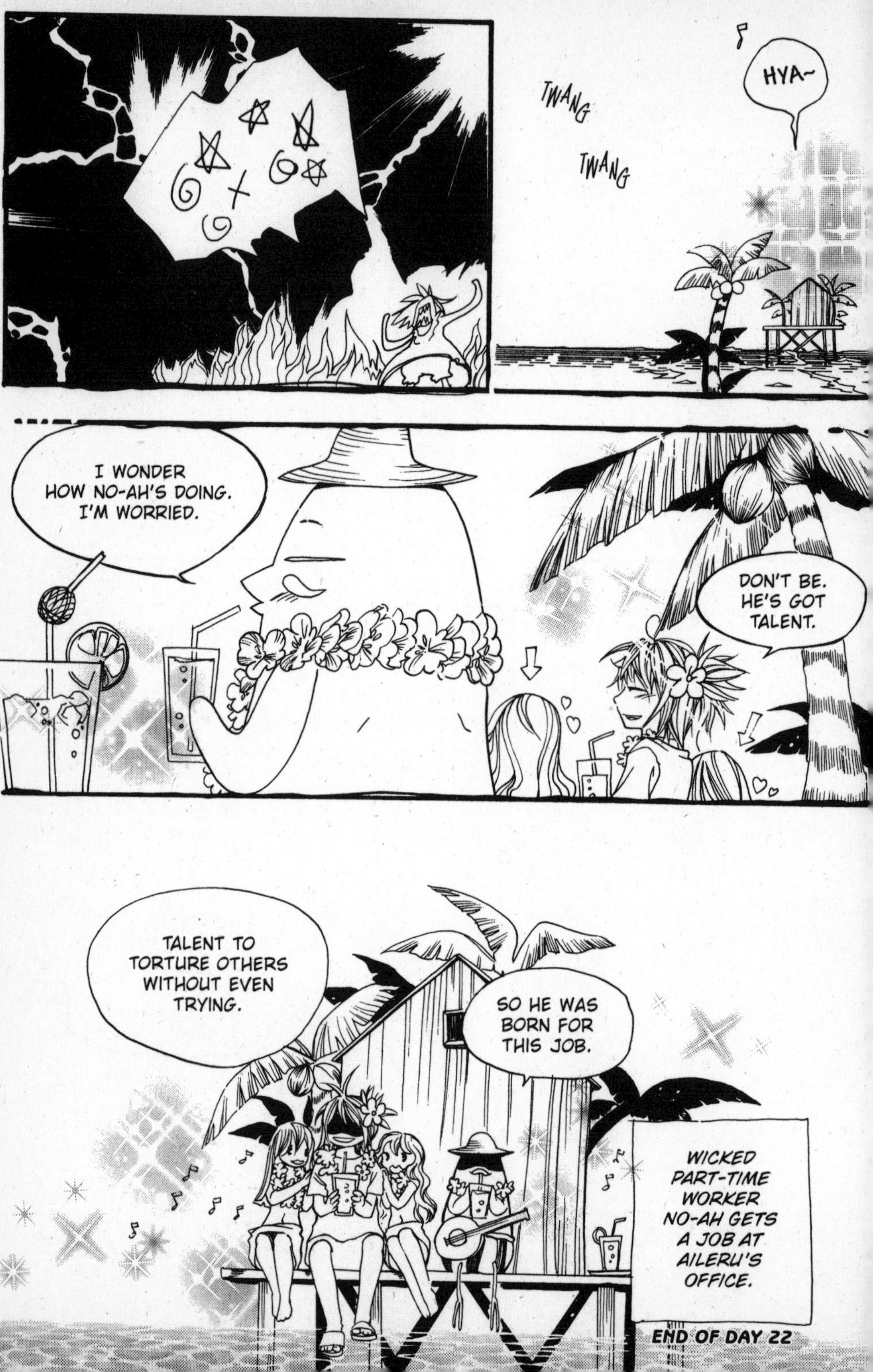
TWANG
TWANG
HYA~
I WONDER HOW NO-AH'S DOING. I'M WORRIED.
DON'T BE. HE'S GOT TALENT.
TALENT TO TORTURE OTHERS WITHOUT EVEN TRYING.
SO HE WAS BORN FOR THIS JOB.
WICKED PART-TIME WORKER NO-AH GETS A JOB AT AILERU'S OFFICE.
END OF DAY 22

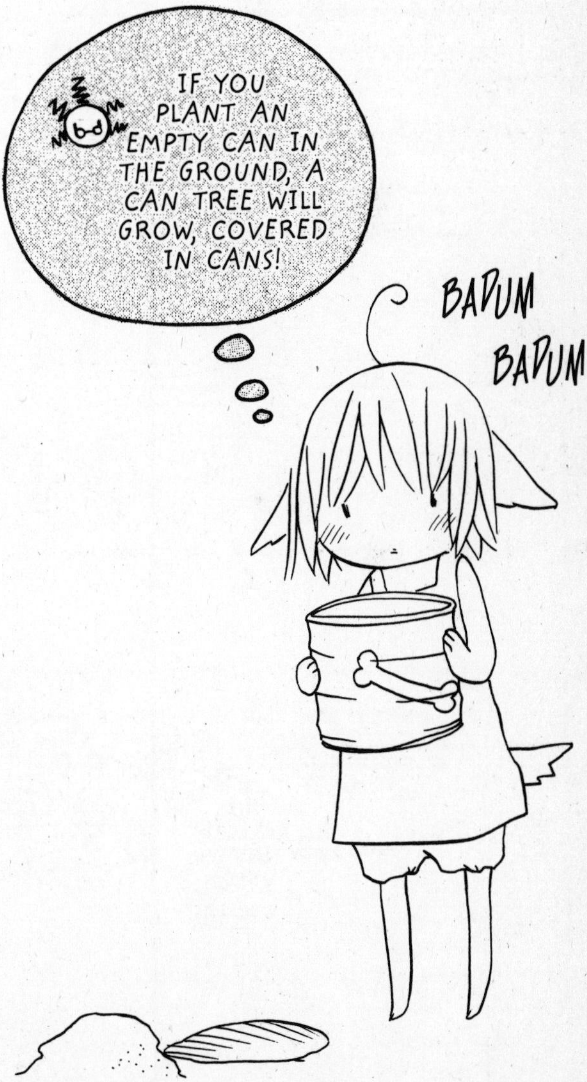
IF YOU PLANT AN EMPTY CAN IN THE GROUND, A CAN TREE WILL GROW, COVERED IN CANS!
BADUM
BADUM

one. SECRET

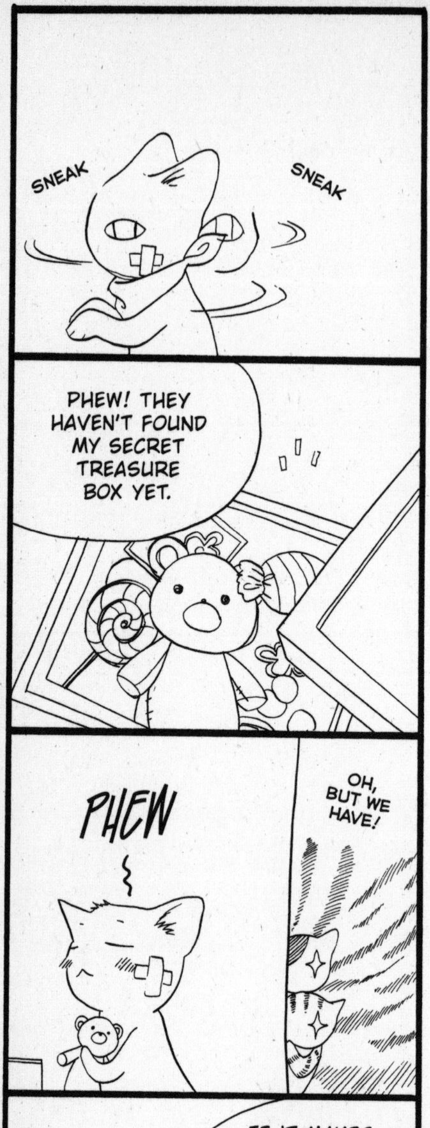
SNEAK
SNEAK
PHEW! THEY HAVEN'T FOUND MY SECRET TREASURE BOX YET.
PHEW
OH, BUT WE HAVE!
HA!
IF IT MAKES HIM THAT HAPPY...LET'S PRETEND WE DON'T KNOW.
OKAY, OKAY.
HA!

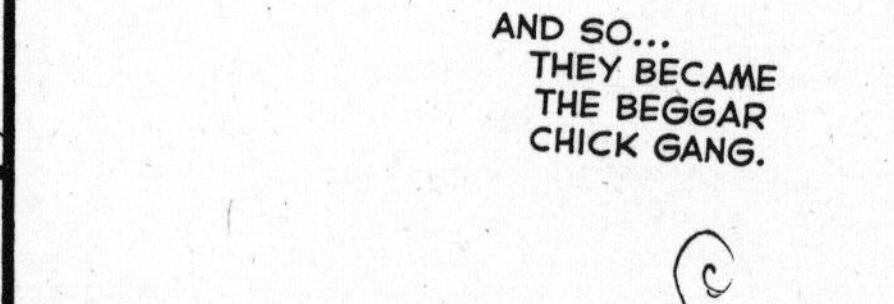
AND SO... THEY BECAME THE BEGGAR CHICK GANG.
GIVE US A PENNY~

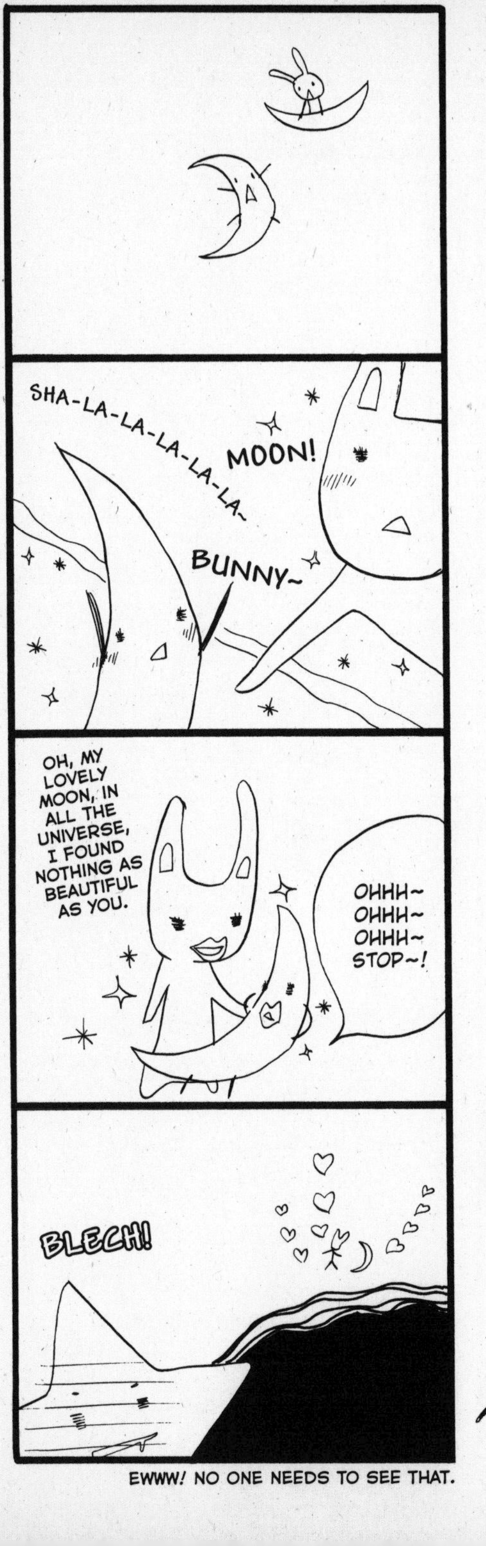
SHA-LA-LA-LA-LA-LA-LA~
MOON!
BUNNY~
OH, MY LOVELY MOON, IN ALL THE UNIVERSE, I FOUND NOTHING AS BEAUTIFUL AS YOU.
OHHH~ OHHH~ OHHH~ STOP~!
BLECH!
EWWW! NO ONE NEEDS TO SEE THAT.

two. FRIEND

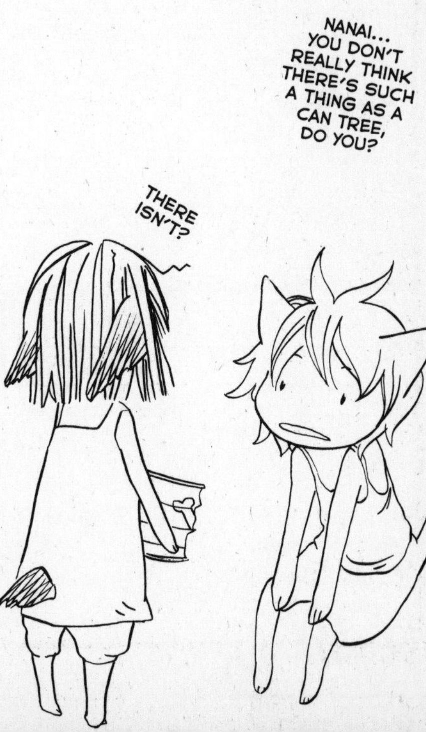
NANAI... YOU DON'T REALLY THINK THERE'S SUCH A THING AS A CAN TREE, DO YOU?
THERE ISN'T?

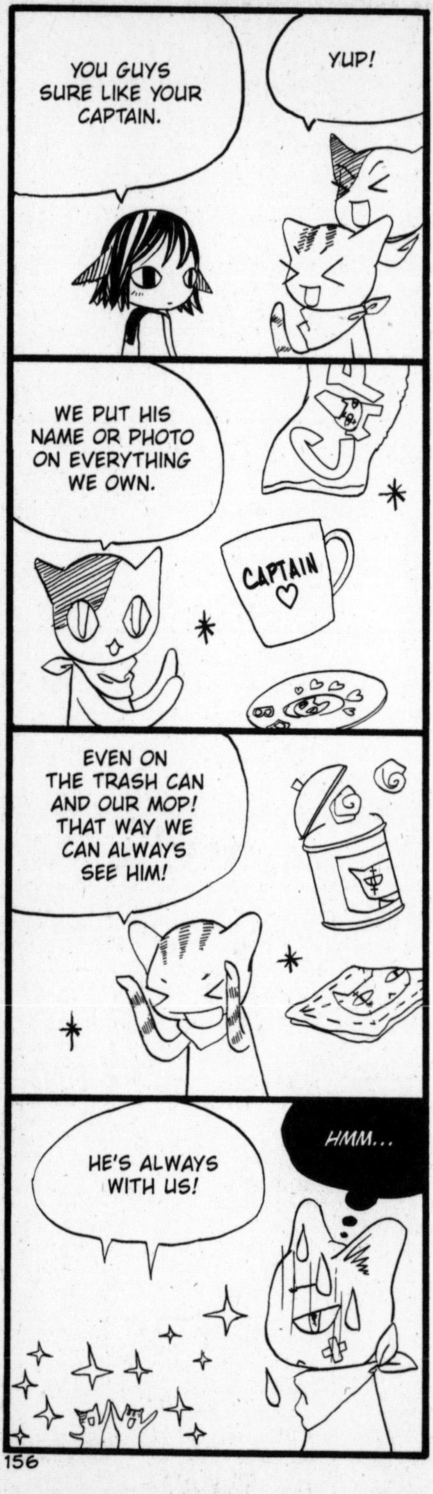
YOU GUYS SURE LIKE YOUR CAPTAIN.
YUP!
WE PUT HIS NAME OR PHOTO ON EVERYTHING WE OWN.
CAPTAIN
EVEN ON THE TRASH CAN AND OUR MOP! THAT WAY WE CAN ALWAYS SEE HIM!
HE'S ALWAYS WITH US!
HMM...

three. OUR CAPTAIN...

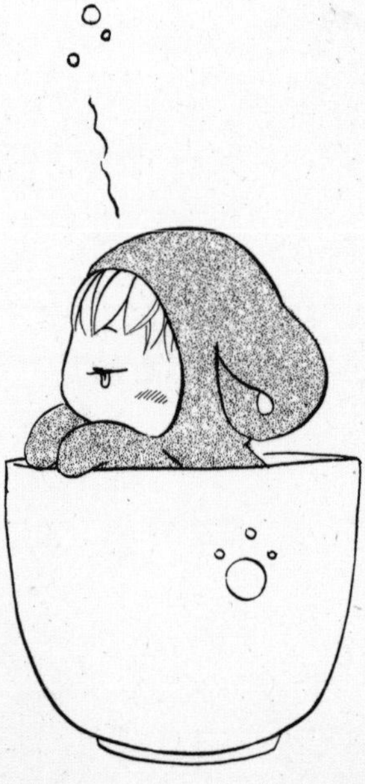

four. THE TRUTH

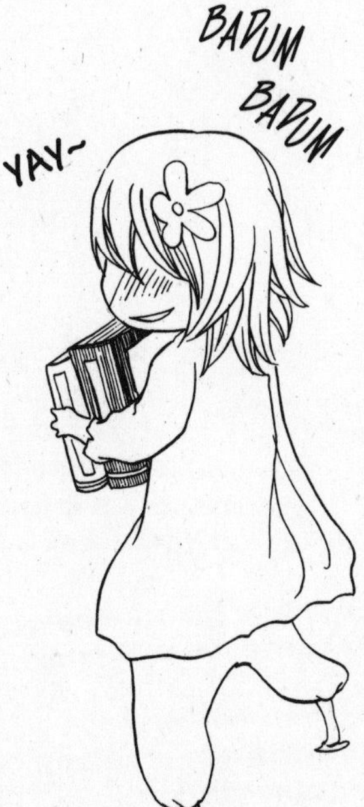
BADUM
BADUM
YAY~

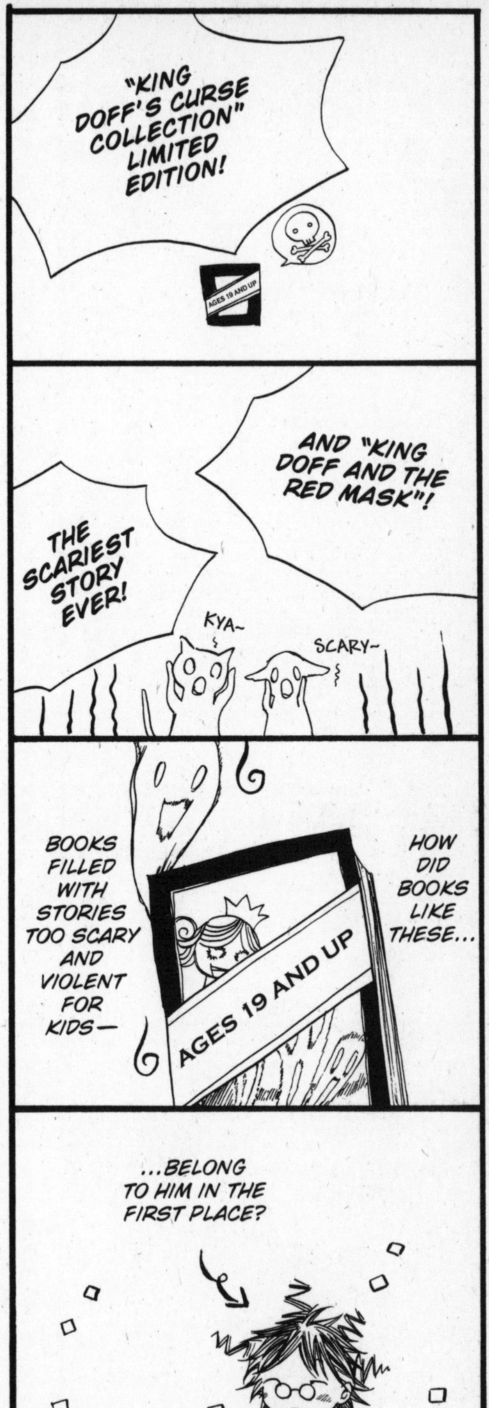
"KING DOFF'S CURSE COLLECTION" LIMITED EDITION!
AGES 19 AND UP
AND "KING DOFF AND THE RED MASK"!
THE SCARIEST STORY EVER!
KYA~
SCARY~
BOOKS FILLED WITH STORIES TOO SCARY AND VIOLENT FOR KIDS—
AGES 19 AND UP
HOW DID BOOKS LIKE THESE...
...BELONG TO HIM IN THE FIRST PLACE?

More adventures await in **one fine day** Volume 3!

Hello! This is YOTSUBA!

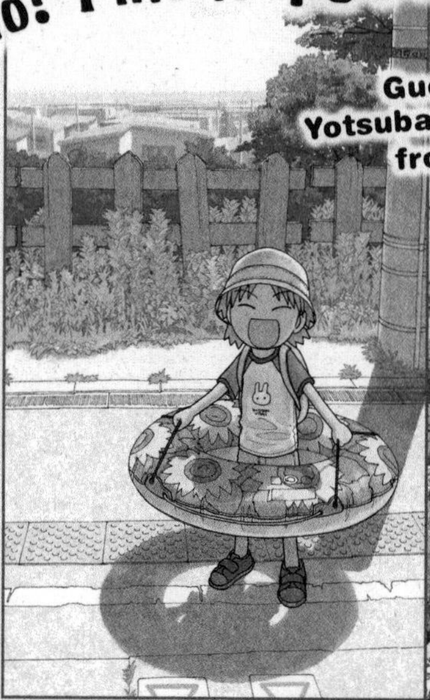

Guess what? Guess what?
Yotsuba and Daddy just moved here from waaaay over there!

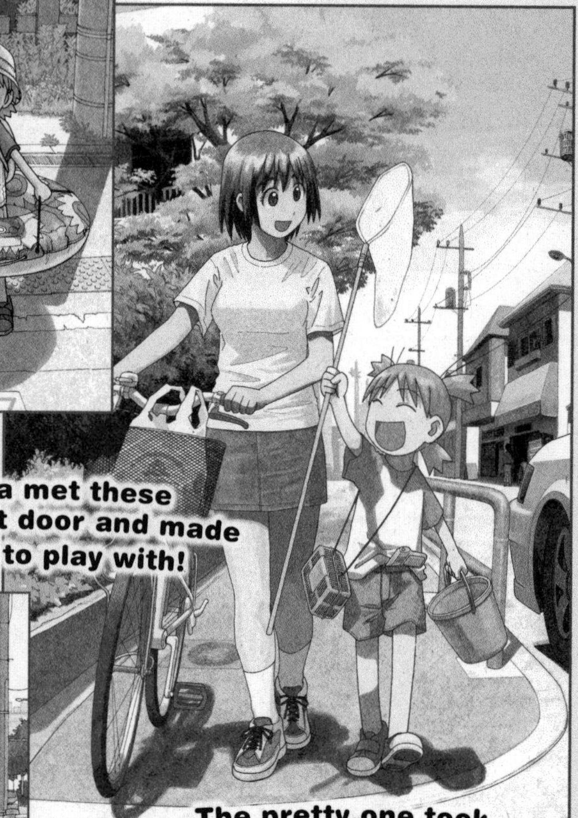

And Yotsuba met these nice people next door and made new friends to play with!

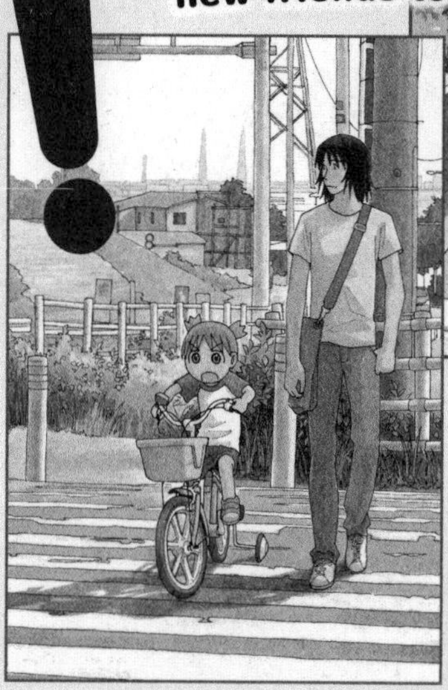

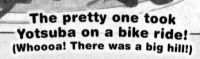

The pretty one took Yotsuba on a bike ride!
(Whoooa! There was a big hill!)

And Ena's a good drawer!
(Almost as good as Yotsuba!)

And their mom always gives Yotsuba ice cream!
(Yummy!)

And...
And...
OHHHH!

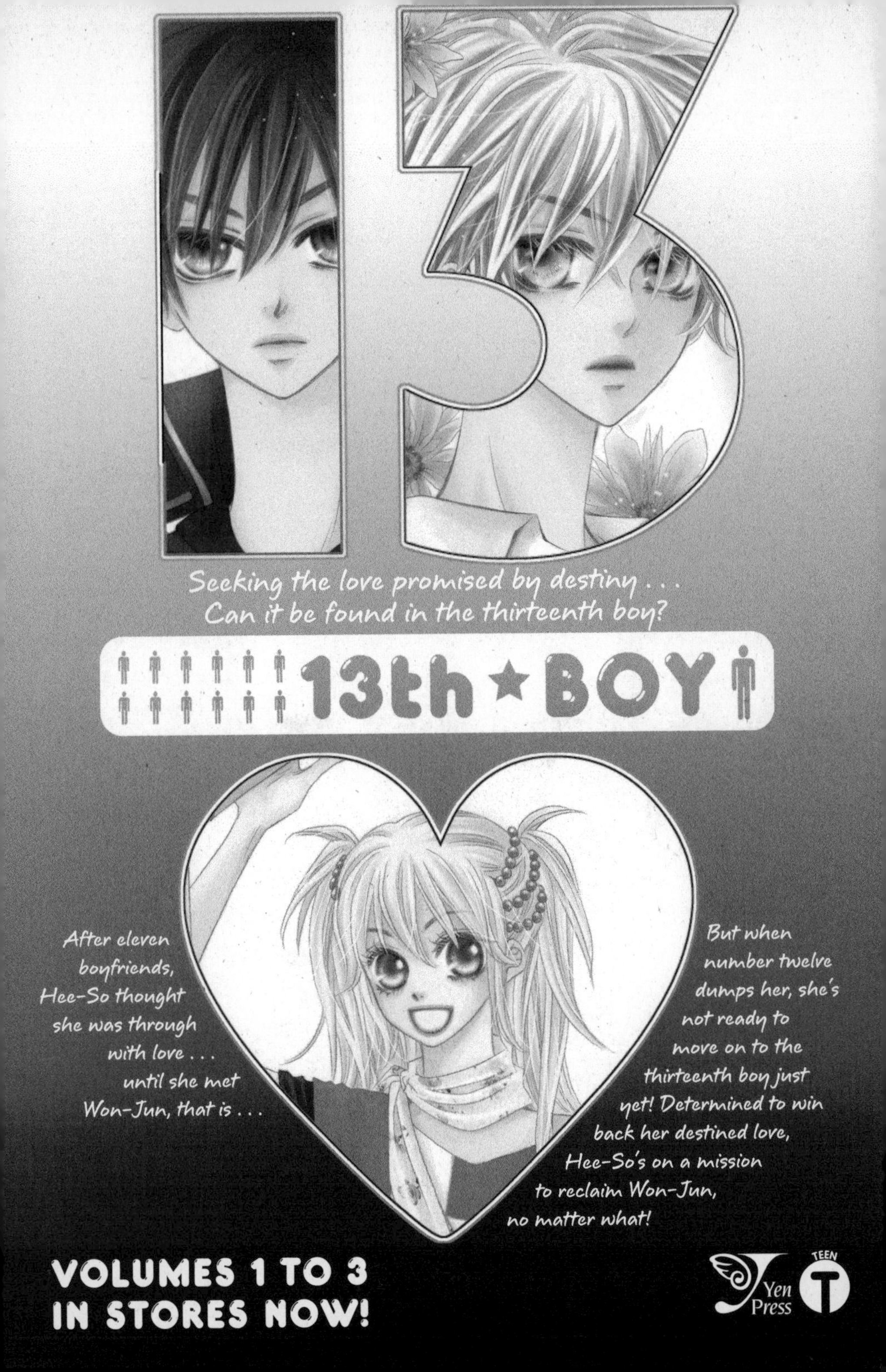
Seeking the love promised by destiny . . .
Can it be found in the thirteenth boy?
13th ★ BOY
After eleven boyfriends, Hee-So thought she was through with love . . . until she met Won-Jun, that is . . .
But when number twelve dumps her, she's not ready to move on to the thirteenth boy just yet! Determined to win back her destined love, Hee-So's on a mission to reclaim Won-Jun, no matter what!
VOLUMES 1 TO 3
IN STORES NOW!
Yen Press
TEEN
T

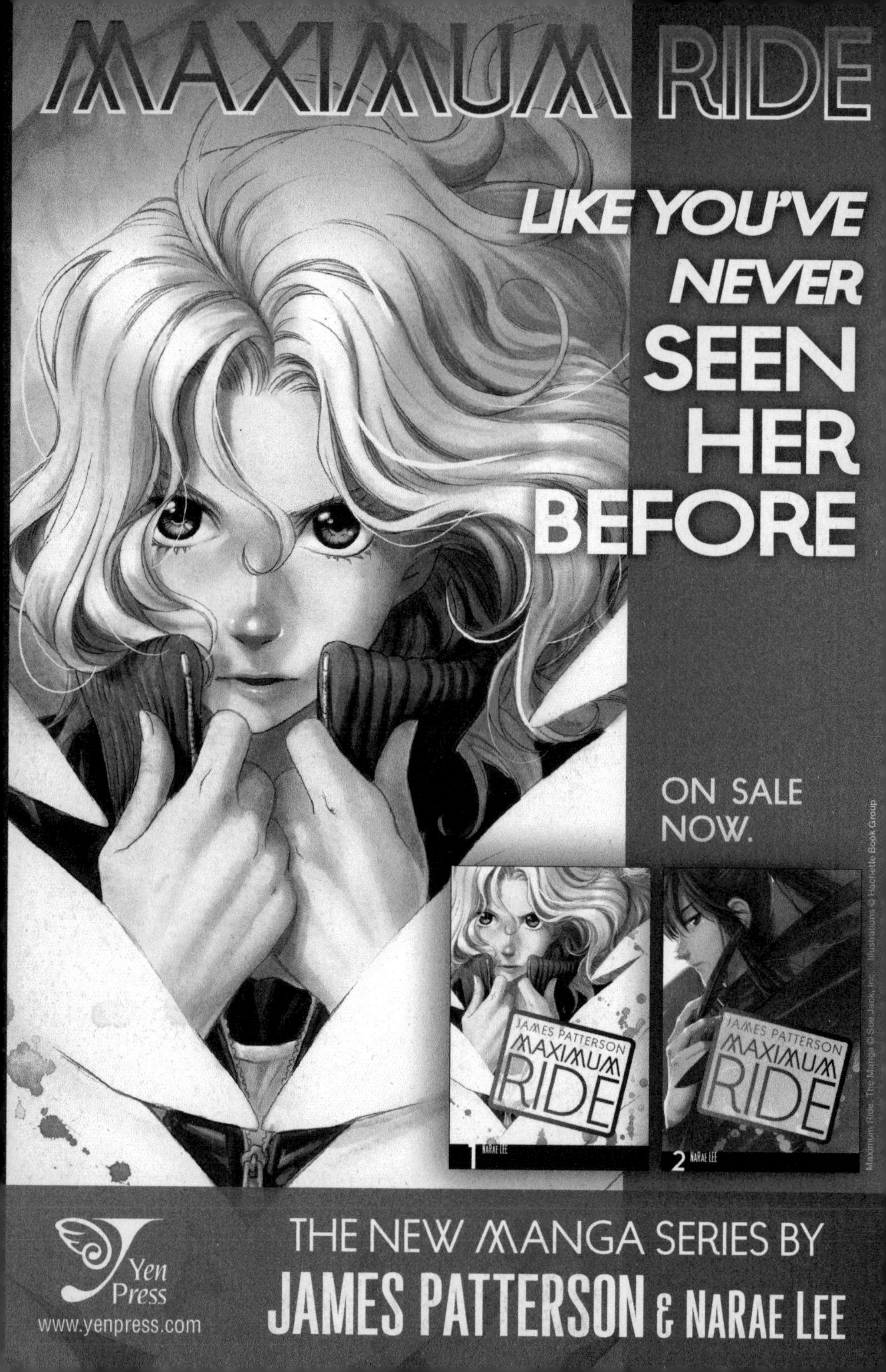
MAXIMUM RIDE
LIKE YOU'VE NEVER SEEN HER BEFORE
ON SALE NOW.
JAMES PATTERSON
MAXIMUM RIDE
1 NARAE LEE
JAMES PATTERSON
MAXIMUM RIDE
2 NARAE LEE
Maximum Ride: The Manga © Sue Jack, Inc. Illustrations © Hachette Book Group
Yen Press
www.yenpress.com
THE NEW MANGA SERIES BY
JAMES PATTERSON & NARAE LEE

ONE FINE DAY②

SIRIAL

Translation: JuYoun Lee

Lettering: Abigail Blackman

ONE FINE DAY Vol. 2 © 2007 by Sirial, DAEWON C.I. Inc. All rights reserved. First published in Korea in 2007 by DAEWON C.I. Inc. English translation rights in USA, Canada, UK and Commonwealth arranged by Daewon C.I. Inc. through TOPAZ Agency Inc.

Translation © 2010 by Hachette Book Group, Inc.

Yen Press
Hachette Book Group
237 Park Avenue, New York, NY 10017

www.HachetteBookGroup.com
www.YenPress.com

Yen Press is an imprint of Hachette Book Group, Inc. The Yen Press name and logo are trademarks of Hachette Book Group, Inc.

First Yen Press Edition: May 2010

ISBN: 978-0-7595-3057-7

10 9 8 7 6 5 4 3 2 1

BVG

Printed in the United States of America